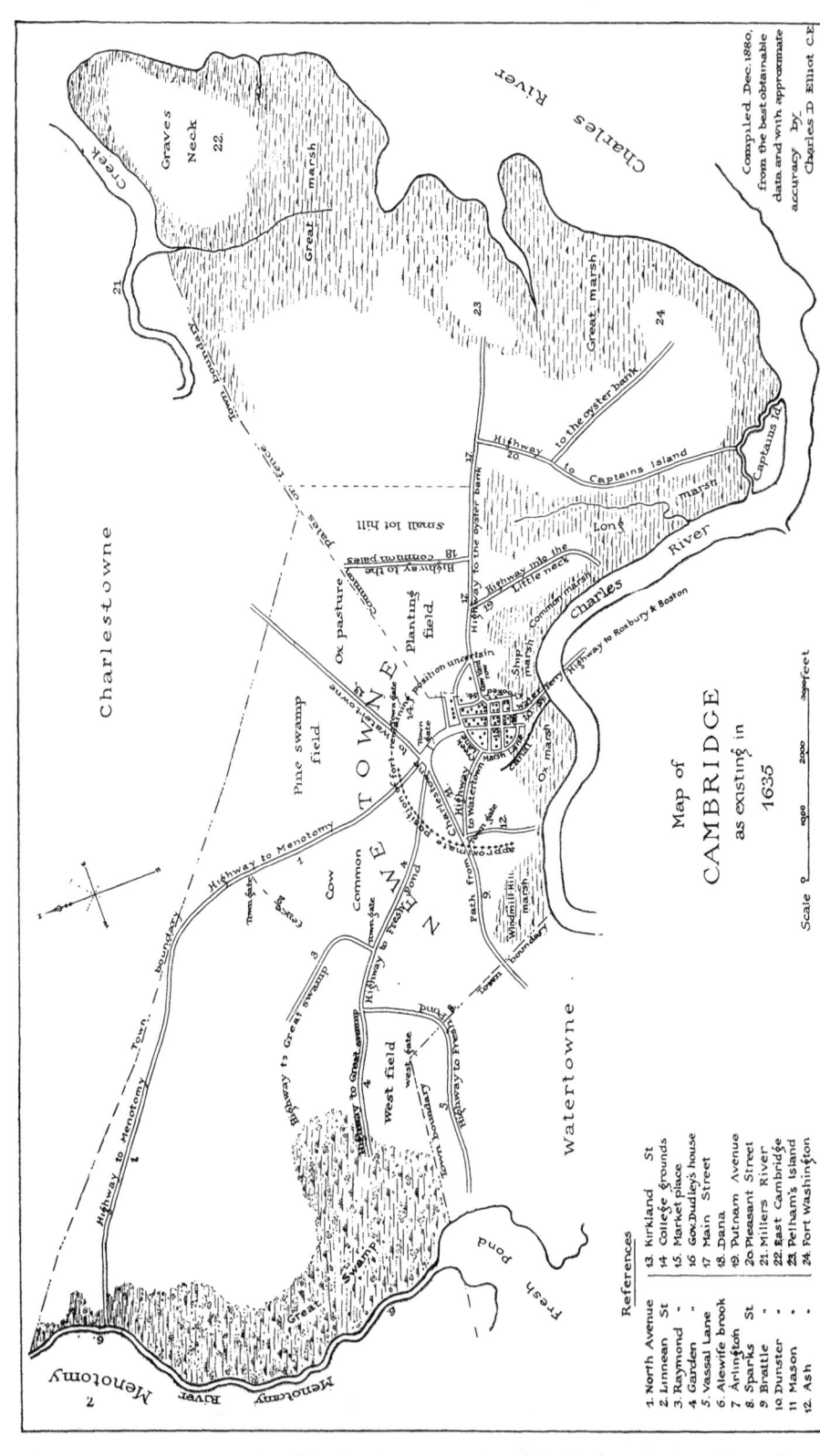

THE RECORDS

OF THE

TOWN OF CAMBRIDGE
(FORMERLY NEWTOWNE)

MASSACHUSETTS

1630–1703

THE RECORDS OF THE TOWN MEETINGS, AND OF THE SELECTMEN,
COMPRISING ALL OF THE FIRST VOLUME OF RECORDS,
AND BEING VOLUME II. OF THE PRINTED
RECORDS OF THE TOWN

PRINTED BY ORDER OF THE CITY COUNCIL UNDER THE
DIRECTION OF THE CITY CLERK

Originally published
Cambridge, Massachusetts, 1901

Reprinted for
Clearfield Company, Inc. by
Genealogical Publishing Co., Inc.
Baltimore, Maryland
2002

International Standard Book Number: 0-8063-5123-3
Made in the United States of America

PREFACE

THIS volume is the second printed book of the Old Records of Cambridge, and, as stated concisely on the title-page, contains "the records of the Town Meetings, and of the Selectmen, comprising all of the first volume of Records."

The period of time covered is from 1630 to 1703.

The general plan and scope of the "Proprietors' Records" — the first printed book of the Old Records — has been followed even to the mechanical features.

It has been the intention to present in this volume *all* and the *same* information which a perusal of the manuscript would present to the reader. No attempt has been made to modernize the text, or to make corrections of any description. From page 1 to page 354 the book is a reproduction of the original, except the introduction of the title, paging, and explanatory marks and foot-notes.

Throughout this volume the dates of the entries do not appear consecutively in all cases, but the dates are published in the exact order in which they appear in the originals. It has not been deemed advisable to place them in consecutive order, except when such order was in agreement with the original text.

The figures at the top of the pages indicate the paging of the transcript. The heavy figures enclosed in brackets represent the paging of the original book in its present condition.

The title " Town Records " has been used, in the belief that the appearance of the book would be thereby improved.

Brackets enclosing a blank space, thus, [   ], signify that something is missing from, or illegible in the original. Carets, ∧, show that a letter or letters in a word are missing. Whenever a star, *, appears on a page it refers to a foot-note on that page.

The task of preparing the index and reading the proofs has been a severe one, due to the worn condition of many of the pages of the original manuscript, and has compelled the greatest care in the translation of the text, that no unseemly errors might creep in.

The proofs have all been read by Miss Sarah S. Jacobs, and have been examined by reference to the original pages, to insure correctness.

As the copy was also prepared by Miss Jacobs, it will be seen that no small part of the work has fallen upon her.

That she was well fitted to perform the task must be evident from her successful effort in the issue of the " Proprietors' Records," published in 1896.

An attempt has been made to produce a complete index, and the forty or more pages devoted to this purpose indicate its thoroughness.

As a frontispiece to this volume, there is printed a map of Cambridge as existing in 1635. This map is, of course, lacking in absolute accuracy, as there are extant few plans or maps which are available for use in preparing a positive reproduction. The compiler, Mr. Charles D. Elliot, now a resident of Somerville, Mass., has, however, taken advantage of the best obtainable data, and even a cursory examination will show its value in determining certain localities which otherwise might be difficult to understand. This plan, too, has the indorsement of Hon. Charles H. Saunders, ex-Mayor of Cambridge, who has given much thought and intelligent investigation to the earliest periods of local history.

It must be understood, however, that the map is in no sense an official one, and that it is published merely as an aid to a more complete understanding of many references throughout the text.

It will be noted that marginal annotations occur on several pages, and, lest it might be assumed that these were penned by the original clerks, it is deemed proper to say, that an examination of the manuscript will show that nearly all of the annotations are the handiwork of more modern scribes. This is proven by the modern method of spelling, as well as the arrangement of the annotations and marks in the manuscripts.

It might not be amiss to state that, in a large number of cases where names are appended to reports, etc., the names are probably original signatures in the manuscript, as in the case of the report of John Watson and Abraham Holman, under date of 8th of June, 1685, in the matter of an investigation into the condition of the highway leading to Concord. (See folio

276.) The antiquarian might discern something of value in this fact.

With this volume, there are published nine reproductions of pages in the original record.

These pages have been selected so as to show in each case, except one, the signature of the Town Clerk for the time being.

The single exception is in the case of William Spencer (1632–1635), whose name does not appear on the page which has been copied. It was difficult to find any page in the record of those earlier years which was sufficiently well preserved to be reproduced, the one selected being probably the most desirable.

For a verification of the dates of service of the several clerks, the compiler is indebted to Mr. William W. Dodge of this City, who gave freely of his experience and time in a close examination of the chirography to establish with some degree of positiveness the names of the recording officers. The compiler desires also to record the able assistance of Mr. William H. Whitney of this City, who has given valuable information with reference to some of the ancient boundary marks.

EDWARD J. BRANDON,
City Clerk.

CAMBRIDGE, MASSACHUSETTS.

Commonwealth of Massachusetts.

MIDDLESEX, SS.
                                    CAMBRIDGE, JULY 20, 1901.

I, Edward J. Brandon, clerk of the City of Cambridge, hereby certify that the following, beginning with page 1, and ending with page 354, is a true and correct copy of the Records, known as the Town Records of the Town of Cambridge (formerly Newtowne), now in the custody of the City Clerk except that the title, paging, and explanatory marks and notes have been added in the printed volume.

                                    EDWARD J. BRANDON,
                                              City Clerk.

Subscribed and sworn to,
        Before me
                DAVID T. DICKINSON,
                        Justice of the Peace.

Town Records

		d
[	] —	— 10
[	] —	1 — 10
[	] —	6 — 00
[	] —	7 — 10
[	] —	5 — 00
[	] —	3 — 00
[	] —	2 — 00

[ ] aboue a year — 1 — 10
[ ] aboue a yeare ould — 00 — 08
swine aboue a yeare — 01 — 00
[ ] aboue a yeare — 2 — 00
[ ] male 20 *d* pr. heade
[ ] for eftate to be made 1ᵗʰ 4ᵗʰ of yᵉ 6ᵗʰ mo.
[ ] prſons yʳ leauy to be payde yearly in yᵉ [   ]

[ ] to be yearly chofen
[ ] to end fmall Caufes 2. Cunftables 5: Townfmen
[ ] one to feal leather one to be [   ]
[ ] meafures, furveyour of high wayes. &c.
           [   ]
           [   ]
           [   ] 138 poles [   ]
           [   ]
           [   ] feilds 168 ac fubdevided   fwamp C ∧
                                          [   ]
                                          [   ]
                                          [   ]

                              s
        [   ]: :   10 — 0
        [   ]   — 04 — 8
        [   ]   — 01 — 6
        [   ]   — 01 — 3
        [   ]   — 08 — 0
        [   ]   — 08 — 0
        [   ]   — 02 — 0
        [   ]   — 03 — 0
        [   ]———————— 25 — 0 d
                £   s   d   ─────────
[   ] ſome is 3 : 11 : 5.   71 — 5

    [   ]
    [   ]
    ─────────────────────────────────
              The perſls of land by yᵉ Farmes [   ]
    [   ] land. 10 s pr acr.
[   ]
[   ] acr.
[   ] pr acr.
[   ] at 20 s
[   ] at 10 s
[   ] at 20 s
[   ] at 10 s

              The Towne   [   ]
              Newtowne
              Inhabitants then
              Tho = Dudly Eſqr
            mr Symon Bradſtreet
            mr Edmond Lockwood
            mr Daniell Patrike
              John Poole
              William Spencer
              John Kirman
              Symon Sackett

The names of offenders agst the orders   [   ]
Knox of Watertowne for felling 20 poul and clapbords for mrs Glouer. was not apointed by his agent for [   ] Goodman Kinſbury of watertowne for encroching [   ] bounds of this town [   ] the line was run.

Iracundia et argentum mutant mores [   ]
Anger   and mony   chang   manners & [   ]

Ri; oldam Died the 9ᵗʰ (dec.ʳ 1655 [   ]
and buried the 20ᵗʰ of the Same m?

	fines	
ₐbout yᵉ meeting-houſe		
[ ] Stone 2. daies cariadge	[ ]	
ₐlip Cooke 3 daies cariadge	[ ] — 05	
[ ] Crackbone 1 day from weſt feild	wayes [ ]	
[ ] miller 1 : day from hence	watch — 10	
[ ] Okes 2. daies and one harf	[ ] — 5	
Joſepth miller mow on load	gunpowder	2 — 00
Wm man.	High wayes 5	
williame: Town (4 daies.	High wayes 1	
Andrew Stevenson one day	4 — 6	
	2 — 19 — 5	
	7 — 5 — 5	

An Agreement by the Inhabitants of [   ] Towne aboute paleing in the necke of [   ]

Impr. that Euery one who hath anny part theₐ on ſhall hereafter kepe the ſame in good and ſuficient repair and if it happen to have annₐ defect he ſhall mend the ſame wthin three daₐ after notice giuen or else pay xˢ a rodd [   ] euery rodd ſo repaired for him.

ffurther it is Agreed that the ſd Impaled grₐ ſhalbe Deuided according to euery mans pₐtion in the ſd pales

ffurther it is Agreed if anny man ſhall [   ] to ſell his part of Impaled ground he ſhaₐ ffirſt tender the ſale thereof to the Towne [   ] Interested who ſhall either giue him the [   ] he hath bin at or else to haue liberty to ſell it [   ] whome he Cann.

4   TOWN RECORDS

The 24th of December 1632.

Ann Agreement made by A Gennerall Conſ∧ for a mounthly meeting.

Impr that Euery perſon under ſubſcribed ſhall [   ] Every ſecond Monday in Every mounth wthin [   ] meetinghouſe In the Afternoone wthin half [   ] ouer after the ringing of the bell and that euery [   ] that make not his perſonall apearannce there [   ] continews ther wthout leaue from [   ] vntill the meeting bee Ended ſhall for [   ] default xii.ᵈ and if it be not paid [   ] meeting then to dobl it and ſoe vntill [   ]

Tho· Dudly   John Haynes and others.

The 7th of January 1632

Its. ordred that noe perſon whatſoeue∧ [   ]   anny houſe in the Bounds of the Towne [   ] leaue from the maiorpart

ffurther it is Agreed by a joynt Conſent th∧ [   ] Towne ſhall not bee Inlarged vntill all [   ] places bee filled wth houſes

ffurther it is Agreed that. all the hou∧ [   ] the bounds of the Towne ſhalbee Co∧ [   ] ſlate or board and not wth thach

ffurther It is ordered that all h∧ [   ] Range eevn and ſtand Juſt fix [   ] owne ground from the ſtreet.

ffurther it is ordred that whoſoeue∧ [   ] A lott in the Towne and dooth not [   ] build vppon it wthin six mounths [   ] his lott to whomſoevr will imp∧

ffurther It is ordred that if [   ] child or ſeruant ſhall [   ] common gate [   ]   [   ] laſt of October [   ]   [   ]

Comon   Pales deuided as ffollo —

John Haynes Eſqr	70 Rodd	Steben Hart	8 Rod
Thomas Dudly Eſqr.	40 Rodd	William Wadſwth	7
mr. Symon Bradſtreet	20 Rodd	George Steele	6
John Beniamen	50 Rodd	Richard Goodman	6
John Talcott	36 Rodd	John Bridg	6

TOWN RECORDS

Mathew Allen	45 Rod	Symon Saket	6
William Weſtwood	30 Rod	Richard Butler	6
James Omſted	25 Rod	Cap: Patrike	5
Daniell Deniſon	25 Rod	Richard web	5
Samuell Dudly	25 Rod	John Maſters	4
Andrew Warner	20 Rod	Antho: Colby	4
William Goodwine	20 Rod	John Clark	3
John White	15 Rod	Nath. Richards	3
John Steele	14 Rod	Richard Lord	3
Edward Stebinge	12 Rod	Abraham Morrill	3
William Spencer	12 Rod	William Kelſe	3
Thomas Hoſmer	10 rod	Jonath Boſwth	2
William Lewis	10 rod	Tho: Spencer	2
Hester Muſſe	10 rod	Garrad Hadon	2
Joſeph Readinge	2 Rod	Edward Elmer	2
Thomas Heate	2 Rod	Jeremy Addams	2

The 5ᵗʰ Auguſt 1633

Lotts Granted for Cowyardes.

Samuell Dudly	$\frac{1}{2}$ 1 Acker	William Wadſwth	$\frac{1}{2}$ akr
Daniell Deniſon	$\frac{1}{2}$ Acker	John Maſters	$\frac{1}{2}$ akr
John Beniamen	1 Ackr	Nath: Richads	$\frac{1}{2}$ akr
ₐiam Peintre	1 Acker	John Clark	1 roode
[ ] Omſted	1 Acker	Capt Patrk	1 akr
ₐilliam Weſtwood	1 Ackr	Symo Sakt	$\frac{1}{2}$ akr
William Goodwine	3 Roods	Will Kelſe	1 roode
John White	3 Roods	Richad Goodn	3 Roods
John Steele	3 Roods	Tho Spencer	1 rood
William Spencer	3 Roods	Jonah: Boſworth	1 rood
George Steele	$\frac{1}{2}$ ackr	Jer: Addams	1 rood
William lewis	$\frac{1}{2}$ akr	Tho: Hoſmer	3 Roods
Heſter Muſe	$\frac{1}{2}$ ackr	John Prat	$\frac{1}{2}$ akr
Edward Stebinge	1 akr		
Steph Hart	$\frac{1}{2}$ akr.		

The 2ᵈ of September 1633

[   ] ˄dered that whofoeuer hath anny tree [   ] Croffe A high˄way and dooth not re˄ it wthin 7 dayes or whofsoever fhal ˄ ter ffell anny tree and let it lye croff [   ] ˄ way one day fhall fforfeit the tree.

[   ] ˄ᵗʰ of October 1633

[   ] whofoeuer maketh an˄ [   ] [   ]
˄hall pay to the [   ] be Deui˄
[   ] [   ] [   ]

[2]   The 4ᵗʰ of November 1633

Lotts for Cowyards granted

John Haynes Efqr	1 Ackr	Richard Lord	1 [ ]
Andrew Warner	1 Acker	mr Hopkins	[ ]
Mathew Allen	1 Acker		
mr Thomas Hooker	1 Acker		
mr Samuell Ston	1 Acker		

The 2ᵈ of December 1633

It is ordered that noe perfon whatfoeuer fhall fell Anny Tree neer the Towne [   ] wthin the path wch goeth ffrom Wattertow˄ to Charles towne vppon the fforfeiture of ffiue fhillings for euery tre soe ffeled

It is ffurther ordered that all the fyer w˄ wch lyeth not onn anny mans ˄ fhalbee ˄ mon to every Inhabetant:

It is ffurther ordered that whofoeuer hath anny Timber lyeing vppon anny mans lott he fhall ffetch it away before the midle of March next or elfe fforfeit his Tymber   Agreed wth mr Symon Bradftreet to make a fuficient Cartway alonge by his pales and keepe it in repaire 7 years and is to haue xˢ for the fame

Granted Tho Dudly Efqr 1 rood whear his h˄ Cockes ftood

The 5th of January 1633.

Granted mr. Tho. Hooker 5 ackers in [   ] to mr Samuell Stonn 4 Ackrs in th˄ more to mr Hooker 3 ackrs in the [   ] to mr Samuel Ston 2 Ackrs in fhip [   ] Granted John Haynes Efqr soe much [   ] by his Cowyard as fhalbee sett out by mr [   ] and John Taylcott

Sould Andrew Warner that Corner [   ] fwampe ground by the ould feild for fo˄ fhillings

The 2d off ffebruary 1633

It is Agreed that the planting ground in [   ] necke of land fhalbe thufe deuided. John Haynes Efqr one Ackr and halfe   John Taylcott 2 Ackrs   John: W˄ [   ]   Andrew Warner 3 Ackrs   Wil˄ [   ] Mathew Allen 2 Ackrs   Mr [   ]   Hefter Mufe 2 Ackrs   Jam˄ [   ]   Stephen Hart 2 Ackrs   Will˄ [   ] Thomas Hofmer 3 Ackrs   Edw˄ [   ]   George Steele 2 Ackrs   for wch ground they are to m˄ [   ] paleinge for euery Ack˄ [   ] rayld six foote aboue ground [   ] before the 1 Aprill next or pa˄ [   ]

The 2d of March 1633

Granted William Spencer the fwampe on the other fide the Creeke

Granted William Lewis the fwampe by the fhipp marfh

Granted John Beniamen all the grownd betwen John Mafters his grownd and Antho Couldbyes prouided that the windmill hill fhall be referued for the Towns vfe and a Cartway of two Rods wyde vnto the fame

Granted William Lewis the vfe of the Comon ground between the fwampe and the ffeild lane vntell they fhall defier it

The 7th. Aprell 1634.

Granted John Pratt two Ackrs by the ould burieing place wthout the Comon Pales —

It is ordered that Euery one whoe hath anny part in the Comon Pales ſhall ſet vpe aſtake at the begining of thr pales wth ther mark vpon it and what ſoever paleing is Judged inſuficient by thoſe wch are Apointed to vew the ſame the owners are after notice giuen to ſend wthin one ower after to mēd the ſame and not to ceaſe vntell it bee ffiniſhed vpon the forfeture of v^s arod to anny one that ſhall mend it for them

The 5th of May 1634

Granted mr Stonn a Garden plot by the meeting house

The 2^d June 1634

Its ordered that the Conſtable ſhall pay James Omſted x^s for makeing the hyeway by William Butlers pales

The 7th July 1634.

[   ] ordered that John Beniamen Daniell $_\wedge$ ſon William Spencer Richard Butler ſh$_\wedge$ [   ] the bounds of mr Atterton Houghes grant

The 4th of Auguſt 1634

[ ] is ordered that whatſoever tree is now [   ] [   ] bounds of the Towne and is not J$_\wedge$ [   ] [   ] the firſt of March next It [   ] [   ] anny man to vſe them or [   ] $_\wedge$ny tree and let it ly abo$_\wedge$ [   ] [   ] for anny man to [   ]

[3] It is ordered that whoeſoever ſhall ffa$_\wedge$ [   ] Tree for Boards Clapboards or fframes of hou$_\wedge$ [   ] fell them out of the Towne ſhall fforfeit for euery [   ] foe ſould xx^s

Granted Symon Williard one the weſt ſide the River one hundrd Ackers

granted John Bridge there 75 Ackrs
granted Tymothy Tomlins there 10 Ackrs
granted Dollard Dauis there 25 Ackrs

Lotts Granted in westend

To John Taylcott 3 acres ½
To Richard ??? the upland beyond John ???
To John Clarke 2 acres
To Guy Bainbridge 1 acre
To George Stocking 2 acres
To ??? Scott 5 acres
To Tho: Judd 4 acres
To John Barnard 5 acres
To Joseph Eason 2 acres
To ??? Evant 2 acres
To Stephen Hart 3 acres
To Jonathan ??? worth 2 acres
To John Maynard 5 acres
To Samuell ??? 5 acres
To Edward Elmer 3 acres
To John Gibbon 6 acres
To Nath: Ely 6 acres
To ??? ??? one roode
To John ??? ??? 2 acres

Lotts Granted in westend ffield

To John Arnold 5 acres   To Will Westr 3 ac:
To William ??? 10 acres   To ??? ???
To Tymo: Standly 6 acres To Took ??? 3 ac
To James Ensigne 4 acres To ??? ???
To Tho ffisher 5 acres
To ??? Drinett 4 acres
To Edmond Garner 4 acres
To Tho: Bull 3 acres
To John Hopkins 4 acres

Granted Joseph Mygatt ??? ??? 7 acres ???
??? ???
ffurther it is ordered that whosoever ???
any hay in the ??? and does not ??? ???
agayne shall pay for every such fact 2s 6d

Lots Granted in Weftend

To John Taylcott 3 Ackrs ½
To Richard Webb the vpland beyond John mafters

To John Clarke 2 Ackrs	To Guy Bambrige 1 Ackr.
To Georg Stockine ½ Ackr	To Tho: Scott 5 Ackrs
To Tho: Judd 4 Ackrs	To John Barnard . 5 Ackrs
To Jofeph Eafon . 2 Ackrs	To Seth Grant . 2 Ackrs
To Chrifto: Kene 3 Ackrs	To Jonatha$_\wedge$ Bofeworth 2 Ackrs
To John Maynard 5 Ackrs	To Samuell Greenhill 8 Ackrs
To Edward Elmer 3 Ackrs	To John Gibfon . 6 Ackrs
To Nath: Elly. 6 Ackrs	To Nicho: Clarke one roode
To John Prince 2 Ackrs	

Lotts Granted In Weftend ffeild

To John Arnold 5 Ackrs	To Will Man 3 A$_\wedge$
To William Peintree 10 Ackrs	To Edmo Hunt 3 A$_\wedge$
To Tymo: Standly . 6 Ackrs	To Robt Day 3 Ac$_\wedge$
To James Ensigne 4 Ackrs	To Garrd Haddon [ ]
To Tho ffifher 5 Ackrs	To Will Kelfy 3 A$_\wedge$
To Humphry Wincett 4 Ackrs	To Edmond Gearner 4 Ackrs
To Tho. Beale– 3 Ackrs	To John Hopkins 4 Ackrs

Granted Jofeph Mygate by the Pyne fwa$_\wedge$ fower Ackers
ffurther it is ordered that whofoeuer fca$_\wedge$ [   ] anny Hay in the Creeke and dooth not cle$_\wedge$ agayne fhall pay for euery fuch falt v^s.

The prime of Septembr 1634

It is Ordered that the Ground lyeinge beet$_\wedge$ the Planting feild and Charls town P$_\wedge$ fhalbee meafuerd and deuided to thofe wch [   ] vfe for it to keep cattell in and that Capta P$_\wedge$ fhall haue one Ackr of it and John Mafters [   ]

Granted John Beniamen the Marfh between [   ] windmill hill and the Creeke next to it.

ffurther it is ordered that Georg St$_\wedge$ [   ] William Spencer fhall measuer out al$_\wedge$ [   ] $_\wedge$ranted by the Towne and have III^d the Ac$_\wedge$ [   ] [   ] fame

TOWN RECORDS

Lots Granted one the weft fide the River

Michaell Spencer 4 Ackrs   Garrad Spencer 4 Ackrs
Stephen Poaft 12 Ackrs   Samuell Wackman 12 Ackrs

The 4th of Octobr 1634

Itt is Ordered that Every one whoe hath anny timbr lyeing vppon Anny mans lott fhall cutt it offe before the ffirft of December next or else forfett the faid timber to thofe wch oweth the lotts

The 3rd of November 1634.

James Olmfted is Choffen Counftable for the yeare followinge and tell a new be Chofen in his Roome and prefently fowrne

John White is Choffen furveior to feethe highways and ftreete kept cleane and in repair for the yeare followeinge

It is ordered that Every Inhabetant in the Towne fhall keepe the ftreet Cleane from wood and all other things againft his owne Ground and whoefoever fhall haue anny thinge lye in the ftreet above one daye after the next meetinge day fhall forfeit v^s for every fuch default

The ffirft of December 1634

Lotts. Granted In Weftend ffeild

To Daniell Dennifon 6 Ackrs   To John Steele 2 Ackrs
To William Andrews 5 Ackrs   To Thomas Scott 3 Ackrs
To mrs Chefter 4 Ackrs   To Bartholmew Green 6 Ackrs
To Samuell Greene 4 Ackrs

Granted William Spencer that Corner of Ground by Jofeph Myats between the Swamps to bee fett out by John Haynes Efqr

The 5th of January 1634

It is ordered that whoefoever hath anny lott Granted by the Towne and fhall not Improve the fame then it is to returne to the Towne or if hee fhall Improue the fame he fhall firft offer it vnto the Towne If they refus to giue him what charges he hath bin att then to haue liberty to fell it to whom he Cann

Granted John Taylcott 5 Ackrs of marſh ‸und lyeing next to John Beniamens an‸ [ ] to haue noe part of the other ground f‸ woorkeing Cattell

Itt is ordered that whoſoever ſhall [ ] keepe anny Swine vppon anny m‸ ‸rownd ſhall forfeit xxˢ for eve‸ ‸h default.

[4]   Lotts Granted behind the Pyne S‸

To John Pratt 5 Ackrs   To John Prince 2 Ackrs
To Antho Couldbey 3 Ackrs   To Nicholas Clarke 3 Ackrs
To mr Pratt 4 Ackrs   To Guy Bambrige 4 Ackrs
To Samuell Whithead 2 Ackrs   To Nath: Hancocke 2 Ackrs
To Georg Stockine 4 Ackrs   To Daniell Abott 3 Ackrs
To James Eſigne 1 rood   To John Hopkins 1 rood
To Humphry Vincent 1 rood   To Tymo: Stanly 1 rood

Itt is ordered that there ſhalbe noe moore Lotts Granted one this ſide the River out of the Cow Comon to anny perſon whatſoever

The 3ᵈ of ffebruary 1634

Att A Gennerall Meeting of the whole Towne Itt was Agreed vppon by a Joynt Conſent that 7 menn ſhould bee Choſſen to doe the whole buſſines of the Towne and soe to Continew vntell the ffirſt Monday in November next and vntell new be Choſſen in their Room ſoe ther was then Elected and Choſſen

      John Haynes Eſqr
      mr Symon Bradſtreet
      John Taylcott
      William Weſtwood
      John White.
      William Wadſwoorth
      James Olmſted Conſtable

Itt is further Ordered by a Joynt Conſent [ ] whatſoever theſe Townſmen thuſe Choſſe‸ ſhall doe In the Compas of ther tyme ſha ſtand in as full force as if the whole To‸ did the ſame either for makeing of new orders or alteringe of ould ones ffurther it is ordered that whatfoever per_∧ they fhall fend for help in anny buffn_∧ and he fhall refus to Come they fhall hau_∧ pow to lay a fine vppon him and to gath_∧ [   ]

ffurther it is ordered that they fhall haue O_∧ to attent vppon them to Imploy aboute an_∧ buffines at a publik Charge

ffurther Itt is ordered that they fhall me_∧ every firft Monday in Mounth at [   ] in the After Noone accordinge to the former [   ]

Alfoe ther was then Choffen to Joyne [   ]

   James Olmfted Conftable
   John Beniamen
   Daniell Denifon
   Andrew Warner
   William Spencer

wch 5 acordinge to the order of Cour_∧ [   ] furvey the Towne lan and enter [   ] a book Apointed for that purpofe

Itt is further ordered that thefe 5 m_∧ meet every firft Monday in t[ ] [   ] at the Conftables houfe in the [   ] _∧t the Ringing the bell

Aprill 21th 1635

*Granted mr Hooker fiue Ackrs of Meadow Grownd in the me next Wattertowne weire

*Granted mr Stonn two Ackrs in the fame meaddowe

*Granted mr Goodwine two Ackers in the fame meadowe

Granted mr Hooker thirty Ackrs of falt marfh one the fouth [ ] Charls River

Granted mr Stonn twenty Ackers of falt marfh in the fame mar both wch to lye next the Lot of Thomas Dudly Efqr

Att A Gennerall Meeting of the whole Towne the 20th August 163[ ]

Itt was ordered that William Spencer and Georg Steele fhou[ ] meafuer all the meaddow ground undeuided belonging to the Ne[ ] towne: and when it is Meafuered and deuided to euery man his propo[ ] cion they are to: meafuer every mans feuerally and Caufe ftakes to b[ ]

*Across these entries a pen was subsequently drawn.

fett at each end and to haue three pence the Acker for the fame and whofoever fhall not pay for meafueringe wthin one yeare then the ground to returne to them for meafueringe

ffurther it is ordered that the fame fhalbee deuided acordinge to every mans seuerall proporcion herevnder written vntell it bee all difpoffed off viz

Tho Hooker 0 Ackrs   Nathaniell Richards 1 Ackr
Tho Beale 1   Sam Stonn 0   Thomas fffsher 1   Abra Morrill 1
Will Goodwine 3   Sam: Greenhill 2   Tho· Heate 1   Capt Patrik 2
Tymo Standly 1½   Sy. Saket 1   James Olmfted 5   Jams Enfigne 1½
Joh Maynad 1   ₍Beniamen 5   John Barnard 1½   Tho Jud 1½
William Andrews 2½   William Kelfy 1   Jo Gibfon 1
₍athew Allen 6   Richard Goodman 1   Tho Scott 4
₍hn Tailcott 5½   Antho' Couldby 1   John Prat 1½
₍uy Bambrig 1½   Tho. Spencer 1   Jo: Hopkins 1½
₍ohn Steele 2:   Richard Lord 1   Ed Gerner 1
₍illiam Pentry 6.   Tho. Hofmer 5   Sam Dudly 4
₍ohn Mafters: 1½   Sam Green ½   Hefter Mufe 1½
₍ndrew Warner 5   John Prince ½   Hmp Vincent 1
[   ] White 2½   Edw: winfhep ½   Jer Adams ½   Robt Day ½
₍liam Lewis 2   Garrd Hadon ½   Nath Elly 1
[   ] Wadfworth 2½   Jofeph Reding ½   Georg Stockin 1
₍phen Hart 2   Nath. Hancok ½   John Arnold 1
₍rd Webb 2   Edmo Hunt ½   Ed Elmer ½   [   ] Steele 1
William Jones ½   Jo: Mygate 1   [   ] Stebing 1½
William Man ½   Will Butler 4   Jona Bofwth ½
₍m Spencer 2½   Jo: Eafon ½   [   ] Butler ½
[   ] Auftin ½   Chr Kene ½   [   ] Daniell Abot ½

[5]   Novembr the 23[th.] 1635

Att A Gennerall Meeting of the whole [   ] ther was then Choffen to order buffines of the whole Towne for the year following and vntell new bee Choffen in their Rooms

  mr Roger Harlackenden
  William Spencer

TOWN RECORDS

   Andrew Warner
   Joſeph Cooke
   John Bridg
   Clement Chapline
   Nicho: Danforth
   Tho: Hoſmer
   William Andrews

 wch nyne men are to haue the power of the whole Towne as thoſe formerly Choſſen hadd as may Apear in the orders made the 3 ffebruary 1634

 ffurther ther was Choſſen and ſworne

 William Andrews Conſtable for the year followinge and vntill anew be Choſſen

 ffurther ther was then Choſſen for the year followin͜

 Barnabas Lambſon: to be ſurveior of the High-wayes

 Itt is further Ordered that the Towne booke ſhalbee at William Spencers house

The 7ᵗʰ of Decembr 1635

  Present
  Nicho Danforth
  Joſeph Cooke
  Will Andrews
  Tho Hoſmer
  Will Spencer

 Itt is Ordered that the mounth ͜ meeting every firſt Monday [   ] Acording to the firſt order ſhall [   ] and whoſoeuer Apears nott w͜ half an ower after the Ringing of the [   ] ſhall pay for the firſt day viᵈ and [   ] day xiiᵈ and ſoe to dobl it every day [   ] a Juſt excuſe ſuch as may give ſatis͜ to the reſt of the Company.

 It is further ordered that ther ſhalbee a ſufici͜ bridg made downe to low watter mark one this ſid the Riuer and a broad ladder one the farther ſide the Riuer for conv͜ Landinge and mr Chapline mr Danforth and mr Cooke to ſee it made

 It is further ordered that the High way by mr Bu͜ ſhalbee mended as alſoe the high way [   ] Clay pitts and anny two of the Townſmen [   ] haue power to Apoint men to doe the ſame [   ] the Charge of the Towne

It is further Ordered that whoefoever h˄ [   ] Ground between the pyne Swamps [   ] fence it Inn before the firſt of Aprell [   ] and whoſoeuer ſhall faile of ſoe do˄ ſhall pay doble to anny one that will doe [   ] ſame or forfeit his Ground

An Agreement by thoſe wch owe the ground [   ] Pyne Swamps that the fence ſhalbee [   ] foote high aboue ground and that mr Bambrigg and William Spencer to vew [   ] fence whether it be ſufficient or not [   ] if it be found not ſufficient [   ] not mend it wthin three days a˄ [   ]   [   ]

The 4th January 1635

˄ſent
˄ C: Chaplin
˄icho Danforth
Jos Cooke
Will Andrews
Andr warner
Jo. Bridge
Tho Hoſmer
W: Spencer.

It is Ordered that John Hopkins ſhall haue the 4 Ackrs of ground by the pyne ſwampe wch mr Prat ſhould have had

It is further orderd that Will Towne ſhall haue the two Ackrs there wch Samuell Whitheade ſhould haue had

It is further Ordered that Edward winſhapp ſhal haue 2 Ackrs ther of that Nicho Clarke ſhould hauehad

It is further ordered that James Hoſmer ſhall haue 2 Ackrs ther prouided he buy a houſe in the Towne ore elſe to Returne againe to the Towne

Granted Tymothy Standly half an Acker moore ther to his garden plott

It is further ordered that the burryinge place ſhalbee palled in: wherof John Taylcot is to doe 2 Rodd Georg Steele 3 Rod and Agate Thomas Hoſmer 3 Rod Mathew Allen — 1 Rodd and Andrew warner apointed to get the Remainder done at A publik Charge & he is to haue iiiˢ A Rodd

It is further ordered that mr Joſeph Cooke ſhall keep the fferry and haue apenny over and Ahalfe penny one lectuer daies

Granted Thomas Hayward about 2 Acks wthin weſtend ffeild gate beyond the Clay pits

It is ffurther ordered that there ſhalbee a foote bridg made over the Creeke at the end of Spring ſtreet and a Caſway and Thomas Hoſmer and William Spencer to ſee it done at a publik Charge

It is ffurther ordered that ther fhalbee a doble Rayle fett vpp from the pyne fwampe fence to weftend feild fence for the Milch Cowes to lyein one nights and that noe other Cattell whatfoever to goe ther ethr fwine goats mares or thelike

It is further ordered that the Remaynder of the Ground betwen William Weftwoods and Jofeph Mygats pales to be fenced in for draft Cattell to be putt in

Reckoned wth John Beniamen for his Conftables Charge and he oweth Juft xx^s

Recd the 8th January of mr Beniamen xx^s

[6]   The 8th February 1635

present

mr Harlackenden
mr Chapline
mr Danforth
mr Andrews
An: Warner
Jo. Bridge
mr Cooke
Tho Hofmer
W. Spencer

Granted Tho Beale A lott in the Towne
Granted mr Green liberty to feed his Cattell Two myles abou Wattertowne Weire this next fomer prouided he dooth not lett them hurt the Moweing ground ffurther it is the intent of the Towne that he fhall not moue there vnles heerafter the Towne fee Caufe to giue him leaue

It is further ordered that the ground lyeinge between Charls Towne path and the Comon Pales foremerly aponted to be meafurd as alfo the Remaynder by watertowne fhalbee thufe deui

To John Haynes Efqr	9	Ackrs
To Tho Dudly Efqr	6	Ackrs
To mr Symon Bradftreet	5	Ackrs
To mr Mathew Allen	5	Ackrs
To mr Sam Dudly	3	Ackrs
To Tho. Hofmer	5	Ackrs
To Will Weftwood	5	Ackrs
To William Peintrey	5	Ackrs
To Andrew Warner	4	Ackrs
To John White	2	Ackrs
To William Wadfworth	3	Ackrs

To James Homſted	5	Ackrs
To Tho. Scott	3	Ackrs
To William Lewis	2	Ackrs
To Stephen Hart	2	Ackrs
To mr Will Goodwine	2	Ackrs
To mr Tho Hooker	3	Ackrs
To mr Dan: Deniſon	3	Ackrs

Itt is further ordered that ther ſhalbee A [   ] Rayle from William Weſtwoods Cowe [   ] to Joſeph Mygats Pales before the [   ] of May next by thoſe wch haue this la$_\wedge$ granted them proportionable to ther Ac$_\wedge$ and thoſe wch are then behinde wth ther fen$_\wedge$ ſhall forfeit ther grownd to the Towne

Itt is further ordered that this ground ſhalbe I$_\wedge$ —preued to noe other vſe but to keepe Catt$_\wedge$ Inn and whoſoever ſhall Improue it to ann$_\wedge$ other vſe ſhall forfeit ther grownd

Itt is further ordered that whoſoeuer ſhall her$_\wedge$ ſett vpp anny houſe in the bounds of the Towne It ſhall not bee accounted as a ho$_\wedge$ to haue the accomodacons of the Towne [   ] anny preuelidge of the Towne vnleſs t$_\wedge$ Towne give liberty to ſett vpe the ſame

Itt is further ordered that whoſoeuer hath or h$_\wedge$ after ſhall haue anny grownd lyeing in [   ] Bownds of the Towne and ſhall defier t$_\wedge$ lett or ſell the ſame he ſhall not Lett or ſ$_\wedge$ the ſame to anny one who eis An I$_\wedge$betant in the Towne or Wilbee wthi$_\wedge$ Twelue Monthes after vppon the forfei$_\wedge$ of all ſuch land vnto the Towne the m$_\wedge$ is land wthout A houſe

Granted William Blunfeld ſix Ackrs on t$_\wedge$ South ſid of the River Agreed wth Andrew Warner and John [   ] to ſett vp A doble Rayle from Weſtend [   ] to the Pyne Swampe for the Cowes [   ] kept in nights and to haue xvi^d [   ] [   ] be done before the midle of A$_\wedge$

Itt is further ordered that ther ſhalbee one Acker Rayld Inn wth doble Rayle for the Dry Cattell to lye In.Anights and John Bridg and will Spencer to hier men to doe the ſame

Agreed wth mr Chapline that his man ſhall kepe the Goats and to haue three halfepence aweek for one goate and apenny aweek for Wethers or kids to begine next Monday.

18 TOWN RECORDS

It is further ordered that the furueior for the high Wayes fhall fee the ftreets kept Cleane acording to the order of the Towne.

The Names of Thofe men whoe haue houfes in the Towne at this prefent as onely are to be acconted as houfes of the Towne

In the Towne

John Haynes Efqr Govr 6 moore in the Towne

Tho Dudly Efqr	6	Richard Beats	2
mr Roger Harlackenden	3	Tho Heywarde	^
mr. Tho: Hooker	4	Will ffrench	1
mr Comfort Starr	3	John Ringe	^
James Olmfted	4	Nath Richards	1
Clement Chapline	3	Widdow Sackett	1
Robt Bradifh	2	Symon Willard	1
George Steele	1		
Edward Stebing	1	In Cowyard Rowe	
Tymo Stanly	2	Nicho Danforth	4
Jonnas Auftine	1	mr Symon Bradftreet	2
Tho. ffifher	1		
mr Peter Buckly	5	In Weftend	
Abrah Morrill	1	Raph Hudfon	2
Tho Beale	1	William Spencer	2
Raph Hudfon	2	Nicho Roberts	1
^ohn Pratt	2	Tho Hofmer	4
William Spencer	2	Symon Crofbey	1
Tho Spencer	1	John Beniamen	2
Barnab Lambfon	2	John Mafters	2
John Arnold	1	John Talcott	4
Tho. Wells	1	John Clarke	1
John Woolcott	1	John Bridge	2
James Enfigne	2	Guy Bambrige	1
Daniel Patrike	2	Richard Champnes	3
Richard Lord	1	Tho Judd	1
^mph Vincent	1	Robert Day	1
John Santly	1	Edmond Hunt	1
Mathew Allen	5	mr Willia^ Wetherall	1
William Andrews	2	John Maynard	1

₄r Tho Shepard	3	John Gibſon	1
₄hn Hopkins	1	John Champnes	1
[ ] Marratt	2	Garrad Haddon	1
₄ill Towne	1	Antho Couldbey	[ ]
₄ath Hancocke	1	William Mann	1
₄niel Abbott	1	William Joanes	1
₄ter Muſſe	2	Joſiah Cobbett	[ ]
[ ] Wadſworth	2		
[ ] Lewis	2	by the Pyne ſwampe	
[ ] Readinge	1	Joſeph Mygate	2
[ ] Beſbeth	1		
[ ] ₄rning	1	On the ſouth ſide the River	
[ ] ₄ke	2	Richard Girlinge	
		William Wetherall (sold to Mr Benjamin & by him to Edm Angier)	

By the ffreſh Pond.

Gilbert Crackbone   Richard Parke
Walter Nicholes   (wch are now)
Will Addams   Widow Grenne

[7]   The ffirſt of March 1635

Agreed wth Richard Rice to keep 100 : Cowes for the ſpace of Three Mounthes to begine when he ſhalbee appointed and is to haue Tenn pounds paid him wthin 10 dayes after the ſhipps bee come in or In June alſo he is to haue 2 men to help him keepe them the firſt 14 dayes and one man the next 7 dayes alſo to have them kept 2 ſaboth dayes and he one dueringe the tyme Alſoe hee is to fetch the Cowes into the Towne every morneinge out of the Comon halfe an ower after the ſone is vpe at the fartheſt and to bring them into the Town halfe an ower before the ſone goeth downe and to pay III^d a Cowe for every night he leveth out anny, alſoe hee is not to kepe anny Cattell for anny man exſept he have leave from the Townſmen vpon the forfetur of v^s a cow he ſhall ſoe kepe alſo he hath liberty to kepe his owne heifer wthout pay

                          Richard R. R. Rice his marke

Agreed wth John Clarke to make a fuffcient Weir to Catch Alwiffs vppo_ Menotomies River in the bounds of this Tow_ before the 12th of Aprell next and fh_ fell and delliver vnto Inhabetants of the Towne and noe other exfept for bayte [ ] all the Aylwifs he fhall take at iii*s* vi_ pr thoufand and fhall at all tymes giue [ ] Notice to the perfons that fhall bee apointed to fetch them away as hee fhalbe dyrected whoe fhal Difchardge the faid John Cla_ of them wthin 24 oures after Notice ore el_ he to haue liberty to fell them to whome [ ] Cann prouided and it is the meaninge [ ] Townfmen that if anny fhall Defier [ ] haue fome to eate before the great quan_ Cometh then he is to haue ii*d* a fcore a_ fetch them thaire ore iii*d* a fcore and he bringe them home ffurther the Townfm_ doe promife in the behalfe of the Towne [ ] make good all thofe fifh he fhalbee dam_fied by the Indians that is fhall himfelfe delliuer vnto them beeing appointed before [ ] the Townfmen how many he fhall delliuer alfo to faue him harmles from anny [ ] he fhall fufteyne by Wattertowne p_ it be not his owne fault he is to haue [ ] mony wthin 14 days after he hath done fifh_

John Clarke

The 13th. of March 1635

Agreed Wth William Patten to kepe 100 Cattell one the otherfide the Riuer for the fpace of feauen Mounthes to begine when the Towne fhall appoint him and to haue Twenty pounds the one halfe paid him In Monny when he hath kept halfe his tyme and the other halfe In Corne when he hath done keeping at the price wch the Comon Rate of Corne goeth when he is to be paid and he is to haue a man to help him the firft 14 days he payinge him for one weeke the Towne for the other alfoe he is to lodg ther exfept once a weeke and to haue aman to keepe them every other faboth day and hee to pay x*s* a beaft for every beaft he fhall loefe and to keepe noe Cattell of anny man exfept the Townf-men give leaue vpon the forfetuer of 5*s* a head for every head he fhall foe keepe

The mark *VP* of William Patten.

Itt is ordered Euery man fhall put his Goats to the keeper before the 20th of March & whofoever dooth not put them to the keeper before that tyme & they be taken In anny mans Corne or hay to pay iii^d a goate for eury fault

The Hog keeper begane to keepe one the firft of Aprill being the 5th day of the weeke at 10^s pr Weeke foe long as the Townfmen pleafe to haue him kepe them and hes to keepe them at Rocky Meadow

The 4th of Aprill 1636

Itt is ordered that Richard Rice fhalbegine to keepe the Cowes the 11th of Aprell 1636

Itt is ordered that William Pattine fhalbegine to keepe the dry Cattell the 14th of Aprell

Agreed wth John Talcott and William Wadfwoorth to haue ther houfe at Rockey Meadowe this year for thee Hogekeeper to abyde in and they are to haue ther cattell goe free from payinge to wards the pound for dry Cattell this yeare

It is ordered that whofoeuer finds a Cocke hen or Turkey in A garden It fhalbe lawfull for them to Requier three pence apeece of the owner & if they Refus to pay then to kill the fame

Itt is ordered that the Common Pales aboute the three Comon ffeilds fhalbee kept in fufficient Repayre and whofoever hath anny defect in th‸ part fhall pay v^s Arodd or ii^d Apale

[　] Chapline to fee the pales about the nec‸ [　] ‸d once euery Weeke

[8] James Enfigne and Richard Champnes to vew the pa‸ about Weftendfeild the firft 14 days and Humph Vincent and Tymo: Standly the next 14 dayes

Itt is ordered that whofoeuer finds either horfe cow goate or anny other beaft In anny of the plantinge feilds after the 2^d day of the next weeke fhall haue vi^d Apeece for bringing them oute

Itt is ordered that whofoeuer finds either Horfe Mare ox goate or fwine In the Cow Comon whear they are to ly anights exfept they: are driueing over the fame or anny Cow exfept before the heard goeth out or after it Cometh home fhall haue vi^d apeece of the owner of the fame beaft for bringing them out

Itt is orderd that Walter Nichols fhall pull vpp the boarded weire In menotemis Riuer

Andrew Warner and Jofeph Cooke to make a rate for the deuifion of the Aylwifs

Itt is ordered that noe man heerafter fhall fett vpe anny dwelling houfe wthin the Bounds of the Towne wthout the Confent of the Maior part of the Townfmen vppon the forfetuer of fiue pounds pr ann: vnto the reft of the Inhabetants for Euery year it fhall foe Continew: The meanin$_\wedge$ of the Towne is that noe man be hindred to add to ther new dwellinge houfes

Agreed W$^{th.}$ mr Bradftreet

The 23th Aprill 1636

Itt is ordered that there fhalbee noe Dry Cattell kept vpp$_\wedge$ this fide the River exfept vppon mens feuerall pr$_\wedge$ prities: and Cows neer Calvinge after the 2^d d$_\wedge$ of the next weeke vppon the forfetuer of ii^s vi$_\wedge$ a weeke or vi^d a Day: & the fame for other yeares

Itt is orderd that all Steers aboue a year and halfe ould at prefent fhalbee kept at Rockey Meaddow $_\wedge$fept fuch as are referued for Draught wch are [   ] be kept in the ox paftuer and that whatfoever fteer is found heer in the Comon after the 4 day of the next wee$_\wedge$ fhall pay vi^d a day or ii^s vi^d a weeke

Agreed wth Andrew Warner to fetch home the ayl$_\wedge$ from the weir and he is to haue xvi^d a Thowfan$_\wedge$ and load them himfelfe for Caredge and to haue power to take anny man to help him he payeinge of him for his woorke

Andrew warner Apointed to fee A Cartway made to the weire

William Refkie Appointed to make Apound

John Bridge Appointed to men$_\wedge$ the penn for [   ] Dry Cattell and make a houfe for the Cow keep$_\wedge$

It is ordered that whafoeuer Dogg is found in [   ] Corne feilds the owner of the Dogg to pay [   ] for euery Tyme or elfe if he Refus then [   ] [   ] $_\wedge$ful for anny man to fhout the [   ]

TOWN RECORDS 23

June the 6 day.

Agreed with Goodman lamfon for his boy for ten pounds foe long as the dry Cattell be kept on the other fyd of the Riuer

Agreed with mr Andrewfe for his man to kepe the Calues for 12^s a weke foe long as we think good onely we are to prouid him a man for the prefent If he fhall Requier It of us

It Is ordered that Thomas hoffmer James benyt and benjamyne bur fhall make a pen for the Calues vppon paine of 5^s a peece

m^r Spencer & thomas hoffmer are to make a fuficyant pale & gate ouer the hey way ouer againft there grownd before the 20 day prefent month vppo$_\wedge$ payne of ten fhillings apece

Octobr the 3^d 1636

It is ordrd that noe Child vnder the Age of Tenn years fhall Carry Anny ffyer frome onehoufe to an other nor anny other prfon vnles It be couerd vppon the forfetuer of xii^d a tyme for euery fuch falt the onehalfe to the prfon that fees it theother to the Conftable

It is orderd that Euery one fhall Ringe ther hoggs before the 20th of this Mounth: vpon the for fetuerof xii^d a day for every day they fhall goe vnrungd after that day

It is ordrd that Euery man fhall fet amarkd ftake at the hither end there fences aboute ay of the Comon feilds before the firft of novmbr next & Returne anoate into the Townfmen betwen who ther fences lye & how much they haue vppon the forfetur 5^s a peece

Agreed wth mr Cooke to take vpe all the ftubbs that are wthin the bownds of the Towne that is wthin the Towne Gates & he is to haue ix^d apeece for takeing vpe the fame & fillinge vpe the holes all above iii inc$_\wedge$ wch he is to doe before the firft of Decembr or elfe to forfet f$_\wedge$
[   ]

7th Novemb.^{er} 1636

Edwd winfhipp is chofen for furveyor of the highwayes for this yeare following

Md, there are chofen for townfmen to order the towne Affayres for this yeare following naimly mr Harleckinden Jofeph Cook m^r Dampforde Richd Jackfon Edwrd Gof$_\wedge$ Symon Crofbee Barnebe Lambfon

24 TOWN RECORDS

M^d there is alfoe chofen for the furveying of all newe lotts [   ] fhall be graunted & purchafes bought & foulde p & keep [   ] book of them & deliv^r into the courte a tranfcrep [   ] the Conftables Jofeph Cook Mr Dampford mr [   ]

[9]   5 December 163

Hogreeve   Its ordered that John Clarke fhall be hogreeve to difcharge that office acco^{r}dinge to the Order of the courte

It is ordered that noe man Inhabiting or not I habiting with in the bowndes of the towne fhall lett or fell anie howfe or Land vnto anie without the confent of the townfme then in place vnleffe it be to a memb^r of the congregatio & leaft anie one fhall fuftaine loffe therby they fhall come & prffer the fame vnto them vppon a daye of ye: monethly meeting & att fuch a Rate as he fhall not fell or lett for a leffer price vnto anie than he offereth vnto them & to leave the fame in there handes in lyking vntill the next Meeting daye in the next moneth when yf they fhall not take it paying the pryce within fome convenient tyme or prvyde him a chapman he fhall then be free to fell or lett ye fame vnto anie oth prvyded the townfmen think them fitt to be received in .

for enter`taynig Inmates   It is ordered that whofoeve^r entertaynes anie p[   ] ftranger into the towne yf the congregation defyr it he fhall fet the towne free of them againe with one moneth aft^r warnig giuen them or elfe he fhall paye 10^s 8^d vnto the townfmen as a fyne for his default & as muche for eure moneth they fhall [   ] Remaine

The lott graunted to the drumm^r M^d: there is graunted vnto ffrannces Grefhold the drummer 2 ac^{rs} of land lying at the ende of Barnebe lambfons pale to^{wde} Charle towne in Regarde of his fervice amongft the fouldiers upo all ocafions as long as he ftayeth with condition yf he depr^t the towne & leave off that fervice with in twoe yeares he fhall leave it vnto thetowne at the charge it hath coft him in buyldin & inclofing

[   ]

ffor prſervg the Timbr in the comon

It is ordered yt noe man ſhall hereaftr fell anie timbr tree i_ the comon or anie place within the bowndeſe of the to_ without firſt leave graunted by the townſmen [ ] maior prt of them att a monthly meeting

And for the bettr fullfilling of the ſame John Bridg to look vnto the prventing of ſuch waſt & wt trees [ ] tymbr he ſhall fynde ſto ceaſe them to the towne_ vſe & thoſe that felled them to paye for a fyne [ ] for eury tree.

ffor preſervation of corn in the Neck

It is ordered that noe cattell ſhall be putt into the neck of lande this winter vnleſſe it be a harde fro_ vppon the forfit of 1s a tyme for eure head & whoeu_ ſhall leave anie of the plantingfeild gates open aftr they [ ] againe Repayred ſhall pay for eure ſuch default 1s.

Mr Harlackingden bar_

Md. There is graunted a place for a barn vnto m_ Harlackingden att the heade of the Creeke next his houſe to be ſett out by nicolas Dampforde & John Bridge

for the ſufficient [ ] of pales

It is ordered that the comon pales in all places yett to be made aftr this day ſhall be done with ſuficient poſt_ & Rayle & not with crotches & likwyſe all that are deca_ ſhall be Repayred in like mannr in paine of wt forſe_ the Townſmen ſhall think fitt

[ ]_ of the _ue ox paſtr

It is ordered that the owners of lande beyond Bar_ Lambſons Planting feild between the cow comon Ray_ [ ] Charleſtowne Rayle ſhall be graunted to ſevrall men [ ] paſture for there draught cattell in manner & forme f_

Edwrd winſhipp ++ 6. o
John Bridge ++ 8. 2
Barnebe Lamſon ++ 6. o
Symon Croſbey ++ 6. o

Teachr ++ 6. _
Sam Sheaprd ++ 8. _
Richrd Jackſon [ ]

Graunt of [ ] the fort hill to Joſeph Cook

Jan 2 1636.

Md It is graunted vnto Joſeph Cooke to have the hill by his howſe wch have bene hithr to prſerved for a place to build a fort vppon for Defence with all the lane leading thervnto prvided yf the towne fhall eu{r} make vfe of it for that ende he fhall yeild it againe or elfe to Remayne to him & his heires for eu{r}

Mr Richard Harlackingto⁸
[   ]

M{d} Graunted vnto m{r} Richard Harlackingden fix hundred Acres of vplande & Meadow at the place called vynebrooke in the midway betweene Newtowne & Concorde vppon condition he fendeth ou{r} his man or ordereth that fome oth{r} may buyld vppon it & Improve it for him the next Sumer aft{r} this next enfuing & now this Spring certaine Intelligence he will foe doe & vppon condition likwyfe that he cometh himfelfe the next Sum{rr} aft{r} being the third from this tyme & yf he fhall fayle in all or anie one of theis 3 conditio_∧ then this Graunt to be voyd

ffeb. 6

Ord{r} for goates mans corne

It is ordered that w{t}eu{r} goates fhall be taken in anie or or garden fhall pay the damage they have done & 3{d} a tyme for eure goate yf fufficiently fenced

Kenballs lande

It is ordered that   Kemball fhall have 2 Ac{rs} of land layd out as fhall hereaft{r} be appointed

The graunt of
∧he lotts for
∧owfes tow{rd}
Watertowne

Graunted vnto mr Grene halfe an ac{r} for a houf_∧ lott next mr Cabots howfe vppon condition y{t} yf he goe awaye it fhall Returne againe vnto the towne only paying him to the worthe of his buylding & fencing & breaking vpp

More graunted vnto   Addams half a acre
Graunted vnto Robert Parker halfe an ac{r}
Vnto Willm Wilcok halfe an ac{r}
Vnto Gregorie Stone halfe an ac
only they fhall paye vnto the Townfmen w{t} cha_∧ they fhall lay out for the lande according to their feverall prportions

∧he graunt of lotts from the
∧eate Swampe
[   ] cowcomon
∧yle & the houfe
∧tts betweene
Migats & Ja
∧fmers

M{d} This prcell of grounde was Layd out in man{r} following

To Elder Champnes 12.ac{rs}

	ac	R
Elder ffroft	6.	0
W{m} ffrenche	2.	0
Thomas Blogget	2.	0

[10] VIth March 1636

Mr Rogg^r Harlacking dens farme

Graunted vnto m^r Rogg^r Harlackingden 5^C Ac^{r}s of Land vnto his Meadowe that m^r Greene made vfe of (for a farme) To be layd out beyonde & about that Meadowe as fhall be thought fit by the Townfmen now in place or thofe they fhall putt in truft to fett it out The meaning is to make vpp that meadowe he hath now in poffefion by waye of purchafe 5C Ac^{rs} with vpland by this graunte on the fouth fyde of Charles Riv$_\wedge$ It is apoynted to be Meafured & layd out by John Bridge & Richard Jackfon as they fhall think fitt

A forfeit of 15 Ac^{rs} of Rocke Mead Edward Goff.
[ ] bought
[ ] Jo Page
[ ] fiue Ackers
[ ] ground
as will appear
[ ] the 29
$_\wedge$f November 1638

M^d feafed this daye to the vfe of the towne as forfet by virtue of a towne order made 8th ffeb^r 1635 Tenn Ac^{r}s Meadow in Rockie Meaddowe fould by m^r Befbeche & fyve Ac^{r}s fould by Ed: Goff both of them to Jo: Page of wat^{r}towne & for the confirm$_\wedge$ of the fame we herevnto fett o^r handes

Roger Harlakenden
Jofeph Cooke
Edward Goff

Richard Jackfon
Nicholas Danforth
Barnabe lamfonn
Simon Crofby

2nd Ap^{r}ill*

M^d Whereas m^r Befbege pleadeth he was Ignorant of the ord^r next above mentioned wee have therfore graunted vnto John Page purchafer vppon his Requeft y^t he fhall quietly enioy the f^d tenn Ac^{r}s: for the fpace of fyve yeares after this daye prvided that when foeu$_\wedge$ aft^r the f^d yeares the Towne fhall Require it he fhall Retourne it back againe with all the Right $_\wedge$tytle he bought of mr Befbege att the fame pryc$_\wedge$ namely 10! & for the fulfiling the fame I the [ ] John Page doe herevnd$_\wedge$ fett my hande

per me John Pag$_\wedge$

* In original MS. a cross was drawn through the entry as noted herein.

May 8

Agreemt for the keeping the milch cowes

Agreed with John Gibſon to keepe 100 Cowes att o[r] directio[n] all this ſum[r] vntill they take them In An[d] he is to [ ] 20[ˢ] the one halfe to be payed him whe he hath ke[pt] thim the[n] halfe of the tyme & thoth[r] halfe in monie [ ] corne at the ende at its then w[th]the & he is to pay 3[d] for evry co[w] he leaveth out a night & x[s] a cowe for eure one that [ ] loſt through his Defaulte he is to take in noe oth[r] cattell without the townſmens conſent he [ ] to dryve them out by 6 of the clock in the morning & to bring them home by ſunne halfe an howre high att night att the lateſt & to bring them into the towne [ ] milking morning & evening he is to have a keep[e] prvided for eurie eache of the ſabbath & whoe eu[r] ſha[ll] putt in anie ſtrange cattell ſhall ſende a helpe for [ ] or 3 dayes & eure man is to putt them into the cowe comon eure morning by the tyme apoi[nted] his owne cowe is to goe free

John Gibſo[n]

An ord[r] for putting the cowes in the comon to goe [ ] by the veep

It is ordered that whoſoeu[r] ſhall not have mil[ked] their cowes by 6 of the clock & putt them into the Comon Readie for the Cowe keep but they be left behynde they ſhall Dryue them to the heard or yf they be fownde att home att 8 of the clock they ſhall be [ten]ded by anie man vntill they paye one ſhilling [ ] poundage & foe for the yeares after *

Aprill: 19: 1637:

It is agreede wth Thomas Marriot and John Moore to keepe 100 Cattell on the other ſide of the Riuer for the whole Summer or for 7 month yf the Towne ſhall ſo thinke fit to beginn the 24th Day[e] of this inſtante = month and the ſaid Thomas Marriot to haue Twentie pounds and John Moore Ten pounds and the one halfe of the ſaid ſommes to be paid vnto the ſaid prties in monie when the tyme ſhall be halfe expired, and the other halfe of the Reſidue and remainder of the monie to be payeable eyther in monie or Corne when the Cattell ſhall be taken vp. And it is further agreed that the Towne is to pruide and alowe a man to helpe each other Sabath to looke vnto the Cowes And there is to be

---

* In original MS. a line was drawn through these last six words.

alowed Ten ſhillinge₍ₐ₎ by the ſaid parties for euery beaſt that ſhall be loſte by their default₍ₐ₎ And that they ſhall not keepe any Cattell of any mans w^{th}out the Towneſmens Conſent vpon the fforfiture of 5 ſhillings per the head for euery ſuch default.

     Thomas marrett
     John Moore

Auguſt 14

John Bridge   M^{d}. graunted vnto John Bridge lib^{r}ty to ſett the porch
his porche   of his barne 6 foote into the high waye.
₍ₐ₎pon his barne
[   ] taking
[   ] ſtubbs   Agreed with Symon Croſbe to take upp [   ] the
[. the ſtreets ſtubbs within the Towne ſtreets in an₍ₐ₎ way of paſſage for horſe carte or man att 4^{d} the ſtub: before the eleaventh Daye of Novem₍ₐ₎ next enſuing

₍ₐ₎ch Mores   Graunted vnto Enoch More a place for a how₍ₐ₎ lott
₍ₐ₎owſe lott   between m^{r} Ruſſells & John Knyghts to be layd out by
John ffrench   Graunted vnto John ffrenche a howſe lott betweene the
s howſe lott   highway to m^{r} Dampſo₍ₐ₎ & the yarde wch was graunted vnto Nicolas Homſteade.

Septemb^{r} 4th

Townſmen   M^{d} There are choſen for Townſmen to order the towne Affayres for this yeare following nly

   Mr Harlackingden   Joſeph Cooke
   Nicholas Dampſ₍ₐ₎   Richd Jackſon
   Edw^{rd} Goffe   John Bridge
   Edw^{rd} Winſhip

₍ₐ₎u^{r}vayor   Symon Croſbey is choſen for the Survayei₍ₐ₎ of the
₍ₐ₎f highwayes   highe wayes for this yeare following
    There is alſoe choſen for the Survaying of a ₍ₐ₎ Newe
Survayors   Lotts th^{t} ſhall be graunted & purchaſed boug₍ₐ₎ & ſoulde
[   ] landes to   pr^{n}: to keepe a booke of them & deliver a Tranſcript into
[   ] the booke   the Courte ſecundum ordine Cur₍ₐ₎ The Conſtables Nly
    Ed Goffe [   ]
     winſhip [   ] John More   [   ]

[11]   1638

Agreed with wm Patten to keepe three fcore [ ] cowes more or leffe vnder 4 fcore att the directio$_\wedge$ of the Townfmen . for all this fum^r vntill they take them in att 10^s a weeke the one halfe to be pd in the firft weeke in July eith^r in monie or good corne & thoth^r halfe when he leaveth of keeping them in monie & thofe that Refufe to paye in monie fhall paye in corne att the price that it is att when it is merchantable he is to pay 3^d for eu^r cowe he leaveth out a night & x^s a cowe for eu^{r}ie one that is loft through his Defaulte he is to take noe oth cattell without the townfmens confent he is to dryve them out by fix of the clock in the morning & bring them home by funn halfe an houre high att night at the lateft & to bring them into the towne eu^{r}e Evening he is to keepe them but eu^{r}ie third Sab^t & thoth to be prvided for as in former tyme & whoe eu^r fhall bring in anie ftrange cattell fhall fynde a helpe for 2 or 3 dayes & the owners to bring them into the common eure morning by the tyme appoynted & his owne cow to be kept free as long as he keepeth them & he is to pay 6^d damage for eu^{r}ie morning that he is not gone out by the tyme appoynted

                               Wm *wp* Patten

The caufey to Roxbery   It is Ordered in Refpect of making a fufficient path from the fouth fide of Charles River from Cambrid$_\wedge$ to Roxberie that the lyne fhall lye righte to the vplande therfore that comon lande that fall within [ ] lyne on m^r Harlackingdens fyde fhall belong vnto him : & his foreu^r & in Refpect of wch foe much of his owne lande as falleth on the outfyde of the lyne he Refigneth vpp vnto the townf vfe   Alfoe in Reguar$_\wedge$ Mr Harlackingden hath vppon his owne prticular Charge made a dicthe he fhall be freed from all [ ] about making a caufey or anie oth$_\wedge$ charge to make that path fufficient & his bowndes to Rem) acording as the Rayle & ditch now is on eu^{r}ie fyde of his lande

                                vth of March

Hoggs Ringed   It is ordered that all the hogges in the towne fhall be Ringed by Wm Wilcok fufficiently before the 27 of Aprill & he is to have 2^d for eu^{r}ie hogg foe Ringed [ ] owners of the hoggs are to afforde fufficient helpe & e$_\wedge$ hogg Ringed by him not fufficiently he is to pay 6^d & w$_\wedge$eu^r fhall Refufe to have their hoggs foe Ringed by him fhall paye befydes the damage they doe for eu^{r}ie hogg [ ] att the firft tyme & 2^s 6^d for eu^{r}ie tyme aft^r as often a$_\wedge$ they be found doing damage

It is alfoe ordered that wm Wilcok fhall take care of all the fence betweene the Plantingfeild in the neck [ ] the ox pafte^r & the owners fhall paye him fufficiently for his w^{r}ke

John Ruffells & Sam: Greene are appointed to loo$_\wedge$ vnto the fence in the weftfeild & Retourne in account to the townsmen

M 2 d: 2

M$^d_:$ It is ordered That whereas there is formerly graunt$_\wedge$ vnto m^r Richard Harlackingden a fearme of 6$^c_:$ ac^{rs} att v$_\wedge$ brooke of
[ ] of farme vpland and meadowe as appeare in an order dat$_\wedge$ the 2 of
$_\wedge$chd vppo Jan: 1637$\sharp$ vppon conditio therin exp^{r}ffed wch cond$_\wedge$ not
Rogg^r being fullfilled it is accordingly fallen back againe vn$_\wedge$
the vfe of the towne whervpon feing that the fearme graunted formerly vnto m^r Rogg^r Harlackingden is not foe fit for pre$_\wedge$ vfe it is therfore now graunted vnto m^r Rogger Harlacking$_\wedge$ his heires for eu^r to poffes & enioye the f^d fearme before gr$_\wedge$ to m^r Rich^{r}d Harlack: Whervppo the fd Rogg^r H hat$_\wedge$ [ ] the fea$_\wedge$ formerly graunted vnto himfelfe now to [ ]

M.2 d:2 1638

Mr Richard M^d Wheras m^r Rog^r Harlackingden gent hath Refign$_\wedge$
Harlacing back againe to the vfe of the towne all his vpland as appeare
dens fearme graunted him (the vith of March 1636) to make vpp his
on the fouth
fyde of meadowe (5^c ac^{rs}) lying on the fouth fyde of Charles Riuer
Charles fometymes in th ocupatio. of m^r Greene for f^r Richrd Richrd
Riv^r Saltingftals cattell It is by thefe prfents now graunted vnto
m^r Richrd Harlackingden Efq & his heires for euer to be layd out according to the former graunte above mention$_\wedge$ & vppon noe other conditions but punctually acording as the fearme att vyne brooke was graunted Jan 2 1636 only the tyme begining att this p^{re}fent date &

enfuing acordingly as there mentioned & m^r Roger Harlackingden hath prmifed to yeald vpp his meadowe att the price it coft him when he purchaf, it to him or anie oth^r to whome it may afterw, be graunted yf it be forfeted by not prforming the conditions And alfoe to yeald vpp to m^r Richard coming within three yeares his fearme charges excepted

The Comon Ox pafte^r   It is ordered that a hundred ac^rs of lande adioyni, to the greate fwampe neare the waye vnto Menotomy River fhall be layd out & enclofed at a gen, charge for comon ox pafter & fo to Remaine for eu^r without Imprpryating & all the tymber to be prferved or made vfe according as townsmen in place yearely fhall difpofe of

The graunt of the 56 ac^rs ,ehynde the ,ewe lotts   It is ordered that fiftie fix ac^rs of lande lying behynde the newe lotts fhall be layd out to thofe of the congregation yt are Impotent & not able to goe farr & to fome that have had none yett neere home & were pr, fome & that to be done by *   in the manner following *

Jofeph Cooke ,dition to menotomy Meadowe   It is ordered that there fhall be Recompence ma, vnto Jofeph Cooke in refpect of fome loffes he ha, fuftained in laying out monie for the towns [   ] & by theis prfents therfore graunted vnto him fome fkirts of land adioyning Menotomye Riv^r on the further fyde wch is to be layd out by Mr Rogge^r Harlackingden & John Bridge according as they fhall Judge neceffa,

M. 3, d: i1

The genall ,ndition of all ,aunts of lotts ,ceforth fro ,e prfent date   It is henceforth ordered that noe howflotts landes or meadowes fhall be graunted vnto anie but vppon this condi, Nly that they fhall neither lett them vnto anie prfon but fuch as [   ] townfmen then in place fhall like of prvided yf they doe not like [   ] fhall take them off att an Indifferent rate as twoe men indifferent, chofen fhall Juge nor fell them except to fome of the congregatio, without the townfmens confent

---

* In original MS., this space is blank; evidently it has been so always.

acording to order made [   ] December 1636 & yf they deprte awaye they ſhall Reſigne them ba_againe vnto the townes vſe att the townſmen diſpoſe. & ſhall onl_be allowed ſuch charges as they have bene att in buylding fencing [   ] anie other waye Imprving as ſhall appeare vppon theire account & yf ſuche accownt cannot be hadd there ſhall be allowed accordin_as ſhall be Judged by 2 men choſen as [   ] prvided allwayes that [   ] the wholl congregation ſhall agree to ſell & deprt it ſhall bynd noe further then that none ſhall allienate contrarie to [   ] agreement of the congregation for the [   ] of the [   ] in the place [   ]

The ould [12] M^d. It is agreed that the ould ox paſt^r y^t lyeth [   ]
_x pſt^r the waye to Charles towhne ſhall have thoth pt on [   ]
[ ] how ſince north ſyde of the path added vnto it & imprpiated to ſome
_mded of the purchaſers & others y^t it now ſtandes in mann^r herevnder written

The north ſyde			On the ſouth ſyde of the path		
				a.	r
The prfessor	++	2.⅔	Mr Eaten	++	2 : 2
Rich^rd Jackſon	++	1. 0	Mr Sheap^rd	++	4. 2
Mr Tho Sheap^rd	++	2. 2	Tho. Dampford	++	6. 0
ffrances Greſhould	++	2. 0	Mr Haines	++	9. 0
Harbert Pellum	++	3. 0	Eld^r Champnes	++	7. 0
Joſeph Cooke	++	13. 0	George Cooke	++	13. 0
John Champnes	++	5. 0	Mr Harlackingde_	++	9. 0
Mr Eaten	++	4. 0	Ed Goffe	++	9. 0
			Mr Buckley	++	5. 0
			John Betts	++	7. 2

M^d the 2 ac^rs & ⅔ above mentioned to the Profeſſor is to the Towns vſe for eu^r for a publick ſcoole or Colledge And to the vſe of m^r Nath Eaten as long as he ſhall be Imployed in that work ſo that att his death or ceaſſing from that work he or his ſhall be allowed according to the Charges he hath bene att in buylding or fencing

It is ordered that that there ſhall be a planting feild fenced in vppon the ſouthe ſyde of Charles Rivver wch ſhall begin foure ſcore Rodd frō the furtheſt prte of m^r Roger Harlackingdens Rayles of his meadow &

that lyne to runne to the hither fyde of the lott wch fhall be graunted unto   Bufh & the other fquare lyne to runne vpp a myle & a quarter into the Countrye & eu^{r}ie man to whome anie lott fhall be graunted fhall beare his equall prportion in the fence & whofoeu^r fhall not have finifhed his fence by fuch a tyme as may be convenient for the fecuring the corne y^t fhall be planted anie other that fhall then doe it to fec$_\wedge$ there corne fhall be payde by him 4^s the rodd [   ] eu^{r}ie Rodd foe done & the laft daye to be the firft of [   ]

Octob^r 26 1638

There were chofen for Townefmen to orde$_\wedge$ the towne affaires for the yeare following

  m^r Harlackenden   m^r George Cooke
  Samuell Shepard   Jofeph Ifacke
  John Bridge & Simon Crofby And
  Edward Winfhip conftables Joyned with them :

    octob^r 26 1638:

Richard Jackfon was chofen Surveyor of the high wayes for the yeare following

To Survey Lands

The fame daye was chofen m^r Jofeph Cooke John More Thomas Mariot

14 January 1638

It is ordered that noe timber trees shalbe felled on this fide Menotamy river wthout a warrant under all the townfmens hands granted at a Generall meeting monthly. Nor noe timber felled beyond menotomy river wthout warrant from the maior part of the Townefmen

Itt is ordered there beinge found muche Damage done by swine in this towne since the order of the Generall Corte was Repealed & they lefte att libertie for eache towne to order: Itt is therefore ordered att A generall meetinge of the townfmen with a generall Confente of the greateft number of the Inhabitants the prefente: thatt is to say thatt none either riche or pore shall keepe Aboue twoo swine Abroad on the Common one sow hog & a barrow or 2 barrows and thefe to be suffitientelye yoaked and Ringed after the iudgemente of the twoo brethren thatt are apointed to see to the executione of this order & to bringe in a note of suche defaultes as they find   And if anye be found defective to breake this order either by keepinge more then 2 hogs and suche hogs soe lett abroade if nott suffitientely after ye order shall pay for euerye breache of this order 2^s vnles in cafe ther$_\wedge$ should be anye failinge by vnexpected prouidence & can foe be proued by suffitiente euidence in thatt case there may be mitigatione of this ffine otherwife to take place without all excufes to thatt end: thatt eache man & this Commonweale may be preferued from dammage by thatt Creature in this our Towne

Itt is ordered y^t whereas mr Paine Granted vnto Goodm$_\wedge$ Shepard a third parte of his yard to build a house vppon itt is Granted 6 Acers of Land to m^r Paines houfe by the Crike to be prefentely settled on itt of the nearest land on th$_\wedge$ other side the water yett vndeuided in lotts

[13]   Aprille 12th 1639.

Itt is Agreed with our brothe$_\wedge$ Ruffells for to keepe the heard of drie Cattell on the other side of the Riuer for the whole summer or 7 mounths as the towne shall thinke fitt and the sayd John Rufells is to haue for his mans seruice to this vfe   pounds the one halfe of the sayde somes to be payd vnto the sayd partie in monye when the time shall be halfe expired and the other halfe of ye Refidue & Remainder of the monye to be payd either in monye or in corne when the Cattell shall be taken vp: And itt is further Agreed thatt the towne is to prouide & alow a man to helpe eache third sabath to looke to the Cattell and there is to be Alowed ten shillings by the sayd partie for euerye beafte thatt shall be lofte by his Defaulte   And thatt he shall nott keepe anye Cattell of anye mans without the Townefmens Confente vppon fforfiture of 5 shillings pr the head for euerye suche Defaulte

Apr 16th 1639

Itt is Agreed with mathew Hichecocke to haue his lad for the summer for to helpe keepe the drie heard ouer the water till the calues should bee fente ouer whiche was the xxth of May. and from thence to keepe the Calues to ye end of the yere And he is to haue for his hire eighteene pounds to be payd either in monye or corne: And further itt is agreed thatt the towne is to prouide one to keepe ye calues eache sabba˄ and there is to be alowed by the sayd mathew 5ˢ for euerye calfe yt shall be lofte by the keepers defaulte

Apr 1639

Agreed with Richard Beckeells to keepe the heard of milche Cows for this yere till they take them in be they more or leffe att the directione of the Townfmen and he is to haue twentie poundes for his wages the one halfe inn Julye either in monye or corne and the other halfe when he leaueth of to keepe them either in monye or corne att the price itt shall be when itt is merchanteable He is to pay 3^d a cow for euerye cow he leaues out a nyghte and 10^s a cow for euerye cow lefte out by his defaulte He is to driue out the cows by fixe a clocke in ye morninge and bringe them home by by sonne halfe an howre high att nyghte att the lateft and to bringe them into the towne euerye eueninge He is to keepe them euerye third sabath & theother to be prouided for as in former time and whoeuer shall bringe in anye ftrange Cattell shall find a helpe for 2 or 3 days an˄ the owners to bringe them into ye Common euerye morninge by the time apointed and he is to pay 6^d damage for euerye morninge yt he is nott gone out by the time apointed And he is to take in noe other Cattell without the Townfmens Confente

Octobʳ the firfte
1639

there were Chofen townfmen to order the towne afaires for the yere followinge: mr Jofeph Cooke Edward Gofe John Bridge Thomas Parifhe Thomas marrett: John more Thomas Briggame Counftables Joined with them

Octob the firfte
1639

Rogger shaw williame willcocke were Chofen surveyors of the high waies for this yere followinge.

To Survey Lands

the same Day was chosen Richard Jackson Roberte Sanders Joseph Isaacke whoo are to meete euery seco⁀ Mondaye in eu{r}ie moneth to enter the severall grauntes & Allienations of landes according to order in that case pr{v}yded.

ffor the ⁀hanging of the Meeting Daye
Wheras It was ordered by the Generall Courte to p{r}vent the hinderannce of the Millitary companie att Boston vppo⁀ the first monday in the moneth that noe other meetings should bee apointed vppon that Daye Its therfore order⁀ that the monthly Daye of meeting for the townsmen & Recorders of the Towne landes shall be on the second Mondaye in euery moneth the one in the forenoone and the other in the afternoone according vnto former orders

An Order for a fine to be payd [ ] all that neglect to record their Landes
And fforasmuch as by the neglect of manie in bringing in the coppies of th{r} landes to bee entered as they are by order enioyned perfect Recordes cannot be kept by our selves nor Transcript given in vnto the Courte but hereupon may growe ocasion of much stryfe Its therfore Ordered y{t} henceforth Whosoeuer shall be sownde to pass two⁀ dayes of this monthly meeting after the graunte or purchase of anie landes shall for the first Defaulte paye five shi⁀ & afterward for euery moneth he shall neglect one shilling vntill entrye be made of the sayd landes

An order for the Restoringe of all lost goods vnto the right owners
Wheras there was an order made the last Session of the Generall Courte helde att Boston in September 163⁀ for the restoring of all lost goods vnto there Right owne⁀ that one should be appointed in euery towne vnto who⁀ howse they shall constantly Repaire for all such goods And an order made by the townsmen for the efecting th⁀ same Theis are therfore to certifye vnto all prsons wi{th} the limmits & bowndes of this Towne that John Russe⁀ is desyred & appointed to take vppon him this care according to the order of Court before mentioned & for h⁀ paines shall receive one penie in the shilling for all such goodes to be paide by the owners before he restore them yf it be demaunded vnles in extreordinarie cases

as for [   ] of greate vallewe or the like that ſhall cauſe anie difference it ſhall bee ended by anie twoe of the Townſmen. And for the better fulfilling this office according to that act of Courte Its now ordered that all prſons as ſh‸ haue anie kynde of Goodes of greater or leſſer vallewe of other mens in their cuſtodie by fynding or otherwyſe as being left att their howſes or borrowed by themſelues or anie of their fammily & forgotten of whome or in their poſſeſion by anie other meanes without the full lycence of the owner therof. that within fourteen dayes after the date of theis preſents they deliuer the ſa‸ vnto the ſayd John Ruſſells and hereafter within [   ] dayes of the knowledge or (finding) of the ſame [   ] or elſe ſháll paye a forfet to the third parte of the vallewe of all ſuche goods not Reſtored accordinly as before mentioned and the ſame to be collected by the ſayde John Ruſſells & he ſhall paye the ſame & Reteurne in his accownt vnto the townſmen eurie daye of the townemeeting

<small>for the fencing the new lotts on the ſouth ſyde of Charles River</small> It is ordered that all that have anie lande in the newe ffeild on the ſouth ſyde of Charles River ſhall be appointed by Joſeph Iſack & Thomas Marret where their fence ſhall lye prvy^{d}ed eu^{r}ie man fenceth att both endes of his lott & the Reſt where they ſhall appointe & w^{t}euer fence is not made before the firſt of marche they ſhall have power to ſett on others to doe it & the owners to paye foure ſhillings the Rodd

<small>for mending the waye in the neck</small> It is ordered that Joſeph Cooke & Edward Goff haue power to cauſe all that haue carrageis that way to come together & mende the highwaye in the neck of lande

<small>an order for the laying ‸he highwayes ‸etweene ‸ownes</small> Wheras an order was made laſt generall Courte att Boſton in September (1639) for the ſpeedie & convenient laying out of all high wayes betwene townes that ✚ ſhould be choſen out of each towne for the efecting the ſame It is therfore ordered that Joſeph Iſack Richard Jackſon Wm Cutter ſhall Joyne with others choſen for other townes to laye out high wayes according as in the ſayde order is expreſſed

TOWN RECORDS

<small>an order yt ^ates fhall not ^oe without a ^eeper</small> It is ordered for the prefervation of appletrees and all other kynde of quickfett in mens yardes or elfewhere for the preventing of all other damage by them & harme to themfelves by fkipping ouer pales that noe goates fhall be fuffered to goe out of the owners yarde without a keeper but yf it apeareth to be willingly they fhall pay vnto anie one that will put them to pounde twoe pence for euerie goate befyde damage and poundage And becaufe the charge would be too greate if only a part of them be kept It is therfore alfoe ordered that whofoeuer fhall not putt forth there goates fhall notwithftanding payetoye keeper within one thirde parte afmuch for euery goate as they that doe put them out untill th^ firft of marche & after that day to the full sa mu^ as anie doe for thofe that are with the herde.

Att a Towne meeting the firft monday in mar^ 1639 theis orders as followed were fome made & them with others made before fubfcrib^ vnto.

It is ordered that all that is not outfyde fence in the weft ffeilde <small>An order for the removing the fence in the weft ffeilde</small> but common ffence betweene that & the other twoe new ffeildes fhall be Remoued by the owners of the fame & fett vpp vppon the lyne betweene Cambrige & watertow^ & to leffen their charges they fhall be abated in eu^rie five Rod^ one Rodd & w^t fhall remaine: to be done att a generall charge as the other Rayles & this to be done before the firft of Auguft next enfuing vppon the penalltie of 5^s a rod for eu^rie defaulte The wch order Thomas Parrifhe & Thomas Briggam fhall fee to be fulfilled vppon the forfit^ of xx^s a man yf they doe not caufe it to be done by the owners of the fence by the daye aforefd: or caufe it to be done by fome other workemen within one moneth after & to effect the fame fhall hereby have power to leavie thofe fynes notwithftanding it is alfoe prvyded that yf anie defy^ to have their ould fence ftand for the Inclofing their land in prticuler they fhall then for eu^rie 5 rodd of ould fence fett vpp three rodds of newe fence in the place before mentioned.

Its ordered that the fence of the feilde on the Southe fyde of Charles River by the pownde fhall be removed by the charges of the fev^rall owners and fett on the out fyde by the highway going to the river & the grounde within being fortie ac^{rs} to be devided as followe

Sifter Crofbye 10 ac^{rs}	Mr Paine 6: ac^{rs}
Edm Hompfte 4 ac^{rs}	Wm Bickleftone 5 ac^{rs}
George willowes 4 ac^{rs}	Mr Sara Symons 6 ac^{rs}

Edw^{r}d: Goff 5 ac^{rs} & all to be finifhed according to the tyme before mentioned for the reft

ffor the keeping the booke: It is ordered that Jofeph Cooke fhall keepe the booke for this yeare & enter all orders before the meeting daye nex enfuing & w^{t}euer fhall be done by the maior parte of the Townfmen prvyded that warning be given vnto all by apointm^t the precedent meeting daye or by confcent of the maior pa vppon anie accedentall ocafions fhall be by their fubfcription be as authentick as yf it were entred & to be entred as before mentioned with the fame handes fubfcribed and all thofe orders being examined wch fhall be done befo^r anie other bufines be tranfacted

granted to Jo: Sell to builde   Granted to John Sell libertie to builde a houfe vppon anie peice of lande he can purchafe prvyded he can buy th libertie of buylding wch is in Goodm whytes hande

an order for one to regeft^r B. m. Brl   Its ordered that wm Towne fhall Regefter eu^{r}ie Birth Mariage Buriall & according to the order of Courte i that cafe prvyded & give it in once eu^{r}ie yeare to be delivered by the Deputies to the Recorder & fhall gather [   ] eu^{r}ie particuler entraunce 1^d for the Recorders fees & [   ] for himfelfe

Its agreed the order made Novemb^r 3. 1634 for clearing the high wayes in the towne fhall be fett vppon the poft & be executed within one moneth

Ther were then p^{r}fent that fubfcribed vnto the forfd orders foure of the feven men }	Jofeph Cooke Edwrd Goff Thoms Br John [ ]

Att a Towne meeting [ ]

<small>fearme graunted vnto Joseph Cooke</small>
Graunted vnto Joseph Cooke a fearme of four hundred Ac^{rs} of the nearest vplande adioyning to his meadowes lyng beyond Cheescake brooke & betwene that & Charles River & alsoe liberty to goe with a streight lyne (on the hithermost syde of his meadowes on this syde Cheescake brook) downe by the edge of the highlande to [ ] Charles River

<small>The Graunte of m^r Samuell Sheaprds ffearme</small>
Graunted vnto m^r Samuell Sheaperd a ffearme of foure hundred Ac^{rs} of vpplande beyonde the afores^d ffearme graunted vnto Joseph Cooke adioyning vnto those meadowes wch were somtymes in the occupation of Brother Grene for Sr Richrd Saltingstalls vse with foure score ac^{rs} of y^t meadowe lying most convenient vppon this Condition that he shall surender vpp vnto the Townes vse & Dispose all those meadowes wch are now in his possession att alewyfe meadowe or Rockey meadowe at the pryce he first payd for them & paying to the towne for the abouesd foure score ac^{rs} of meadowe prportionably according to the Rate m^r Rogg^r Harlackenden payde for the wholl & for this Reason bec the Towne is to Repaye the wholl to his successors

<small>The Graunts $_\wedge$f fearnes to [ ] Cooke $_\wedge$wrd Goff [ ] John Bridge</small>
Graunted vnto Captaine Cooke & Edwarde Goff eache of them sixe hundred ac^{rs} of vpland & meadowe to be layd out to them by the appointment of the Townsmen about the outsyde of the boundes betweene watertowne Concord & Charles towne & John Bridge with them three hundred ac^{rs} & fifty of vpland & meadowe in manner afforsayde but all three of them vppon this condition that they shall surrender vpp vnto the Towns vse all those meadowes in their prsent possession in Rockey & Alewyse meadowes at the same price they first purchased the same

There were then p^{r}sent six of the seven Townsmen that subscribed vnto theis Grauntes n^{++}ly	John more Thomas Briggam Thomas Marret Edw^{r}d Goff John Bridge Joseph Cooke

[16] Att a Towne meeting the fecond monday in may Theis things following were ordered

Jofeph Ifack graunt of fkirtes of m^rfhe to his lott
Graunted vnto Jofeph Ifack the fkirtes of mrfh adioyning vnto his lott prvyded that he leaveth the high waye foure Rodds wyde vizltt betwene the marfhe on the fouth fyde of Charles River & the newe lotts there graunted

The order for hoggs
Its ordered that after the fixt daye of this p^rfent weeke there fhall be libbertie graunted vnto all fuche as fhall Defyre to keepe hoggs abroade with a keepr but yf anie fhall refufe to keepe hoggs with the heard they fhall be conftrayned fufficiently to yoake them & Ring them & in cafe anie dammage fhall come by their going abroade without a keepr though yoaked & Ringed the owners of the hoggs fhall paye the one halfe of fuch dammage & the owners of the fence the other prt of it And that to be according vnto the Difcretion of twoe men Indifferently chofe_∧ & for fuch hoggs as fhall be fownde to goe abroade without yoakes or Rings out of the owners owne grown_∧ they fhall paye for eu^rie fuch hoggs fix pence vnles with a keepr as aforefd :

Graunted vnto John Sell
Graunted vnto John Sell (in Refpect of his graunte in march laft paft to buylde a houfe where he could purchafe a peice of land convenient) yf he could purchafe the houfelott in John whytes hande) that now by this p^rfent order he may make a Tenement of one prt of his howfe to improue to w^t vfe he will in letting or felling in fteade of the forefd howflo_∧ he hath now purchafed enioying the libertie belong_∧ vnto it

The ordering [ ] neck fence
Wheras it is found that by Reafon of diverfe changes & allienations of lotts in the neck of lande that fome prt of the fence hath noe own_∧ & fome have more for an acc^r then others wch is contrarie to the firft order made the 20th of March 1632 nly that eu^rie one fhould beare for   & all after that prportion Its therfore ordered that Jofeph Cooke Edw^rd Goff & Thomas Mar_∧ fhall meafure all the neck fence & fett out to m^r Hough his prt & to Charleftowne their halfe prt betwene o^r plantingfeild & theirs & devyde the oth_∧ according vnto their beft Difcretion prportionable to the fd firft order of the wholl foe now equally of the remainder

The Recorde of their Retourne

Theis three men chofen as aforef[d] doe bring in this Retourne as followeth

[17] X[th] Novemb[r] 1640

Att a Towne meeting generally of all the Inhabit, according to former order made 3[d] of ffeb: 1634 nly that all Towne Officers fhould be chofen the firft monday in novemb[r] & fince Altered with all other towne meetings by an order made at a Gen[r]ll Courte to be on the fecond monday in the moneth There were chofen for Townfmen as followeth
Conftables for this prfent yeare } M[r] Andrewe,
                                  } Ed Anger

And for Townfmen with them } Tho: Marret
for this yeare   } Thoms Parrifh
                              Thomas Briggam
                              Joh Stedman
                              Abrahm Shawe

Chofen to Recorde the towne landes } Jofeph Cooke
& delivr in a Tranfcript to the Gen[r]all } Edw[r]d Collings
Court for this yeare enfuing   } Robert Saunders

Chofen for Surveyors to mende the } Robert Daniell
high wayes for this yeare   } George Hutchin,

And all theis feuerall Officers to have power for the difcharge of their feu[r]all Offices accordin, to Orders prefcrybed in this booke as others hau, had before them in the fame places

At a Towne meeting this prfent 13[th] of July 1641 It was agreed by the Townfemen then in place that John Page fhall haue free & full poffeffion of the 10 acers of meddow the which he bought of M[r] Befbeg, & that was formerly in the towns hands for 5 yeares prouided they payd him 10*l*

Agreed with Richard Beckeells to keepe the heard of milch Cows for this yeere, till they take them in be they more or leffe att the direction of the townfmen, and hee is to haue 16' for this yeere & hee is to haue the on halfe in July either in mony or corne & the other halfe when hee leaueth of to keep them, prouided he fullfill the Conditions of the agrement made with him in the yeere 1639

Agreed with Goodmā Oaks for his man to keepe the drie heard on the other fide the water at 12ˢ pr weeke & he is to receiue his paymen when he leaue of keepe by the direction of the townſmen, In like manner is it agree with Richard Shaw for his man to keep the calfes, at the fame wages;

Agreed this prſent 26ᵗʰ of March 1641 by the Townſmen now in place that what euer Hogges ſhall be found either in ſtreete or Commo without a keeper not fufficiently yoaked and rung they who are the owners of fuch hogs for euery defalt are to pay 6^d and if found in Corne or gardens they are to pay the damma & in cafe the defalt ſhall appeare to ly in the fenfe they ſhall recouer their dammage vpon the part yt oweth yt fenfe.

It is ordered by the Townſmen now in place this prefent ſecond monday in auguſt 1641 that all the fenſſes belonging vnto the necke ſhall fufficiently be kept as was ordered the laſt yere by the townſmen then in place vntill the 5 day of Nouember next enfuing after the date hereof, I fay thus ordered by us

Granted vnto Goodman Thefington a peece of march liing right before his doore frō his gate to a ſtake, the townſmen now in place fet, vnto the other corner of his yarde next vnto Goodie Crofbys yarde, by us now in place this prſent yere 1641;

Graunted to Thomas Parriſh one hundreth acrˢ of land lyinge on the left: hand of the great playne toward mʳ Haynes his farme between the two brookes on the fouthweſt fide of Chef=nut hill the Comon furrounding it with a fwampe vpon the foutheaſt

Graunted vnto Thomas Danforth four & twenty Acrˢ of land on the fouth fide of Charles=river, neer vnto the lands formʳly graunted to Thomas Parriſh to be layd out by the Townf=men in Confideraĉon of his allotment in thofe lands alredy layd out on that fide the river

RECORD MADE BY JOSEPH COOKE, TOWN CLERK, 1636–7; 1639–1641

(See Folio 45)

TOWN RECORDS 45

Graunted vnto Thomas Danforth fourteen Acr^s of vp=land adioyninge to each fide of his meado$_\wedge$ att Alewife meadowe layd out by m^r Jofeph Cooke & Edward Goffe by the appoyntmt of the reft of the Townf=men 1644

Itm granted in like manner vnto Edward Winfhip fortie Acr^s of vpland adioyninge to his meadow at Alewife meadowe layd out alfoe by m^r Jofeph Cook & Edward Goffe

Itm Graunted to Richard Champny eight Acr^s meado$_\wedge$ and vpland more or leffe, fkirts of his meadow at alewife meadowe Anbutted highway to Concord Southweft Richard Parke north weft, Edward Winfhip and the Comon northeaft: Thoms Danforth foutheaft.

[18] 8th Novemb^r 1641

Att a towne Meeting vppon the daye abovewritten accor$_\wedge$ to former order made 3^d ffeb^r 1634 namly that all Towne Officers fhould be Chofen the firft monday in november And fince Altered with all other Towne meetings by an order made att a Gen^{r}all Courte to bee on the feconde munday in eu^{r}ie moneth: There were Chofen for Townfmen for this prfe$_\wedge$ yeare & furvayers lande & furvayers of highway$_\wedge$

Chofen for Conftables for
this p^{r}fent yeare — } Edw^{r}d Goff
Edward Collins

ffor Townfmen,
theis five are chofen } Jofeph Cooke
Thomas Marret
Rich^{r}d Jackfon
John Bridge
Rogger Shawe

Surveiors for the townflande
that are to deliv^r in the Trafcript
to the Gen^{r}all Courte for all the
prticuler prcells of landes graunted
& Alienated are Chofen } Jofeph Ifack
John Ruffells
Hezechiah Vfher

Surveyors for the highwayes
for this prfent yeare — } Robert Danniell
George Hotchins

Decemb 13^(th.) 1641

Att a towne meeting vpon the day aboue written It is agreed vpon that Robart Holmes and John Stedman ſhall take ceare for the making of the towne ſpring againſt m^r Dunſters barne a ſufficent well, with timbar and ſtoone fitt for the uſe of man and wattering of Cattell. Allſoe richard Jackſon is to be an afsiſtant to them by way of advice if they ſhall require it

[19]   8 9^(th) mon^(th) called Nouem: 1642.

Att a towne meeting vpon the day aboue written according to former order made 3 ffeb 1634 namely that all towne officers ſhould be choſen the 1 monday 9^(th) m^(th) and ſince altered w^(th) all other towne meetings by an order made att a generall courte to be one the 2^d 2^d day in euery monthe theire were choſen for townſmen for the prſent yeare w^(th) Conſtable & feruayors of highuaies as heere vnder written

ffor Townſemen theiſe fiue are choſen	George Cooke
	John Bridge
	Sergent Winſhepe
	Roger Shawe
	John Ruſſell
ffor Conſtables for this p^rſent yeare	Thō Briggam
	Edwa: Oakes
ffor Suruaiores of the highe waies this prſent yeare	John Stedman
	Roger Bancroft

Agreed by the towneſmen mette together vpon the 9^(d^) of the 11^(th) monthe that Joſeph Cooke Edward Goofe, Rich: Jaakſon Tho Marrett ſhould conclude of a way for the payment of the debt due frō the Towne to Natha: Sparowhawke & Edm: Anger.

further it is agreed att the ſame meeting by the ſame towneſmen that
Ric Jaakſon   Rich: Jaakſon haue ritte to a houſe lott that was Rich:
houſelott gr   Buttlers that ſometimes laie in the necke of lande:

TOWN RECORDS 47

Ric Jaakſon ye vſe of meadow gr
ffurther it is agreed that Ric: Jaakſon ſhall haue the vſe of 2 or 3 acres of meddowe lieing in the common meddowe called alewife till it be deuided by lott:

an order about oute fences
ffurther it is agreed that all the oute fences that lie w^{th}in the compaſe of the towne cattle (that is to ſay all fences betwene corne & paſture ground) ſhalbe made ſufficient againſt all lawfull cattle betweene this [ ] the laſt of the next 1 monthe: but it is agreed that the fencing ſtuffe ſhalbe laied redie att the fartheſt by the 1 of the 1 moth- wee aduice this fence to be made with a ditch 4 foo_∧ wide att the topp & 2 foote & a halfe deepe wch w_∧ iudge to be the beſt fence being moſt ſecure: the penaltie for not prformance of w^t is heere ordered is $3^s\ 6^d$ for euery Rodd of fence that is faieling.

Joſeph Cooke Edw: Gooſe & william Willcoke are deſired & haue conſented to take care that this order ſhalbe prformed & they are to iudge of the ſufficienciencie of the fence

George Coke.　　　　　Roger Shawe
　　　　　　　　　　　　Edward Winſhipp
John Bridge　　　　　　John Ruſſell
Thomas Briggam　　　　Edward Oakes

It is ordered that according to an order of courte made the laſt generall courte for the towneſmen to ſee to the educating children) that

the diuiſion of the towne for ye looking to ye well educating children
John Bridge ſhall take care of all the families of that ſide the higheway his owne houſe ſtandes on to my brother Winſhepes & ſoe all the families frō Gouldi_∧ More to m^r Holeman & Carie Lathums ffamilie: & Sergent Winſhepe is to ſee to the families on the other ſide the comōn to Griffall next Bro: Bridg_∧ [ ] is to ſee to all the ffamilies that the lane goeing ffrō the meeting houſe downe to the Riuer & ſoe the lane that goeth ffrō the meeting houſe to [ ] bro: Dunſtars houſe & ſoe water towne ward [ ] his owne houſe John Ruſſell to ſee [ ] bet_∧ that high way & the high [ ]

George Cooke to take care of all the ffamilies betwene that way & the highe way goeing ffrō the meeting houſe into the necke by Tho Dauenporte & my brother ſhawe all the reſt betweene that & the Riuer & my bro: Oakes all one the other ſide the Riuer

<small>Corne due to ye Indians</small> Att a towne meeting the 10th of the 2 monthe agreed wth Indians by the prſent towneſmen to pay to Squa ſachem 8 bh of Indian corne after next harueſt   It is agreed likewiſe that George Cooke being att the charg to make a fence of 2 ſufficient railes in the towne line about halfe a mile in lengthe the fence to beginn att the outſide of George Cookes land runing out northeward to meet Captaine Gibbines his fence to ſecure the Indians Corne   It is agreed that the towne will pay for the making the fence

Att the ſame towne meetinge John Betts was fined by us 19^s 6^d for his hayeſtakes & cowe houſes and dunghills that he anoyde the ſtreet befor his dore wth & thoughe often warned to cleere the ſtreet yett denied to doe it

The ninth of the eight month 1643 : at a Towne meeting graunted to Willm Towne the vſe of a prcell of ground adioyninge his owne land on the ſouth ſide of Charles river of about one Acr for his ſervice of goinge on the townſ=mens errands as they ſhall haue occaſion to imploie him, and as formly he hath done for payment by them, he is now to prforme that ſervice for the vſe of that land whileſt he have yt.

The 11 of ye 9th monthe

The prſent townſemen haue agreed that the towne ſhall pey Edmund Anger 4^l 3^s 1^d which is of a rate he was to gather when he was Conſtable & is as followeth

	l	s	d
George Cooke abated of his rate being ouer rated	2	18	00
Roger Shaws rate ye towne being in his debt ſoe muche	00	19	04
Will : Townes rate the towne being in his debt	00	03	09
Bro : Manning ſenior his rate abated	00	02	00
the totall	04	03	01

It is agreed y^t y^e cowe keepers ſhall pey 6 bh of corne to Squa ſachem for y^e Damage done by the cowes to her corne vpon y^e ſaboth day throughe the neglect of the keepers in the yeare 1642

RECORD MADE BY GEORGE COOKE (PROBABLY), TOWN CLERK, 1642–1643
(See Folio 49)

[20]   13th of ye 9th mth 1643.

Att a towne meeting vpon the day aboue written according [   ] a former order made the 3d of ye laft monthe 1634 namely tht all towne officers fhould be chofen the firft monday of ye monthe & fince altered with all other towne meetings by an order made att a generall Courte to be one the 2d day in euery monthe: theire were chofen for townefmen for this prfent yeare with Conftables & feruayors of highwaies as herevnder written

ffor townefmen theife fiue were chofen	mr Jofeph Cooke George Cooke John Bridge Edw: Oakes John Ruffell
ffor Conftables for this prfent yeare	Edw: Goffe Serg: Winfhepe
ffor feruayors for the highwaies for this prfent yeare	Herbert Pellam Efqr John Stedman Enfigne

This prfent day John Betts was reckoned wth, about harmes done in his corne by the towenheard of cowes to the valew of 3^l which fome is clearely payd I fay 3^l

John Betts

Att a towne meeting the 13 3d mth 1644 It is ordered that noe oxen nor drie cattle fhall henceforth goe to feede in the cowe common vpon the penultie of 3d a day for euery beafte that fhalbe founde a trefpaffer in that kinde for this prfent fummer the fame order to continue from yeare to yeare vntill further order be taken

The ixth of the vth month 1644

It is ordered at a genrall meeting by the Townfmen that Capt Cooke & Edward Goffe doe take view of the new fence in the ox pafture in the neck of land & what they fynd not fufficient that they forthwith give notice to the owners therof

[21] The 11 of 9 ᵐᵒ 1644

Att a towne metting According to and or‸ made 3 of 9 mō 1634. there was chofen theife feuerall offecers as followeth

ffor townfemen	Richard Jackfonne
	Thomas Marritt
	Edward Oakes
	Roger Shawe
	Edward Wenfhepe

| Conftables | John Bredge |
| | Edward Goffe |

| Servaiors of hywayes | Harbut Pellam efqr |
| | John Stedman |

Seuerall men chofen to enter the elenation of lands	John Ruffell
	William Cutter
	Thomas Damforth:

Granted to m^r George Phillips of watertowne liberty to make ufe of the high way and Comon land annent his meadow for the erecting of a fence to fecure his meadow, dureing the pleafure of the Townfmen

It is Ordered by the Townsmen that no person with his family fhall come as an Inhabitant in to o^r Towne, with out the consent of the major part of the Townfmen for the time being, under the penalty of 20ˢ for eu^rie weeke,

And for preventing all inconveniences herein, it is Ordered by the Towsnmen that no man fhall Let out his house to any person comeing from any other place to settle him or her self as an Inhabitant in o^r Towne, with out the consent of the major pr^t of the Townsmen for the time being, under the penalty of twenty fhillings a weeke for eu^rie fuch default

1645 . 14. 2. mo.

Granted unto Roger Shaw 200^{ac} of upland lyng between ye South weft fide of Capt. Cooks farme & ye greate fwamp neere unto ye Eaft

Corner of Concord boundes, which fwamp is heade of part of Shaw fhine river & all that medow adjoining to yt Swamp which fhall fall with in our Boundes & this farme to be layd out, by Herbert Pelham Efqr & Capt. Cooke.

this farme of Roger fhawes a part of It being fould to michaell bacon and he building his houfe vpon the townes land betwene the farme and his medow It was agreed vpon by the felect men with the fayd Bacon that hee fhould haue twelue akers of land wheare his houfe ftand that fhould Rune from the farme to his medow in way of exchang for eightteene akers of his farme to be layed to the towne land againe on the weft fide of his farme and david fifk was appointed to doe the fame which the fayd fifke did and made his Returne of the fame vnto the felect men in the yeere 1670

      Ed: Winfhipp
      Edward Oakes
      Edward Goffe
      John Bridge

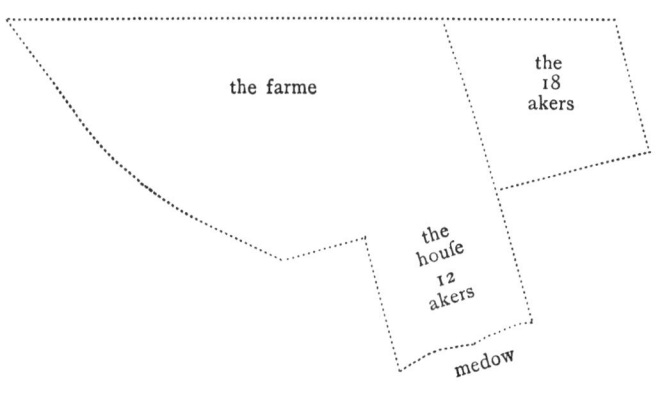

[22]   12th. 9. ^{mo} 1645.

At a towne meting according to An order ma$_\wedge$ y^e 3^d of y^e 9th mo. 1634: there was then chofen theis$_\wedge$ feverall officers as followeth

      Herbert pelham Efqr
for Townfemen   Roger Shaw
      Edward Oakes
      Tho: Beale.
      Richard Hildreth.

for Cunftables.	m^r Jofepth Cooke
	Thomas Danforth
Surveyours of land to be Joyned with y^e Cunftable	John Ruffells
	william Cutter
	Roger Bancroft
Surveyours of Highwayes	John Stedman
	John Cooper

15 (11) 1645:

according to a former act of the townfmen in y^e yeare. 1643. (2) mo: as appeares vnto v$_\wedge$ by there acknowlegment vnder there Hands. yt is now alfoe Ratified By Theefe perfons a grant vnto John Bridge Senior. of twen$_\wedge$ acres of plow land. on this fide Vine Broo$_\wedge$ eaftward nere vnto y^e place where His ftacks of Hay Did ftand. in lew of his lot in y^e necke, viz: unbroaken land onely with y^e timber & wood.

It is ordered By y^e townfmen that noe man Hath Any Right for to fell or difpofe of any wood or timber, which belong$_\wedge$ vnto this towne Comon, out of y^e towne It is Therfore ordered That whoever fhalbe found to trefpafs in felling cary$_\wedge$ or difpofeing of any wood or timber of y^e Comon to any other towne, fhall pay for every Cart loade of wood 5^s & of timbe$_\wedge$ ten fhillings: This order extendeth To Both fides of Charles River.

12. (12) 1645.

Wheras formerly orders Haue Bin made by This towne for y^e well yoaking of all fuch fwine as are let goe at liberty, wh$_\wedge$ haue not attained y^e ends amed at, but ftil$_\wedge$ the labors of many men, who can leaft fpa$_\wedge$ It, haue bin yearly in great part deftroyed; as by the many Complaints which Dayly haue Bin Brought vnto us is too apparent, we Doe Therfore order that all fuch perfon or perfo$_\wedge$ as fhall keepe Any fwine fhall Caufe them to be well & fufficiently Ringed, before y^e Third day of y^e firft mo: next enfueing: & from The twenty Day of the fame mo: vnto fuch time as Indian Corne be gathered in they keepe them at home in a clofe yarde or elfe fend them forth with a fufficient keep$_\wedge$ And if any fhalbe found or Taken eith$_\wedge$

[ ] The towne or Comon, or in any garden pafture medow or planting feilde, eyther vnringed or without a fufficient keeper as afor‸ faide, That then they fhall pay fix pence a pece for every fuch Default Together with Sattisfaction for fuch damage as fhalbe done By them And Therfore we Doe not Injoine any man to fence againft any fwine.

At a towne meting: $8^d_.$ (4) $^{mo}_.$ 1646:

Edward Goffe Delinquent in the Breach of the hog order about fome feven times (two Hogs) & ten at feverall times befides with out keeper & some vnringed Richard Jacfon granted liberty for to fell two Clapbord trees uppon y^e Comon beyond Menotime

Vppon y^e requeft of m^r Henry Dunfter f. affee in truft of ye eftate y^t belongs to ye Children: It is agreed that Richard Jacfo‸ & John Stedman fhall fet a price what is worthy to be allowed for ye rent of ye marfh in ye necke to ye Children

Richard Jacfon & John Stedman make returne That they Judge ye marfh being about 40: ac‸ There is worthy to be allowed twelve pence pr acre: & if uppon meafure there appear‸ to be more or leffe, y^n to haue after 12^d pr acre.

Thomas Brigham delinquent in ye Breach of the order about hogs. viz: for his wiues rescuing of two Hogs from ye Impounder when He fhould a driuen them to pound, for ten at one time & two at another being unringed, & thre being impounded allfoe for two oxen of his: Breaking ye order

Robert parker Delinquent in felling two trees uppon ye Comon with out leaue:

Henery prentice delinquent in the Brea‸ of the order Concerning oxen & for ye refcuing of them from ye hand of ye impound‸ two feverall times:

Elder Champnies granted liberty for ye felling of fome timber for ye repare of Bro: Goulden moores Dwelling houfe: & for his Barnes.

Edward Goffe for his delinquency in ye Breach of the Hog order to pay. — 00 — 08^s — 0

54   TOWN RECORDS

Thomas Brigham for yᵉ Breach of ye Hog order to pay for yᵉ two refcued away by his wife vˢ & for yᵉ other   oo — 07 — 6.

Robert parker for Breaking yᵉ order about felling of timber, fined — oo — 0.5 — o

Henery prentice to pay according to ye order for yᵉ Breach of yᵉ orders about oxen — o — 2 — o
& for his two refcues.   — oo — 10 — o
There is taken of his fine. — 6ˢ·

[23]   4 (9) ᵐᵒ 1646.

Severall men fined [   ] Breach of the orders concerning oxen & hogs.

		s
Bro: Cooper fined for 4 oxen once & 3 another		— 02 — oo
Bro: Winſhop: fined for 4 oxen twice & his hogs:		— 03 — oo
Bro: patten, fined, for one hog without keeper, thrice	— o — 1 — oo
Bro: Brigham. {for 10 hogs at one time & 4 at another & 3 at another with out a keeper & ſome unringed}		s 4 — oo
Will: Man, for one hog twice without keeper.		— oo — o6
John Kendall, for 3 hogs at one time & 4 at another, & 5 at other times with out keeper		s — 03 — oo
Robert parker for one ox uppon yᵉ Cowe Com̄o feeding thrice being taken. & often times befides.		— 1 — 6
Bro: Gibſon {for breaking yᵉ order Concerning yᵉ oxen at 3 feverall times with 2 oxen twice & one at an other, is fined}		— o — 2 — 6
Bro: Crackbone {for letting his 2 hogs goe with out a keeper being taken twice, & one unringed, & for letting his heifer feed on yᵉ Com̄on is fined — 2ˢ.}		s — 2 — oo
Richard Cutter, {for letting his hog goe loofe without a keeper, being taken 4: times — 2ˢ}		s — 2 — o
Bro: Cane. for letting his hog goe feverall times with out keeper being taken once		— oo — 6

Elder froſt	for letting his 2 oxen goe to feed on yᵉ Comon. taken once is fined: 1.ˢ —	— 01 ✻ 00
Bro: Bancroft	for his 2 hogs, being taken once with out a keeper is fined. 1.ˢ	— 01 ✻ 00
Tho: Hall	for his heiffer & hog being once taken uppon yᵉ Comon, Contrary to yᵉ order, is fined. 1ˢ	— 01 — 00
Bro: Micherſon	for one hog being taken twice with out a keeper is fined 8ᵈ	— 00 — 08
mʳ Pelham	for his hogs being taken in yᵉ planting feildes is fined. 1.ˢ 6ᵈ	— 01 — 06
Abram ſmith	for his heiffer being taken in yᵉ planting feilde is fined, 6.ᵈ	— 00 — 06
Robert Stedman	for one hog being taken twice with out a keeper, 8ᵈ	— 00 — 08
Daniel Stone for	his hog taken keeper, is fined.	04
Samuel Greene	for ſuffering his 4 oxen at 3 ſeveral times being taken on yᵉ Cow Co͞mon is fined	— 04 — 00
Tho: Welſh.	for one heiffer being taken in yᵉ planting feild, is fined, 6ᵈ	— 00 — 06
Bro: Withe	for one hog being taken with out a keeper 4 times & once vnringed & his two oxen taken uppon yᵉ Cow Co͞mon beſides ſeverall other times is fined	— 3 — 0
Bro: Willowes.	for his 2 hogs being taken twice uppon ye Comon with out a keeper	1 — 6
Robert Broadiſh,	for his 2 oxen thrice & 2 hogs twice being taken Contrary to the order is fined 5s.	04 — 00
Bro: Angier.	for one Heiffer being taken Contrary to yᵉ order & his reſcue is fined 2.ˢ 6.ᵈ	2 — 6
Dauid fiſke.	for two Hogs being taken Contrary to yᵉ towne order is fined 8.ᵈ	00 — 8
Siſter Bittleſtonn.	for one Hog being taken 6 times Contrary to yᵉ order, is fined	— 01 — 06

Bro : Hutchine.	for one heiffer being taken Contrary to y{^{e}} order is fined. 6{^{d}}		— 00 — 06
Philip Cooke.	for his hog being taken twice without a keeper, is fined, 1{^{s}} —		— 01 — 00
Bro: ffrench.	for 2 hogs at one time & one at another & 2 at another with out a keeper, is fined		1 — [ ]
John Stedman	for 2 hogs at one time & one at another & 2 at another taken without keeper is fined		— 2 — [ ]
William Cutter	for one being taken with out a keeper is fined 6{^{d}}		[ ]
John Thrumble	for his 2 hogs being taken tw$_\wedge$ [ ]		[ ]
John Bontaile	for swine being without a keeper is fined 6{d}.		— 0 — 0 — 6
Goodman knowls,	for his swine Divers times goeing with out keeper is fined 1{^{s}} — 6{^{d}}.	{s}	— 0 — 1 — 6

It is ordered By y{^{e}} Townsmen that Richard Hildreth & Thomas Danforth shall gather up the fines for this present yeare.

5 (9) 1646:

It is ordered by y{^{e}} Townsemen that there shalbe fifty shillings payde vnto Tho. longhorne for his service to y{^{e}} Towne in beating y{^{e}} Drum this two years last past.

      Herbert Pelham
      Richard Hildreth
      Edward Oakes
      Thomas Beale
      Tho : Danforth.

[24]   (9) 9. 1646.

At a Towne meeting according to an order made y{^{e}} 3{^{d}} of y{^{e}} (9) mo. 1634. there was then Chosen these severall officers as followeth.

for Cunstables. { Edward Goffe.
       { Edward Winshipp.

(9) 9: 1646.

At a Towne meeting according to an order made ye 3d of ye (9) mo. 1634. there was then chosen these severall officers as followeth.

for Cunstables. { Edward Goffe.
{ Edward Winshipp.

for Townsmen. { John Bridge.
{ Thomas Marrett.
{ Edward Oakes.
{ John Cooper.
{ Tho. Danforth.

Surveyors of land to { John Russell.
be joined with ye townsd. { Tho. Chesholme.
{ Roger Bancroft.

Surveyor of high wayes { John Stedman.
{ Gilbert Crackbone.

11 (10) 1646: There is liberty granted unto David Fiske for to fell some timber for ye use of his trade uppon ye common beyond Fry pond uppon ye rocks this liberty to continue untill may day next.

RECORD MADE BY THOMAS DANFORTH, TOWN CLERK, 1645-1668
(See Folii 56-57)

for Townſemen
{ John Bridge.
Thomas Marret.
Edward Oakes.
John Cooper.
Tho. Danforth.

Surveyors of land
to be joined with
yᵉ Cunſta —
{ John Ruſſell.
Tho. Cheſholme.
Roger Bancroft.

Surveyor of high ways { John Stedman.
Gilbert Crackbone.

---

11 (11) 1646: There is liberty granted vnto Dauid fiſke for to fell ſome timber for ye vſe of his trade uppon yᵉ Comõn beyond Spy pond uppon yᵉ Rocks this liberty to Continue vntill may day next.

There is leberty Granted to B. Sell to the number of twelue tres for fencing and building, to be felled by may day next.

Leberty Granted to mʳ Pellm and Bro Jackſonne to fell ſoe many tres as may ſeure to fence betwene them on the backſide of Bro Jackſonne houſe between this and next may day.

Leberty Granted to B. Wyeth to fell tember to build him a barne: betwen this and may day next

Liberty granted vnto goodman kempſter to fell two clapbord trees uppon yᵉ Rocks provided yt be done before may day next.

Liberty granted vnto ffrances Moore ſenior to fell ſome timber to fence about his yard & his land in the weſt feilde.

Liberty granted vnto Elder Champnis to fell ſome timber uppon yᵉ Rockes againſt his meadow for to fence in his meadow withall.

Liberty granted vnto Abraham Erington to fell ſome timber for ground ſells for his houſe & to fence his yard with all.

Granted liberty to mʳ Aires to fell a Clapbord tree

Ordered that what land there is on yᵉ other ſide yᵉ water, between yᵉ weſt Corner of Edmond Angers farme & yᵉ weſt end of mʳ Andrews furthe_∧ raile more then Edmond Angers proportio_∧ mʳ Sparahauke ſhall haue the rem_∧ [   ] of his proportion

11 (11) 1646: It is ordered by the Townſmen that what ever prſon or prſons ſhall cut downe or Cause to be Cutt downe any tree or trees whatſoeuer, whether liveing or dead in ſwamp or upland, on this ſide Menottime River, (the greate ſwamp only exempted, ſhall forfett for every tree ſoe felled ten ſhillings: this order to Continue vntill further order be taken by ye Townſmen.

It is allſoe further ordered that whatſoever prſon or prſons, who hath had any land at menottime laid out vnto himſelfe or his houſe wherin he Dwelleth, shall after the 12th day of this preſent month Cutt out or take away directly or indirectly any wood or timber on this ſide the path which goeth from ye mill to water towne, every such prſon shall forfett for every such loade, if yt be timber, fiue shillings pr loade, & if wood, 2s. pr loade provided that there is liberty granted vntill the twentith day of this prſent month for ye fetching whome of what is all ready Cut out, & after that what ever is found to be forfett:

Edward winſhop & John Coopr are appointed by the townſmen to ſee vnto ye execution of theſe two former orders & to fetch away & ſeaſe upon what ever wood or timber they finde Cutt out Contrary to ye order.

Edward Gofe & Edward Okes are appointed By the Townſmen to deuide the land on the South ſide of the water vnto thoſe ſeuerall men vnto whome It is granted By the towne.

8. (12^m) 1646:

It is ordered By the townſmen that Edward Goffe Edward Oakes & Tho: Danforth shall lay out the land that is due to the towne houſes at watertow̄ mill on y^e ſouth ſide Charles river.

There is liberty granted vnto m^r Edward Jacſon for to fell two ₍ₐ₎ Clapbord trees. on ye Com̄ons before may day next.

There is liberty granted to John Jacſon to fel two Clapbord trees before may day next.

there is liberty granted vnto Samuell greene & Thomas Swetman to fell ſome fencing stuffe for there yards before may day next.

It is agreed by ye Townfmen that the farmes of m^r Jofepth Cooke & m^r famuell, shalbe layde out By the major part of the townfmen :

the order Concerning goates being this day agitated It is Concluded by the Townfmen that the former order made (1639) shall stand in full force & that none are to fuffer there goates to goe at liberty with out a keeper, but they shalbe liable for to pay all damages vnto the full vallue though there be noe fence & therefore the order made in 36 is herby repealed.

Granted by the Townfmen vnto Nathanel hancocke foure ac^r of upland & swamp more or leffe lying in the weft feilds Butted uppon the greate fwamp north the High way at the foote of John Betts lott west & By fouth. the high way from ould Bucks to John moores lott fouth eaft the land of Nich: Withe Eaft & By North: ∧t is further declared to be the true intent of [   ] shalbe a High way left. at the end of John Betts lott. two rod on the north fide the ould pales, allfoe two rod with in the ould pales according to the ould high way. allfoe that goodman Hancocke shall leave a High way where now It is for a convenient paffage for wood to the fwamp, throw the midle of his lott. & foe is to haue all the land with in that Bounds formerly mentioned downe to the fwamp fide. to be staked out By Tho: Danforth, who is appointed by ye Townfme^n for this prticular.

8 (1) 1646.

liberty granted vnto Edmond ffroft for to fell fome timber for the Building of an houfe, before the laft of the 3^d mo :

There being granted vnto Tho. Danforth by the Townfmen twelve ac^r of land to be multiplied by eight at ye end of 5 mile It is by these prfents Confirmed vnto him & he is to take It either at the fide of m^r Sparahauks furtheft divifion next vnto the weft fide of It or elfe adjoining vnto fome of the land that is there all ready layde out

     Edw Goffe
     Thomas Marrett
     Edward Winfhipp
     Tho. Danforth.

12.^day (2)^m 1647.

It is ordered by the Townſmen that thoſe whoe haue land in menotime feild ſhall make vp there out fences Before the 25. day of this prſent month or elſe. It is declared By this prſent order, that there lotts are fforfet vnto the Towne who will take Care to get It vp.

there is liberty granted vnto Renold Buſh for to ffell halfe a duſſen trees for fencing ſtuffe on the other ſide the water vppon the Comōns

Bargained with Waban. ye Indian for to keepe about ſix ſcore heade of dry Cattle on y^e ſouth ſide of Charles River, & he is to haue the full ſome of Eight pound, to be p^d as followeth viz : 30^s to James Cutler. & ye reſt in Indian Corne at 3^s p^r buſhell after micheltide next.

he is to begin to take Care of them the 21. day of this prſent mo. & to keepe them vntill 3 weeks after michelmas. & if any be loſt or ill he is to ſend word vnto the towne & if any ſhalbe loſt through his Careleſſnes he is to pay according to the vallue of the beaſt for his defect.

his [mark] mark
Waban.

It is agreed that w^t Eng. Comodity ſhalbe layde out By Bro Goffe to the dry heard keeper or peage he ſhalbe ſattiffied to ye full for the ſame [   ] corne according as It will purchaſe [   ]
[   ] to be allowed beſides for the forbearance [   ] his money. the goeing of two Cattle.

8^d (3^m) 47.

ordered that the fence belonging to menotime feilde ſhalbe devided equally vppon the ac^t through out the whole feilde beyond the firſt prticular incloſiers

It is ordered that all the hogs in this towne ſhalbe ſufficiently yoaked and Ringed, or elſe ſhutt up.

Bro: Crackbone is appoynted for to fee vnto the executi͜ of this order for all the Hogs, except thofe with in the towne pales & to fee vnto the weft feilde that ther͜ be noe Cattle let goe at liberty with in the bounds of the Com̃on fences

Tho: Hall is appoynted for to looke vnto the pine Swamp feildes

& Bro: Beale is appoynted for to looke vnto the Hogs with in the Towne pales

& m^r Ruffell is appoynted for to looke vnto t͜ necke of land that there goe not any Cattle at liberty that may indanger any Corne or meadow Contrary to any former towne orders.

It is further ordered that what ever Hog shalbe found vnringed or vnyoaked, aboue eight weekes ould, shall pay vnto him that pounds them 3^d pr heade for every such default.

allfoe what ever beaft shalbe found in any planti͜ feilde Contrary to the former towne orders fix pen͜ pr heade for every fuch default except ye Townfmen vppon Juft Complaint shall fee Caufe for to remitt any part or the whole fine

Bro Hildreth is appoynted for to fee that the Cow Com̃on be kept Clear of any steeres or any dry Beafts & what ever shalbe found Contrary to the former towne orders the owner of the fame shall pay 3^d pr heade except the townfmen uppon Juft Complaint shall finde Juft Caufe for to remitt It.

7th: 4mo: 1647.

Ordered by the townfmen that the land on the fouth fide of the water abutting uppon the Eaft fide of m^r Sparahauks feildes about 40. ac^r more or leffe. is by theefe p^{r}fents fould vnto Richard Champnis to be prifed by the townfmen at a valuable price

Allfoe there being granted vnto him one hundred acrs of land to be an adition to his farme, By 12 men that were deputed to difpofe to euery man his portiō of the Com̃on lands, It is by thefe p^{r}fents Confirmed to him, & he is to haue It on the eaft fide of the further deiufion on the further fide of the water & is to allow vnto the towne what It shalbe thought more worthe then if he had It by his farme on the other fide.

[26]   30. (5) 1647:

Where as formerly many orders haue bin made for the well yoaking & Ringing of all fwine wch hath not yet attained the End amed att, but the labors of many haue bin & is much fpoiled, as the many Complaint‸ that are brought to the townfmen doe daily teftify:

It is therfore ordered by the townfmen that every p^rfon or p^rfons who keepeth any fwine shall forthwith eyther shut them vp or elfe fend them forth with a keeper in the day time & shutt them vp euery night,

& further it is ordered that what euer fwine shalbe taken in any Corne feilde the owner of the fame shall pay fix pence pr heade for the bringing them out together with full sattiffaction for what ever damage is done.

11th. 8. 1647.

It is ordered that Edward winfhip & Tho: Danforth shall deuide the fence belonging to notime feilde on the Charlftowne fide, to the feverall proprietors according to each Mans proportion of land there through out the whole feilde, after the deuifion of the faid fence is fet out betwen Charlftowne us.

ordered that Elder Champnis shall pay to the towne 20^s pr ac^r for the vpland lying By m^r Sparahauks raile &. 6^s. 8^d pr ac^r for the fwamp.

allfoe he shall allow for the hundred acres in exchang‸ for that by his farme eyther 20^{li}. or elfe let the wood by Comon to the towne.

allfoe It is ordered that Bro Goffe & Tho: Danforth shall meafure out the land that m^r Sparahauke had of the towne & take in his account.

It is ordered that Bro. Goffe & Bro: Ed: Oakes shall gather vp the fines due to Bro Cane for his fines of the oxen.

	s	d	
of Robert parker.	— 0 — 8 —	2	according to this account every man is Bated one third prt of what he ough˄ to a payde By the towne order wch is 3^d pr heade. & we haue Concluded that every man shal˄ pay according to this.
of Tho : Brigham.	— 0 — 7 —	8	
of. Nicho. Withe	— 0 — 4 —	4	
William Man.	— 0 — 2 —	8	
William Hollman	— 0 — 1 —	8	
of Elder ffroft	— 0 — 2 —	6	
of Sam. Greene	— 0 — 3 —	0	& foe he pay but 2d. pr. heade. for every default. & theefe men are to be sattiffied out of the fines for there gathering of them vp.
of Tho : Danforth	— 0 — 0 —	8	
of Bro. Crackbone.	— 2 —	2	
of Rich ffrench.	— 0 — 0 —	10	
of. Bro. Holmes.	— 0 — 4 —	8	
of. Bro. Shaw.	— 0 — 2 —	0	
of. Bro. Gipfon	— 0 — 1 —	10	
of Bro. Hildreth	— 0 — 0 —	8	
of. Bro. Coopr.	— 0 — 1 —	0	
of. Bro. Oakes.	— 0 — 0 —	4	
of goodman Broadifh	— 1 —	8	
of Elder Champnis.	— 0 —	8	

It is ordered that the Conftables Edward Goffe & Edward winfhip shall Make the towne rate, that is due to the treafurer & the Captine of the Caftle. & gather It off the towne according to the order of the Court.

Granted by the Towne of Cambridge vnto Grigory Stone a prcell of land about. 200 ac^r more or leffe Abutt uppon the Heade of the (8) mile line towards Concord It is to run vpon a prpendicular line to y^e (8) mile line vnto a greate Rocke ftone being ye Bounds betw˄ Edward Goffe & him, & from thence in a ftraite line to ye Brooke, & Croffing the Brooke, ftill to Run allong By Another Brooks fide, running on ye weft fide of a plaine, vntill he Come to the end of ye pla˄ & from thence he is to run along By the further fide of the meadows that ly about a greate pine Hill, & foe to Continue vntill he Co˄ to a marked white Oake nere Concord

˄rom thence a line to be drawn being a paralell [   ] the other weft End oppofite vnto the fame, vntill he Co˄ vnto the eight mile heade line.

8 (9) 1647

There is liberty granted vnto Philip Cooke for to fell fome timber on ye Comon for an addition vnto his dwelling houfe, & one Clabord tree.

the 28th 10th mo. 1653:

The proprietors of the wood Lotts meeting together agreed to devide the remainder of the wood Lotts apperteyning to there Lotts formerly Devided in to foure Squadrants, wch was accordingly done by lott being in·eurie Squadrant thirty acres

at the Same time there was allowed to Jno: Stedman more then his du proportion in confidera∧ of wt his former Lott fell fhort foure acres.

and to Nicholas withe two acres.

In ye firft Squadrant begining at ye necke of Land next to James Skidder.

Jno: Bridge	— 03½
Richard Jacfon	— 02½
Robert Homes	— 02¾
Mathew Bridge	— 02
Richard Ecles	— 01½
Samll. Greene	— 02¾
Jno: Cooper	— 02¾
mr Parkes	— 01¼
Jno Shepard	— 01½
mr Collines	— 01½
Robt: Broadifh	— 02¼
Edw: Michelfon	— 02¾
	27

In ye 2: Squadrant		In ye 3d Squadrant next Ri: Hassell		
mr Cooke	— 05	5	Tho: Danforth.	— 10¾
Jno: Stedman	— 07	1	mr pelham	— 01¾
Nich: withe	— 03½	8	Jno: Glour	— 02
Deac: ftone	— 03¼	4	Edw: Goffe	— 06
Jno watfon	— 01¼	6	Colled.ge	— 02
Dan: ftone	— 02¾	2	Wm Wilcocke	— 02
wm Manning	— 01¼	7.	Wid. Wilkinson	— 01½
Gilbt: Cracbone	— 01	3	mr Day	— 01
Elder ffroft	— 02			27
	27			

12 (11) 1660. lotts were drawn for this fquadrant, beginning ∧ the ∧ lott at Spy pond.

TOWN RECORDS 65

In ye 4th Squadrant next Spy pond

Tho: Oakes	— 02
Edw: winſhip	— 02½
m^r Michell	— 06
Abra: Errington	01¼
ffranc: whitmore	— 00¾
Ri: Champny	— 03½
Tho: Cheſholme	— 04
The towne Lott	— 01½
Tho: Brigham	— 02
Jno: ffeſſington	— 01¾
Andrew Belſhar	— 01½
	26¾

[**27**]   In the year. 1646:

Severall lotts granted by the Towne for wood lotts vnto divers prſons, But the land to ly in Comon for ye townes vſe.

In the ould ox paſture.

Granted vnto.

m^r Sam: Shephard.	11. ac.^r +
Gilbert Crackbone	+ 04 ac. —
John Ruſsell	+ 07 —
Robt Homes	+ 11 —
Tho: Brigham	+ 08 —
— Ed. Goffe	+ 24 —
John Coopr	+ 11 —
— John Glover	+ 08
Mr Parks	+ 05.—
for a towne lott	+ 06
An Tomſon	+ 08 —
m^r Joſepth Cooke	+ 20
Ed: Micherſon	+ 06 —

TOWN RECORDS

On the other fide menotime Bridge,

Granted vnto	ac^r roods.
—John Betts.	— 08 + 00
—Widow wilkerfon	— 06 + 00
—Herbert Pelham Efqr	— 07 + 00
—John Stedman.	— 12 + 00
—Nicho: Withe	— 06 + 00
—Grigory ftone.	— 13 + 00
—Nathan Aldis	— 04 + 00
John ffeffington	— 07 — 00
—Sam. Greene	— 04 + 00
—Umphery Bredfhew	— 5 + 00
—Mr Philips houfe	— 7 + 00
—Tho: Marrett.	— 11 + 00

Thefe following Butt. the firft of them vppon the South End of the other.

Imprimis. Ed. Collins.	—06 + 00—
—Goulden Moore	— 08 + 00
—William Cutter	— 05 + 00—
—Tho: Chefholme	— 08 + 00
Tho: Parrifh	— 08 + 00
—Roger Shaw	— 10 + 00—
—John Gipfon	— 07 + 00—
Edmond ffroft.	— 08 + 00
Edward Winfhip.	— 10 + 00

Tho: Crofby.	— 06 + 00

this lott Butts uppon Tho: Marret. & foe thefe follow in order.

Robert Broadifh.	— 09 + 00
Eliath Corlet.	— 7 + 00
Mr Tho: Shepherd.	— 24 + 00
Edward Goffe	— 06 + 00
m^r Dunfter	— 05 + 00
[ ]	Bridge [ ]

	ac^r
John Bridge	— 14 + 00
The Colledge	— 08 + 00
Richard Parke	— 3 + 00
Elder Champnis	— 14 + 00

Richard Jacfon — 10.^{acr} for the wch the Towne granted him the one halfe of the Ylands amongft the Swamps Betwen m^r Sparahauks farme & Menotime River, with all the Swamp, that Butteth upon the Meadow on the foueaft the path from the farme Through the Swamp on the weft, & soe along the Swamp & both fides of the Brook that Runeth into little Spy Spond;

& vnto Tho: Danforth 12 ^{acr} for the wch the Towne granted him the other halfe of the aforefd Ylands & Swamp, to Be Equally devided Betwen Rich Jacfon & him. Allfoe he is to haue for the makeing up his number of ac^r the Yland in ye Swamp on the nor weft fide of menotime River, namely all the wood apertaineing vnto it.

TOWN RECORDS 67

In the yeare 1645.

There being 5 more Chofen by the Towne to joine with the feven felect men that were then in place for the ordering of fome fpeciall affaire of the Towne: there were then thefe feverall lotts granted.

Imprimis feverall lotts on the other fide of Menotime according as is entred in the Tranfcript, vnto the feverall prfons with there number of acres.

Alfoe granted the land on this fide the water lying beyond (5) miles, vnto the feaventh mile for fmall farmes. the names of the prfons & quantities followeth, onely they that fall by lott betwen the 5th & 6th mile, there quantity is to be multiplied by 8: & they that fall betwen the fixth & feaventh mile there quantity to be multiplied by nine. & what the land on this fide the water Cometh short to make up the prties prportions here after mentioned of the land on ye other fide the water, to begin at the nereft, & foe on.

		ac
Itm. To Herbert Pelham Efq^r late m^r Bucklies houfe.		— 13 — 00
1	lott. Tho: Brigham.	— 10 — 00
2	Vfher & Sanders houfe.	— 08 — 00
3	Tho: Skidmore	— 05 — 00
4	Tho: Marrett.	— 10 — 00
5	John Rufsell.	— 08 — 00
6	Mr Philips houfe.	— 10 — $\frac{1}{2}$
7	m^r Jofeph Cooke.	— 06 — 00
8	Nich: Withe.	— 06 — 00
9	Tho: Chefholme.	— 04 — 0$\frac{1}{2}$
10	John Gipfon.	— 07 — 0$\frac{1}{2}$
11	George Cooke.	— 09 — 00
12	Ould Crofby	— 06 — 00
13	Edward Micherfon.	— 08 — 00
14	John ffifhenden	— 04 — 0$\frac{1}{2}$
15	Robt. Broadifh.	— 12 — 00
16	The Colledges	—
17	John Betts. for two houfes	— 09 — 00
18	John Coopr	— 10 — 0$\frac{1}{2}$
19	Edward Collins	— 13 — 00

20	Carath Lathan	— 03 — 00
21	Mrs Glouers childrens houſe	— 18 — 00
22.	Will. Cutter	— 06 — 00
23	Nathan Aldis	— 06 — 00
24	John Stedman	— 12 — 00

The Names of thoſe whoſe prportions are to ly next vnto there purchaſed meadows

	acr.
Robert. Homes	— 13 — 00
Ed. Goffe & widow wilkerſon	— 13 — 0½
Sergent winſhip	— 12 — 00
Goulden Moore & his wiues children.	— 13 — 00
Rich Jacſon	— 09 — 00
William Wilcocke	— 04 — ½

It was allſoe granted vnto Edward Winſhip he haueing bought the prportions Both of Tho: marret & John Ruſſells that they should be layde out by his owne By his purchaſed meadow.

Granted vnto Tho: Danforth the Skirts of meadow, that m^r Haines farme leaueth to y^e Como– of the meadow, Comonly Called alcocks meadow, with all thoſe ſeverall ſpots [ ] meadow that ly vppon that Br$_\wedge$

Granted vnto John Betts six ac^r of the nereſt Comon meadow for what he Came Short of his prchaſed meadow.

Granted vnto Tho: Danforth. twenty ac^r of land in reſpect of his father, to Joine vnto his land on the other ſide the water.

Agreed that all the Comon Meadow not formerly diſpoſed of, shalbe layde out to each man his due prportion as may be moſt Convenient for his farme.

Granted vnto John Steadman liberty to take 5 ac^r at menotime & ſoe there remaineth but Eighte to be layde out for his farme. I say eight acrs.

land laide out on the ſouth ſide the water by m^r Pelhams farme.

	ac^r
To Edmond Anger ⎱	
m^r ſparahauke ⎰	— 39 — 00
Herbert Pelham Eſq^r	— 35^{acr} — 00

Geourge Hutchine	— 09	— 00
John Thrumble.	— 06	— 00
Ed. Shepherd,	— 08	— 00
William Manning	— 5	— 00

Layde out vnto feverall men on the other fide the water nere watertowne Mill.

	ac^r	
To John. Jacfon.		— 10 — 00
Renold Bufh.		— 10 — 00
John Kendalls houfe.		— 10 — 00
Ould Clemans houfe.		— 10 — 00
redfins house, about	7^{acr}	— 07 — 00
Richard Parke.		— 11 — 00

Granted vnto Rich: Jacfon the peice of meadow wch he hath formerly occupied by his farme vppon Condition that he attend the laying out of the fmall farmes.

[ ] Shepards grant.   Granted vnto m^r Tho: Shepherd, Paftor. six ac^r of meadow lÿng next vnto John Betts at ye end of ye purchafed meadow.

We doe alfoe agree & giue the land at menotime for their full prportions of all the lands in ye Towne except Rich: Jacfon: John Betts: & Tho: Brigham

---

Agreed that all thofe whoe shall refufe to pay for the laÿng out of their lands, all such lands shalbe forfet in to the hands of the Towne, & y^e Towne shall pay for the meafuring of y^m.

To the widdow Crofbyes houfe was granted twelve acres to be multiplied as the other
and to her other houfe three acres & halfe.

Severall Officers Chofen to order the prudentiall affaires of this Towne for this prefent yeare Enfueing the date herof. 8$^{th.}$ 9th. 1647.

Conftables. { Edward Goffe
              { Tho: Danforth.

for Townfmen.	{ John Bridge Tho: Marret. John Stedman Tho: Brigham. Tho: Beale.
Surveiours of high waies	{ Robert Daniel. Gilbert Crackbone John Coopr.

There is liberty Granted vnto m^r Dunfter for to fell fome ffenceing stuffe vppon ye Comon for to make vp a peice of fence againft his feilde about fome 20. rod.

There is liberty granted vnto Tho: Danforth to fell fome raile trees on ye Comon to fence about his yard.

13th of ye 10th. 1647.

It is ordered By ye Townfmen that Edward Goffe & Edward Winfhip, shall meete with Charlftowne owners of menotime feilde, & deuide the fence betwen Cambridge & them. Belonging vnto y^t feilde, and according vnto y^r owne prpofition, lay out to Charlftowne twenty rod more then to Cambridge & they are allfoe in ye name of ye Towne to declare vnto them that we will engage or felves, for ye makeing of y^t fence noe longer time then o^r towne shall fee good for to ma Improvement againft that feilde in a prpriety again them & Take a note of It vnder the hand of the Townfmen of Charlftowne

further It is ordered that when they haue thufs done they shall deuide the fence vnto Each prprietor, according vnto the nomber of there ac^r in the whole feilde foe far as It refpecteth Cambridge, to be done before the 1th day of ye 1th month next Enfueing.

It is ordered By ye Townfmen that what ever prfon or prf shall haue dry Cowes goeing with the heard on this fide the water, or any Dry Cattle on ye other fide of ye water with the Heard there, any part of eyther of the halfe yeares, he shall pay for the whole halfe yeare & the halfe of the 1 part of the fommer to end uppon ye laft day In July.

There is liberty granted unto Tho: Marrett. for to fell fome fencing stuffe on ye Comon for his Comon fence. allfoe two Clapbord trees for his houfe

There is liberty granted vnto Richard Jacſon to fell ſome fencing ſtuffe for his Com̃o fence.

There is liberty granted vnto Edward Goffe for to fell. ſix timber trees on yᵉ Com̃o for yᵉ building of his veſsell,

There is liberty granted vnto Mʳ Dunſter to fell ſome timber for the new ſcoole houſe.

10 (11) 47: There is Liberty Granted vnto Thomas Oakes for to fell ſome fencing ſtuffe to mend the fence belonging vnto Thomas Parriſhes land.

Liberty Granted vnto Robert Stedman to fell a [   ] tree for his houſe Covering:

10 (11) 1647.

There is liberty Granted vnto wartertowne to fell ſome timber on yᵉ Com̃on on the other ſide the water towards yᵉ makeing of the Bridge over the River Att yᵉ mill, to be ordered by mʳ Jacſon & his Bro: this liberty to Continue n_{∧} longer than the latter End of aprill next.

liberty Granted vnto Bro Withe to fell ſome timber on yᵉ Com̃on for to Builde him a Barne, before the laſt of may next

ordered by the Townſemen that All thoſe who haue not formerly had there prportions on the other ſide the water, shall haue It layde out vnto them 4 acʳ for each pʳſon in eyther deuiſion as others formerly have had of there Ranke,

Allſoe there is 3 acʳ in each deuiſion, Granted vnto Richard Ecles in Conſideration of a former Grant on this ſide the water the which is to Be layde out vnto his other lott.

It is Agreed vppon by the Townſemen, that All that land which fall to be deuided Into Small farmes Att the heade of mʳ Andrews farme with In the Compaſſe of three miles from the Towne shalbe multiplied. foure for one At menotime

Wheras there was A former Grant made By the Towne of All the wood on this ſide the path that Goeth Betwen Capt. Cookes Mill & Watertowne vnto the ſeverall men who now haue there ſeverall wood lotts layde out of that portion of wood & there Being yet ſome over plus Beſides what is deuided vnto Every man the which by the former Grant doth Belong on thoſe ſeverall prprietors In the ſame It is By this order

Confirmed & stated vppon Each man his right In the fame over plus according to his prportion, In the fame to them & thires & no other as though It had Bin added vnto his lott.

It is ordered that the former order made In (1642) be Published Concerning out fences & who ever be delinque$_\wedge$ shall pay according to the penalty therin p^{r}fcribed.

It is ordered that whofoever shall Cutt or Caufe to be Cut downe In the Comon Greate Swamp Any wood shall Cleare away All the vnderwood & Brufh & who ever shalbe delinquent herin & not doe It with In one weeke After ther wood is fetcht out of the Swamp, shall pay for every loade twelue penc$_\wedge$

14th of the 12th mo: 1647.

At a Generall meeteing of the whole towne

It was agreed that there fhould be a dry heard keep^r hired for this yeare Enfueing & that If Any fhall put ther Cattle over the water without a keep^r, they fhall pay as much as thofe pay that haue there Cattle kept, & if there be not Enough of theefe, to make up the keepers wages, then all those that put there Cattle vnto any other place fhall Each of them there prportion according to the number of Cattle that they haue, make up the fame

further It is ordered, that euery man, that Putteth any Cattle to the Dry heard, fhall Bring In for Each Beaft one pecke of Corne vnto the houfe of Edward Goffe Cunstable before the laft of the (2) mo: next & If any fhall Be delinquent herein Euery fuch prfon fhall pay fix pence more uppon a heade, then the Comon price of the wages, unto thofe that lay It out for them to be leuied By the townfemen

the fame day It was ordered By the townfmen there being a former Grant of (600) ac^r of land unto m^r Natt: Sparahauke now deceafed & he haueing receiued fattiffaction In land on the fouth fide of the water for (230) of the fame   It was ordered that the remainder, viz: 370: ac^r fhall forth with be layde out By thofe men formerly appointed In that worke on the fouth fide of the water, Betwen his owne further deuifion of land & Bofton line.

13th:(1) $\frac{1647}{1648}$

liberty granted to William Rusfell for to fell fome timb for a barne with two clapbord trees, & (2 raile trees uppon the comon before the laſt of may next.

It. to fell three trees for to ground fell Tho: Marriots houfe.

It. to fell fome for to make a lentoe for Bro. fwetman

It. There being due to Timothy Haukins of watertowne, fome timber that he vfed about John ffrenches houfe, he hath liberty to take fiue trees of the comon, before the laſt of aprill next.

It. Granted liberty to Robt. Stedman to fell fome timber on the comon for an adition to his houfe.

It. granted liberty to Robt. Homes to fell fome timber for an adition to his houfe before may day next.

Chriftopher Cane hath liberty granted him to fell fome timber to fence in his garden about his houfe.

Roger Bancroft hath liberty granted him for to fell fome timber uppon the comon for to fence with:

Whereas It hath bine formerly ordered & publifhed that all out fences be fufficiently made by the owners therof before the laſt of this p^{r}fent month. & the penalty of 6d pr rod, for euery rod that is found faileing: It is now ordered that there fhalbe 12^d a month penalty for euery rod that fhalbe found delinquent after the laſt of this p^{r}fent month is expired: to be demanded of the owners of fuch fence from time to time the faide monthly fine vntill fuch time as the fence be made fufficient.

Edward Goffe & Tho: Danforth are appointed to fee this former order executed uppon the owners of the necke fence.

John Stedman &   are appointed to fee this order executed uppon the fence belonging to pine fwamp feilde.

John Bridge Tho: Marritt. Tho: Brigham. and Tho: Beale are appoynted to fee this order executed uppon the owners of the fence belonging to the Weft feilde.

(10) 2mo 1648.

It is ordered by the townfmen that all fwine that goe at liberty With in the Bounds of this towne be at all times fufficiently yoaked & ringed,

& the penalty is fix pen, for euery default herein, & if any fhalbe found in any Corne or corne feilde, the owner or proprietor in the fame fhall hereby haue Power for to impound the fame though yoaked & ringed, & require & recouer of the owner ther of fix penc, pr heade for bringing them out with all the damage done by them Prouided, allwaies if the owner of the fwine can make it appeare by fufficient proofe that they eyther did or might ordinarily, Come in to fuch Corne by reafon of the infufficiency of the fence apperataineing to the fame the which fhalbe foe accounted if being veiwed by Indifferent men they Judge it not fufficient to keepe out a well yoaked Pig of ten Weekes ould then the owner of the fwine fhall haue power for to recouer all fuch damage as fhalbe Caft uppon him by reafon of the trefpaffe of his fwine of the owner or owners of all fuch fence proportionably prouided there be Notice giuen them if liueing With in the bounds of this towne within two dayes after fuch damage be done, that there fence is found defectiue that foe further damage may be preuented & if they defire it they may Chufe one man for to Judge of the fufficiencie of the fame.

8th. 2th. mo 1648:

there is liberty granted to Robt. Parker for to fell fome timber for the building of a dwelling houfe & fome for a barne & fenceing: prvided it be felled all before the laft of the 7th mo. 1648.

9th. 2th mo. 1648:

It was agreed, At a Generall meeteing, When the whole towne had fpeciall warneing to meete, for the difpofeing of Shawfhine, that there fhould be a farme layde out of a thoufand acres, to be for a publick ftocke & improued for the Good of the Church, & that part of the Church that here fhall Continue, & euery prfon or prfons that fhall from time to time remoue from the church: doe herby refigne up there intreft therein to the remaineing prt of the Church of Cambridge.

1000 acres at Shaw Shine for ye use of ye Chh.

this. 1000. ac^r of land giuen to the vfe aforefd fhall be layde out eyther all together, or elfe feuerally prt in one place, & prt elfewhere, according to the difcretion of the men that are apointed to lay out that land.

further it was then Granted, that thofe who doe, eyther refigne up there fmall farmes for the good of the towne, or doe want that they Can not be fuplyed With in the bounds of the eight mile according to the nature of there grant, that all fuch fhould haue there prportions, for quantity & quality at fhawfhine

allfoe there was then granted to feuerall brethren that had no houfe right in the town if they did defire it. farmes, at fhaw fhine.

Imprimis Capt. Googine a farme if he buy a houfe in the towne. all foe to Bro Edward Oakes. Tho: Oakes & Richard Hildreth Each of them a farme, for there Incouragement, if they fee it may make for there fuport, & defire it. prvided allwaies, uppon this Condition if they or any of them fhall depart the towne then there land to fall into townes handes againe, & then they fhall haue no Power to fell, alinate, or giue to any other there right therein if they depart, from this place, onely the towne fhall pay them for what it fhall then be found better by there Improuement of It being valued by Indifferent men.

ffurther it is Granted to m^r Henry Dunft, & m^r Edward Collins, liberty to haue there fmall farmes, at fhaw fhine, and to be Confidered in there quantity more than others, in regard of there worke, & place.

ffurther it is ordered at this meeteing of the towne that Edward Goffe, John Stedman, Thomas Beale, John ffefington & Tho: Danf, fhall according to there beft Judgement & difcretion, lay out to euery man there proportiō, according as may make moft for the good of the prprietors therein, & the publick. Allfoe they with the reft of the townfmen to order how much euery of thefe fhall haue for quantity.

quantity ordered in page 34

[31] 19th of the 3th mo. 1648.

It was ordered by the townfmen that that prt of the fence which belongs to the ould ox pafture on the fouth fide the High Way. Both againft Charlftown feilde, & the High Way, fhould be meafured, and pro-portioned to the feuerall prprietors, Begining at Tho: Danforths lott, & foe ending at John Betts according to there number of ac^{rs} therein & they whoe haue more then there prportion of fence againft the High way to haue foe much according to ther prportiō deducted of ther end fence agst Charlfton & they whoe haue not there prportiō of the fence agst the High Way according to ther number of ac^{rs} to make foe much the more agst Charlftoñ feilde according to which order, the fence was thufs deuided agst Charlftow̄ feilde, there belonging to the ox pafture 51. pole & agst the High way 147 Pole. Begining next to Charlftowne pt of that fence.

1 : John Betts. — 19 pole.
2 : m^r Herbert Pelham. 22¼
3 : m^r Jofepth Cooke. — 04¾ 3 foote.
4. Robert Holmes. 0 — 1¼
5. Edward Michelfon. 01½
6. John Glouer. 02½

& vnto Edward Goffe there did belong 2 ^{p}¾. but Tho: Danforth haueing three rod of fence agst the High Way more then his prportiō, he agreed with him, to doe that prt of fence wch his ox pafture lott was to beare agst the neck in lew of it. & thefe 197. pole of fence, belonging to 69. ac^r [   ] land, it Cam to by deuifion. 2 pole ¾ 1. foote. pr ac^r

12th of ye 4th mo: 1648:

Vppon the Complaint, of Edward Goffe, againft Richard Cutter for wrongfull detaineing of Calues, impounded By him of the faid Edward Goffes wherein Samuell Eldred wittneffeth, Edward Goffe defired his Calues of Richard Cutter, promifeing to pay all damages & Coft as two men fhould aprehend to be right. but the f^d Richard Cutter denied to let him haue them, except he would tak$_\wedge$ a Courfe with his Boy & promife they fhould neuer Come there againe & a fecond time, being defired to let Edward Goffe haue the Calues, he Anfwered noe: the townfmen haueing Confidered the buifines they thufe order that Edward Goffe fhall pay 14^d Damage to Richard Cutter & Richard Cutter fhall pay for the Cofts of the fame & wittneffes, foure fhillings & feuen pence.

liberty Granted to John Stedman to mow a prt of ye Comōon meadow nere unto the path from Vine brooke to Watertowne.

11th of the 7th mo. 1648.

Granted vnto John Thrumble. 10. ac^r of land in Confideration of land he hath left out for a high way: which is to be the Juft Bredth that the high way is, betwen m^r Cookes pale & Goodman Betts pale, & foe quite through all his marfh. he is to haue his land the one half of it in the lower & the other half in the vpper deuifion next vnto y^t which is alrea˄layde out on the fouth fide charles riuer towards ftrabery hill:

more Granted to him 8: acr to be layde out adjoyneing to [   ] other, 4: ac^s in each diuifion.

Seuerall men Chofen for officers to the Towne No. 13. 1648: for the following yeare:

for three men to end fmall Caufes: m^r Jofepth Cooke. m^r Edward Jacfon.   Edward Goffe.

for Cunftables. John Stedman. John Ruffell:

for Townfemen. Edward Goffe. Edward Winfhip: Ed. Okes   John Cooper. Thomas Danforth:

for to fee to the order about leather fealeing: ffrancis Moore: ——

for Clearke of the market: Tho: Beale

13th 9th mo. 1648:

It was agreed at a meeting of the Whole Towne, that there fhould be land fould of the Comon for the gratifying of m^r Corlet, for his paines in keepeing a fchoole in the Towne. the fume of Ten pounds, if it can be attained. prvided: it fhall not prjudice the Cow comon: —

20th 9th 1648.

John Kendall for breakeing the towne order, by his hogs, was fined. 3^s. 6.^{d} to be leuied by ye Cunftables:

It is agreed by the Townfmen, that the Cunftables fhould make a Rate equivolent to the p^{r}fent Country Rate, & leuy it of the inhabitants of the Towne for paying the Towne debts.

It is agreed that Natt. Hancocke fhould haue fome wood out of the Weare, to be Cut out and fetched home by the Cunftables at ye Towne Charge:

It is ordered, that there fhalbe an eight peny ordnary prvided, for the Townfmen, euery fecond munday of the mo: uppon there meeteing day. and that Whoeuer of the Townfemen, faile to be prfent With in half an houre of the Ringing of the Bell, (Which fhalbe half an houre after eleuen of the clocke) he fhall both lofe his dinner, & pay a pinte of facke or ye vallue, to the prfent Townfmen: and the like penalty fhalbe payd by any that fhall depart from ye reft with out leaue. the Charges of ye dinner fhalbe payd by the Cunftables out of the Towne ftocke.

11th 10th mo. 1648:

Liberty granted to William Man to fell fome timber to mend up his Comon fence, and finifh his houfe pruided it be before may day next.

alfo to m^r Jacfon to fell fome Cedars, for pofts for his garden.

fould by the Townfmen to m^r Edward Jacfon forty acre of land, adjoyneing to that which is already layd out unto his Bro· John Jacfon and to himfelfe for Redfins houfe prvided he fatiffie Ten pounds to m^r Corlet for the Townes ift to him:

[32]   11th 10th mo. 1648:

William Man for Breach of Towne order, by felling a tree on the plaine on this menotime was fined foure fhillings to be levied by the Counftables.

There is liberty granted to Bro: Goffe to fell fix timber trees on the Comon Towards the building of his barne.

Granted by the Townfmen to John Gibfon the ufe and prfit of the Weare, and Weare land for two yeare enfueing, uppon condition, that he ferue the Towne with fifh, at ninepence pr thoufand and if he afford helpe for loading them to be allowed ten pence pr 1000:

Liberty granted to John Stedman, to fell fome timber on the Comon for the makeing up fome 15. p. of Comon fence about m^r Dunfters Land.

Liberty granted to John Cooper to fell fome for a leant

At a publicke Towne meeteing ye 21th of the tenth month. 1648:

Impr. It is agreed, by the the Inhabitants of the Towne that the Cow Comon fhalbe ftinted.

and for the better regulateing thereof, It being found that there is many blotts, uppon many figures in the Record of the former affeffment of the Comon that it can hardly be difcerned, what is euery mans Right and intreſt, and there being an ould Copy of the originall extant, with out blotts or blurs, It is therefore agreed by the Towne that there fhall fiue men be chofen, to veiw and examine th_ ould Records, and foe neere as they can to Regulat_ the fame according to the firft originall, the which being done, they fhall enter the fame, fairely written, in words at length, and not in figures, there to Remaine, as the true and prper intreft of euery of the Inhabitants, in the Cow Comons; Whofe names are here under written: Mr Henry Dunfter. Mr Richard Champny. Edward Goffe. John Ruffell. Thomas Danforth

alfo it was agreed that thefe fiue men, Chofen, fhould according to there beft difcretion, apoynt a prportiō of cow Comon unto fuch as they finde none granted in the former Records, prvided it be to fuch as haue liberty of building from the Townfmen.

alfo it was voted, and agreed by the Major part, that if they faw Juft Caufe, they might then ad unto fuch as they did aprehend had too few, Confidering there place, and publicke Charges.

alfo that Noe man fhall put on to Comon aboue his Number foe Recorded by thefe men, and if he fhall put on any other beaft eyther horfe, ox, ftere, goate, or fheepe, it fhalbe after fuch a prportion as fhalbe allowed in the Roome of his Cowes, and not exceed, uppon the forfeture of fuch penalty as the Townfmen fhall Impofe;

alfo it is agreed that Noe man fhall fuffer any Hogs to goe at liberty, exceeding the Number [   ] thefe men fhall order for each houfe.

8th. of the 11th. 1648:

Liberty granted to Andrew Steuenfon to fell fome timber on the Comon for the repare of his houfe and garden fence prvided it be before June next Enfueing:

Liberty granted to Thomas Brigham to fell fome timber on the Comon for the Repaireing of his houfe and out fences, prvided it be before the firft of June next Enfueing : Alfo the Like liberty is granted to Robert Parker. alfo to Edward Winfhip for the building of a Barne : the like liberty was granted to Wm. Rufsell for his necefsary ufe.

12th (1) $\frac{1648}{9}$

Liberty granted to Edmund Angeir for to make a gate uppon the high way on the fouth eaft fide of his farme prvided he maintaine it Convenient for pafsengers, at his owne prper coft.

Liberty granted to Edward Okes to fell fome Timber uppon the Comon lands for his necefsary reparations.

Edward Goffe and John Stedman are appoynted to execute the Towne & Court orders, Concerning fences, about the necke of land.

In like mañor Edward Goffe, & Edward winfhip is appoynted for the pine fwamp feilds, & Edward Winfhip and Richard Hildreth for menottime feilds

alfo John Rufsell & Tho. Danforth are in like mañour appoynted for the ffences about y° weft feild :

14th 3th mo. 1649

It is ordered by the Townfmen that Richard Ecles, & Richard Haffull to gether with any other of the Towne as occafsion is offered to them haue hereby full power and authourity giuen them to cleare the cow common belonging to the Towne of all dry Cattle that are kept by any of the Inhabitants of ye Towne uppon the fame, alfoe to Impound them if need require, alfo to impound all fuch Cattle appertayneing to any of watertowne as they fhall finde kept uppon any prt of our bounds, or turned uppon the fame by the owners thereof and we doe further order that the owners of all fuch Cattle fhall pay thre pence for euery beaft that fhalbe found trefpafsing herein, to fuch prfon or prfons as fhall execute the fame.

Liberty granted to Richard Cutter to fell foure trees for his trade on, the fouth fide the Riuer upon the comon next to Bofton line.

20th 3$^{th.}$ mo. 1649 :

Andrew Steeuenfon, & Willm Patten, are appoynted by the Townfmen to execute the Towne order concerning Hogs, & to Levy of all fuch as fhalbe found Breaking that order, the Juft penalty of the fame, y^r in prfcribed.

m^r Jofepth Cooke, John Bridge & Thomas Danforth are appoynted to meet with Dedham to Run y^e line betwen the Townes, & to fettle the fame, as they fhall find to be right & Equall, according to the Grant of the Court.———————

[33]   16$^{th.}$ 12$^{th.}$ mo. 1648:

At a publique meeting of the Inhabitants of the Towne it was then voted, and Joyntly agreed, as followeth.

Imp^r that every perfon fhould make up his fence, appertayneing to any of the Comon feildes, before the fixten day of march yearely, and foe maintaine the fame fufficiently untill the corne be all out: uppon the forfeture of fix pence for every Rod that fhalbe found defectiue, to be leuied by the apoyntment of the Townfemen:

2. alfo that euery perfon fhall pay for every of his beaftes whether ox, ftere, goate, fwine, fheepe, Calfe, horfe, Cow, or other, that fhalbe found at liberty, or trefpafsing in any of the Comon feildes, after the fixten day of march. fix pence unto him that bringeth them out befides all Juft damages:

3. alfo that all fuch as keepe any fwine, fhall fufficiently Ring, and yoake the fame yearely at or before the fixten day of march, and foe mainetaine the fame uppon the penaltye, of three pence for want of euery yoake, and 3^d for a Ring that is otherwife found whether in towne or Comon to be leuied by the appoyntment of the townfemen and that noe pigs goe at liberty untill they be fufficiently yoaked and Ringed:—

4. It was left to the Townfemen to giue what confideration they might think meet to Bro. Richard Jacfon for his expen$_\wedge$ of time for the Townes publique occafions:

5. that the Townfmen fhould profecute fute in law agft fuch of the inhabitants of watertowne, as haue Trefpafsed in o^r greate fwamp.

$$12^{th.} (1) \frac{1648}{9}$$

Liberty granted to George willowes to fell fome Timber on the Comon for y^e repare of his houfe.

whereas I Sam: Straiton of Water-towne haue by bill under my hand ingaged my felfe to pay fifty fhill: for wood that I haue taken out of the greate fwamp with in Cambridge boundes, the faid bill being hereby voyd, with all Conditions on eyther prte then prmifed, I doe hereby Ingage my felfe to [   ] at the houfe of Richard Jacfon in Cambridge Thirty fhillings, in Ten Bufhells of Indian Corne before the laft of this p^{r}fent mo. dated 12 (1) 4$\frac{8}{9}$.

Samuell Z ftraiton his marke.

Whereas I w^m Clarke of water=towne haue by bill und$_\wedge$ my hand ingaged my felfe to pay 14^s 8^d for wood y^t I haue taken out of the greate fwamp in Cambridge bou$_\wedge$ the faid bill being hereby voyd, I doe hereby Ingage my felf$_\wedge$ to fattiffie fiue fhillings fix pence to Richard Jacfon of Cambridge, dated 12 (1) 4$\frac{8}{9}$. his Õ marke

Wm Clearke.

9th — 2th mo 1649.

vppon the Removall of the high way on the fouth fide the Riuer which pafseth from the mill at watertowne, to m^r Hibbins farme It being now layd on the Eaft fide of Richard Danas land, betwen him & the Indians, It is agreed that Richard Dana fhall haue the high way formerly appoynted betwen him & Samuell Hides onely he is to allow Samuell Hides a high way of 24: foote in bredth from the high way that is now lay$_\wedge$ out foe far as his own land, & make & mainetaine fuffici$_\wedge$ gates, or Barres, at eyther end for Cart, horfe & man, alfo he is vz Richard Dana: granted by the Townfmen that prcell of land wch was formerly prt of his lott on the fou eaft fide of the high way allowing foure Rod in Breadth for the high way foe far [   ] it lyeth in his lott:

At a meeteing of the Townfmen with fuch other perfons as were nominated by the Towne to determine of the Quantity of acres for the farmes Granted formerly by the Towne to Seuerall prfons at Shaw Shine Aprill 1649. It was then thus agreed viz.

That m^r Henry Dunfter prfident of Haruard Colledge fhould haue fiue hundreth acres, whereof foure hundreth is granted by the Towne to his owne perfon & heyres to Injoy freely foreu^r, & the other one hundreth acres for the vfe of Haruard Colledge.

Shawfhine farmes.

It. unto m^r Daniell Googine, fiue hundreth acres.

It. unto m^r Edward Collins in Lew of his Small farme with in the

TOWN RECORDS 83

Towne boundes, with fome addition in refpect of his place in the Deacons office, It was agreed y^t he fhould haue fiue hundreth acres.

10th of ye 4th mo. 1649:

It is ordered by the Townfmen that all prfons prvide that there dogs may doe no harme in corne or gardens by fcrapeing up the fifh, uppon ye penalty of 3^d for euery dog that fhall be taken damage faifant with all other Juft damages:

Richard Withe (uppon requeft to the Townfmen) in regard of the ftraitenes of his yard, & danger of fire, hath liberty granted him by the felect men to let his Barne Range uppō ye Comō. beyond his fence about (3) or (4) foote.

Edward Goffe & John Stedman hath each of them liberty granted them to fell one clap-bord tree a peece for there ufe, prvided it be before the laft of Sept. next Enfueing:

John Stedman Edward Oaks, & Tho: Danforth are appointed by ye Townfmen to meafure out unto m^r Edward Jacfon The forty acres of land formerly fould him by the Towne for the payment of m^r Corlet Ten pound as a Gratuity frō y^e Towne.

Edw: Goffe & John Rufsell are apoynted by the Townfmen to lay out a high way to the feverall lotts in wigwam necke when it may be moft conuenient for the seuera$_\wedge$ owners there of.

There is liberty Granted by the Townfmen, to John Hafteings: Willm̄ Patten, & Tho: ffox, for this prfent hay time to mow of the Comōn meadow at Shawfhine, prvided they intrench uppon noe prpriety.

The Difference betwen the Townfmen & Chriftopher Cane is referred to the heareing & determination of m^r Jofepth Cooke & m^r Ed. Jacfon:

Edw: Winfhip is apoynted by the Townfmen to prfent ye names of all fuch prfons to the felect men, as fhall trefpafse uppon any of the Towne Comōns, eyther by Cattle, or takeing away wood or timber with out lawfull right & liberty for ye fame.

10 (10). 1649:

The Townfmen doe grant to Tho: Marret, the timber and firewood uppon the high way that lieth betwen the fenced feild that was m^r Sparahauks and m^r Norcras land on the fouth fide the Riuer

Roger Bancroft hath liberty for fenceing ftuffe

[34] At a Generall Towne meeting. Novem. 1649.

There was then chofen thefe feverall officers for the yeare enfueing: ffor Comifsioners to end fmall caufes under forty fhillings.
m^r Jofepth Cooke, m^r Edward Jacfon, & m^r Edw. Goffe.
ffor Cunftables. Robert Holmes. Roger Bancroft.
ffor Townfmen, Edw. Goffe. John Bridge. — — Jno. Stedman. Edw. Okes. & Thomas Danforth.

10th 10th 1649

Liberty granted by the Townfmen to Edw: Hall to fell fome timber on the Comons to Raile in his lands about his houfe.

At a Generall meeteing of the Inhabitants of the Towne Novem. 1649. it was then agreed that m^r Edward Jacfon John Stedman and Tho: Danforth fhall veiw the land m^r Hibbins defireth and if they find it not prejudicial to the towne, then the Town doe giue to m^r Hibbines forty acres of land to be fet out by the aboue named perfons, uppon condition following: viz. that neyther m^r Hibbins nor any of his succeffors fhall heard uppon any prt of or bounds lying in Comon, nor take any liberty by vertue there of to prejudice any prt of our bounds, uppon the forfeture of the land in to the hands of the towne againe. ———

10 . 10. 49.

Liberty granted to John Jacfon to fenc croffe the high way on the north fide the Indians land uppon condition to make conuenient passage for passengers and to lay open the fame againe uppon notice of the fame from the townfmen.

also to fet his hay on the upland fenced in by m^r Philips ags^t his meadow, and make ufe of the timber to fence in his meadow.

14. 11. 49,

The townfmen doe agree that there fhalbe a ràte made and gathered by the Cunfta: Equivolent to the prfent country rate.

Thomas Danforth was then chofen to feale the weight$_\wedge$ and meafures for the Towne.

11. 12. 49:

The Townſmen doe giue liberty unto Edw: Goffe, Edw: Winſhip, Thomas Danforth, W^m. Ruſſell & Henry Prentice to fell timber on the Comōn for there p^rſent uſe in buildin_∧ and fenceing.

The requeſt of Richard ffrances for remitting the p^rſent town_∧ rate in regard of gods viſſitation by ſicknes on himſelfe and familie is granted.

Mr Edmund Angier execut^r of m^r Nathanell Sparauhau_∧ for & in conſideration of a debt from his Eſtate to the towne reſigneth up in to the Townes hands ſoe much of the farther deuiſion as the Indians haue Incloſed of y^t land, at fiue ſhillings pr acre, in prt of payment of the ſaid debt. w^o is ſixty 3: ac^r. of the lan_∧

Surveyo^rs of high wayes.
The Townſmen doe order that what euer prſon or prſons being an Inhabitant of this towne, & lawfully warned by the Surveyours of the High waies to attend the comō_∧ worke of the Towne, eyther perſons or other help of ther teames, or ſufficient pay for the Hire of ſuch labor as they haue notice giuen them to [   ] assist with all, and ſhall refuſe or neglect to doe it euery ſuch perſon ſhall forfet to the uſe of the Town_∧ double the price of ſuch labor as he had warneing to ſend To be levied by the appoyntment of the Townſmen.

It is further declared that ſix dayes ſhall be accou_∧ lawfull warneing:

At a Gen^rall meeting of the Inhabitants of the towne.

18. 12. 49:

Repairing meeting house
Voted and agreed by a gen^rall conſent that the meeting houſe ſhalbe repaired with a 4: ſquare rooffe and couered with ſhingle, and the charges thereof levied uppon the Inhabitants of the towne by Equall rate. also Edw: Goffe. Tho: Marret, Jno· Stedman, Robt Holmes, & Tho: Danforth, are choſen by the towne to overſee and carry on this worke, to agree with workmen, and to levie the charge of there ingagements for the worke, uppon the Inhabitants of the towne.

11th (1) mo. 16 49/50

Reconsidered & voted to build a new one 40 feet quare
At a Gen^rall meeting of the wholl Towne, it was then voted and agreed that the fiue men choſen by the Towne to repayre the meeting houſe ſhall defiſt from the ſame and agree with workmen for the building of a new houſe, about

forty foot ſquare, and couered as was formerly agreed for theother, and levy the charge of there Ingagements uppon the Inhabitants of the Towne.

It was alſo then voted & Generally agreed that the new meeting houſe ſhall ſtand on the watch houſe hill:

11. (1) 49.

The Townſmen doe grant liberty to Tho: Hall to fell timber on the Comon for building him a Barne,

also to Daniell Kempſter 4 trees for his trade

also to John Haſtings for repayreing his houſe.

Edw: Goffe, and Thom: Danforth are apoynted by the Townſmen to agree with the Cow keepers for the milch heard. Also to Agree with Roger Bucke about the weare for one yeare enſueing:

$8^{th}_{?}$ 2th. mo. 1650:

liberty granted unto Goulden Moore to fell ſome fenceing ſtuffe: on ye Comon:

John Bridge is appoynted to make up ſoe much of Abraham Morrills comon fence as lyeth agſt his land that he bought of him & Abram to Sattisfie him for the ſame.

Philip Cooke hath liberty granted to fell timber on the Comon for a barne,

Gilbert Cracbone and Thom: Okes are appoynted to looke unto the fences about weſt feild,

Willm Towne & John Cooper to pine ſwamp feild.

Edw: Goffe & John Steadman to the necke of land.

they are all Injoyned to make return of all deffects of all or any of the ſaid ffences with the names of the perſons and place of defect, & Quantity thereof, unto the Townſmen each towne meeting day.

Richard Ecles & Andrew Stevenſon doe agree with the townſmen to keep the milch heard this pᵣſent ſumer, they are to keep them at the appointment of the townſmen, and attend it dilligently ſpending there wholl time about the ſame, not onely at firſt but alſo the latter end of the ſumer when the Cattle come in to feildes, and to keep them ſoe long as the townſmen ſhall ord^r them in the latt^r prt of the yeare to be allowed 12^s. each of them each other weeke, and ſix pence for eu^{r}ie beaſt, in prt of the ſaid ſum in mony, butt^r, or wheat.

[35]   9. (7) 1650:

The land on the ſouth ſide Charles Riuer, now planted by the Indians, & aſſigned unto the Towne by the executours of m^r Nathaniell Sparauhauke, for the payment of a debt due to the Towne from m^r Sparauhauks eſtate being about fifty acres more, or leſſe, at fiue ſhillings pr acre, wee the Townſmen in the behalf of the Towne aſſigne and ſet over the ſaid land unto Edward Goffe & Thomas Danforth who are hereby Ingaged to ſattisfie the ſaid ſum̄e of fiue ſhillings pr acre for the uſe of the Towne unto the workmen about the meeting-houſe.

<blockquote>
John Bridge.
John Stedman
Robt. Holme.
Roger Bancroft:
</blockquote>

Chriſtopher Cane agſt m^r Joſepth Cooke for deteyneing of (2) oxen

John Betts agſt m^r Joſepth Cooke, for debteynein$_\wedge$ his (2) oxen and three Cows.

---

11. (9) 1650:

Seuerall officers Choſen for the yeare enſueing:

ffor Cunſtables: John Cooper, John ffeſſington: John Jacſon

for Townſmen: Edw: Goffe, Edw: Winſhip: Roger Bancroft, and
    Tho: Danforth:

for Surveyours of high waies: Richard Robbins: Ri: Hildreth and
    Tho: ffox:

for the ending Small cauſes 3 Com̄iſſioners. m^r Joſepth Cooke.
    m^r Edw: Jacſon. m^r Edw: Goffe. ———

The Townſmen doe giue liberty to willm Hamlet to fell (3) trees for to worke out, and (2) clapbord trees, but he is not to fell any prt of it out of the towne

John Parker for not attending the high waies is fined 3^s.

Robt: Browne for not attendance one day, one ſhill: 6^d

Edw: winſhip and Richard Hildreth are appointed to veiw the complaintes of ſev^{r}all on ye other ſide the water, and make returne to the townſmen, alſo to bound w^m Clemance meadow which he bought of Tho: Danforth nere alcocks meadow, alſo to veiw the Complaint of w^m Clema Senr for want of land.

The Townſmen doe giue w^m Clemance liberty to fell timber on the Comon for fencing agſt the high way. ———

9 (10) 50: Whereas dreadfull experience ſhews the inevitable danger and great loſs not only to prtic: prſons, but alſo to the wholl town, by the careles neglect of keeping chimnye clean from ſutt and want of lathers in time of need the ſelect townſmen takeing the ſame into there ſerious conſideration doe therfore order that eu^{r}ie person inhabiting within the bounds of this towne, before the 10th of the next mo: prvide one or more Sufficient lathers at all times in a readines to reach up to [   ] top of his or there houſe, and forth with and at all times hereafter ſee that there chimnies be kep clean ſwept at leaſt once eu^{r}ie mo: uppon the penalty of two ſhilling ſix penc for eu^{r}ie months neglect herein:

9. 10. 50:

m^r Jacson Richard Robins, and Samuell Hide are appointed by the Townſmen to lay out a high way where it may be moſt convenient from Roxbery high way to the Meadows.

Tho: Longhorn hath liberty granted for fencing ſtuff on the Comon.

Agreed by the Townſmen that Dedham high way ſhall ſtill remaine in the old place.

The Townſmen did agree that the grant of m^r Tho: ſhepards farme, ſhould be entred in the Towne book, viz: the Towne hath formerly giuen to m^r Tho: Shepard there late Paſtor, three hundred acres of land beyond watertown mill, adjoyning to that which was m^r Mailmes, also 200: ac^r more neere m^r Samuell Shepards farme.

300 acres

The Townſmen doe giue liberty to Philip Cooke in regard of the inconveniency of his owne yard by a water courſe that flowes it neer his barne, to set his new barne beyond his Pale about fiue foot:

13 (11) 1650:

The Townſmen doe agree and order that the high way from John Jacſons houſe to mʳ Hibbins farme ſhall ly betwen Richard Dana and Sammuell Hides where it was firſt laid out, and Soe from thence continue in the neereſt and moſt conuenient place through John Jacſons lott, untill it meeteth with the high way that leadeth to Dedham:

Agreed that John Jacſon ſhall haue soe much land adjoyneing on the comon added to his lott as the high way taketh away from his lott.

The Townſmen doe conſent that one of the Elders and two of the Deacons at the requeſt of John Betts ſhall Determin whether in Equity any sattisfaction ought to be rendered by the towne unto the Said John Betts for the land on which the new meetinghouſe ſtandeth and with ther Determination the ſaid John Betts prmiſeth to ſet downe Sattisfied.

The Townſmen doe giue liberty to Tho: Swetman Wᵐ: Man, John Coopr, Edw: Winſhip, Wᵐ Ruſſell and wᵐ Bucke to fell timber on the Comon for there neceſſary outfencing and building,

13. 11.1650   The Townſmen doe grant unto Tho: Danforth the uſe and Improuement of the reſerved Comon meadow at ſhawſhine for this next yeare Enſueing:

[ ] (11) 50   The Comon land recouered from Dedham not formerly granted or diſpoſed of by the Towne or Country is ſould By the Towne to mʳ Edw: Jacſon: Edward Goffe. John Jacſon & Tho: Danforth for twenty pound according to the agreement made by the Towne the 25ᵗʰ (10ᵗʰ) 1650 wᶜʰ was as followeth

[36] At a Genʳall meeting of the Inhabitants
the 25ᵗʰ 10ᵗʰ 1650: It was then voted
and agreed, as followeth.

Agreed that the land recovered from Dedham lying in Comon ſhalbe ſould by the Townſmen to ſuch of the Inhabitants, as are willing to allow twenty pound for the uſe of the towne prvided they ſhall not fell the ſame againe unto the towne of Dedham ſoe as to pʳjudice the towne, by the land not being improued, but in caſe after ſuch perſons haue purchaſed it, they find it not for there prfit to improue the ſame they tendering of it to the towne againe ſhalbe allowed there 20ˡˡ againe.

A proclamation of the fame on the meeting houfe. It being Agreed by the Towne that the land lying in Comon neere Dedham fhalbe fould to fuch of the Inhabitants as are willing to purchafe the fame, and improue it as they fhall fee beft. It is therfore defired that all fuch as doe defire or are willing to Joyne in the purchafe of the fame, would come and make agreement with the townfmen for the faid purchafe at there next town meeting day which wilbe, 13. 11th mo. 1650.

13 (11) 1650

Gilbert Crackbone and Tho: Beall are appointed by the Townfmen to looke over the ffences appertaining to weft feild and to attend the order of t Gen^rall Cort concerning ffences [   ]

In like manner Edw: Winfhip and Rich: Hildre are appointed for the ffences about menottime ffeild

also John Coopr and Ed Hall for the ffences about pine Swamp feild.

also Edw: Goffe and Tho: Danforth for the ffences about the neck of land.

John Russell is appointed by the Townfmen to take notice of all defects for want of Ladders and p^rfent the fame to the Townfm and giue all fuch perfons as are deffective from time to ti notice to attend the Town meeting to anfwer for themfelues and he is to be allowed for his paines 4^d of each perfon th the Townfmen fhall judge worthy to pay there fine.

George Willowes hath liberty to fell fome Timber on the Comon to repare his ffences againft the Comon and for his houfe.

10. (1) $\frac{1650}{1651}$

Chriftopher Cane ag^{ft} m^r Jofepth Cooke for deteyneing of two oxen, the Townfmen did judge Chriftopher Cane to pay m^r Cooke the Towns order fix pence a beaft. Captine Gookin hath liberty to fell some timber on the Comon to fence in his garden.

Thomas Danforth dissent.

Edward Micherfon liberty granted for to fell ground fells for his houfe on the Comon.

m^r Jofepth Cooke hath liberty granted him to fell fome timber on the Comon for to fence in his orchard and Clapbords.

m^r Henry Dunfter hath liberty to fell timber on the Comon f_∧ carying on the fchooll and fencing in the yardes about it.

Thomas Longhorne hath liberty to fell timber on the Comon for Clapbord mr^s Tompfons land.

Grigory Stone hath liberty to fell fome timber on the Comon for his fence againft the Comon.

10. (1) 1650/1651

The Townfmen agreed with Daniell Cheaver to keep the milch heard this p^rfent fumer enfueing and to allow him eleuen fhillings 6^d a weeke and he is to begin and leaue of at the Townfmens appointment and to goe forth with the heard before funne half an houre high each morning.

The Townfmen doe determine that the Quantity of Richard Hildreths ffarme granted him by the Towne at Shawfhine fhalbe two hundred acres adjoyneing to the other farmes allready determined:

Edward Goffe and John Cooper are appointed to fee the pound raifed againe at the burying place with all convenient fpeed and to take of the neereft timber on the Comon for the fame. — —

A Pound erected - -

It is ordered by the Townfmen that the pound keeper fhall receiue of the owners of the Cattle that fhalbe impounded after this rate: viz. of euery perfon that fhall haue one beaft impounded two pence and for two beafts of one man ye fame for three beafts 3^d. and for foure beafts, 4^d. and not to exceed 4^d. of one man at one time:

Regulations of it

John Jacfon Richard Oldam and Tho Danforth are appointed to attend Roxbery men in runeing the line between the two townes.

Perambulation

Thomas Danforth and Mathew Bridge are appointed by the Townfmen to attend watertowne men in Runeing the line betwen water towne and this towne.

14 (2) 1651

the Townfmen doe giue Tho: Beal liberty to fell timber on the comon for an addition to his dwelling houfe.

Thomas Beal and Gilbert Crackbone are appointed to fee the order executed concerning fwine.

The Townfmen doe agree that fiue acres of land fhalbe laid out to william Clemance fenior for and in confideration of what he hath haid giuen him fhort of his due prportion of that land adjoyneing to Elder ffrofts farme.

The Townfmen doe order that m[r] Boman, Richard Hassull & Ric Hildreth and william Hamlet looke to the Cow comon, that no cattle trespasse uppon the fame to the damage of the Cow heard, and in cafe they or any other of the inhabitants fhall find any cattle foe trespassing they may impound the fame either in the towne pound or there owne yards prvided they giue the owners notice and require of the owners of fuch cattle, 3[d] a head

12. (3) 1651:

The Townfmen doe giue liberty to Daniell Kempfter to fell Timber on the comon for the ufe of the Towne, to improve in his trade.

The Townfmen do order Bro: Angier to sattisfie twelue fhillings for the makeing up his fence in pine fwamp feild, and in cafe he fhall refufe do order the Cunftables to levie the fame

The Townfmen do agree to call the inhabitants to gether the next 4th day to confider of Shawfhine, and some other publique occassions of the Towne

27. (8) 1651

The Townfmen do grant liberty to Tho: Danforth to fell fome Timber on the Comon for ffencing and building & repairing his houfe. ——

[37] Receiued by the Towne of m[r] Richard Champny forty fix pound fix fhillings eight pence in full fattiffaction for the purchafe of the land whereon his houfe ftands, adjoyning to the land of Nathaniell Sparahauke on the weft being by eftimation about forty acres more or leffe, Also in exchang of one hundred acres of land granted him by the Towne nere m[r]. Sam[ll] Shepards farme, for one hundred acres of land adjoying to the fmall lotts to be laid out at the fouth fide of Roxbery high way adjoyneing to fouth fide of Nathaniell Sparauhauks feild, To

TOWN RECORDS 93

haue and to hold both the faid prcels of land with there appurtenances to the faid Richard Champny his heires & affignes for eu.ͬ

10th of the (9) mo. 1651.

There was Chofen thefe Seuͬall officers of the towne for the yeare enfuing

☞ ffor 3. Comiffioners to end fmall caufes.

mͬ Jofeph Cooke mͬ Edw. Jacfon. mͬ Edw. Goffe.

Townfmen for the prudentiall affaires of the Towne. Edward Goffe. Edw. Winfhip Roger Bancroft, and Thomas Danforth.

To Joyne with the Townfmen. John Stedman Thomas Beall Richard Roberts. Cunftables

Surveiours of high waies. Edw Okes. William Manning and Tho: ffox.

To fize Cafke. william Manning.

The Inhabitants did confent that the fiue men that were deputed by the Towne to make the agreement with the Carpenters ffor building the meeting houfe, fhould confider of there Complaints, and allow them wͭ they may Judge equall, not exceeding forty pound.

Representative without pay ☞ The Inhabitants do confent to make bro: Ri: Jac₍₎ allowance ffor his attendance at the laft Seffions of the genͬall Court.

8th 10.th mo. 1651.

Town clerk his pay The Townfmen do choofe Tho: Danforth for there clarke, and do allow him the ufe of Shawfhin meadow as formerly.

The Townfmen do giue liberty to mͬ Shearman to fell and cary away 200. of hop poles in fome comon fwamp before may day next.

The Townfmen do agree that there fhalbe a towne rate made equiuolent to yͤ Country rate.

The Townfmen do giue liberty to mͬ Michell, Edw. Goffe. John Stedman, and Tho: Chefholme to fell fome timber on the comon for there ufe in building and fencing

Edward winfhip did declare to the Townfmen that the high way through menottime feild was altered and therfore he would not be any longer ingaged to maintein the fence on the high way.

William Mannings prposition for wharffing at the head of the Cricke, is referred to the next meeting of the inhabitants of the Town then to be confidered of.

The 9th. 12. 1651.

The Townfmen do giue liberty to Edw: Winfhip Robert Parker John Cooper to fell Timber on y̆ comon for y̆ neceffary fencing and building.

The Townfmen takeing into there confideration a complaint made by divers of the great ftroy made of Timber lying in comon by feverall who with out refpect to the publique or future weal of this place haue done much ftroy in felling downe of multitudes of young Trees for firewood whereas in the meane while much wood that lies downe is yearly burnt up by fires in the woodes, Doe therfor order that no perfon or perfons what foever after the date here of fhall either directly or indirectly fell or caufe to be ffallen, any Tree uppon any prt of The bounds of this Towne lying in Comon without the confent of y̆ major part of y̆. Townfmen for fire wood or any other ufe, excepting only fuch trees as are old and decaying and meet for no other improvement but for fire wood, uppon the penalty of five fhillings for every tree foe fallen contrary to this order, the great fwamp only excepted.

Mannings wharf
11. 1651. William Manning is granted liberty by the inhabitants of the Towne at a gen'all meeting to make a wharffe out of the head of y̆ Cricke towards m^r Pelhams barne, and build a houfe on it to come as high as the great pine ftump, and range with m^r Pelhams fence next the high ftreet in to Towne.

[38] At a gen'all meetings of the inhabitants the 26. 12. mo. 1651. was granted and voted,

Church farm at Shawshin leased
That the Deacons and Edw. Goffe and Tho: Danforth fhould leafe out y̆ Churches ffarme at Shawfhine.

To John Stedman his requeft for fetting out his leanto about fix or 8 foot into ftreet.

To Tho: ffox to Take in the high way anent the land he bought of wm. Sims that was mr Sparhauks.

To ffrances moore fo much of the Comon land annent his dwelling houfe to be fet out by Edw. Goffe. & John Stedman, & Tho: Danforth; That the Townfmen fhall make fale of the land whereon the old meeting houfe ftood.

10 (3) 1652:

Liberty is granted by the Townfmen to m^r Dunfter for to fell fome timber on ye comon, about 2: tun for ye repare of his houfe & fences but not for the ufe of the Colledge to take any of the comon: There was a prpofition made by Thomas ffuller: of woburne for ½ a mile fquare of [ ] plaine neere m^r Dudlies farme, and for further incouragement to make a plantation:

It was agreed by the Townfmen that they would prpound this prpoffition to the Church the firft opportunity they could.

Whereas many complaintes are made to the Townfmen of the unreafonable practife of divers perfons to keep cattle ordinarly in comon feilds amongft corne, uppon fwamps or other peeces of graffe wherby much damage is done to many perfons and yet know not how to attaine fattisfaction for the fame the Townfmen do therfore order that what eu^r cattle fhalbe taken in any comon feild after fuch time as all fences by Towne orders are to be fecured except it be in fuch lands as are fufficiently fenced in by themfelves or fuch cattle as are at fuch time when they be there kept improved for the tilling of fome part of the land and by the owners therof fecured by a fufficient keeper aboue fixten yeares of age, the owners of all fuch cattle fhall be liable to fattisfie Double damages and fix pence pr head to fuch perfons as fhall bring them out, prvided allwaies that if it fhall appea_∧ fuch cattle trefpaffed through the infufficiency of any prt of the Comon fence apperteining to the fame feild the owners of the cattle fhall then be freed from all damage & coft, and the fame required of the owners of fuch infufficient fen_∧ through which in prbability fuch cattle might or di_∧ trefspaffe.

The Townfmen uppon the examination of the fale that John Thrumble hath fould to Elder Champnies of eighte_∧ acres on ye fouth fide the Riu^r do find that there was fo much granted by the Townfmen to John Thrumble, prt of it in lew of his prportion of the 1400 acres that was devided on ye fouth fide [   ] and the remainder in lew of a high way [   ]

that the faid John Thrumble did yeld to the Towne on the weft fide of m^r Pelhams Marfh on ye Eaft fide of Jonas Clarks houfe from the high way that runneth downe by m^r Cookes & fo to continue downe to the Riu^r:

Bro: Kempfter Bro: Marret & Deacon Marret haue liberty granted them to fell fome timber on ye comon for their ufe;

Ferry boat   The townfmen do agree that the Cunftables fhall purchafe a new ferry boat.

The 9th. 4mo. 1652.

It was agreed by the Church that Shaw fhine fhould be devided as followeth.

{ Ministerial   To m^r Michell, fiue hundred acres
{ Grant   To Edw. Okes, three hundred acres

To Thomas Okes one hundred and fifty acres;

It was agreed that theis 3 aboue named fhould haue their lotts laid out by a comitte, with as little prjudice to any lott as may be, and fo not to draw any lott.

☞   Alfo the Church doth agree that although the land be by grant of the Gen^rall Court peculiar to the Church only yet the wholl towne vzt fuch as are owners of houfe and land in ye Towne fhall come in to ye devifsion thereof.

Alfo it is agreed that eu^rie man fhall haue a prportion of the land more or lesse, according to his prportion now allotted him.

Alfo that eu^rie man fhall haue a prt of the meadow in prportion, with his upland to be laid out after the fame rule y^t the upland is, both by lott, & quantity

Alfo it is agreed that after the ffarmes fformerly granted are laid out the remainder of the land fhalbe deuided into 3. breadths, vzt. 2. of ye faid breadths to ly betwen ye rivers & the 3^d on this fide Shaw Shine Riuer

The firft Lott to begin uppon a line continued ou^r Shaw Shine Riu^r, ye fame yt is betwen woburn and us runing towards Concord untill it

TOWN RECORDS 97

meet wth m^r wintrops farme, and fo ye faid 1. lott to butt, fouth uppon y^t line and on Shaw Shine river, and mr wintrops farme and fo each lott to prceed one after another by due parrellells untill they come cleare of ye farmes allready laid out, and then to extend in two devifsions betwen ye riuers and a 3^d deuifsion on the eaft fide shaw fhin Riu^r and fo eu^{r}y mans lott to follow one another takeing all the 3 breadths at once the neareft land to the firft Center being ftill alwaies the next lott in order.

The Number of eu^{r}ie mans lott, and Quantity of acres is as followeth on the other fide.

[39] The Deuifsion ot

	Shaw Shine : 4 (4) 52	acres			acres.
1	Daniell Cheauer	020	25	Josseph Miller	015
2	William Clemance fen	030	26	Jonath : Hide	020
3	Daniell Kempfter.	080	27	Dauid ffifke	060
4	william Bull	015	28	Wid : Hancocke	010
5	Roger Bucke	010	29	And : Stevenfon	060
6	Thomas ffox	080	30	m^r Elijath Corlet	100
7	Humphery Bredfhew	015	31	Dauid Stone	050
8	m^r Boman	020	32	Tho : Danforth	220
9	william Clemance	030	33	Rich : Frances	060
10	Richard Cutter	080	34	John Parker	010
11	Thomas Longhorne	060	35	Jonath : Padleffoote.	015
12	Daniell Blogget	040	36	Edw : Hall	070
13	Robert Holmes	150	37	Ri : Oldam	060
14	Th : Hall	020	38	Gilbart Cracbone	090
15	widdow Banbricke	040	39	Robert Stedman	090
16	John Jacfon	050	40	Tho : Swætman	070
17	wm Homan	050	41	Wm. Bordman	060
18	Nath : Grene & mother	080	42	John Betts	090
19	Richard ffrench	020	43	John Shepard	060
20	John watfon	080	44	Daniell Stone	050
21	Richard woodes	010	45	John ffrenches Child^n.	030
22	John Taylor	060	46	John ffownell	100
23	Wid : Wilkerfon	060	47	Sam^{ll} Hides	080
24	Leift Willm : ffrench	150	48	Tho : Marret	200

7

TOWN RECORDS

		acres			acres
49	Edw. Wenſhip	200	87	william Patten	090
50	Goodm. Hamond	015	88	Beñ. Bower	020
51	Steven Day	050	89	Tho : Briggam	180
52	John Gibſon	080	90	John Russell	080
53	Edw. Goffe	450	91	Will Bucke	020
54	william Man	070	92	Richard Ecles	070
55	Ri : Jacſon	200	93	m^{rs} Sarah Sims	050
56	Willim Dixon	080	94	m^r Jakſon	400
57	George Willowes	060	95	m^r Andrews	150
58	Tho : Cheſholme	100	96	Abrã. Errington	070
59	m^r Edmund ffroſt	200	97	widd : Cutter	040
60	John Hall	020	98	ffr Moore ſen^r	050
61	Edw : Michelſon	150	99	m^r Joſseph Cooke	300
62	And : Belcher	050	100	Wm Wilcocke	090
63	John Swan	020	101	Chriſtopher Cane	080
64	Phil. Cooke	080	102	Rich. Dana	020
65	ffr : Moore Juni^r	050	103	m^r Angier	300
66	Widd. Sill.	040	104	Vincet Drufe	15
67	Robert Parker	060	105	Rog^r Bancroft	100
68	willm Manning	060	106	John Cooper	140
69	Richard Haſſull	060	107	Edw. Shepard	080
70	Nicho : Withe	090	108	Tho : Bridge	050
71	Willm Hamlet	060	109	Ranold Buſh	010
72	Willm Towne	070	110	Tho : Prentiſe	150
73	Samll Greene	080	111	Math : Bridge	080
74	Robert Browne	040	112	Golden Moore	100
75	John Boutell	020	113	Robert Brodiſh	080
76	John Bridge	250			
77	Tho : Beal	100		Mem There is theſe two prſons over ſlipped, vzt	
78	Richard Parke	100	28 91	Richard Robbins	080
79	ffranc^e Whitmore	050		Daniel wines	010
80	Jonas Clearke	060		theis 2 lotts muſt come in there due order	
81	John Hastings	080			
82	Henry Prentiſe	080			
83	Elder Champnis	350		The Towne do giue to Gregory Stone adjoyneing to his ffarme one Hundred acres	100
84	Nath : Sparhauke	140			
85	John Stedman	300			
86	Willm Russell	060			

At a Genrall meeting of the Inhabitants the 8th (9) mo. 1652.

The Towne do choofe mr Richard Champney, Gregory Stone, Tho: Marret Ri: Jacfon, and Gilbert Cracbone to draw up inftructions ffor the Townfmen, and prfent the fame to the Towne 4th 10th 52. to be allowed or diaflowed by a Genrall Vote of the Towne then met.

Edw: Okes, Tho: ffox and willm Manning are chofen Cunftables.

Edw: Goffe, John Bridge, John Cooper and Thomas Danforth are chofen Townfmen

Ri: Hildreth. Ri: Robbins, and Phil. Cooke are chofen Surveyors of highwayes

Edw: Okes, and Tho: Danforth are chofen to meet with Roxbery men for laying out a high way betwen there towne & or.

John Shepard is chofen to gage Cafke

Ri: Jacfon, Edw: Goffe Ed Okes, Tho: Danforth, & Tho: ffox are chofen to veiw Shaw Shine, and make report to the Towne.

agreed the 4. 10th. 52. to meet the whole towne to gether againe.

At a Genrall meeting of the Towne ye 4th (10) 1652.

Theis prpofitions here under written were voted, and joyntly agreed uppon by the Inhabitants, for the inftructions to be giuen to the Townfmen.

Impr. That wt eur worke or buifsines is by order of Court assigned to the Townfmen or injoyned on the Towne That the Townfmen fhall take due care to effect the fame fo as may beft conduce to a publique good and no damage by neglect thereof

2. That as often as they fhall fee needfull, they fhall giue publique notice to the inhabitants to meet together and wt eur orders or determinations fhalbe paffed by a publique vote of the Towne, or are already made by the Towne or ye felect men, that the Townf- men take due care to execute fullfill and accomplifh the fame with out refpect of any mans perfon, according to yr beft wifedome.

3. That wt eur damage they fhall conceiue or apprehend to come to the Towne, by any perfon with in or with out the Towne by appro- priating intruding or damnifying or exceeding there owne due prportion in any wife, any of the Comons, landes or woodes, or other publique ftocke liberties or interefts of the Towne according to there beft difcretion they fhall prvent and remoue the fame.

[40] 4. That they take due care for the maintenance and reparation and well ordering of all such thinges wherin the Towne hath a Comon interest, as the meeting house Comon gates and high wayes, Comon heards and ye like.

5. That they make such wholesome orders and impose such Penalties, and duly publish and execute the same as may best effect the execution of the premises

6. That the necessary charges y^t shalbe expended in ye execution of the p^{r}emises be yearly discharged by an equall rate, made by the Townsmen, and leuied by the Cunstable on ye seu^{r}all Inhabitants

7. That The Cunstables giue in a yearly account of w^t they receiue of the publique stocke of the Towne by rate or otherwise, and how they haue disbursed the same, the same to be done before ye yearly Election of the Townsmen, and kept uppon Record in a booke fairely written and in case the Cunstables shall faile herein, then to Continue in there office another yeare, except the Towne shall see meet otherwise to dispose

8. That the Surveyours of the high wayes take due care for the reparation of all the Comon high wayes with in ye towne, and keep uppon Record the names of Such persons as are improued therin during ye yeare, and deliu^r the same in a list fairely written to the Townsmen then in place at y^e end of there year, that so no man may be wronged in doing more then his due prportion.

At the same time the buisines about stinting y^e Cow Comon was debated, and by a publicke Voted agreed that it should be refferred to y^e magestrates of the next County Cort in Midlesex, to determine wheth$_\wedge$ o^r Cow Comon were already lawfully stinted.

also there is chosen for a comitte to effect this buisines with the Magestrates by prsenting y^e true state of the buisines, m^r Joseph Cooke John Bridge, Gregory Stone, Edward Goffe Ri: Jacson and Edward Winship.

27. 10 : 1652

First Tavern   The Townsemen do grant liberty to Andrew Belcher to Sell beare and bread for enterteinment of strang^{rs} & the good of the Towne.

14 (12) 1652

Robert Parker hath liberty to Sell fome timber for his ufe, as alfo John ffessington, for enlarging his barne, and Tho: Brigham for railes.

Edw. Goffe: Edw. Okes & Tho: Danforth are appoynted to lay out Elder Champny his land on Strabury hill.

Alfo they are appoynted to lay out m^{rs} Sar$_\wedge$ Simes 4. ac^r. land formerly granted her by the Towne.

At a meeting of the Inhabitants of this Towne 13th of the 9th mo. 1653:

There was then chosen these seu^{r}all officers of the Towne for the yeare ensueing:

ffor Townsemen. Edward Goffe. Jno: Steadman
  Tho: Beale, and Tho: Danforth:
ffor Cunstables: Jno: Hasteings: Tho: Oakes: and Sam^{ll} Hide.
ffor Surveyours of the high wayes: Philip Cooke:
Jno: Watson: and Richard Oldam.
ffor Sealear of Leather ffrāces moore Senior:
ffor gager of Caske. Jno: Shepard:

19 (10) 1653

{ Town Clerk's compensation } The Townsmen do grant to Thomas Danforth, [in prt fattisfacon for his conftant care and paines in being their Clerke] The use and benefit of the Comōn meadowes not yet devided about Shawshine bounds.

13th. 12. 1653

John ffessington and Thomas Oakes are desired by the Townsmen to take notice of the breaches of the Towne order concerning ftroy of timber on the Comōn and p^{r}sent the names of Such prsons to the Townsmen:

order for p^{r}fervation of wood. see 15th 8. 1656. whereas many Complaintes are made to the Townsmen of the vnreasonable ftroy that is yet made by many persons of the wood and timber wch lieth in Comōn in this Towne, not with ftanding all orders that haue formerly bin made for the pʳservation thereof, It is therefore ordered by the Townsmen that no man fhall cutt of the boughes of any tree, nor fell any tree uppon the Comon for fier wood, (excepting only Such as are dead and fare); uppon pœnalty of fiue fhillings forfeture for euʳie tree fo felled or ftowed contrary to this order. Richard Hildreth and Tho: ffox are desired to fee this order executed, and are to haue thᵉ one fourth part of the fines for their Labour.

It is ordered by the Townsmen that all fwine that go at liberty within the Limitts of this Towne fhalbe by yᵉ owners thereof: conftantly & sufficiently ringed vpon pœnalty of paying all damages done by such fwine, wth 3ᵈ a Swine to Such person as shall find such swine damage faisant, either to the Comon or his owne prticular.

The Townsmen do order that all ffences againft Corne, meadowes, or gardens fhalbe made sufficient againft all lawfull cattle at the sight of the Select Townsmen, or Such as they fhall appoynt to veiw the ffences of any of the Comon feilds, and so conftantly mainetaine the Same, so long as any grasse, Corne, or garden ftuffe fhalbe on the ground vpon [41] vpon pœnalty of paying all the damages, that shall come throw neglect therof with Six pence per Rod for every weeks neglect to Such person as fhalbe damnified thereby. ─────

Representative how paid.   The Townsmen doe Order the Cunstables to pay Bro: Richard Jacson 2ˢ pr day for twenty eight dayes that he was Deputy for the Towne at the Genʳall Court held at Bofton 1653:

mʳ Edward Jacson, Edward Oakes and Thomas Danforth are appoynted by the Townsmen, to lay out all necessary high waies on the South Side the water, and agree with the proprietors of the Land for the fame by exchange for comon Land or otherwise according to their discretion.

Elder ffroft, Jno. ffessington, Daniel Cheauʳ, Philip Cooke, and John Shepard haue liberty granted them by the Towne to fell timber on the

Comon for their building and reparation of their ffences. with in the Limitts of this towne, as also Jno: shepherd ffor his trade.

Vpon Complaint made to the Townsmen of the great Damage that is yearly fuftained not only by the Cow Keeper, but also by the Cow heard, by the great negleƈt of many persons in not paying in Season w^t is justly due to the Cow Keeper for his labor. The Townsmen do therefore order that eu^{r}ie person wch hath any beaft in the milch heard belonging to the Towne, fhall at or before the firft of may next, deliu^r in at the houfe of Daniell Cheaver Cow Keeper or Jno. Haftings Cunftable, for each beaft one pecke of Corne, And also at or before the laft of november next following make up the Said pecke of Corne the juft Sume of three shillings six pence, in maner following vzt. for each beaft one pecke of wheat, and the remainde$_\wedge$ in Corne or other Sattisfaƈtory pay to the content of the Cow Keeper, uppon pœnalty of paying foure fhillings for each beaft, with all cofts & damages for obteyning the Same.

Daniell Cheaver agreeth with the Townsmen to begin his going out with the milchheard, by the fiften day of April at furtheft, and continue his conftant care over them one month after michelmas.

Also Daniell Cheaver agrees to find all necessary help$_\wedge$ and prvide two sufficient bulls, to be allowed out of his wages of 3^s. 6^d. pr head.

---

[42] The Townsmen do agree with Thomas Eames that he fhall haue the vse of the wares for three yeares next enfuing, vpon condition that he fhalbe carefull to Catch all the fifh that the wares will afford, and deliuer the Same to the towne at nine pence per 1000: also he hath liberty to make vse of any timber or wood that growes on the ground for fecureing the Land, and he is to Leaue notice at Jno. Haftings when there is any fifh.

John Stedman hath liberty to fell some timber on the Comon for his vse in the Towne.

Att a meeting of the Select men
the 13th of the 1st mo 1653.

There being Twenty pounds due to mr Pelham for damage done him by high ways layd out throw his ffarme on the South Side the Riuer the one to Roxbery two Rod wide, entering in to Edmund Angiers ffarme at the north weft Corner of his ffence, and the other Leading to Elder Champnyes Land, The Townsmen do agree and grant to him for Sattisfaction thereof one hundred acres of Land adjoyneing to Bofton Line. provided alwayes if the Towne fhall make payment of Twenty poundes in Corne or Cattle with in twelve monthes next after the date hereof to mr Pelham or his Lawfull Atturney and giue him notice of Such their intent with in six months that then the aforesaid hundred Acres of Land fhall returne to the vse of the Towne againe:

<small>vide. ye act of ye felect mèn. 20. 11. 58 ye wood is referued to ye towne of this 100. acrs</small>

John Stedman and Richard Robbines are appoynted by the Townsmen to Lay out the aboue said 100 acr of Land.

Robert Broadifh and Tho: Longhorne are appoynted by the Townsmen to veiw the ffences apperteyning to the necke of Land and to drive the necke of all cattle that fhalbe found trespassing therin.

John Cooper and Nicholas withe are in like manner appoynted for the weft feild

[42] John Watson and Robert Browne are appoynted by the Townsmen to the execute the order of the Towne concerning Swine.

Richard Hildreth and Tho. Hall are appoynted to veiw the ffences about Winottime ffeild.

Edw. Hall & william man are appoynted to veiw the ffences about pine Swamp feild.

11. (2) 1654:

The Townsmen do grant Liberty to John Swan to fell some timber on the Comon for fencing in his garden.

Humphery Bredfhew is granted allowance for his Land that wobourne high way throw winottime feild, doth take away from his Lott, after 20s. pr acre to be allowed him out of his pfent towne rate.

Humphery Bredfhew is granted liberty of ffencing ftuffe, for his Lott about his house.

Manning's wharf

The Townsemen do allow William Manning fiue pound out of the p̃nt Towne Rate vpon Condition that he make a sufficient wharffe from his ware house to the Lower part of his Land, that he hath their ditched in, ſo as to keep the Tide of the high way, and to mainteine the Same in like good condicon for twenty yeares next ensueing the date hereof· ——

   At a meeting of the Select men
    the   day of the 3.m̊: 1654:

Edward Goffe and John Cooper are appoynted by the Townsemen to Lay out and Determine all differences about the high wayes leading to the Seu{r}all Lotts of marſh towards m{r} Haughs ffarme.

     12. (4) m̊ 1654:

The Townsmen do grant liberty vnto m{r}: pelham to fell Some clapbord trees on the Com̃on for the reparation of his house.

[**43**] Att a meeting of the Inhabitants of this Towne
   in May 1650:

It was voted and consented vnto by the Towne that the house wch m{r} Philips built annent Charlestowne lane, wth the land adjoyneing & wood lott ſhould be Sould to Thomas Danforth for fifty pounds to be payd by him to m{r} Philips or his assignes, in Current Country pay, vpon Demand at the ſaid house. The said Tho: Danforth to Enioy the said house & land to him his heyres & assignes for eu{r}.

In witnes whereof we the ſelect men do put to o{r} hands this 11: (10){ber} 1654.

       Edward Goffe
       Richard Jackſon
       John Stedman
       John Cooper.
       Gilbert ƥ Cragbone
        his marke

[43] 13th (9)mo 1654:

The Towne being met for Eleccon of their yearly Towne officers, there was then chosen

Conftables.	Jn? Stedman Tho: Prentice Gilbt. Crackbone
Townsmen.	Edward Goffe Richrd. Jacson Thomas Danforth. Jn? Coopper.
Surveyo^rs of high waies.	Jn? ffessington Tho: ffox. Jonath. Hide.
Comission^{rs} to end smal caufes.	m^r Joseph Cooke Edw. Goffe Tho: Danforth

Voted affirmative at the meeting of the Towne that the Townsemen fhall Levy about forty Pounds, for the Incouragement of the Gramer Schoole mafter. — — —

Att a meeting of the Inhabitants of this Towne the 29. (11) 1654.

The towne consented that twenty pounds fhould be levied vpon the feverall Inhabitants and given to m^r Corlet for his pñt Incou^ragement to continue with vs; & the form^r vote for forty poundes thereby to be dissanulled.

In Ans: to a Lrē: sent to the Towne ffrom o^r Neybours of Shaw Shine alias Bilracie, wherein they desire that whole tract of land may be disingaged from this place, & be one Intire body of it selfe The towne consented to choose five persons. — a Comittee to treate & conclude wth them conc^rning y^r requeft therein. at wch time was chosen m^r Henry Dunfter, Elder Champny, Jn? Bridge. Edw: Goffe, & Edw: Winfhip. —

[**44**]   At a meeting of the Select men
the 12. (1ˢᵗ) 165$\frac{4}{5}$

The Townsemen do appoynt Jn͡º Stedman & Tho: Danforth to lay out to David ffiske forty acres of land neere adjoyneing to his fathers farme in leiu of fixty acres granted him at Shawfhine, and also to veiw a peece of meadow that he desires and make report to the towne.

The Townsmen do grant liberty to Edw: winfhip to fell 2. or 300. of Railes on the Com̄on land lying on the weft fide his farme to fence in his meadow.

The Townfemen do grant to Richard Robbines the vse of a peece of meadow or marfh land lying on the South fide the Cricke by mʳ Andrews farme, and to hould the fame dureing the pleasure of the townfemen.

Jn͡º Hafteings. wm Man. Jn͡º Coφper and Tho: ffox had liberty for fencing ftuff of the Com̄on.

In anfwer to the requeft of fome of oʳ Beloved Brethren and Neighbours the Inhabitants on the fouth fide the River, that they might have the ordinances of Chrift amongft them diftinct from the Towne. The Townfemen not well vnderftandeing wᵗ they intend, or do desire of the Towne, nor yet being able to conceive how any thing can be granted by the Towne in that respect, but yᵉ fraccͩon will prove deftructive to the whole body, Do not fee ground to give any incouʳagement for any divissio_∧ of the Towne. Also wee hope that it is not the desire of oʳ Bretheren fo to accom̄oda_∧ themselves by a divission as thereby vtterly to dissinable and vndoe the Church of Chrift with whome they have made fo follemn an ingagement in the Lord, wch is apparent to us wilbe the effect thereof and theref_∧ do desire that wee may Joyne both in hand

[**44**] hand & heart to worfhip the Lord together in one place vntill the Lord fhalbe pleased to inlarge & fhow vs oʳ way more cleare for a divission.

Tho: ffox. Nicho: withe, & ffranc· moore are appoynted to veiw the ffences about the weft feild.

Jno. Hafteings & wm Towne are appoynted to veiw the ffences in pine fwamp feild.

Edw. Goffe & Jno. watson are appoynted to veiw the ffences about the necke of land.

Jno. Cooper & Robert Parker are appoynted to veiw the ffences about the ffeild where their houses ftand.

Enfigne Winfhip and Serg^t Hildreth are appoynted to veiw the ffences about Winottime ffeild.

Robert Browne and Daniell Cheaver are appoynted to fee the Towne order executed conc^{r}ning Swine.

Richard Jacson and Jno. Stedman are appoynted to Bargaine with a heardfman for the Towne Cowes. —

---

[45] At a meeting of the Inhabitants of this Towne for the Eleccōn of Townfemen. Conft: Cōmiss^r. &c. 12th 9 mo. 1655.

There were then Chofen, Conftables ⎧ Richard Robbines
⎨ Jno. ffessington
⎩ Philip Cooke:

Townfemen. ⎧ Edward Goffe.
⎨ Jno. Stedman
⎨ Edw: Oakes
⎩ Thom^s. Danforth.

Surveyo^{rs} of high wayes — —   Jno. Watson.
                                        Saml. Hide. — — —
Comission^r, to end fmall caufes — ⎧ m^r Joseph Cooke
                                                ⎨ m^r Edwrd Jacfon
                                                ⎩ Thom^s. Danforth.

14th (11) m^o 1655.

The Townfemen do order that Jno. Bufh fhall pay a fine of Twenty fhillings for comeing as an Inhabitant in to the Towne with out the leave of the Townfmen, and his ffather Renold Bufh fhall alfo pay the like fine of Twenty fhillings for Enterteyneing him with out confent as afore faid.

And Richard Robbines Constable is appoynted to levy the fame.

10th $\frac{12}{mo}$ 55.

Jn? Cooper, & George Bower have liberty granted them to fell timber on the Comon for reparaccon of y^r houfes & ffences in this Towne bounds.

Jn? Cooper & Gilbert Cracbone are appoynted to veiw the ffences about the weft feild for the yeare Enfueing.

Robert Parker & wm Man to veiw the ffences about the ox pafture feild.

Richard Hildreth & Enfig: Winfhip for Winotti$_\wedge$ feild, and wm Patten.

Edw. Goffe & Robert Holmes in like manner for the neck of Land.

Andrew Steevenfon & Daniel Cheavers are appoynted to fee the orders conc^{r}ning fwine Executed

Whereas this Towne about 5 : years now paft bargained with Thomas Danforth for that houfe wherin he now liveth, vpon Condiccōn that he fhould pay to the Assignes of m^r Philips of Wrentw. the Erector of the faid houfe: the Sume of fifty pounds in Currant Country pay vpon demand in Camb^r. And whereas the faid money have hitherto neyther been payd nor demanded, but the faid Thomas Danforth doth demand a deed of Sale to be made him by the Townfemen, pleading y^t m^r Dunfter hath rec^d forty pounds in part thereof The Townfemen do hereby declare y^{m}ly, that the contract being made by the whole Towne with ye fd Thomas, they conceive it not in their power to Abrogate or Alter the fame, and therefore fhall expect the prformance y^r off from the faid Thomas according to his Covenant, and fhall accordingly give the faid Thomas

security
[46] Security for the peaceable Inioym^t of the faid houfe with its appurtenances.

Alfo whereas m^r Dunfter hath made a prposiccōn to the Townfmen for the acquitting and discharging of the faid forty pounds fo received as before p^{r}mifed [by the faid Thomas,] vpon the acc^t of his out laÿng for the fchoole houfe. The townfmen do hereby declare ym^y that as they cannot yeld to the fame for the Reafons before mentioned, yet never the lefs if m^r Dunfter fhall pleafe to p^{r}sent any prpoficcōn to the

Towne when mett together, they fhalbe willing to further the fame according to Juftice & Equity. —

10 march 165⁵/₆

m^r Edmund Angier, w^m Dixon, Robert Stedman w^m Ruffell & Jno. Stedman have liberty granted them by the Townfemen to fell fome timber on the comon for the necefsaray reparaccõns of their fences.

[46]   21th Aprill 1656.

Complaint being made to the felect men of this Towne of the necessity of a high way to be layd out on the South fide the River, leading from Roxbery path to the Pines, by Charles River, wherevpon the Townfemen going over the River veiwed the said way and alfo the high way, that leadeth from the Pines along by the meadow fide, & having confidered the Advantages & inconveniences of both, do Judge it beft that the high way be layd out in ye line betwen the land of Nathaniell Sparhauke and Richard Dana, the whole length of their land, two Rod in Breadth, and alfo a high way to ly crofse Richard Danas land, about 50 pole, and from thence to be continued throw Richard oldams land, for a high way to watertowne. The wch high wayes the owners of the land adjacent are to have liberty to mainetaine gates convenient for travellers, both for man & beaft and not to turne any cattle at liberty therein.

Alfo Richard Dana agreed with ye Townfmen to take five pounds in full sattisfaccõn, for his land in both wayes. the long high way that leadeth from the Pines to Roxbery high way being to ly wholly in his land, and th^e other crofse way thwart his land to Watertowne mill fo far as his land reacheth, alfo Richard Dana is granted liberty to make vse of the high way annent the Springs at the Pines, and to take the Same in to his owne land by fencing the Same, vntill the Townfemen fhall fee meet to require the fame to be left open againe.

Alfo the Townfmen do grant vnto m^r Edward Jacfon liberty to take & fence in the highway & Comon land annent his meadow, dureing the pleasure of the Townfmen & vntill fuch time as they fhall require the fame to be fet at liberty againe, vpon condiccõn that he fhall pay vnto

Richard Dana five pounds for the purchafe of the other high wayes before named, prvided alwayes when the Townfmen fhall fee meet to recall the high way againe, they fhall then repay the faid five pounds to the faid m^r Jackfon his Heyres or Assignes. ———

June 9.th. 1656.

The Townfmen do confent that Thom^s Dosse fchochman serv^t to Ens: Winfhip, fhall have liberty to mow the grasse in the Swamp annent the north end of Spy pond.

The Townfmen do appoynt Jno. Stedman & Jno. ffessington to accompany Deacon Bridge in ftakeing out the high way betwen the Weft feild and Water = Towne line. —

Octo. 13. 1656.

The Townfemen do grant liberty to Bro. Jno. Stedman to fell fome timber on ye comon for fencing ftuffe.

[47] At a meeting of the Inhabitants of this Towne
10th 9th mo. 1656. ffor the Eleccon of Towne offic^rs.

Richard Jacfon, Jno. Cooper, Jno. ffessington &' Thomas Danforth are chofen felect men for the ordering of the prudentiall affaires of the Towne for the yeare enfueing.

Richard Parkes, Edward Shepard and Robert Parker are chofen Conftables for the yeare enfueing, and to Joyne with the aforesaid Select men.

Jno Hafteings, Thomas Wiswall and Abra^m Errington are chofen surveyo^rs of the High wayes for the yeare enfueing.

At a meeting of the Townfemen. 20th 9 mo. 1656.

Jno. Stedman & Jno. Watfon, are chofen to veiw the necke ffences, the yeare enfueing.

Thomas ffox and ffrancis moore are appoynted to veiw the fences about weft feild.

Enfigne Winfhip, Willm Russell, and Philip Cooke are appoynted to veiw the fences about the Winottime feild.

The Townſmen do agree that the Conſtables do forth with take effectuall care for the repaire of the meeting houſe, and ſchoole houſe.

It is ordered by the Townſemen that whatſoever perſon or perſons, whether at prñt Inhabiting or hereafter ſhall come to inhabit within the limitts of this Towne, not haveing Towne prviledges eyther by gift or purchaſe, or otherwiſe by conſent of the ſelect men for the time being, every ſuch perſon ſhall have no power to give either vote or ſuffrage in any Eleccon of any Towne offic.ʳ Deputy or repʳsentative nor yet in ordering or dispoſeing any of the Comon intereſt of the Towne, nor making of Towne orders, nor yet be allowed wood or comonage from of or vpon the Towne Comons. excepting only in such eleccons, or caſes, where any are impowered by yᵉ Genʳall Court.

24ᵗʰ 9ᵐᵒ 1656.

At a meeting of the Select men It is ordered that the Inhabitants of this Towne be all warned to meet to gether the Second Monday of the next mo. by Eight of the Clocke in the morneing to conſider and agree about theſe Seuʳall things hereafter mentioned. vzt.

Concerning the pʳservaccon of wood & timber.

Concʳning Comon fences, and orders about Swine. and for the Publiſhing of thoſe orders made at the last towne meeting:

Alſo concerning imprvemᵗ of families in ſpinning and cloathing;

[48] At a Genʳall meeting of the Inhabitants of the towne, the 8ᵗʰ. of the 10ᵗʰ. mo. 1656.

The order made by the Selectmen the 10ᵗʰ of the 9ᵗʰ m.ᵒ laſt being publiquely read, is conſented vnto by the Inhabitants. excepting only theſe words, by the liberty of the ſelect men is hereby made Null & voyd And it is hereby declared that none have power to enterteine Inhabitants to yᵉ pʳviledges of the towne, but only the ffree Inhabitants of yᵉ towne.

It is ordered, conſented and agreed by a Joynt vote of the Towne, that the ſecond Munday in march, by nine of the Clocke in the morning ſhalbe Annually the time for the bringing in of votes By yᵉ ffreemen of this towne for yᵉ Nominaccon of Mageſtrates, choyce of County Trēr.

and Choyce of Deputyes for the Gen^{r}all Court. and alfo the fecond Munday in Novem.^{r} at ye aforesaid time in the morning fhalbe Annually the time for Elecc͠on of all Towne offic^{rs}, and all perfons concerned therein are to attend the said times respectively without expecting any further Notice only it is agreed that Notice fhalbe publiquely given thereof the Lecture before going or else Pofted on the meeting houfe.

The Towne do Mutually agree and confent that the felect men fhall prporc͠con to eu^{r}y man fuch a number of Swine as may be moft convenient for eu^{r}y family to keep. and none fhall fuffer a great^r quantity then fuch their prporcc͠on by y^m determined to go at liberty on any part of the towne Com͠ons. and that all fuch fwine as go at liberty fhalbe at all times fufficiently ringed, and in the feafon there of yoaked: the fufficiency of both yoakes & rings to be determined from time to time by the Judgm^t of the Hog reeves. and that all Penaltyes impofed by ye felect men for the breach of this law, as alfo any other Penall law or order for ye good of the Towne, be from time to time, and at leaft twice eu^{r}y year, levied by ye felect men vpon all offenders, without any partiality.

The Inhabitants of this Towne do confent to pay each one their prporc͠con of a rate to ye fum͠e of 200^{li} oo. oo. towards the building a Bridge over Charles River. vpon condicc͠on the fame may be effected with out further charge to ye towne: voted on ye affirmative.

Capt. Gookin, Ed: Goffe, Jno Stedman and Thomas Danforth, are nom͠inated a Com͠ittee to exfecute & effect ye fame.

The Towne do agree and confent that there fhalbe a rate made to the vallue of 108^{li} 10^s and levied of the feu^{r}all Inhabitants, for the paym^t for the fchoole houfe provided eu^{r}y man be allowed w^t he hath already freely contrebuted thereto, in part of his prporcc͠on of fuch rate.

[48] At a meeting of the Select men
the: 15th of October 1656.

The Townfemen do grant liberty vnto Andrew Steevenfon to fell fome timber on the Com͠on to fence in his yard.

Alfo the Townfemen do grant liberty for the felling timber on the Com͠on to fence in the yardes about the houfe of correcc͠on:

Bro: Richard Jackson: Jn:º ffessington and Robert Parker are granted liberty to take Timber on the Comon for fencing ftuffe and reparac͠cons:

Whereas not withftanding former orders that have been made for the pʳservaccon͠ of wood and Timber lying in Comon with in the bounds of this Towne yet there is much ftroy made of both, wch will in time appeare to be a great damage to the Publique weale of the Inhabitants.

It is therefore Ordered by the Select men as an Addition to the formʳ Orders made the 13ᵗʰ of the 12.mº. 1653 : That all such Perfons as fhall hereafter fall any tree or trees vpon any part of the Towne Comons, whether for timber or firewood, fhall from time to time cutt out and eyther Coard, or fett vp an end, fit to load into a cart all the whole tree both body and top, vpon penalty of paying two fhillings for every tree that fhall ly vndone above ten dayes after the falling thereof, excepting only thofe trees wch are for timber and not for riveing, the timber being cutt off, and top cleared away, they may then have liberty to lett such timber ly, foure monthes before it be fetched away, and if it fhall exceed, fuch time, it fhall then be lawfull for any other perfon, that hath right to Towne pʳviledges, to make vfe thereof.

Provided alwayes if any part of any tree fhalbe fo full of knotts, as that it fhalbe vncapeable of riveing and fhalbe fo Judged by him who fhalbe appoynted for the time being to fee this order executed, with in ten dayes after the falling thereof, In such cafe such perfon as feld the fame fhalbe free from the Penalty of this Order respecting the fame.

2ly. That no fmall tree or trees vnder 12 inches the diameter, two foote above the ground be fallen for timber vpon penalty of two fhillings for every Tree, excepting the felect men give liberty.

3ly. That in cafe any perfon or perfons by reafon of the Extremity of the feafon in winter time fhalbe forced to fell any wood for the fire, they fhall then take such as are decaying trees, and not fitt for timber, and fhall pay to the vfe of the towne twelve pence for every load.

price of wood

And in cafe any perfon fhall otherwife tranfgreſse vizt. eyther by falling trees for firewood that are fit for timber, or fhall faile to pay the said twelve

[49] Twelve pence a load, or to give notice thereof more then foureten dayes after the falling of fuch tree or trees, to fuch perfon as fhalbe from

time to time appoynted to fee this order executed every fuch perfon fhall then forfeit five fhillings pr load, to the vfe of the Towne. to be levied by the Conftable, by the appoyntm^t of the felect men ———

William Hamlett and Jno. Swan are appoynted by the felect men to execute this order for the yeare enfueing. ——

Edw: Goffe, Jno. Stedman, Enf. Winfhipp Thomas Swætman. & Jno. Jackfon are nominated and appoynted by the felect men to execute the order of the Gen^{r}all Court, for the imprvm^t of all the families with in the limitts of this towne, in Spinning and cloathing, and each of the faid perfons are to fee to the execuccon of the faid order in their refpective quarters of the Towne.

Spinning

Roger Bucke is granted liberty by the felect men to fell timber on the Comon for the imprvem^t of his trade.

Enf: Ed: Winfhip, Jno. Cooper. Willm dixon and Willm Rufsell and Thos. Hall have liberty to fell timber on the Comon for repareing their out ffences.

Jno. Shepard have liberty granted him to fell fome timber on the Comon for the vfe of his trade.

Enfigne Winfhip and Philip Cooke are appoynted to Execute the Order concerning Swine. and Jno. Stedman and Jno. Watfon are appoynted to Joyne with them, and they are to p^{r}nt all defects to the townfm once a m^o. vpon the towne meeting day.

The Townfemen do agree and confent that Ed: Goffe. Ri: Jackfon. & Thomas Danforth or any two of them fhall fett out to Willm Hamlett, fo much of the Rocks annent his houfe, as they fhall find him to be damnified by the high way crofsing his land.

Saml. Hide is appoynted to execute the order conc^{r}ning fwine, on the South fide the River: — — — ——

[49]   At a meeting of the felect men
       Jan. 5th. 1656.

Robert Stedman hath liberty granted him to fell fome timber on the comon for repaire of his dwelling houfe. — — —

Jno. Stedman hath liberty granted alfo for plankes for his ftable. —

The Townfmen do order that all fuch swine as are taken with out rings on the north Weft fide of the path leading from Watertowne to

Capt. Cookes millne in any part of our bounds, except vpon the own^{r}s prpriety, the owners of such swine fhalbe liable to pay the penalty of twelve pence a swine, for want of each Ring:

9. (1) 165$\frac{6}{7}$

Jno. Haftings hath liberty granted him to fell fome timber on the comon for reparaccon of his out fences.

Thomas Swætman hath liberty to fell one tree on the Comon for clapbords.

Thomas Beale, & Widow Bowers have liberty granted them to fell fome timber on the comon for reparaccons of their houfes & fences.—

William Rufsell being fined — 2^s — 6^d. for want of ringing his swine, he is allowed the fame in part of sattisfaccon for the land taken away by the High way at the north end of his lotts. and the Towne is yet his d^r for that land being in all about twenty foure poles: 2^s 6^d.— —

Jno. Swan hath liberty granted him to mow the Swamp on the north end of Spy pond, this prnt yeare. 1657.

Humphery Bredfhew & Jno. Addams, have liberty granted them to fell fome timber on the Comon for reparaccon of their out fences. — —

Daniel Cheaver have liberty granted him to fell a clapbord tree on the Comon — —

James Hubbard hath liberty granted him to fell fome fmall timber on the Comon for the making him a loome.

Abram Errington hath liberty granted him to fell fome timber on ye comon for fencing his gardens.

The Townfmen do give m^r Cooke liberty to fell fome timber on the Comon for repareaccon of his mill & mill houfe.

Jonathan Padlefoote hath liberty granted him to fell fome timber on the comon for repairaccon of his out fences

the townfmen do give John Marrit and John greene liberty to fell fome timber for clapbord and ground filling

Liberty granted to brother Kemftere to fell fome timb^r for his trade.

John Palfraye hath liberty granted to fell a tre or two for his trade.

4. (7) 57: Thomas Gleiſon being a delinquent, by leaveing yᵉ tops of 5: trees, uncutt out contrary to towne orders, yᵉ fine being 10ˢ and for his ſwine 6ˢ he appeared before yᵉ townſmen and acknowledged his fault, & submitted himſelfe, where vppon yᵉ townſmen abated him 9ˢ and ordered yᵉ Conſtable to levy seaven shillings of him

[50]   Philip Cooke is fined 12ᵈ for breach of yᵉ Towne order by his swine.

Jnᵒ Greene	00 — 00 — 6
And. Belcher.	00 — 06 — 06
mʳ Angier	00 — 07 — 00
mʳ Stedman.	00 — 07 — 06
Wᵐ Barrett.	00 — 01 — 03
mʳ Day	00 — 01 — 06
Wᵐ Patten.	00 — 02 — 06
Richard Cutter.	00 — 02 — 03
Wᵐ Russell.	00 — 01 — 00
Jno. Swan.	00 — 02 — 00
Jno Gibſon	00 — 02 — 03
Charles ſterns	00 — 01 — 06
Th: Beale	00 — 00 — 09
Th: Longhorne	00 — 02 — 06
Ed: Goffe	00 — 03 — 03
Nich: Withe	00 — 02 — 06
Th: Cheſholme	00 — 01 — 06
Roger Bucke	00 — 00 — 09
Wᵐ Man	00 — 00 — 06
Wᵐ Manning	00 — 01 — 06
mʳ Andrews Alias Dauid G.	00 — 00 — 06

9 (12) 56. formʳly fined

David ffiske		00 — 01 — 03
Abram Holman	×	00 — 02 — 06
Rich: Cutter		00 — 02 — 06
Jno. Addams		00 — 07 — 00

	Humph: Bredſhew		00 — 02 — 00
	Bro: Cooke	×	00 — 02 — 00
	ffr. Moore		00 — 01 — 06
	Th: Browne		00 — 00 — 09
	Wm Russell	×	00 — 02 — 06
	m^r. Dunſter		00 — 02 — 06
	Wm Russell		00 — 00 — 03
	Jno. Addams		00 — 00 — 06
	Jno. Swan		00 — 04 — 06
	Geor. Polly		00 — 01 — 06
[50]	Gilbert Crackbone		00 — 02 — 03
	Wm Bull.		00 — 00 — 09
	Wm Man		00 — 01 — 00
	Ch: ſternes		00 — 01 — 03
	Jno. Gibson.		00 — 00 — 06
	Wm Patten.		00 — 01 — 09
	Nich: Withe		00 — 02 — 03
	George Willows		00 — 00 — 09
	Math: Bridge.		00 — 01 — 03
	Edw. Winſhip		00 — 01 — 00

4. (7) 57 Saml Goffe is fined for felling a tree on ye townn land in ye neck } 00 — 05 — 00

Richard Jackson for neglect to cut out tops of trees is fined } 00 — 04 — 00

17th 7th m? 1657

The Townſmen do grant liberty vnto Richard Jackson to fell timber on the Common for reparaccon of his out fences.—

The Townſmen do Order that the high way into Pine Swamp feild, begiññing at Edw: Halls houſe, ſhalbe continued where it hath form^rly vſed for divers years paſt, to ly about one pole in breadth ſo as that two carts may meet wthout damage each to other.

Whereas the Conſtables of this towne are put to great trouble and expence of their time by seu^rall perſons that either obſtinately refuſe or carelefly negleƈt to pay their refpeƈtive fines or rates, haveing ben lawfully demanded.

The Townfmen do therefore Order and hereby impower the Conftable or any other perfon impowred for receiveing such fines or rates to levy the same by diftrefs, vppon th' eftate of fuch perfon fo refufeing or negleƈting, and wth the fame for his paynes and travell two fhillings, for each rate or fine so taken by diftrefs. — — — —

Enf: Edw: Winfhip informed the Townfmen of thefe feu^rall perfons vnder written, for breach of the town‸ orders, whofe fines according to the towne order are as followeth

Jn?. Swan.	00 — 18 — 09
Jn?. Addams.	00 — 01 — 06
Wm Bull.	00 — 00 — 03
Tho: Gleifon	00 — 05 — 09
Wm Munrow	00 — 00 — 06
Wm Rufsell	00 — 02 — 06
Rich: Cutter	00 — 00 — 03
ffra: Whitmore	00 — 00 — 09

ffra: moore hath liberty to fell timber on the comon for reparaccon of his out fences. ———

[51]   13. (8) 57

At a meeting of the seleƈt men

Bro: Edw. Goffe, for breach of the towne order about fwine is fined.   00 — 04 — 03

Jn?. Swan is abated of his fines. 12.^s 6.^d   00 — 12 — 06

At a meeting of the Seleƈt men 2. (9 mo) 1657.

Bro: Watson gave in the names of these perfons vnder written, for Breach of Towne orders respeƈting swine, for negleƈt in yoaking & Ringing.—

m^r Angier	00 — 01 — 06
B^r Goffe.	00 — 02 — 09
Th: Longhorne.	00 — 01 — 00
Andrew Belcher.	00 — 02 — 09
m^r ftedman	00 — 05 — 00
Bro: Greene Jno.	00 — 00 — 06
Wm Michelfon.	00 — 00 — 06
Thomas Chefholme.	00 — 02 — 00
Gilbert Crackbone	00 — 01 — 00
Goodm̄. fternes.	00 — 01 — 06
Rich. Cutter.	00 — 02 — 09
Wm Man.	00 — 01 — 00
	01 — 02 — 03

Jno. Swan is abated his fine of 12^s — 6^d for labor & time spent in surveying ye woodes & com̄ons.

Jno. Watson is allowed. for his paines & travell in executing the Orders concerning fwine, three pounds. the wch he is to receive out of the fines. and in cafe any refufe to pay he is to take ye fame by diftrefse: with 2^s pr head, according to towne order. Alfo he is to gather all fines due, from ye feu^{r}all Inhabitants for breach of towne orders conc^{r}ning fwine, timber & wood.

The Select men

At a gen^{r}all meeting of the Inhabitants of this Towne, It was voted affirmative, that Enfigne Edward Winship shall have the swampy peece of land annent his houfe, towards Spy pond. prvided he shall not take in the Well. nor yet pound or otherwife damnifie any greate cattle apprteyning to this towne for trespassing on the fame at any time or times w^t soeu^r.

The select men do grant vnto Richard Eccles in confideracc̄on of the dam̄age done him by the High way going crofs his lott, that he fhall have the vfe & benefit of the High way anent his lott in recompence of yt dam̄age he Suffereth thereby. ———

[51] At a Publique meeting of the Inhabitants
Novem.^r 9th 1657

There were chofen thefe publique officers of the Towne for the yeare enfueing.

Mr Joseph Cooke, m^r Edward Goffe & Thomas Danforth Comifsion^rs for ending Small cafes.   Comifsion^rs

Edward Oakes, Thomas Danforth, John Cooper, and John ffessington, Select men.   Select men

Thomas Hamond, Robert Holmes, & John Watson Conftable   Conftables

m^r Stedman, m^r Sparhauke & Robert Browne Surveyo^rs of the high wayes.

Voted affirmative that Deacon John Bridge, Deacon Stone, Edw. Goffe, & John ftedman, Edward Oakes, and Thomas Danforth, are chofen a Comittee to divide the wood on the Eaft fide Winottime River, (i e) to leave about one fix^t part of the trees ftanding for the vfe of the Towne and to divide the reft. alfo they are to take order for clearing the fhrubs and fmall young trees in the ox pafture.

voted affirmative, that the deacons, Townfemen, m^r Jackson, Edw. Goffe, m^r Stedman & Edw. Winfhip are appoynted to make a levy of two hundred and forty pounds for the main- tenance this yeare, and for the paym^t of the debts, of our Reverend Pastor m^r Michell.   Paftors levy.

£240

☞

At a meeting of the Select men,
14th of decem^r. 1657

Wm Rufsell hath liberty to fall fome timber on the comon for his out fences, & fome building.

liberty is granted vnto m^r ftedman m^r Angier &c. the owners of the Catch Triall to fell fome timber on the Comon for a warehoufe.

John Cooper hath licence granted him to fell fome timber for his building & reparaccon of his out fences. & Robert Homes hath the like liberty.

m^r Edw. Jackson, Deacon Bridge, Edward oakes & Thomas Danforth are appoynted a Comittee to lay out & settle Such High wayes as they find necefsary on the south fide the river

[52] Samuel Hastings hath liberty granted him to fell timber on ye comon to fet a fhop on his fathers land at his Homeftall lott.

11th 11th m^o 1657.

Mr Edward Jackson, Jno Jackson, Richard Parkes & Samuel Hide are appoynted a Comittee to lay out and fettle the high wayes in refference to the proprieto^{rs} at that end of the Towne, prvided they p^{r}judice not ye Towne, otherwife then by crofsing vppon any part of the comon, as need shall require.

Jno Greene hath liberty granted him to fell timber on the comons for an addition to his dwelling houfe.

Jno watfon hath liberty granted him to fell timber on ye comon for ye repaire of his barne & other buildings.

George Polly hath liberty granted him to fell timber on the comon for repaire of his out fences. —————

There being nineten ac^{r}s of land due to be layd out to Eld^r Champny on the south fide the river, the Townfmen do grant him liberty to have the same layd out on ftrawberry Hill adjoyneing to the other nineten ac^{r}s that he hath on the f^d Hill. — — — —

The above s^d 19. ac^{r}s to be layd out by Edw^{r}d oakes, & Thomas Danforth.

Deacon Jno. Bridge hath liberty to fell fome timber on the Comon for repayre of his out fences. — — — — —

The marfhall hath liberty granted him to fell fome timber on the Comons for repaire of his houfeing. — — —

Goodm Gleifon hath liberty granted him to fell fome timber on ye Comon for repaire of his out fences agft o^r Comon. — — —

Andrew Belcher hath liberty granted him to fell fome timber on ye comon for fencing & reparaccon of his houfes. — — — —

daniell Cheauer hath liberty granted him to fell fome timber on the Common for repayering of his outt fence

15th 12mo 1657:

The Townſemen do grant liberty vnto Thomas Gleiſon to fell ſo many trees on the com̄on as may be sufficient for a barne floare for Thomas Beale, vppon condic̄c̄on y^t he obſerve ye towne order therein.

Jno. ffessington & Thomas Danforth have liberty granted them to fell Timber on the com̄on for the reparac̄c̄on of their Houſes & fences:

[52] Thomas ffox, Robert Parker, and ffrancis moore are appoynted by the Townſemen to survey & regulate the ffences apprteyneing to the weſt feild.

Bro. Edward Goffe, and B^r. Jno. ſtedman are appoynted by the Select men to survey & regulate the ffences apprteyneing to the necke of land.

Willm Russell & Ensigne Winship are appoynted by the ſelect men to survey & regulate the fences apprteyneing to the Com̄on feild beyond Winottime River. — —

Daniel Cheavers is appoynted to ſee the order of the Towne Executed in refference to yoaking & Ringing of swine.

It being teſtified to the Townſemen that Nicholas Withe had a Towne right or liberty of building him a houſe in ye Towne granted him about 19: years now paſt, the wch right was ſold by the ſaid Nicholas withe to Jno Cooper, the ſelect men agreed & conſented that the ſaid grant ſhould be entred vppon Record, as a Towne grant. to have p^{r}viledge in y^e Towne as other grants of y^e ſame n^r. that were granted by the ſelect men. — —

At a Towne meeting of the Select men the 8th of march 165$^{7}/_{8}$.

Thomas Swætman hath liberty granted him to fell some timber on the Com̄on for repaire of his out fences and addition to his buildings.

Daniel Kempſter hath liberty to fell ſome 6. or 7. trees on the Com̄on for the vſe of his Trade.

Charles Sternes covenanteth wth y^e ſelect men to keep there milch heard this p^{r}nt ſum^r. beginning his charge on the 20th of Aprill next & to continue vntill the 20th. of October. & to find all the help that he ſhall need for the carefull discharge thereof, and to pʳvide two sufficient Bulls, & to burne the woodes feafonably & carefully. In confideraccon whereof the felect men do covenant to allow the said Charles three fhill. & Eight pence pr. head. to be pᵈ in mannʳ following: (i e) to receive it of the feuʳall owners of the cattle, th' one halfe in wheat. at 4ˢ 6ᵈ pr bufh. Rie at 3ˢ 6ᵈ pr bufh. and Indian at 3ˢ pr bufh. in all or either yᵉ sᵈ graines at or before midfum̃ʳ next, & th' other halfe in such graine and at fuch prifes as the next Country rate is payd in.

memʳ. It is to be vnderftood yᵗ yᵉ agreemᵗ is yᵗ for each Cow yᵉ Cow keepr fhall have one pecke of wheat, or two pound butter & the reft of yᵉ paymᵗ to be in any graine excepting only pease in yᵉ firft paymᵗ.

his ⊓ marke
Charles Sterne∧

Cow keeper his pay.

[53]   8 (1) 165⁷⁄₈

The felect men do nõminate & impower Bro: Goffe, & Bʳ ftedman, to veiw and determine the matter in difference between the neighbours on the fouth fide the Rivʳ about the Highway neere Jno. Wards Houfe.

Bro. Edw: Hall hath liberty to fell timber on the Com̃on for fencing his orchard.

Peter Towne hath liberty to fell fome trees on the Com̃on for the vfe of his Trade before the laft of may next.

---

12. (2) 58

John Swan hath liberty granted him to fell fome timber on the Com̃on to fence in a garden plott, and to build an adition to his houfe. ——

John shepard hath liberty for two load of timber on yᵉ Com̃on for his trade.

At a Towne meeting the 8ᵗʰ Novemʳ 58.
for choyce of Towne officʳˢ.

Jno. Cooper, Nathaniell Sparhauke and Jnº Shepard are chofen Conftables for the yeare enfueing.

Edw: Goffe Edw. Oakes & Thomas Danforth are chofen Comifsion⁽ʳˢ⁾ for ending fmal cafes.

Edward Oakes, Thomas Danforth, Jn°. ffessington & Thomas ffox are chofen Select men to gether with y⁶ Conftables for y⁶ yeare enfueing. —

Jn°. ftedman, Ric. Robbins & ffrancis Moore Jun.ʳ are chofen Surveyo⁽ʳˢ⁾ for the yeare enfueing.

Tho: Danforth is nominated to be p⁽ʳ⁾fented vnto y⁶ County Court to ☞ be impowred in mariages, & giveing oathes in Civill cafes.———

The Towne do grant to David ffiske a prcell of meadow, neere to Deacon ftones farme, about fix acrs. more or lefs in cafe the artillery grant do not deprive him of the fame.

[53]   At a meeting of the Inhabitants
         the 10ᵗʰ of $\frac{11\text{th}}{\text{mo}}$ 1658;

Thefe following propoficcons were voted by the Towne in the affirmative:

1. That the great Swamp lying with in the bounds of this Towne, on the Eaft fide of frefh pond meadow, & Winottime brooke, fhalbe divided into prtic⁽ʳ⁾ alotments & prpriety.

2. That no person that hath any part or parcell thereof granted vnto him or fhall purchafe any part thereof, fhall alienate the Same to any perfon not inhabiting wᵗʰ in the bounds of this Towne, on penalty of forfeiting the Said land vnto the vfe of the Towne, & that no perfon shall alienate or difpofe of the wood of any prt yʳ of to any perfon not Inhabiting within the bounds of this Towne, on penalty of forfeiting so much by the load as if he had sold it from off the comon. And that vpon no other Condiccons then thefe above named shall any perfon hold any prpriety therein.

<small>Fresh pond meadow</small>

3: That vntill it be divided it shall not be lawfull for any perfon to fell any prt thereof on penalty of forfeting 2ˢ pr load.

4. That the Deacons, Townfemen, Ri: Jackson. Jn°. ftedman Jonas Clark & David ffiske, with all convenient speed make the divifsion thereof according to their best difcretion, as alfo to determine how farr it shalbe divided, & how farr it shalbe left in Comon. ———

At a meeting of the Select men, 20th $\frac{11}{mo}$ 1658

It was agreed by the select men, & confented vnto, by Thomas Danforth, m^r Pelhams Attorney that m^r Pelham fhould have one hundred acc^r of land, according to the former grant of the select men 13: march. 53: vpon confideraccons therein exprefsed, But the wood & Timber thereon to ly in Comon to the vfe of the Towne. — — —

[54] At a meeting of the select men.
14. (12) 1658:

Widow Daniell, Thomas Longhorne, Robert Parker. Willm Man & Edw. Hall are granted liberty to fell timb on ye Comon for reparaccon of their out fences & Houfes.

Ens. Winship is allowed to take 4: trees vpon the Rockes in lew of his right in y^t wood y^t was divided to ye towne on Winottime Playne.

Granted to Br. Kempfter liberty to fell fix trees on the Comon for to repaire his Houfe & trade. & to Deacon Marritt for repair of his Houfe & adition of a leanto.

B^r Cooper hath liberty to fell fome timb on y^e Comon for repaire of his out fences.

B^r. Ri: Jackson hath liberty granted to fell some timb on the comon for repaire of his fences.

At a publique meeting of the Inhabitants
of this Towne, 18. (12) $\underline{58.}$

ffor the p^{r}venting of further ftroy of wood in the great Swamp, It is ordered by the confent of the Inhabitants, That henceforth all perfons that cut any wood therein from time to time shall duly obferve thefe following direccons., vizt.

1. They fhall Anually enter vpon fuch part thereof as the select men for the time being shall appoynt.
2. They shall cutt downe all the brufh as they go along, & shall cutt out the great wood, the fame day they fall it, & alfo faggott vp the Brush, on penalty of forfeiting five fhill pr load, for neglect thereof,

more then three dayes: as alſo for cutting in any other part or place of yᵉ ſwamp. then ſhalbe appoynted them as above ſaid. the one halfe of wᶜʰ fine ſhalbe to yᵉ informʳ, and the other halfe to yᵉ vſe of the Towne. And in caſe any perſon shall have any wood fallen, & vncut out & ſet vp an end more then three dayes, or vnfetched out of the ſwamp more then ſix m̊ it ſhalbe lawfull for any other perſon to take the ſame.

Freſh Pond

3. That none do cut down any prt of the ſecond growth, or pass through the ſame with a cart, on penalty of paying twelve pence for euʳy tree, hop pole or hoope pole,

and

[54] and five shill, for euʳy time they shall paſſe throw the ſame with their cart.

4ly That ſuch as will ingage to ſubdue it for meadow, and ſhall accordingly give in their names to yᵉ ſelect men wᵗʰ in a fortnight, ſhall have a prcell ſett out vnto them by the Com̄ittee formʳly appoynted to divide the ſaid ſwamp not exceeding one accʳ & halfe to any one perſon. And that ſuch perſons ſhall have no intereſt in the reſidue of the great ſwamp, that lieth wᵗʰ in the fence now to be ſett vp for the ſecureing of the weſt feild. — All theſe prticls were voted on yᵉ affirmative.

Where as mʳ Tompſon had two ſmall farmes granted by the Towne, wᶜʰ were not determined by lott, in the ordering the diviſsion of the farmes. The wᶜʰ farmes were ſold by mʳ Tompſon to Joseph Juitt of Rowley, & one hundred accʳs thereof ſold againe by the ſaid Juitt to mʳ Angier, & by mʳ Angier to mʳ Wilcocke, as attorney of mʳ Wᵐ Tannʳ, of Coxall, & by mʳ Eake attorney of yᵉ ſᵈ Tannʳ, ſold vnto Thomas Danforth, to gether wᵗʰ the farme where Ri: Haſsull is. The Towne did vote it; that the ſaid hundred accʳs ſhould be layd out beyond the farmes already layd out on the ſouth ſide the rivʳ: neere into the great pond by mʳ Haynes farme. —

Voted on the affirmative, That the Elders, Deacons, & Select men for the time being, ſhalbe a conſtant & ſetled power for regulateing, ye ſeating of perſons in the meeting houſe, from time to time as need shall require.

At a meeting of the select men,
21. (12) 58.

It is ordered that all persons that either already have, or hereafter shall fall any

[55] any tree, vpon any high way, do forthwth cleare away the same, on penalty of paying five shill. for eu^{r}y trespass herein. This order was published by posting on ye meetinghouse. 23: (12) 58:

Richard Robbines & Jno Jackson are impowred to excecute the orders conc^{r}ning swine, on y^e south side y^e Riu^r

Ens. Winship. Jno. Watson, & Rog^r Bucke, to execute the orders about swine on the north side y^e Riu^r All wch are to p^{r}sent the names of all delinq^{ts} eu^{r}y towne meeting da$_\wedge$

Nicholas Withe, Robert Parker, & David fiske, are to survey the fences about West feild for this yeare ensueing, and Jno. stedman & Thomas Longhorne are in like mane^r appoynted for the necke of land, And Ens. Winship &   for Winottime feild.

The 14th of march. 165^8/$_9$.

Granted liberty to m^r Joseph Cooke to take 70: Railes & 40: postes of the comon in lew of so many that was taken of his p^{r}priety for the fenceing his yard & orchard.

The difference between the prprietors of the new ox pasture lotts, & Ri: Jackson being referred to y^e select men, & Deacon Bridge by ye mutuall consent of both prtys. they do judge meet & determine that during the time the said Ri: Jackson shall imprve it for feed of draught cattle, according to the native grant, or otherwise suffer it to ly in comon, he shall maintaine a sufficient fence. twelve pole in length, betwen Jonathan Padlefootes lott & that, & in case he shall againe imprve it for corne, he shal$_\wedge$ then make & mainteine th' one halfe of the said Particcon fence:

[55] Jno. stedman, & Thomas Danforth are appoynted a comittee to consider of the complayntes of Tho: Hamond & wm Clemance conc^{r}ning the want of land that of right belongeth to them on th' other side the river, and to make them such allowance as they shall find just. ———

June 20th 1659.

It is ordered by ye Selectmen, that all ye Inhabitants, whofe cattle do feed vpon any part of our Cow comon, within five miles of the meeting houfe, on the north fide of the river, fhall pay to the heardsman, whether of Cowes or fheep, prporēconable to ye no. of cattle fo feeding, any formr law, coftome, or vfage to the contrary not wth ftanding, — Excepting only fuch farmes as cannot with convenience put their cattle to any heard. — — — —

August 8th. 1659.

Whereas complaynt is made of great ftroy of Corne in the necke of land not wth ftanding all formr orders yt have bin made for reftraint of vnruly cattle, & prvission of fufficient fences. The feleƈt men do therefore order that Henceforth wt eur cattle fhall be found damage faifant in the faid feild, the ownr thereof fhall pay vnto the occupier of the land whereon the trespasse is comitted, or to the comon pinder, (i e) to fuch of them as fhall bring them out of the faid feild, Eighten pence for each beaft, & in cafe it be proved that any perfon hath voluntarily turned his cattle or beaft in to the sd necke of land, he fhall then pay five fhillings for each beaft to fuch perfon as fhall bring them out. prvided alwayes where the default is meerly in the fence, & the cattle fo found are not illegall in fuch cafe ye owner of the cattle shall go free, & the ownr of the fence throw wch they trespassed fhall pay all cofts & charges, fines & damages, wch otherwife the own'rs of the cattle ought to have fattisfied. And mr ftedman & Tho. Longhorne are [56] appoynted to be the comon pinder of all cattle found in the faid feild for this prfent yeare — *

[56]   Novemr. 1659.

At a genrall meeting of the Inhabitants for choyce of
Towne officers.

ffor Townfemen for
the yeare enfueing

{ Thomas Danforth
Edw. Oakes
Jno. Cooper
Jno. ffifhenden

* Remainder of page blank.

Conſtables — { ffrancis moore
Thomas Longhorne
Thomas cheny

Jan. 23. 1659

At a publique meeting of the Inhabitants, It was voted on the affirmative that the remote inhabitants on the south side ye Riu^r, should annually be abated the one halfe of y^r prporc̃on to the miniſtryes allowance dureing the time they were prvided of an able miniſter according to law. — — —

ffeb.^{r} 13. 1659.

Liberty is granted by the Townſemen to Willm Towne George Willowes. Jno Cooper, & Thomas Danforth, to fell some fencing timb. on ye com̃on for their vſe, according to Towne order, in like mann^r, to Deacon ſtone, & to Jno ſteadman for planke fencing & a leantoo. for a barne floare & to Jno. Goave a Clapbord Tree & to Jno Palfrey 3. trees for his trade. To Daniel Cheaver for fencing & a clapbord Tree.

Willm man being complained on for defficiency of his fence, anent y^e Weſt feild, is to pay David ffiske the surveyor of that fence two ſhill. & three pence; & in cauſe he ſhall refuse, to pay on demand the Conſtable is to take it by diſtreſs. — — —

March, 19. 165$\frac{9}{60}$

Nicholas Withe acknowledgeth that he hath covenanted wth Gilbert Crackbone to make & maintaine for euer five rod of com̃on fence, apprteyneing to y^e land of y^e ſaid Gilbert lying anent the yard of the said Nicholas withe. — — —

[57]   14. (3) 1660.

It is ordered that who euer turnes any ſheep into o^r com̃on, that is not an Inhabitant of y^e towne, ſhall pay 5^s a head for the Sum̃erfeed thereof.

Samuel Goffe being convicted of disorderly falling & takeing away sundry loades of wood, from y^e towne lott in y^e ox pafture is ordered to pay to the vfe of the towne fiften fhilling$_\wedge$

Samuel Goffe, Tho. Beale, Daniel Kempster, Jno Bowtell, Ri: Haffull. are granted libty to fell timb. for repair of y^r comon fences & buildings. & to Daniel Kempfter 6 trees for his trade. — — —

22. (3). 1660.

The Townfmen agreed that Thomas Browne fhould haue foure acc^r of the neereft comon land not form^{r}ly granted by the Town, in confideraccon of a high way to be left & made through his land leading from ye houfe of Thomas cherry towards Water-Towne milne.

The Townfmen agreed that the quantity of land given by the Town to Jonas Clarke fhould be five acc^{r}s to be layd out wth Thomas Browne foure acc^{r}s, if he defired it.

m^r Edmund Angier makeing of it appeare y^t his farme houfe on the south fide the Riu^r is an old p^{r}viledged houfe, is granted libty to fall timb on y^e comon for making his out fences. — — — —

28. (3) 1660

At a gen^{r}all meeting of the Inhabitants. voted on the affirmative. That there be a fence errected vpon Water=Towne line from Willm Hamletts land, vnto Rockie meadow fence.

2. That y^r be a comittee of 7: men chofen to confider & determine, the ordering, makeing & mainteining of that fence, & y^t y^e charge thereof be levied vppon the prprieto^{r}s of the Comon, according as they fhall Judge equall.

3. The comittee for this worke chofen by papers, are Thomas Danforth, Deacon Jno Bridge, Deacon Gregory ftone, Ri: Jackson, Leift. Edw. Winship. Jno Cooper & Jno ffessington. — — — —

12. (4) 1660.

At a meeting of the Select men, seu^{r}all persons fined for felling & ftroying timb on ye comon lands, are

Henry Rainer.	0 — 8 — 0
Saml Rainer.	0 — 5 — 0
David stone.	0 — 7 — 0
Saml stone.	0 — 2 — 0

[57] Thomas Longhorne hath liberty to fell timb on the comon for his barne. — — —

---

liberty is granted to Peter Towne for two trees for his trade, & for w̅ᵗ he needs for the repayre of his houſe

---

At a Publique meeting of the Inhabitants
the 12ᵗʰ of novemʳ 1660.

Thomas Cheſholme, Jnº. Ward, & Richard Eccles are choſen Conſtables, for the yeare enſueing.

Capᵗ Daniel Gookin, Thomas Danforth, Edward Oakes, Jnº Cooper, John ffiſhenden & Thomas ffox are choſen Select men for the yeare enſueing.

Thomas Browne, Jonath. Hide, Joſeph Mirriam, Walter Haſtings, & Robert Holmes are choſen Surveyoʳs of high wayes.

Thomas Danforth. Jno. ſtedman. Jnº ffiſhenden & Thomas ffox are appoynted a Comittee to veiw the land deſired by Deacon ſtone being about 30. or 40. accres. & if they ſhall ſee meet to ſet a price of it, or otherwiſe as they ſhall ſee meet.

The Land in the necke wᶜʰ the Towne bought of Deacon Jnº Bridge, by eſtimaccon abᵗ 7. accʳˢ more or leſs, is ſold to Thomas Longhorne, on Condiccon that he pay ten pounds & five ſhillings in Corne or Cattle, to the vſe of the towne.

As a finall iſsue of all complaints referring to mʳ Dunſters Expences about the ſchoole houſe, all though in ſtrict juſtice nothing doth appeare to be due, it being done by a voluntary act of prticular Inhabitants, & mʳ Dunſter: & alſo the Towne haueing otherwiſe recompenced mʳ Dunſter for his labor and expences therein yet yᵉ Towne conſidering the caſe as its now circumſtanced, and especially the Condiccon of his relict widow & children, do agree yᵗ thirty pounds be levied on the Inhabitants of the Towne by the Select men, & payd to mʳ Dunſters Execcutoʳs, & yᵗ on Condiccon yᵗ they make an abſolute deed of ſale of yᵉ

Said Houfe and land to the Towne, with a clear acquittance for the full payment thereof. —— ——- ———

Edward Oakes, & William Manning, are chofen to Joyne wth the Comittee form^{r}ly chofen ye eight of decem^r 1656. for the profecuteing & effecting a Bridge over Charles Riue^r.

[58]   At a meeting of ye Select men
12. (9) 1660.

prefent
Capt. Gookin,
Thomas Danforth,
Jno Cooper
Edw. Oakes.
Jno ffishenden
Tho. ffox.
Tho. Chesholme.
Ri: Eccles.

Capt Gookin m^r ftedman, William Manning. David ffiske. Deacon Marrett Ri: ffrancis & Humphry Bredfha. Haue all of them libty to take timb on ye comons. for repaires of y^r houfes, out fences & orchards.

Robert ftedman hath hired of the felect men, the land wth in ye necke gate called the clay pitts, for 7 years. on Condiccon to secure w^t cattell he shall put y^m by a sufficient fence and to pay 10^s pr ann^m to the vfe of the Towne.

Tho: ffox, and ffrancis moore Junr are appoynted to lay out to David ffiske, forty accres of land, form^{r}ly granted him at ye head of ye Eight mile line.

At a meeting of the Select men

p^{r}fent.
Thomas Danforth,
Edw. oakes,
Jno Cooper,
Jno ffishenden,
Tho ffox,
Th^o. Chefholme,
Ri: Eccles.

Deacon ftone, Jno Cooper.
Rich. Eccles, Tho. ffox, wm pattin.
Jno. Goave, Jno watson. ffr. whitmore haue all of them libty to take timb. for repair of fences & reparaccon of y^r houfes.
ffrancis whitmore hath leave granted him to take fome pines in the Swamp to build him a barne.

Jno. shepard hath liberty granted to take two trees for his Trade.

Deacon Bridge, Thomas fox & ffrancis Moore Jun.ʳ are appoynted to Joyne wth fome of watertowne to marke out yᵉ line between oʳ bounds in yᵉ great Swamp.

The Townfemen do order that no Tradefmen fhall be allowed above two trees pr Ann. out of the Comons for his trade.

[58] ffebruary the 4th. 1660.

At a publique meeting of the Inhabitants of this Towne,

Great Bridge.
The form^r propoficcons & votes that had paffed for the building of a Bridge over Charles Riuer, were againe confidered & debated, and the Queftion being propounded, whether the Towne did agree & confent that the faid worke fhould yet be further profsecuted, and that 200^ls should be levied on the Inhabitants of this towne towards the effecting thereof, the Vote passed on the affirmative. ———

Sundry young men haue liberty granted them to build a gallery on yᵉ South beame, on condiccon that they shall not dispose their feates therein to any other, but leave them to yᵉ order of thofe yᵗ are appoynted to regulate yᵉ fitting of perfons in yᵉ meeting houfe.

20. 12th. 1660.

The townfmen ordered, yᵗ none cutt out any of yᵉ wood fallen for yᵉ Bridge, on penalty of 3ˢ 6ᵈ pr load, wth out leave of yᵉ the towne, & that Edw. Oakes & Jno. ffishenden, make fale of such as is vfefull to ship carpenters, for yᵉ publique good of yᵉ Town.

Jnº. Watson hath liberty to fell timb on yᵉ Comon for his building, & for fencing ftuffe, on condiccon yᵗ if yᵉ Towne at a publique meeting confent not to yᵗ for his building. He shall pay the worth yʳ of to yᵉ Towne.

At a Publ: meeting of the Inhabitants,
the 2. munday in novem^r. 1661.

The Towne being mett together, did choofe thefe feu^rall offic^rs for the yeare enfueing.

for Select men, Capt. Gookin, Thomas Danforth Edw. Oakes. Jn̊. Cooper, Jn̊. ffessington. Thomas ffox.

for conftables. { Richard Dana.
Abrām Errington
Walter Hastings

for Surveyo^rs of Highwayes
Leift. Winfhip.
Jofeph Mirriam.
Thomas Longhorne.
Wm Robbins.

p^rfnt.
Capt Gookin
Edw. Oakes
Tho: Chefholme
Jno: ffifhenden
Jno: Cooper
Th: ffox
Ri: Eccles

[59]   13th of May, 1661.

The Townfemen do Judge meet to grant the request of Thomas Danforth for the removall of the Towne gate y^t ftandeth agft Thomas Swætmans, that it may be removed below Jno: Taylors orchard, prvided He do the Same at his owne charge, & for the mayntenance of the Same for the future they do agree to allow him two shillings pr. Ann. vntill such time as the Towne shall orderly dismisse Him from any further care or charge about the Same.*

[59]   At a meeting of the Inhabitants.
Janu^y 13th. 1661.

The Towne do order & confent that the land beyond Dedham path, leading between watertowne mill, & Leift. Prentices, on the north side thereof, be fold to thofe of that pr^t of the Towne that belong to ye new meetinghoufe there: on condicc̄on that they give good security to the Towne for payment of twenty pounds pr Ann for ever to the vfe of the other prt of the Towne belonging to the old meetinghoufe on the north fide the Riu^r: the wch condicc̄ons being prformed, the Towne do

* Remainder of page blank.

grant that all thofe Inhabitants beyond foure miles diftante from the old meetinghoufe, fhall be wholly free from the Towne, In cafe the Gen^r^all Court fhall rattify & confirme the faid agreemt.

Capt. Daniel Gookin. Thomas Danforth, Gregory ftone, Jno: ftedman, & Edward Oakes, are nominated & impow^r^ed by the Towne to treat wth o^r^ Brethren & neighbo^r^s on the fouth fide the Riu^r^ & to ifsue the matter wth them according to the above named propoficcon made & agreed by the Towne.

The Towne do agree & confent that all the comon lands on the South fide the Riu^r^, on th' eaft fide of dedham Path, shall be divided into prpriety to the feu^r^all Inhabitants that haue an intereft therein, as alfo such comon lands as ly in the Seventh mile on the north fide the Riu^r^ alfo 'tis agreed that the neere lands on the Head of m^r^ Andrews farme on Bofton Line shall be divided to each perfon his fhare y^r^in & the other parcells to be divided in one divission to each one y^r^ fhare.

Alfo tis agreed that all the Swamps within the bounds of this Towne, not wth in the compasse of form^r^ divissions & not prfitable for feed, be forth wth divided, to such of the Inhabitants as haue an intereft therein.

The Towne do agree that the Deacons, felect men, Jno. ftedman, Ri: Jackson, & Leift. Edw. Winship, shall & are hereby impowred a comittee, for the determining of w^t^ Swamps & other lands they Judge meet to divide, & to divide the Same to the Inhabitants that haue an intereft therein both for quantity & quality as they fhall Judge equall: The Towne do agree that fuch as will ingage to make meadow of y^r^ fhare of Swamp, may haue it layd out together.

The Towne do agree & confent by their vote in publick meeting to all thefe divifsions above named, on condiccon, that neither wood, timb^r^ or land be fold or passed away from the Towne, on penalty of forfeiting the fame to ye vfe of the Towne againe.

The

[60] January. 13. 1661

Grant to Rev^d^ M^r^. Mitchel

The Towne do grant to Capt. Gookin & to m^r^ mitchell, twenty acc^r^s of land apeece, to be layd out to ym on the neere lands on the fouth fide the Riu^r^ where it may be convenient for y^r^ imprvemt by Tillage.

At a meeting of the Select men.
13th (11.) 1661

The Townsmen do grant libty to Saml Goffe, Leift. Winship, widow Beale, Ranold Bufh, philip Cooke, Edw: Shepard, Thomas Danforth, & Capt. Gookin, to fell some timb, on the comons for the repayre of y^r houfes & out fences. alfo to Robert parker. Thomas Chefholme, Ens. Greene, wm Barratt, & walter Haftings Abram Errington, & to Peter Towne one Tree for his trade, & alfo for his fencing & a leanto. to Jno. fhepard two trees for his trade. to Jonathan Kane 2. trees for his trade.

To Elder ffroft libty for repayre of his out fences & of his buildings.

To Jno. ffessington & Thomas ffox, libty for fencing ftuffe.

To mathew Bridge for covering his houfe.

To Zachariah Hicks libty for timb to repayre his Houfe.

Philip Cooke for falling 4 trees on ye Rocks wthout licenfe is fined, 2^s 6^d a tree, — 10^s 0^d

Alfo Philip Cooke for falling trees in ye Swamp beyond Winottime Riu^r. wth out licenfe is fined thirty fhillings. — — —

Renold Bufh is granted libty to take timb. of the comon for repayreing his houfe, takeing such trees as Saml Hide shall marke out for such vfe, & alfo for fireing taking such wood as is fallen: & not felling any young trees vnder 6 inches diameter.

At a meeting of the Select men,
10 (12) 1661.

Wm. Dixon, widow Russell, Jno. Boutell, James Hubbard, ffrancis moore, Jno. Bridge haue libty to take timb^r. for y^r fencing & building.

Seu^{r}all fined for falling trees on the Comon wth out licenfe.

Jno. watfon, — 18^d Nicholas withe six fhill: ffrancis moore, two shillings.

An order was pofted prhibiting all felling any wood or timb. on the lands divideable on the South Side on penalty of five fhillings a tree.

Jno. Boutell hath libty for 5. load wood on y^e South side y^e Riu^r of y^e tops fallen.

a fine of 12^d **[60]** George Willowes for not attending the Towne meeting being warned is fined twelve pence.

Philip Cooke abated of his fine laſt towne meeting, ten ſhillings.

20th of March. 166$\frac{1}{2}$.

Jno. Cooper, Thomas Marritt. & Robert Browne is grantad libty for fencing ſtuffe.

Deacon ſtone is granted a ſwamp Oake on y^e eaſt ſide winottime Riu^r.

grant of a tree to Rev Mr Mitchil for a cyder mill.   m^r mitchell is granted a tree for a ſider preſſe.

The Townſemen do order that the Constables do levy a rate on the inhabitants, each perſon the one moyty of his Country Rates & ſuch as be not in the Country Rate, that they be added therevnto.

25. of march, 1662.

The Townsmen taking into their consideraccon the equity of allowance to be made to mr Corlett for his maintenance of a gramer Schoole in this Towne, especially considering his pʳſent necessity, fewnes £10.00 by reason of the <u>fewnes of his ſchollars</u>, do order & agree that ten pounds be payd to him. out of the publicke ſtocke of the Towne.

14. (2) 1662.

liberty is granted to m^{rs} Dunster to fell timb for repayre of the Comon fence agſt. wm Bulls.

The Townſmen conſented at ye requeſt of m^r Richard Champny, y^t ye lands granted him, at Alewife meadow, not excepted for Highwayes, or ſold to ffrancis whitmore, be entred in ye name of m^r Edm: ffroſt.

It is ordered by y^e ſelect men, y^t none fell any trees on ye High wayes of this Towne except for publ: vſe, on pænalty of forfeiting 20^s a tree.

3. 9. 1662.

The Townſmen do order that yᵉ wood lotts granted to Samˡ Goffe. Andr. Belcher, & yᵉ Colledge. Six Accʳ a peece be layd out at yᵉ north-end of mʳ pelhams 100 accʳ successively one after another. Andrew Belcher yᵉ firſt lott. & Samˡ Goffe yᵉ ſecond.

[61] Alſo mʳ Pelhams 20 accʳs to be layd out on yᵉ South end of his 100 accʳs. ⫽

At a publick meeting of the Inhabitants,
the Second munday in Novemb. 1662.

Capt. Daniel Gookin.
Thomas Danforth
Lt. Winſhip.
Edw. Oakes. } for ſelect men
John Cooper
Thomas ffox

John ffishenden
Robert Holmes } Constables
Jonath. Hide

Gilbert Crackbone,
Thomas cheny
Zach. Hicks. } Surveyoʳˢ of High wayes
Math. Bridge,
Thomas Prentice, Junʳ

---

10. 9. 62.
Jno. ffiſhenden grant.

The Towne do grant to Jno. ffishenden the land between the runet of water & his garden pale, to be ſet out by yᵉ ſelect men.

Jno. Greene.

The Towne do grant to Jno. Greene the High way annent his houſe: provided Hee do not injure Thomas fox by pʳventing his passage to yᵉ lands beyond it.

[61]   22. 10. 1662.

At a meeting of the Selectmen.

James Hubbard is granted libty for timb. to build an end to his Houfe, & for fencing his orchard.
Thomas marritt for two clapbord Trees.
Robert Holmes Timb. for a Cart & wheeles. ———

The Names of such as are returned by Lt. Winſhip for defect in yoaking & Ringing their Swine.

,,	Widow Russell. — —	00 — 07 — 03
	John Browne. — — —	00 — 07 — 00
,,	Tho: Rosse, & Wm Row.—	00 — 13 — 09
,,	Wm Bull. — — —	00 — 01 — 03
,,	John Adams. — — —	00 — 04 — 06
	John Swann. — — —	00 — 11 — 06
	Robert Wilson — —	00 — 05 — 03
,,	m^{rs} Dunster. — — —	00 — 05 — 00
,,	Richard Cutter. — —	00 — 03 — 06
,,	James Hubbard. — —	00 — 02 — 00
,,	ffrancis Whitmore — —	00 — 02 — 03
,,	wm Dixon — — —	00 — 02 — 06
,,	Thomas Hall. — —	00 — 06 — 00
,,	Lt. Winſhip. — — —	00 — 01 — 06

$$\underline{\underline{03\,!! = 13: =: 03 =}}$$

12. (12) 1662
At a meeting of the Select men

Edwd Shepard is granted liberty to take two trees of the comon for his vfe: Alfo Jno. shepard is granted two trees for his trade.

De: Grigory ftone is granted liberty to take some fencing on the Comon, for ab^t. 60: rayles.

to m^r Angier for a Hogs coate: & Br Cooper for some fencing & to Thomas fox for fencing.

TOWN RECORDS 141

Thomas Danforth & Jn.º ffishenden appoynted by the Towne at a publ: meeting. Novem.ʳ 12. 1660, to veiw a parcel of land defired by Deacon ftone, made report yᵗ they had veiwed the land defired, & found that yᵉ quantity is by their eftimaccon about twelve accʳ more or lesse, & is bounded wᵗʰ yᵉ High way from Joseph mirriams Houfe to Concord on yᵉ north. mr flints farme on yᵉ South. & yᵉ sᵈ Deacon ftones land East & weft. the wᶜʰ land they find will be a conveniency to yᵉ reft of his lands there, & that yᵉ same may be granted him wᵗʰ out any pʳjudice to yᵉ Towne: & that according to yᵉ truft repofed in them they had layd out yᵉ fame to him bounded as aboue faid.

The Townfemen do order yᵗ a High way of 20: pole in breadth be allowed & left in comon adjoyneing to yᵉ weft fide of yᵉ farme yᵗ was Edw: Goffes, to rune from Deacon ftones farme to water towne line.

[62] At a meeting of the Selectmen,
19ᵗʰ of January, 1662.

The Townfemen do order that the High way leading from mʳ Pelhams caufey throw mʳ Angiers farme, be repaired there where it was orderly layd out by the Comittee of the feuʳall Townes that was appoynted to lay out the High way betweene Cambridge & Roxbery:

liberty is granted to George Willowes to take timb: to repayr his garden fence & for his fonnes Garden fence. =

Ri: Eccles libty for two trees for rayles.

The Townfemen do order that if any prfon do leave open the gate on the Bridge over the River, or turne any cattle at liberty on yᵗ fide, except on his owne prpriety, or the lands in comon with out all prpriety, euʳie such person fhall pay for euʳie fuch default & trespasse, twelve pence, & twelve pence for euʳie beast so found trespassing on any mans prpriety.

Granted to Ri: Dana in lew of damage He hath sufteined by yᵉ High way anent his houfe, a prcell of comon land adjoyneiₐ to his about 20: poles more or leffe. =

The Townfemen do order that the charges for the High wayes & caufyes be defrayed by a Rate on the Inhabitants, & for that end that a rate be forthwith levied to yᵉ quantity of 3: fingle Country rates, &

such as are excepted therein, be added by Th: Danforth Jn° ffishenden & Jn° Cooper.

Jonath: Cane for felling trees on yᵉ Comon contrary to Towne order is fined, 30ˢ & wm Pattin for falling trees on yᵉ comon contrary to Town order is fined, 20ˢ.

mʳ John Stedman, Edward Oakes, Thomas fox and Edward Shepard, are appoynted to attend the laying out of the High way, from our bounds leading towards Roxbery, as the law directeth, and as they ſhall haue warneing given them by thoſe concerned therein:

[62] At a meeting of the Select men,

9. 12. 1662.

In conſideration of Damage Done to Mʳ Thomas Danforth in his marſh by the high way paſſing throw it, to the bridge ouer Charles Riuer,

☞ The Towne do grant him (in conſideration & for ſatiſfacktion of his accre of marſh lying in the ſaid place) all that peece of marſh below william Mannings, betwen that & the riuer, a conuenient high way, and accomadation to the warhouſe, being reſerued, and as for mʳ Pelhams accre of marſh lying not farre from the cauſy, leading to the bridge, they do agree to allow him four pounds for it in caſe hee bee willing to part wᵗʰ it & to leave it in como for the Towne.

Voted by the Townſmen the day & yeare
aboue written atteſted by

DANIEL GOOKIN

liberty granted to Daniel cheaver to fell one clapbord tree & 2. trees for a pʳ wheeles.

9ᵗʰ of march. 6$\frac{2}{3}$

Lᵗ Winship, Robert Parker, John Browne, Thomas Hall, John fiſhenden, Robert Browne, haue liberty granted them for repayreing yʳ houſe & fences. & 2. trees to Robert Browne for a pʳ Wheeles.

Jno. Shepard & Thomas Longhorne are appoynted to veiw the necke fences

TOWN RECORDS 143

Nicholas Withe, John Gibson, & Jno. Watson for the Weſt feild.
Thomas Hall & Willm Pattine for the Menottime feilds.
ffrancis Whitmore & Wm Dixon are appoynted to See ye orders conc^{r}ning ſwine execcuted, on the weſt ſide Menottime, & In the Towne John Goave and Peter Towne
And for the Comon Richard ffrancis
And in caſe they find any not Ringed and yoaked, or ſhall Judge them not ſufficient they are to returne their Names to y^e Towne eu^{r}ie month day.
And for the South ſide the Riu^r Richard Robbins & Wm clemance Senr

[63]   12 — (2) 166$\frac{2}{3}$

Peter Towne hath two Trees allowed Him of the Comon for His Trade.
Andrew ſtevenson & Richard Garden haue liberty for timber on y^e Comon for their out fences.

23. (2) 166$\frac{2}{3}$

At a publique meeting of the Towne
voted on y^e affirmative.

Bridge painted — That the Bridge be layd in oyle & lead provided that it exceed not forty pounds charge to the Towne

The Townesmen, m^r ſtedman & m^r Andrews, are Appoynted to see this worke effected, in caſe they find it feaſeable.
Edward ſhepard, & Thomas White are appoynted to drive the necke and are injoyned to returne ye names of all ſuch as they ſhall find treſpassers eu^{r}ie month day of y^e ſelect men meetin͓
ordered that all swine be yoaked wth a crotch yoake or wth 2. croſs peeces & y^t y^e ſame be in length & bredth prporc̃onably to the bignés of ye Swine
Thomas Danforth. & Jno. fishenden are appoynted a comittee to lay out m^r Mitchels farme, & Thomas Oakes farme at Shawſhine. //
Ordered that none fetch away any ſheep or lamb from the Comon flock wth out notice given & Sight of the ſhepard on penalty of two shillings a peece, to be payd to shepr^d whereof th' one halfe ſhall be in prt of his wages, or in the ſhepards abſence on y^e ſight of Edw. Hall. ⸺

[63] ordered that all the sheep put to y*e* Comon flocke be eare marked or Wooll marked, on penalty of bearing their lofs, in cafe they be not distinctly marked, by y*r* owners. =

Robert ftedman hath liberty for timb for his out fences, & a Cart.

Ordered that in cafe the Hogreeves fhall neglect their truft, for the Excecuccon of the orders conc*r*ning fwine, on complaynt made by fuch as find themfelves agreived, fuch perfon fo neglecting his truft fhall pay double the fine that the delinqu*t* party ought to haue pd in cafe the Towne order had been excecuted, th' one halfe whereof fhallbe to y*e* complay*nt* & th' other to the poor of the Towne.=

<small>order for Hogreeves.</small>

Elder champny, Edw. oakes, & Richd Robbins, are defired to veiw the High way on the south fide the Riu*r* throw the new lotts, & to fettle y*e* fame where it may be moft convenient & leaft p*r*judice to y*e* proprietors.

The Townfemen do order that a peticcon be drawne & figned in y*e* name of the felect men by y*r* clarke, requefting the Coun*t* Court of Suffolk that in some orderly way the High way between this Towne & Roxbery may be fetled so as may be for y*e* eafe & fafety of Travellers attending to y*e* Gen*r*all Courts order, & that the fame be prefented by Edw. Michelson, Marfhall.

Thomas Longhorne hath liberty to take timb on y*e* comon for making him a Cart:

ordered that if any man be convicted that his dog is vfed to pull of the tayles of any beafts, and do not effectually reftreine Him: He fhall pay for eu*r*ie offence of that kind twenty fhillings in cafe that further complaynt be made

[64] At y*e* requeft of Andrew Belcher y*t* His wood lott may be layd out according to y*e* Towne grant to Him, the Townfmen do order that David ffiske do lay out the fame, at y*e* north end of m*r* pelhams 100 acc*r*, & y*t* y*e* fame be accounted the firft lott.

---

13. 2. 1663.

At a meeting of the Select men, granted Liberty
☞ To y*e* Colledge for pofts & rayles to fence in the yds. & a clapbord tree.

To Jonas clarke timb for a warehoufe.
To Daniel Kempfter, 2. trees for his trade,
To Wm Pattin for a payre wheels.
To Thomas Danforth a clapbord tree.
Richard Cutter fined for felling fome warnut trees on ye Rocks. two fhill.

---

24. 2. 1663.

ordered by the Select men, as followeth.

That Richard ffrancis do drive the weft feild for the yeare enfueing.

That no cattle be kept in a Heard with in any part of our Towne Comons, with out confent of the Townesmen firft had & obteined excepting only fuch as fhall keep y^m on y^r owne proprietyes, with out drift over the comons, on penalty of paying five fhillings pr head for all fuch cattle as are taken from other Townes, & for other cattle that belong to ye Towne, as the Towne fhall hereafter conclude.

[64] 16. 3. 1663.

ordered by ye felect men that what eu^r cattle shall be found trespassing on ye Cow comon, It fhall be lawfull for the heardsman or any other of ye Inhabitants to bring them to pound, & they fhall be allowed for their paynes by the order of ye Townfmen for the time being, & in cafe any fhall prfume to keep them on o^r bounds they fhall pay for eu^rie beaft fo found twelve pence a head, one halfe w^rof shall be to fuch as bring them to pound.

At a meeting of the Select men.
June 29th. 1663.

Jane Bourne making her complaynt to the Select men that fhee can find none in the Towne that is willing to enterteine her to their fervice, & craving their favor that fhee may haue liberty to prvide for Her felfe in some other Towne, with fecurity to fuch as fhall fo enterteine her. The Townfmen do grant her requeft in man^r following vizt So as y^t fhee place her felfe in some Honeft family, & in cafe fhee ftand in need of Supply, or the Towne whether shee fhall resort do fee reason to returne Her againe vpon this Towne, fhee fhall be ftill accepted as one of the poore of this place, & this to be enderftood & taken as bynding to the Towne for one yeare next after the date hereof, any Law, vfage or coftome to ye contrary notwithftanding.

13th (5) 1663.

Ordered by ye feleɕt men of this Towne y^t any perfon finding any cattle damage faifant in his owne land in any cornefeild of this Towne, or other inclofure, fufficiently fenced as the Laws of ye Country & orders of the Towne do require, & impounding them, may require of the own^r of the beaft, Eighten pence for his labor & expence of time for each beaft fo impounded, with full fattisfacɕon for all damages, any Law, vfage, or coftome to y^e Contrary not with ftanding, & the like allowance fhall be made to y^e comon pinders. =

[65]   At a meeting of the Seleɕt men.
20th of July 1663.

Complaynt being made that the woonted paſſage throw m^r Angiers farme is obftruɕted, It is

ordered by the Seleɕt men that Edward Oakes and Thomas fox, do ftake out the High way leading from the Bridge throw m^r pelhams & m^r Angiers farmes, two Rod wide, attending so farr as it may ftand with convenience & ye accomodaɕɕon of paſſeng^{rs} & the improvem^t thereof, the agreem^t of the Comittee that layd out the fame for the vfe of the Country about ten years since, of which comittee the Said Edward Oakes was one imployed by this Towne, and the faid High way fo ftaked out the Surveyo^{rs} are forthwith to repayre, y^t fo all further complaynt of that kind may be p^{r}vented.

Cambridge. 19. 8 : 63.

The Townsemen do order that the Surveyo^r of the High wayes do forthwith repayre to Goodm Woodward & Goodm Robbins, & acquaint them that the High way layd throw his farme is required to be layd open, and that the damage thereby accrueing to them they fhall on all demands fattisfy as the law of the Country for y^t end direɕteth, and in cafe they fhall refuse to confent thereto, the said Surveyo^r is required to make the faid way passable, for both foote, Horfe & carts as the law requireth. — — — — —

At a publick meeting of the Towne
14. 10. 63. //

The Towne agreed that all the comon lands belonging to this Towne towards the falls fhould be divided to ye Inhabitants according to their respective interefts & that thofe Inhabitants on the fouth fide the river adhering ftill to ye Towne in all charges, be considered & allowed a share therein, as the Comittee fhall judge meete. & y^t notice of the Townes intent herein be given to thofe o^r neighbou^{r}s at ye end of ye Towne, with a tender to purchafe it before ye divifsion if they defire it.

[65] Novem^r 9. 1663.

At a publicke meeting of the Towne for choyce of Towne officers: Capt. Daniel Gookin, Thomas Danforth, Edw. Winship

Edw. Oakes, Jno. Cooper, & Jno. ffisenden were chofen felect men.

Gilbert Crackbone, Edward Hall, and Thomas Browne chofen Constables.

Thomas fox. Ri: Robbins & Isacke Williams and ffrancis whitmore, & Samuel ftone Surveyo^{r}s.

The Towne granted to philip Cooke the peece of land that he hath fenced in before his barne, on condiccon that Hee for ever mainteyne the High way good & fufficient in the wett & miry place agt his ground on the north side of the ware Bridge.

At a meeting of the Select men
9. 9. 63.

Granted to francis moore an Afh for his trade

To francis Whitmore timb for his fence, To m^r Angier liberty to take timb on m^r pelhams 100. acc^r for fencing ye High way layd throw his farme.

Capt. Gookin, mʳ ſtedman & Edw. Oakes are appoynted to lay out the High way through Ri: Robbins farme, for the vſe of yᵉ lotts lately layd out.

At a meeting of the ſelect men.
14. 9. 63.

mʳ Edward Jackson & Samuel Hide by the mutuall conſent of yᵉ ſelect men & mʳ Angier are nominated to consider & determine of the allowance to be made mʳ Angier for the passage of yᵉ High way throw his farme.

Granted to yᵉ Coll: liberty for timb: to shingle the rooffe, & to Joseph Scill some for repayring his houſe.

Jno. Addams is fined for non appearance befor‸ the Townſmen according to warneing, three shill: foure pence & to be warned againe by the Conſtable to appeare next towne meeting day.

At a meeting of yᵉ Select men
11. 11. 63.

Jnº Adams appearing before, yᵉ select men, his excuſe for non appearance laſt day is accepted & his fine remitted, & being convicted of falling trees

[66] trees on the Comon contrary to Towne order is fined five shill: & to pay it in to yᵉ Conſta‸ with in a mº. or else to pay double.

Jeremiah Holman hath liberty to fall ſome timber on yᵉ Comon for an adition to his mothers houſe.

Daniel cheavers hath liberty to take timb on yᵉ Comon for a pʳ of Wheels.

Jnº Browne is to be warned to appeare next Towne meeting to Anſwʳ for falling trees on yᵉ Comon.

Jnº ffisenden liberty for timb. for a worke houſe.

Jn:° Cooper liberty for timb for fencing.

Granted to Jn:° Goave liberty to mow the High way by ye frefh pond, & ag^t his owne lott, vntill the Towne fhall otherwife difpofe y^r of;

At a meeting of the felect men,
8th. (12) 1663.

Granted to Wm Pattin & to Jn:° Marritt liberty to take timb on ye Comon for each of them a cart. To Tho: Hall a tree for pofts. Alfo granted to Thomas Hall the vfe of ye patch of meadow called little Rock meadow vntill it be otherwife difpofed off:

Mathew Bridge & David fiske are licenfed to keep a dry heard on ye Comon lands ab^t their farmes, but are prhibited taking of cattle from other townes.

compl^t being made by Thomas Danforth y^t throw a mistake prt of his wood lott lÿng agt Juft: Holdens farme is layd into ye fmall lotts, Lt Edw. Winfhip, & Jn:° Cooper are appoynted by the felect men to veiw the land that is taken away from Him, & to lay him fo much as may be a meet recompence for ye lofs y^t he thereby fufteyneth out of that fwamp that yet remaineth in Comon, adjoyneing to Richard Hafsulls farme.

Whereas Capt Gookin, Thomas Danforth & Richard Jackson, are poffessed of y^r wood lotts lÿng neere to Juft Holdens farme, & by the orriginall grant the Land of the faid lotts yet remaineth

to

[66] to the Towne. The faid Capt Gookin Thomas Danforth, & Richard Jackson are granted the propriety of the Land to be to y^r owne propper vfe afwell as the wood. & the fame to be in lew of their fhares in the Swamps wch ye towne haue agreed to divide.

By the Select men as attests.

Edward Winfhipp
Gilbert Crackbon   Edward Hall Cunftable
John ffifhingdin   John Cooper

At a meeting of ye Select men.
10. 12. 63.

Lt Edw: Winſhip hath liberty for timber to build Him a ſtable Thomas fox for a p^r of Wheels.

Alſo the Deacons & ſelect men did ſettle the Liſt for o^r paſtors maintenance for the yeare enſueing.

14. 1. 1663.
At a meeting of the Select men.

ffrancis Whitmore, Widow Ruſsell, & Ri: Haſsull. Deacon ſtone, Jno Shepard, Thomas fox. Capt Gookin, Robert Parker Richard Jackson, & Ri: ffrances, haue liberty to take fencing ſtuffe on the comon for y^r out fences, orchards & reparaccons of y^r houſes. alſo Lt Winſhip & Joseph Ruſsell.

Jno Shepard haue two trees given Him for his trade.

Roger Willington complained of for falling trees on the comon, and is to be warned to the next Towne meeting.

Willm Bull for falling wood on the comon is to pay eighten pence to the Towne.

Jno Browne appearing and being convicted of falling a tree on the comon contrary to order is fined two shillings and six pence:

Jno Cooper & Thomas Danforth are granted liberty on ye comon for reparaccon of out fences, & Thomas Danforth for an addition to his barne.

Jno Marritt haue liberty for fencing ſtuffe for his out fences,

John Adams, & Benj: Crackbone haue liberty granted them to take timb. on the comon for y^r out fences.

Wm Pattin is abated of his fine five shillings.

[67] At a meeting of the Select men
march 24th: 1663.
4

Robert Stedman & Jno Holmes are appoynted to veiw the necke fences, & to see the Towne orders execcuted referring to that comon feilds.

Thomas fox & Walter Hastings are appoynted to veiw the fences about the weſt feild, & to see the Towne orders excecuted as the law requireth for the preventing of damage therein.

philip Cooke and Wm Dixon are appoynted to veiw the fences about Winottime feild, & to fee the Towne orders excecuted as the law requireth for the preventing of damage therein.

Samuel Hide & Richard Dana are appoynted for veiwers of fences as the law requireth on the South Side the River.

ffrancis Whitmore, & Willm Bull are appoynted to excecute the Towne orders conc^rning Swine on ye west side of the River of Winottime.

Robert Parker is appoynted to look to the Swine on the Comon.

Benjamin Crackbone is appoynted for the Towne.

Richard Woodes is appoynted to excecute the Towne orders concerning Swine on the South Side the River.

At a meeting of the Select men. 9. 2. 1664.

At the motion of Cap:^t Hugh Mason the Townfemen confented that water=Towne pond heard might pafs by the fide of o^r bounds, not p^rjudiceing o^r Cow comon, & Ri: Eccles & Daniel Cheavers are nominated to veiw the place & to make returne of y^r thoughts to y^e Select men.

m^r Cooke hath liberty to take fhoares for his barne & Daniel Cheavers for an afh to make a Cart.

Richard Cutter is fined ten fhillings for carÿng hoop poles from of o^r Comon to Charleftown, & to be admonifhed that he be not taken in the like fault againe. & in cafe he pay it not before the 30th. of octob. next, then Hee fhall pay 20.^s

Richard Cutter is granted 2. trees for his trade, & timbe_∧ to repayre his barne.

Nicholas withe is granted timb. for repayreing his out fences.

Robert Stedman pleading y^t Hee hath ben injured by not haueing his due proporcčon in form^r alotm^ts. the Select men do grant him liberty to mow the grafs in ye High way on ye South Side ye rive^r, for this next yeare as heretofore. & do conceiue it equall this his plaint be confidered in the next divifsion

Br Oakes. & Br fifhenden are nominated to veiw the land defired by mr Angier, & to make report to ye next towne meeting.

The Townfemen do order yt if any man chofen to veiw fences, or excecute ye orders of ye town conc^{r}ning swine, fhall refuse the fame, He fhall pay 20^s fine to ye towne, & some other fhall be appoynted in his ftead.

[67] At a meeting of the Select men. 6. 4. 64.

complaint being made of much damage susteined by reafon of the insufficiency of fences ag^t towne feilds, It is ordered that where any fences are in height lefs then foure foote from the ground, all Such fences fhall be accounted insufficient ag^t Such cattle as do pafs over the fame. — — — —

Richard Robbins being complained of for clofeing vp the ancient comon High way leading from the High way neere m^r Angiers farme to Boston feild, It is ordered that he open a free pafsage throw the Said High way, thwart his farme within Six dayes, on penalty of twenty fhillings fine for eu^{r}ie weeks neglect after y^t ye conftable hath given him notice of this order. —

[68] At a meeting of the Inhabitants of this Towne
November. 14th 1664.

Thomas Chefholme, John Greene, & Isacke Williams were chofen Constables.

Capt Daniel Gookin, Thomas Danforth, Edward Oakes, John fisenden, John Cooper, & Thomas fox were chofen Select men for ordering of the prudentiall affaires of the Towne.

Jno Jackson, Richard Robins, philip Cooke, Samuel stone, and John Shepard, were chofen Surveyo^{r}s of the Highwayes.

Voted, on the affirmative that all the comon lands on the South side the River be divided and that Edward Shepard, Richard Robbins and David fiske, do attend, & effect the Same.

Voted on the affirmative that m^r Elijah Corlet fhall be allowed & payd out of the Towne rate, annually twenty pounds, for so long as Hee continue to be schoolemaster in this place.

9. 11. 1664.

p^rfent
Capt. Gookin.
Th. Danforth.
Th. Chefholme.
Jno. ffisenden.
Th. fox.
Jno. Greene.

At a meeting of the select men.

Liberty granted to sundry for timb. from of the Comons.
To Capt Gookin for 40. rod out fences.
To Jno. Addams for 9: rod out fences.
To Roger Bucke for a clapbord tree.

To Abram Errington for an adiccon to his houfe end & fencing his yards, and ag^t his lott, towards watertowne & a clapbord tree, & groundfill. Alfo he is granted liberty to pafs throw ye high way that leadeth to his lott throw Ri: ffrancis land by ye brickill:

To Thomas fox for fome of his outfences.

To Thomas Danforth, for a frame, over a Cellar ab^t 16: foote square, & for 100: pofts.

p^rfent.
Capt. Gookin,
Th. Danforth,
Th. Chefholme
Jno. fisenden
Th. fox.
Jno. Greene.

At a meeting of the Select men 16. 11. 1664.

After a full hearing of the complaynt made by Benoni Eaton, & Jno. ftedman Junr ag^t Sundry for breach of ye Towne orders, conc^rning cattell & fences referring to ye necke of land, this laft sumer.

The Townfemen ordered, that thofe under written fhall pay them ye s^d Eaton & ftedman damages for neglect of y^r fences.

Mr Joseph Cooke —	twenty fhillings.
Andrew Belcher —	eight fhillings
Walter haftings —	foure fhillings
Goodm ftratton —	foure fhillings
Nicholas Withe	foure fhillings
the whole is —	02 — 00 — 00

[68] And for damages by cattle trespassing in the necke.

Andrew Belcher.	— 0 — 01 — 06
Sam.ˡ Goffe.	— 0 — 04 — 00
Edw. Michelson	— 0 — 04 — 00
Mʳ Corlet,	— 0 — 01 — 00
mʳ Angier	— 0 — 02 — 00
Zach. Hickes	— 0 — 02 — 00
Jnº Shepard.	— 0 — 01 — 00
Capᵗ Gookin	— 0 — 02 — 00
mʳ Mitchell,	— 0 — 02 — 00
mʳ Oakes	— 0 — 02 — 00
mʳ Andrews.	— 0 — 01 — 00
	1. 02. 06

liberty granted to seuʳall for timber,
To Deacon ſtone for a pʳ wheeles.
To Ri: Eccles for fenceing his orchard.
To Jonath. Cane for repayre of his houſes & fences abᵗ ye ſame.
To Jnº watson for a leanto & fence.
To mʳ pelham for fence agᵗ Jnº Taylors

Robert Wilson, Wᵐ Bull, Jnº Adams James Hubbard, ffrancis Moore Junʳ. ffrancis Whitmore, Joseph Russell, Jnº froſt, & Humphry Bredſha, are granted two accʳ, to each of them of Swamp on yᵉ north ſide of Menotteme Riuʳ on condicc̃on that they cleare it for meadow with in five yeares, or else to returne againe to the Towne com̃on as before this grant. alſoe it is hereby expressly declared that this ſhall not be interpʳted as any allowance for their building in the Towne, or the giving them any further right in the com̃on rights of the Towne. —

Jonathan Cane is abated ten ſhillings of his fine on condicc̃on if he pay yᵉ remainder being 20ˢ within foureten dayes next, ſo as to discharge ſo much of Some of yᵉ Towne debts, or else to haue no abatemᵗ. —

[69] At a meeting of the Selećt men
13. 12. 64.

Liberty granted to Sundry for timber from of the com̃on. (i e)
To Jnº Holmes for fenceing his yards

To Thomas Danforth for a payre Wheels
To Thomas Longhorne for fenceing ftuffe.

m^r Edward Jacson, Capt Thomas prentice and Jonathan Hide are nominated a comittee to consider what High wayes are meet to be ftated on that fide, & make returne to the Townefmen.

The Constables are ordered to allow Juft: Holden 10^s towards a woolfe killed partly in water=Towne, & partly in this.

He had ben in y^e towne ab^t a weeke in this Towne. Thomas Gleifon being fent for to appeare before the Select men, was warned to provide Himfelfe, the Townfemen not feeing meet to allow of Him as an Inhabitant in

At a meeting of the Inhabitants &
prprietors of the Towne Comons.
January. 20th 1664.

It is agreed among them that the perfons hereafter named, be a comittee to draw vp the list of the names of such Inhabitants as haue intereft to the said comon lands, as neere as may be according to the order & agreem^t of the thirten men, Recorded in the Towne booke, or according to any other righteous rule as they fhall fee meet, and to proporccon to each Inhabitant aforesaid their juft right for number of acres in the comon lands on the south side the river yet vndivided, alfo in a diftinct list to prporccon, & alott in a way of free gift so much of the s^d lands vnto other Inhabitants of the Towne that haue no intereft with respect to their quality, defert, or ftanding in the Towne, & beareing publique charges, according as the said comittee fhall think equall & juft, and the said comittee haueing drawne vp this lift, as aforesaid to call all the aforesaid Inhabitants together, & prefent the same vnto them for their finall approbaccon, at wch meeting the Major vote; either affirmative or negative fhall be conclusive in this matter.

The comittee are as followeth, viz.

All the Select men of Cambridge. Deacon ftone, Deacon Bridge, m^r Jno Stedman Lt Winfhip
Edw:
[69] Edward Shepard, Richard Robbins, philip Cooke, Jno Shepard, David fiske.

.And if it fhould so appeare, that the Major vote of the aforesaid Inhabitants, do vote in the affirmative & agree to what is to them p^rfented, then their fhall be a prceeding to draw lotts, according to what is agreed; in Such a method & mann^r, as shall be prpofed by the said comittee for the divission of all the comon lands on the South Side the River. And the comittee are defired to dispatch this work, as soone as conveniently they can, the Townfemen to appoynt time & place of meeting.

       Voted in the affirmative the day and yeare above written.

 It is agreed by the major pr^t of the Inhabitants that the defire of francis moore Junio^r, for a peece of Land neere his houfe, for prefervaccon of his houfe & barne from danger of fire, be referred to the aforesaid comittee, for the quantity of land, & the price thereof, to be granted him.

 Vpon defire of Edw. Michelson sen^r in behalfe of his Brother Willm Michelson for a small peece of land to build a houfe vpon, & for a garden; It is referred to the aforesaid comittee to appoynt a place, & quantity for y^t end. If they Judge it convenient, & not p^rjudiciall to the Towne.

 Vpon the request of Jno Bowtell for liberty and ground to fet a barne vpon, neere his houfe in the High way, It is referred to the comittee aforesaid to consider of his motion and if it be not p^rjudicciall to the Towne, to appoynt him a place to fet a Small barne in for his necessary vfe.

 The Commity Confidering of the defire of francis More Junr for a peece of land on the weft side of his houfe in the ox pafture for the preferuation of his houfe and barne from danger of fire they granted him an Aker of land hee paying three pound for the fame which he did by order of the felect men and John Cooper was Chofen by the faide Commity to lay It out which accordingly was done to his Content.

      [70] 14: 12: 1652.

 It is agreed betwen Ri: Jacfon, Tho: Brigham on the one prty and m^r Joseph Cooke, Edward Goffe, and Tho: Danforth on ye other prty, y^t all differences about the fence in the necke of land, apperteyning to Cambridge; fhall be refferred to the hearing and determination of Deacon Monfell and Tho: Perce of Charles Towne, to determine the matter in difference betwen the marfh and upland, each prty to procure one of the faid arbitrators at or before the 10th of march next enfueing.

     Jofeph Cooke   Richard Jackfon
     Edward Goffe   Thomas Brigham
     Thomas Danforth
     ———————8

At a meeting of the Select men. 27. (1). <u>1665</u>

Thomas Longhorne, and Jno Bowtell are appoynted surveyo$_\wedge$ of the fences about the necke of land, and alfo to cleare the feild of all cattell from time to time as need fhall require.

Gilbert Crackbone & Jno Watson in like manner for y^e Weft feild.

Willm Pattin, & Willm Bull, in like mann^r for the feild beyond Winottime river.

Jno Jackson, & Jonathan Hide are appoynted veiwers of fences on the South Side the river, and Richard Woodes to excecute the orders conc^{r}ning Swine on y^t fide.

Jno Goave, Peter Towne, and Joseph Russell are appoynted to excecute the orders conc^{r}ning Swine on the north fide the river.

ordered that all persons y^t do contribute to ye miniftry of this place do vpon the firft second day of may next appeare before the Deacons & felect men to cleare the paym^t of their dues for time paft; or fend in writeing a receite yr of, inder the hand of o^r Pafto^r or Deacons. ☞ and y^t for y^e future, eu^{r}ie one do annually attend the like order, at y^e Same time, y^e place $_\wedge$f meeting to be at y^e meeting houfe. and the time by eight of the clocke in the morning.

And in cafe any be behind, or do not then appeare to cleare the same how they discharged their dues, The Conftables fhall give fuch persons notice to appeare at y^e next meeting of y^e felect men to anfw^r their neglect. and they fhall besides the paym^t of y^r dues fattisfie all the charges that fhall be expended in the levÿng of the Same.

[70] At a meeting of the Select men
Aprill, 12th. 1665.

The Select men of this Towne, being enformed of great damage to ye comons by Sundry persons y^t for their owne private conc^{r}nes do greatly p^{r}judice the publique. do order & appoynt as followeth, vizt.

1. That H:forth no person fhall be allowed any grant of timb from of ye comon for the repayre of any fence vntill the necessity thereof do appeare by the teftimony or informaccon of thofe y^t are appoynted to veiw the fences, or such other as shall be appoynted thereto.

2. That if any on p^{r}tence of leave for falling on ye comons fhall cutt downe any timber tree & let it y^r ly vnimprved for ye end for wch they had leave to fell it, for more y^n 4. months such person shall pay two shillings six pence for eu^{r}ie such tree to the vfe of the Towne. and it fhall alfo be lawfull for any other person that haue an intereft in the comons to fetch away the fame for his owne vfe, as was before by a towne order made octob. 15th 1656. and in cafe any timber fhall ly in the woods after fallen more then six months, it fhall then be lawfull for any perfon circumstanced as above with Towne. priviledges, to take away the Same. any labour y^t may be beftowed thereon not with ftanding. —

3. That Henceforth it fhall not be lawfull for any perfon or perfons what so ever. to convey any bark out of the Towne, that was taken from of any of the comons of this Towne and in cafe any fhall p^{r}fume so to do they fhall forfeit five shillings pr load to the vfe of the Towne. //

[71] *

[71] 1665. At a publ: meeting of the Inhabitants for choyce of Conftables & select men &c there were elected for the yeare enfuing

Conftables { Andrew Belcher, John Watson, & Thomas Parkes.
Thomas fox chofen in lew of Andrew Belcher

Townsmen. Capt Daniel Gookin. Thomas Danforth. Jno Cooper, John fisenden, Thomas fox & m^r Edward Jackson.

Surveyo^{rs} of High wayes. Isacke Sternes. Wm Dixon, Robert Browne. Ri: Dana John Fuller.

---

* This page is blank in original manuscript.

At a meeting of the Select men.
novemb. 20th 1665

The Townsmen do order the constables to make a convenient horfe block at the meeting houfe. & causey to the doore & to get the windowes & roofe repayred by the firft opprtunity. —
 Granted liberty to seu^rall perfons to fell timb on the comon.
 To the Colledge for pofts & rayles.
 To Capt Gookin, for sleepers & orchard fences.
 To Thomas Danforth for pofts & rayles.
 To Edw. Hall for groundsills
 To m^{rs} Dunfter for repayreing her barne.
 To Robt parker for wheels & cart.
 To Wm Dixon for a cart.
 To ye repayreing of Jerah. Bowers houfe.
 To Jno Cooper for building a leantoe.
 To ffrancis Moore for a leanto & porch.
 To Peter Towne for a porch.
 To Wm Pattin to build a leanto, & an end to his barne
 To m^r Cooke groundsills for his barne
 To Deacon ftone for 100 rayles & pofts for y^m for his out fences, & some groundsills.
 To Jno fisenden groundsils for his barne
 To Jno paulfree, two trees for his trade. —

[72]   At a meeting of the Select men
January 8th. 1665.

The highway in the great Swamp lÿng between Ri: Eccles, and Walter Haftings is granted to the said Eccles, the Herbage and grafs thereof. on condiccon that he cleare the brufh of the fame, and that the faid way do remayne free and vninterupted for the vfe of the Towne as any may haue occasion, and this grant is in lew of damage done him by the high way pafsing throw his lott.

Benjamin Whittamore for pulling downe a bench of a feate in the meeting houſe is fined five shillings. and the Constables are to require the Bench of him and fet it vp againe.

Granted liberty to fell timber on the comon

To the { Coll. for mending y^r fences ab^t ye p^rſid^ts garden.
{ Joseph Ruſsell 2: trees for wheels, & for a cart.

Samuell Goffe for 200. rayles.

Elder frost for repayre of his out fences

Walter Haſtings for repayre of his mill & fences.

Thomas Hall one tree for wheels.

The Conſtables are to warne to ye next meeting. Lt Edw. Winship: and Mathew Bridge. to anſw^r for breach of towne orders ab^t wood and timb.

☞ Alſo sundry young men are to be warned to appeare to anſw^r for their liveing from vnder family governm^t.

☞ And sundry persons were ordered their setting in the meeting houſe.

At a meeting of the Select men.

ffebr. 12. 1665.

Liberty granted to sundry Persons for felling of timber on the Towne comon.

☞ To Lt Edward Winſhip for repayreing of his out fences, & for a small table.

To Mathew Bridge for repayre of his out fences.

To ffrancis Moore Senr for a frame of a dwelling houſe.

To Thomas Danforth for the frame of a houſe ab^t 24. foot long.

To Richard Jackson for ground selling of his houſe.

☞ Jacob Coale, Arthur Henbury & John Jackson single men & inmates in this Towne being ſent for before the Select men to give an account of their abode, & orderly cariage, were appoynted at the next meeting of the Select men, in march. to give them Sattisfaccon of their orderly Submiſsion to family goverm^t, or otherwiſe they muſt expect that they the Select men will order their abode as the Law enioynes

☞ [72] Jacob Coale submitted himfelfe to the family governm^t of francis whitmore, who engaged to respond his rates, & orderly cariage dureing his abode their.

To John Marritt liberty to fall timber for ab^t forty Posts & 60 rayles.

To Thomas Longhorne for a ftable he hath liberty to take timb on ye comon

To Andrew Steevenson, & Jonathan Remington liberty for fencing ftuffe for their gardens

To John goave, liberty for to take timb on the comon for a Cow houfe, & a payre of wheeles.

☞ Lt. Edward Winship, being by his owne confession convicted of selling wood out of the Towne, from of his lott, granted him on the South fide the River. The Townsemen do declare, that according to the condicens on wch the said lotts were divided into prpriety, the same is forfeited to the vfe of the Towne.

---

prefent
Capt Daniel Gookin
m^r Edward Jackson
John Cooper
John fifenden
Thomas fox

At a meeting of the Select men the 26th of march. 1666.

William Clemance Junr is ordered to fill vp the Sawpitt that he hath digged in the high way neere his land, before the next Town meeting day. the second munday in the next m^o on penalty of 20^s.

James Prentice & Thomas Prentice Junr are appoynted to excecute the Towne orders conc^{r}ning fences and swine, on that part of the Towne.

m^r Jno Stedman, & Thomas Longhorne are appoynted to see the fences about the necke of land made vp according to Towne order.

Jno Goave & Peter Towne are appoynted to cleare the necke of all cattle according to Towne order, & to looke to the yoaking & ringing of Swine in the Towne.

Gilbert Crackbone & John Gibson are appoynted to see the fences about the weft feild, made vp according to Towne order, and are alfo to cleare the feild of all cattle.

Alfo the Townfmen do order, that all places with in the compafs of any of the corne feilds, that are fenced in for Pastures, thofe that are appoynted to veiw the out fences fhall see that the fences about the fame be sufficient to secure the feild from damage. & in cafe of defect, their turneing of cattle in to such paftures fhall be accounted as though they turned them into ye comon feild, & fhall be prceeded ag^t accordingly.

[73] Lt Edward Winship, & John Addams, are appoynted to veiw the fences about Winottime feild, & William Bull to cleare the cattle out of the feild, & to look to the Swine on that part of the Towne

Prefent
Capt Daniel Gookin.
Thomas Danforth.
John fishenden.
John Cooper.
John Watson.
Thomas fox.

At a meeting of the Select men, Aprill. 9th 1666.

Nathaniel Boman appearing before the Select men confessed that this laft winter, he had one tree, a great white oake, the top affording him two cord and a halfe of wood, from of our comon, neere to his fathers houfe. And being charged with falling thirten more trees, the yeare before, he said he would neither confesse nor deny it, but confessed y^t the fame yeare he fold and deliu^{r}d two load of bark to Capt mason.

Samuel Reyner is appoynted Surveyo^r of the woods & comons on that quarter where he liveth, and to enforme the Select men from time to time, as he fhall find any stroy to be done thereon.

Jonathan Cane confesseth that he did fall on the comons 4. trees, for ☞ fencing stuffe, according to liberty granted him by the Townfmen. but hath neglected to improve the same.

Richard Cutter hath liberty for timber on the comon for repayreing his out fences.

Thomas Danforth hath liberty for timber on the comons to build him a Porch to his houfe.

m^r Joseph Cooke hath liberty for timber on the Comons to build him a dwelling houfe.

Robert Wilson hath liberty to take timber on the comon for repayreing his out fences.

m^r Elijah Corlet haue liberty to take timber on the comon for repayre of his out fences.

Lt Edw. Winship hath liberty granted him to take timber on the comon for a payre wheeles.

Ordered by the Select men, that the Towne order made 16th 3th m.º 1663. for the secureing of our Cow comons from damage by cattle that go at liberty, fhall be excecuted, according to the intent thereof.

20. 2. 1666. m^r Joseph Cooke & Daneel Cheaver, together with Thomas Peirce sen^r, John fowle of Charlstowne, went the line between the Townes and agreed on the Antient bounds.

Perambulation with Charlestown and Woburn

Also Mathew Johnson & James Convars Joyned wth them in like mann^r for rivifeing the bounds between this Towne & Woburne.

[73] At a meeting of the Select men, may the 14th 1666.

prefent.
Capt Gookin.
m^r Jackson.
John fifenden
Thomas fox.
John Watson.
Th: Danforth.

Robert Browne and Thomas White are appoynted to excecute the orders of the Towne conc^{r}neing Swine.

John fifenden, David fiske, & Walter Haftings are appoynted together with the owners of the Small farmes adjacent to o^r Towne comons to veiw settle & new marke all their bounds for the preventing of damage to the intereft of any, by the neglect thereof; the charges y^{r}of to be sattisfied the one halfe by the Towne and th' other halfe by the proprieto^{rs} of the farmes.

liberty is granted to Willim Dixon to fell some timb. on the comon for a leantoe, & a clapbord tree

To Jno Watson a tree for Pales and to repayre his fences.

At a meeting of the Inhabitants
the 12th of november, 1666.

m^r William Manning, m^r Samuel Andrew, & James Trowbridge, were chofen Constables for the yeare enfueing.

Capt Gookin, Thomas Danforth, Edw: Oakes. Jno fiffenden, Jno Cooper, & Thomas Fox, were chofen Select men, for the yeare enfueing.

Gilbert Crackbone, Zach. Hicks, Jno fuller Richard Woods, & Isacke Sterns, were chofen surveyo^{rs} of highwayes.

Prefent.
Thomas Danforth
m^r Andrews
m^r Manning
Jno Cooper
Jno fissenden
Thomas Fox.

At a meeting of the Select men.
12th of novemb. 1666.

On Complaynt of Richard Dana, Elder Champny is ordered to pay him 3^s 6^d & the widow Woodward, alfo to pay him 3^s 6^d for y^r defect in high way worke, w^n orderly warned Philip Cooke hath liberty for 100 railes. Jno Cooper, Edw. Hall, Ri: Jackson. william Bordman, Abram Errington, Jno Watson, Robt Parker, Walter Haftings haue all of y^m licenfe to fell timber on the comons for fencing stuffe, & building.

[74] Jno Watson is complayned ag^t for falling Seaven trees on the comon lefs then a foote diameter.

Nathaniel Bowman is to be fent for to refpond his falling timber on o^r Comons.

Willm Dixon motioned that in letting the wares, care might be taken to secure Winottimes Corne feilds. — —

☞ Thomas Fox is ordered to looke to the youth in time of Publ. worfhip vntill the next monthly meeting, & to inform agt such as he find disorderly.

☞ The Conftables are ordered to repayre the glafs aboute the meeting houfe, & to get the pinning mended.

At a Towne meeting. decemb. 10th 1666.

Daniel Cheavers is granted timber for a barne.
Wm Pattin, timber for a Cow houfe, & halfe a 100. of rayles.
Wm Barratt timber for a barne.
Mrs Dunster timber for a Cow houfe.
Jeremiah Holman Timber for a payre wheels. 2. trees. & one tree for Pales.
Robert Stedman timber for fencing.
John Bowtell timber for a barne.
The Townsmen considering the need that will be of timber for the maintenance of the Bridge do order that no more oaken timber be fallen on that part of the 100. acc^{r}s wch is reserved still in comon for the vfe of the Towne. on penalty of ten shillings for every tree.

At a meeting of the Select men.
Jan. 14th 1666.

m^r Stedman, m^r Andrew. Tho. fox, & Th. Danforth or any two of them are appoynted to lay out vnto Jn:º Benjamin ten acres of meadow to him yet resting in the comon meadowes

Liberty is granted for falling timber on the comon.
To Humph: Bredsha for repayreing his houfe.
To Thomas Danforth for a slead.
To Roger Bucke for finishing his houfe, & trade.
To George Willowes for fencing.
To John Palfrey two trees for his trade
To Nath. Hancocke for groundsils, & clapbords.
To Daniel Andrews fencing stuffe.
To Jn:º Marritt for fencing.
To Peter Towne two trees for his trade.
To
[74]   To Jonathan Remington two trees for his trade.
To Samuel Goffe fencing stuffe.

m^r Angier is granted three acres of Swamp Land, adjoyneing to the lots layd out on the west Side winottime river. — —

At a meeting of the Select men,
ffebr. 11th. 1666.

Cap:^t mason, & Ens: Shearman, are nominated by the mutuall consent of Elder Wiswall, and the neighbours there, to veiw the necefsity of a highway through the Elders land, to the lands beyond towards Dedham, and Edw: oakes and James Trowbridge are defired to accompany them.

Mathew Bridge is granted liberty to take timb from of the comon, for building an end to his barne, & a leanto, & fencing stuffe for his orchard. with reference to the Priviledge y^t belong to his fathers houfe which he hath now Pulled downe.

To Gilbert Crackbone liberty for timber for fellowes for wheels.

Nicholas Withe complayneing that he is injured by not haueing his full due granted him on the South Side the river neere Boston line, by reason y^t a part of the Townes grant was layd into the prpriety of Richard Parkes.

for sattisfacc̃on whereof, the Towne do grant him the propriety of the land wch is his wood lott, lÿng within the Swamp on the west Side of winottime river.

Nicholas withe appearing before the Select men acknowledged that he stood ingaged to make a parcell of fence ag^t his owne land, ab^t six rod more or lefs, for wch he had receiued full sattisfacc̃on for the making & mainteyneing of y^e fame forever. the above said fence form^{r}ly apperteyneing to Gilbert Crackbone.

At a meeting of the Select men March 11th 166$\frac{8}{7}$

liberty granted for timber on the com̃ons.

To Nicholas Withe a tree for Posts.

To John Greene for fencing his orchards.

To Thomas Longhorne for 100 Rayles.

Nathaniel Bowman, being convicted of tranfgrefsing the orders of the Towne, by falling timber on the com̃ons is fined thirty shillings, and to be im̃ediately levyed by the Constables. —

[75] John Swann hath liberty granted him for timber from of the com̃on for repayreing his barne

Thomas fox for mending his fences.

m^r Charles Chauncey for his fences.

Sister Cane for groundselling her houfe. and fencing of her yards.

Thomas Danforth for a payre wheels.

Richard Jackson Timber for repayreing an out houfe.

John Marritt Timber for ringing a p^r wheels.

Daniel Cheavers for his yards.

Thomas Andrews for his out fences.

Lt Winship & Wm Pattin are appoynted Surveyo^{rs} of ye fences about winottime feild.

Richard Cutter, & John frost to oversee the Swine there.

John Watson, & Walter Haftings, are Surveyors of the fences about west feild.

m^r Joseph Cooke & Thomas Longhorne are Surveyo^{rs} of the necke fence, and to drive the feild.

Daniel Cheavers is overseer for the excecuting the orders about Swine, for the whole comon on the north side the river.

At a meeting of the Inhabitants of the Towne.
May. 27. 1667.

It was voted by the Towne, that the Proprietors of the ware houfe at the water fide, or any of them that fhall repayre & keep vp the wharfe that is ag^t the ware houfe, fhall haue the wharfe & ground for their owne propriety.

It was alfo agreed vpon by the Towne that there should be a stone Wall made between Goodm Hafsull & Rockie meadow for the fecurity of the Cow comon, and that the charge thereof fhould be levyed vpon the Cow comons, and is left in the Townfmens hands to contrive and effect the accomplifhm^t thereof.

[75] At a meeting of the Inhabitants of this Towne
the 11th of novemb. 1667.

There were chofen for offic^{rs} of the Towne for the yeare enfueing, thefe following Persons.

for Constables, m^r Joseph Cooke, Willm Dixon & Gregory Cooke.

for Selectmen. Capt Daniel Gookin. Thomas Danforth, Edward oakes, John Cooper. Willm manning, & Thomas fox.

Surveyours of highwayes — for Surveyours of the highwayes, John Ward Peter Towne, Willm Pattin, Saml Stone, and Richard Robbins.

At a meeting of the Select men, January 13th 1667.

There is liberty granted for to fall timber on the comon.

To m^r Stedman, ffrancis Moore Senr Thomas fox. John Cooper. Deacon Stone. Wm Manning, Samuel Andrews, Richard Eccles, Jno Marritt, Jno Swan, Jno Goave, Humphry Bredsha, Roger Bucke, Ri:

Jackson, Joseph Ruſsell. Widow fiſenden, Ri: Haſsull, L:t Winship, W:m Dixon for the repayre of their out fences, garden fences, & buildings & for wheels, as they respectively do need.

Granted to Deacon Stone, a Hollow tree on the comon. To L:t Winship a Walnutt tree for the feres. To Jn:o Haſtings liberty to fell timber for his Barke mill. To Jn:o Marritt, liberty to fall a tree for a Cider preſs.

At a meeting of the Select men, feb:r: 1667.

The Townſemen do order that the priſes of corne for payment of the Towne rate, ſhall be the same with the Country rate for this yeare.

[76] At a gen:rall meeting of the Inhabitants
of this Towne, January 20:th 1667.

The Question conc:rning the Diviſion of the wood on the Rocks, being againe debated, the Towne do gen:rally agree that it is for the Publicke good to divide it into propriety. On such cautions & in such a way, as may be a furtherance to the ends intended, w:ch is to be determined by following votes.

vizt. That none Sell any wood or timber out of the Towne, on penalty of forfeiting their lotts, backe againe to the Towne.

☞ And that none ſhall alienate the propriety of his wood lott from his houſe right to which it is firſt granted, with out the conſent of the Select men for the time being.

Theſe were voted on the affirmative the Day & yeare above written.

Some of the Inhabitants, alledging that it was not a full meeting of thoſe conc:rned, It was agreed to meet againe the 3:th of the twelfe month, to consider further of theſe above written propoſals. & put an iſsue thereto.

At a meeting of the Inhabitants of this Towne,
febr. 3:th 1667.

It is againe agreed by the gen:rall vote of the Inhabitants, that the vote that was written and voted in the affirmative at laſt Towne meeting, touching the divideing the comon woods & timber with in the Cow comon beyond winotteme shall be now confirmed.

Alſo it is agred that the Select men, Deacons. and Jonas Clarke, ffrancis Moore Jun.ʳ with John Shepard ſhall be a com̄ittee to order the Survey of it, and the most convenient way how it may be divided and to prepare lotts, to be drawne for it. according to the rules of Justice.

At a meeting of the Select men,
march. 9ᵗʰ. 166 7/8

Granted to Andrew Belcher some timber for repayreing of the necke fence.

Gilbert Crackbone hath liberty for two groundſils

To John Shepard two trees for his trade.

Thomas Hall 2. groundsils for a barne.

[76] At a meeting of the Select men.
13. 2. 166 7/8.

Thomas Longhorne, & Robert Browne are appoynted to veiw the fences about the necke of land for the yeare enſueing. and to cleare the feild of all cattell.

for the west feild, ffrancis Moore Junʳ and Gilbert Crackbone. and Jeremiah Holman to cleare the cattell out of yᵗ feild,

for Winottime feild, ffrancis Whitmore & Joseph Ruſsell. and they to cleare yᵗ feild of all cattell.

for Hogreeves Robert Parker, Peter Towne, Richard Woods, & James Prentice.

for surveyoʳˢ of fences, on the South ſide the River, Jonathan Hide & Jnº Ward

for Hogreeves beyond winottime, Humphry Bredsha.

At a meeting of the Select men.
Granted vnto John Taylor five Trees on the com̄on for his trade.

22ᵗʰ of Aprill, 1668.

The Select men of this Towne being deſirous yet further to experience all possible means for the preservation of the wood & timber yet growing on o^r comons although former endeavours haue not been effectuall to y^t end. Do therefore order that after the Publication hereof no person whatsoever shall fall any tree or trees on any part of the comons of this Towne vntill the Said tree or trees haue been Set out by the comon Wood reeves, on penalty of payng five shillings for every tree, fallen contrary to this order, And for allowance to the Wood reeves for their paynes. they shall pay either foure pence an houre, or two pence a tree at the choyce of the wood reeves.

Also for the further encou^{r}agem^t of the woodreeves to dilligence and faithfulnes in the discharge of their trust. they shall be allowed th' one halfe of all the fines that shall be levyed for the breach of this or any former orders that are made for the preservation of the towne comons. Also the wood reeves shall not be injoyned to attend any mans desire for the excecuccon of the aboves^d order, Save only vpon the third day of eu^{r}ie weeke, haueing at least two dayes notice before hand from thofe that defire to haue them attend the s^d worke.

John

[77] John Paulfere is granted two trees for his trade.

Deacon Cooper is granted timber for a payre of wheels.

At a meeting of ye Select men.

21. 7. 68.

Deacon Jno Cooper is appoynted to fee a sufficient pound errected ag^t fpring next & is to take the timber on ye comon.

m^r Cooke hath liberty for fencing ftuffe for his orchard.

Tho: Danforth hath liberty to take timber to make a hovell for his sheep.

Wm Manning hath liberty granted to take timbr for repayring his houfe.

m^r Cooke and Deacon Cooper are appoynted to settle ye necke fence.

At a meeting of the Select men.
12. 8. 1668.

m^r Richard Champney appearing before the Townfmen, declared that he had refigned vp all his intereft in the houfe right that apprteyned to Wm Wodsworth houfelott vnto his sonne in law Jno Haftings, to haue & to hold the fame to him his heyres & afsigns for ever.

Granted to Wm Patten timber from of ye comon to repayre his old houfe at towne.

Granted to Steeven Day libertye for timber to build him a leanto to his dwelling houfe.

Abraham Holman appearing before the Select men, declared that in cafe any would make vp his mothers prt of fence ag^t ye weft feild, being ab^t 18 poles soas might be sufficient & secure, he would Ingage himfelfe to pay thofe that were appoynted by the Townfmen to overfee thofe fences.

Joseph Holmes appearing before the Townfmen, is ordered to pay Gilbert Crackbone & ffr. Moore, for repayreing six rod of his prt of fence in weft feild twelve shillings.

The choyce of Townfmen was omitted to be entred, & is in ye following pages.

[77]   At a meeting of the Select men. 14. 10. 68.

Lt Edward Winship and Richard Hafsull are defired to fet out to Mathew Bridge so many trees out of the Coll: lot of wood as the Prefidt had out of his, & in cafe there be not enough there to supply to make vp what is wanting out of the comon.

Mathew Bridge is granted timber from of the comon for repayreing his houfing at the farme, inlew of the houfe he hath taken downe at Towne.

M^{irs} Dunster is granted liberty of timber on ye comon to repayre the houfe wherein shee live.

for ifsueing the difference betweene thofe whofe cattell went in Winottime heard, & Lt Winship, ye s^d L^t is ordered to pay for all his cattell (excepting 3 : calves) in prporccon with others.

John Goave is granted liberty for timber to fence his yards, and two for his trade.

Richard Eccles is granted two trees for Posts for his orchard

Richard Jackson is granted two trees for clapbords.

Richard Haſsull is granted liberty for to take timber on the comon, to build an end of a barne.

Lt Winship is granted liberty for timber to make a leanto, & to make a p^r wheels, & to mend another payre.

ffrancis Whitmore is granted liberty for a clapbord tree.

It is ordered by the Select men, that Henceforth no perſon whatsoever shall fall any tree, on any highway within the bounds of this Towne, on Penalty of ten shillings, for every tree so fallen, with out speciall licenſe firſt had & obteined from ye Select men of the Towne, for the time then being.

At a meeting of the Select men. 21. 10. 1668.

There is granted liberty to sundry persons to fall timber on the comon as followeth, i e.

To Richard Cutter for a p^r of Cart wheels.

To Thomas fox, for a cart body.

To Deacon Stone for mending his out fences.

To Elder frost for repayreing his fences.

Richard Cutter, appearing before the Select men and being convicted of falling 4. trees on the comon, contrary to ye Town order made in Aprill laſt, is fined ten shillings.

Ephraim Winship appearing before the Select men, and being convicted of falling foure trees on the comon contrary to ye Towne order made in Aprill laſt. is fined ten ſhillings.

January 11th 1668.

At a meeting of the Select men.

Richard Whitney being accuſed of falling sundry trees on the High way leading from Jno Jacksons to Jno Wards, and by his owne confession convicted of falling 4: trees, & 2. dead bodyes, is fined 20^s Twenty shillings.

Jn.º Watson being convicted of falling firewood on yᵉ comon, contrary to order, by his owne confession three loads, is fined ten shillings.

Wᵐ Dixon being convicted of falling firewood on yᵉ comon contrary to Towne order is fined for two load six shillings and eight pence.

[78] There is liberty granted to Jn.º watson to fall timber on the comon to repayre his fences, according as the Surveyoʳˢ shall Judge he ſtand in preſent need of, and for a cart and wheels.

Reſolved vpon the Queſtion that it belongs to yᵉ constable to repayre the great Bridge, over charles River, at the publcke charge of the Towne. —

Granted vnto Wᵐ Bull liberty to mow the graſs on the meadow called cheavers meadow, towards Concord bounds.

There is liberty granted for falling timber on the comon, as followeth. vizt.

To Capᵗ Gookin, thomas Danforth, mʳ Corlet, & thomas fox for repayreing their out fences.

To Richard Jackson ſo much fencing ſtuffe as the surveyoʳˢ shall make return he stand in prt need of.

Jn.º Addams, Jn.º Swann, & Jn.º Paulfere, are to be warned to the next meeting to anſwʳ for falling trees on the comon, contrary to towne order.

Richard Cutter. and Ephraim Winship are abated four shillings apeece of thoſe fines impoſed on yᵐ at yᵉ laſt Towne meeting.

The Towne being called together this day, among other things it was prpoſed to them, that the farme on the South ſide of the river, form'ly belonging to mʳ Andrews dec͞cd, now apperteyneing to mʳ thomas Danforth was prejudiced by lotts granted to some of yᵉ Inhabitants of Cambridge, and about twenty acres thereof taken away thereby. The Towne conſidered of the matter, and it was acknowledged that old mʳ Andrews had fifty acres of land granted to him sundry years since, by way of addition to the old farme that he had bought of one mʳ Girling. and to find out the right it was conceiued that the beſt expedient is to vſe the beſt means that may bee, to get the knowledge of yᵉ old line of the farme before the adition was made, & yᵗ being done, then to procure a sufficient surveyoʳ to lay out the fifty acres adjoyneing to it, and for the effecting whereof the Select men have chosen Deacon Stone, Lt Winship, Edw. Oakes, & ffrancis Moore Junr a comittee to informe themselves the best they can about the old line of the farme and to prcure an able surveyo^r to lay out the fifty acres vpon the head of it touching upon Boston line, and then to make report to the Townsmen what they haue done in the premises, and what damage the said farme doth susteine by any grant of the Towne to particular persons.

m^r John flint is nominated to be the Surveyo^r.

[78] At a meeting of the Selectmen
febr. 8th 1668.

Samuel Hide appearing before the Select men to answ^r for falling trees on the highway ag^t his land pleaded that on exchange of land he condicconed to referve the timber & wood to himfelfe, and was promifed the fame, by John Jackson, Jno Ward & Jno Parker.

Samuel Hide complaynes ag^t m^r Jackson for leaving out of his Invoyce in the Country rate 15 : acc^r meadow. 15. acc.^r Englifh grafs. & 120 acc.^r of inclofed Pasture.

Ditto. ag^t Jno Jackson for leaveing, 10 acc.^r of meadow out of his Invoyce and an ox.

Liberty is granted to fall timber on ye Comon.

To John Watson, for 50. rayles. & 28. pofts.
To Wm Dixon for his orchard fence.
To Tho: Danforth for a ftable.
To m^r Angier for his houfe & fences.
To Jno Swan for his orchard, wheels & Cart.
To Jonath: Remington for his orchard fence.
To Samuel Haftings for his barne.
To Thomas Hall for his orchard fence.
To John Haftings for his orchard fence.
To Humph. Bredfha for a garden fence.
To Jno Marrett for a leanto & orchard fence.
To Ri: Cutter for his out fence.
To Daniel Cheaver, a groundfell & for his fences.

John Swan being convicted of falling seaven trees contrary to Towne order is fined thirty-five shillings, according to Towne order, Apr. 22, 1668.

John Paulfere being convicted of falling one tree contrary to Towne order is fined five shillings.

ordered that ye Constables warne the Inhabitants to provide thems: of ladders within 2: months on penalty of paÿng according to ye Towne order referring thereto.

for Katechiseing the youth of this Towne.

Elder Champney. m^r Oakes are appoynted for those familyes on ye South side the Bridge.

Elder Wiswall, m^r Jackson, & John Jackson for those at the new church.

Deacon Stone & Deacon chesholme for those at the remote farmes.

Lt Winship, Wm Dixon & ffr: Whitmore for those on West Side winottine.

[79] Deacon Stone, & Deacon Cooper for those familyes on the west side the comon. & for Watertowne Lane, as farr towards ye Town as Samuel Hastings.

thomas Danforth, & thos ffox for those familyes on the East side the Comon.

Richard Jackson, & m^r Stedman for those familyes on ye West side of ye Towne.

Capt Gookin & Elder frost, for those familyes on ye East side of ye Comon Water streete leading from the meeting house to ye Waterside being the particcon.

Entry of choyce of Selectmen. omitted at ye time of choyce,

At a meeting of the Inhabitants

Novemb. 8th — 1668.

Chosen for the Publique offic^{rs} of the Towne for the yeare ensueing, as followeth.

for Constables. ffra: Whitmore, Peter Towne, & John Spring.

for Select men. Capt Daniel Gookin, Thomas Danforth, Edward Oakes, John Cooper, Thomas fox, & Willm Manning,

for Surveyo^{rs} of high wayes. Wm Barratt, Humphry Bredsha, Isacke Sternes.

for the South fide the River, Surveyo^{rs} are Thomas Hamond Junr and Thomas Browne.

15. 12. 1668.
At a meeting of the Select men.

Samuel Goffe, & Thomas Longhorne are appoynted overfeers of the fences about the necke for this following yeare,

And John ftedman Junr is to drive the necke

Gilbert Crackbone, Jno Watson, & ffr. Moore Junr are appoynted over Seers of the fences ab^t weft feild & Jeremiah Holman to drive it for this following yeare.

Willm Dixon, & Jno Addams, are appoynted overseers of the fences ab^t Winottime feild, & Wm Row to drive it for

[79] this following yeare.

Robert Parker, Robert Browne, Joseph Rufsell and Richard Woods are chofen hogreeves for this following yeare, william bull is Chofen to Joine with Jofeph Rufsell to looke after the fwine over menotime for this prefent yeere

Thomas Andrews is granted liberty to take timber on the comon for to build an end to his dwelling houfe.

Peter Towne, is granted 2: trees on the comon for his trade, & a Walnutt for hoopes.

At a meeting of the Select men.
26. 1. 1669.

John Watson, Walter Haftings, & Daniel cheaver are appoynted to Joyne with thofe y^t are deputed by Charlstowne to rune the bounds between them and o^r Towne. And they are alfo at ye same time to rune the bounds between o^r Towne & Woburne.

m^r Cooke is appoynted to Joyne with thofe y^t are the overseers of the fences about the necke of land.

John Goave is appoynted to afsist John Stedman in driveing the necke.

Mathew Bridge & Samuel Stone are appoynted to Joyne with such as shall be deputed by Concord to rune the bounds between them & vs.

Deacon John Cooper is nominated Clark for the select men for this following yeare.

finis

Tempore omnia mutantur.

at a meeting of the select men
12 (2) 1669

liberty granted to feuerall to fell timber on the Common ——
To Captaine Gookins a ground fill and fleepers for a flooure ——
to daniell Cheauer for an addition to his houfe.
to widdow beale for her land and gardin
to walter haftins a 150 railes and pofts for his fence ——
Vmphry bradfheere being Convicted for felling 6 trees Contrary to the towne order is fined fifteene fhillings.

[80] Nathaniell patin Convicted for felling A lode of ded woode is fined fiue fhillings

March th 30 1669

A Generall meeting of the towne to Confider about making fatiffaction for the land taken away by the fmall lots from m^r thomas Danforths farme on the fouth fide of the River the towne made Choyfe by voyte of m^r John ftedman deacon ftone lewetenant winfhip and francis More Junr aded to the felect men to bee a Committy to make fatiffaction for the faide land to m^r danforth of fome of the Common lands excepting thofe lands that the wood of them is allredy layed out ——

Granted to Roger buck this preafent yeere to mow the medow by the fwamp neere littill fpye ponde

At A meeting of the felect men   Aprill the 19 1669

Richard haffell Daniell Cheauer and thomas White are Appointed to driue the Cow Common and to take of the delinquints according to the towne order being three pence pr hed

Andrew fteuenfon is Appointed by the felect men to be the fealer of leather : ——

May th 10 1669

liberty granted to Richard Cutter to fell twoo Clapbord trees for the Repayering of his dwelling houfe. ———

10 (3) 1669.

at A meetting of the felect men

It is ordered by the felectmen that if any horfe be founde in the Corne fields and the owners haue notice giuen them that theare they are and they doe not forthwith fetch them out the Common driuer or any other that is trefpafed thearby may hire as many as hee fee meete to fetch them out and the owner fhall pay all the Chargis thearof ———

[80] and in Cafe any horfe bee knowne to breake A fence that is fufifhent fuch A horfe fhall bee Crofe languled or not fufered to goe againeft the Corne feild fence on penalty of paying fiue fhilling a time for euery time they are taken in any of the Corne feilds befides all damage to the party trefpafed thear by ———

the felect men taking into Confideration upon the Comeplaint of fome of the Idolnes and carlefnes of fundery perfons in the time of publicke worfhipe upon the faboth day, by keeping with out the meeting houfe, and theare vnprofitably fpending theare time, whearby Gods name is difhonered: they doe Order, for the time being, that the Cunftable fhall fet Awarde of one man during the time of publicke worfhip, one in the fore noone, and another in the afternoone, to looke unto fuch perfons that they doe attende vpon the publicke worfhip of god; that gods name and worfhip be not neglected, nor profaned by the evill mifcarage of futch perfons.

15 (4) 1669

liberty granted to Nathanill pattin to fell fome timber to repayer his out fences: ———

5 (5) 1669

At A publicke meeting of the Inhabitants of the towne to Confider of fupply for the miniftry, ———

1 It was voted on the firmative that the felect men and deacons and Richard Jackson and m^r ftedman and m^r Angier are appointed A Commity to take preafent Care to purchas or build A Conuenient houfe for the Entertainment of the Minifter that the lord may pleafe to fende vs, to make vp the breach that his afflicting prouidence hath made in this place; and that the Charge theareof be leuied on the Inhabitants as is Vfuall in proportioning the maintinains to the miniftry

<small>A ministry house</small>

the fetelling of the houfe on the minifter, or ftating it on the miniftry, is left to further Confideration as the matter may require ——

2 that Care be taken for prouifion of payment of the pafage of m^r Oakes family If It pleafe the lord to fende him to vs, and A leuy for that purpofe be made vpon the Inhabitans to the vallew of fixty pounds which euery one is to prouide in money that it may be in a redines on demand. Voted on the firmatiue

[81] July (5) 1669

3 It was voted on the firmatiue that the Vfuall proportion payed to the minifter of this place be payed into the Deacons as formerly: and that out thearof thofe that labour among vs; and Miftris Mitchell haue A competence allowed her, as the Commity aboue named fhall appointe; and the Remainder if any, be to goe towards the difburfment as is aboue exprefed for a houfe

<small>Mrs Mitchell</small>

Auguft th 9 1669

At a meeting of the felect men ————

liberty granted to Edward hall to fell fome timber for A leantoe and for the body of A Cart ————

September th 9 1669

Church farm sold for building a (house of public worship) Parsonage houſe

At a Church meeting to conſider about the felling of the Churchis farme at bilrica for the building of houſe for the miniſtry It was Voited on the firmatiue, that the ſayde farme ſhould be ſould, and Improuement made of It, for the building of A houſe for the Miniſtry ———

ſebtember (27) 1669

At A meeting of the Commity Choſen for to take Care for the building of A houſe for the Miniſtry the ſayde Commity agreed with m^r Thomas danforth to Cary one the ſame — —

---

4 (8) 1669

at A meeting of the ſelect men m^r william Maning and petter Towne was appointed to agree with workmen to take downe the ſcholehouſe, and ſet It vp againe; and to Cary the ſtones in the ſeller to the place wheare the houſe for the miniſtry Is to be built — —

October th 11 1669.

At a meeting of the ſelect men
liberty granted to thomas Cheſholme to fell ſome timber for a leantoe and to John holmes timber for a leantoe and to francis whitmore for a leantoe

27 (8) 1669

At A meeting of the ſelect men granted to Goodman Coller two Clapbord trees for to Couer his houſe with all ———

th 1 (9) 1669

At A towne meeting all the Inhabitance being warned — —
_{when church}

It was Concluded by a Vote that the Comittee Namly the felect
men then in being, and the deacons, and m^r John ftedman
Richard Jackfon, and m^r Edmond Angier that weare
appointed to make Accomodation for the miniftry, are
appointed to giue and figne a deede of fale of the Churchis
farme at fhawfhin, in the name of the Church and the towne

<small>Committee chose to sell shawshin farme</small>

November th 8 1669

at A Generall towne meeting for the Choyfe of Cunftabls felect men and furueyors ———

for Cunftabls { walter haftins
Richard Ecels
John fuller

for felect men { Captaine Gookin
m^r thomas danforth
m^r John ftedman
william Maning
thomas fox
John Cooper

furueyors of highwayes   Samuell Gofe
John Addams
daniell bacon
Dauid fifke

---

8 (9) 1669

At A meeting of the felect men liberty granted to Mathew bregd fix trees for building timber to make an adifhon to his dwelling houfe at his farme

---

Allowed to m^r Corlet out of the towne Rate fourty fhillings for the Repayering of his houfe, wheare hee keepe fchoole, becaufe the fchoole houfe is to bee taken downe.

---

13 (10) 1669

at A meeting of the feleƈt men m^r thomas danforth and walter haftins weare appointed to goe and fee what damage was done by the owners of goodman fhawes farme to our lands adioing thearto and make Report to the towns men theare of ─────────────────

[82]   th 13 of defember. 1669

at a meetting of the feleƈt men libertie granted to feauerall to fell timber to Andrew fteuenfon for to build a barne to Jonathan Remington for an ende to his houfe to m^r ftedman for a payre of wheeles to deacon ftone to fence his yarde and A tree for pales to John Goue fence for his land in the weft feild

to Elder froft timber for out fence
to Richard Jackfon timber for A Cart
to John Marrit timber for A leanto

---

20 (10) 1669

ministers house

at A meeting of the Commity appointed to take Care for a houfe for the Miniftry, It was agreed vpon by the fayde Commity, and A Rate was made according to the voyte of the towne, of which fayde Rate, A part of It to be gathered by the deacons for the fuply of m^r Chancy, and fuch as labour among us in preaching the word, and a part of It to Miftris Mitchell according to the fume ordered by the fayde Commity to the deacons which sayd fume was fifty pound to m^r Chancy and 30 lods of wood, and what fhould be Conuenient to any other that weare helpfull among vs; and thirty pounds to Miftris Mitchell; and the Remainder of the fayde Rate with an adifhon of halfe a yeere more to be aded and forthwith to be gathered by the Counftables, and

Mr Chauncy

£50.

difpofed of towards the building of the houfe by thofe Imployed for the Carieng on of the worke

---

27 (10) 1669

---

at A metting of the felect men liberty was granted to m^r thomas danforth to fell timber for to build A barne at his farme wheare Richard hafell did fume times liue

---

defember th 10 1669

at A meeting of the felectmen liberty granted to petter towne to fell two timber trees for his trade and liberty granted to Richard Cutter to fell fome timber to build an Ende to his houfe

---

defember th 12 1669

At A meeting of the felect men liberty granted to deacon ftone to fell fome timber to groundfill his houfe and to John Cooper to fell fome timber to ground fill his barne and to faw for planke to floure his barne and to faw for borde for the houfe for the miniftry and to make fome ladders

---

14 (12) 1669
At A meeting of the felect men

liberty granted to thomas longhorne to fell timber to build and ende to his houfe

and to John Jackfon a lode of Afh timber to make plowes from of the hundred akers

granted to John holmes liberty to fell timber to make A payer of wheeles

[82] th 14 of Jenuary 1670

at A meetting of the felect men:

liberty granted to william Maning to fell fome timber to fence his garden and to thomas fox to Repayer his out fence and to thomas hall to Repayer his out fence and to John Cooper to Repayer his out fence

granted to John fheaperd two trees for his trade and fencing timber for his gardin ———

granted to thomas one tree for pofts

granted to thomas poft fencing timber for his gardin

ouer feers of the fence in the necke m^r Jofeph Cooke and thomas longhorne

and for the weft field Gilbert Crackbone and John watfon —

and for Menotime field Edward winfhip and william dixon —

and to driue the necke m^r Jofeph Cooke and John ftedman Junr

and to driue the weft field Jeremiah holman —

and to driue Menotime field Nathaniell pattin

and for hog Reeves for the towne daniell Cheauer and for the Common Edward hall

and for Menotime william bull

and for the fouth fide of the Riuer thomas prentis Junr

---

at A meeting of the felect men
th 11 (2) 1670

---

liberty granted to feauerall perfons to fell timber —

to vmphry bradfheere to Repayer his out fencis and his barne and Cow houfe

to petter towne to Repayer his fence about houfe — and to John holmes to Repayer his fence to the weft field — —

to John watfon to Repayer Edward winfhips fence belonging to the weft field

to m^r Jofeph Cooke for an out houfe —

to Jonathan Remington to Repayer his out fence

to m^r Angier to Repayer his gardin fence

to John Addams to Repayer his out fence

to Jeremiah holman a tree to lay Crofe the Riuer at the ware and fome timber to make hurddles to fet downe the Riuer to ftay the fifh —

November ye 14. 1670

att a publicke meeting off the Inhabitants
off the towne to chuse towne officers

for Counstables { Samuell Hose
{ Thomas prentis Jun
{ Samuell Champnis

for selectmen { Captaine gookins
{ John stedman
{ William Maning
{ Edward Oakes
{ Thomas fox
{ John Cooper

Surueyors off { John Bone
high wayes { Joseph Russell
{ Jeames Cutler sen
{ Thomas Oliuer

granted to the owners off the kettles
that are to builded in the towne
liberty to fell timber vpon the
Common for the building off the
sayd kettles at that publick meeting
that was for the chosye off towne
officers

RECORD MADE BY JOHN COOPER, TOWN CLERK, 1669–1681
(See Folii 185–186)

th 9 (3) 1670

liberty granted by the felect men to feauerall to fell timber
to Jonathan Cane 4 trees to Repayer his houfe and out fencis —
and to Edward hall to build A leanto
and to daniell Cheauer timber for a Cart
and to John haftins timber to Repayer his out fencis
and to Nathaniell hancok two trees for fills for his houfe

[83] th 16 of may 1670

at a metting of the felect men

liberty granted to m^r ftedman to fell timber to make a Cart and wheles ant to Repayer his garden fence and for A leanto

liberty granted to william dixon to fell timber to fence his Orchyard

8 (6) 1670

At A metting of the felect men

liberty granted to Jonathan Remington to fell fower trees for groundfills for his barne

October th 10 1670

at a meeting of the felect men

liberty granted to Jonathan dunfter to fell two trees to make a payer of wheeles — — — —

× · × · × · × · × · × · × · × · × · × · ×

Nouember th 14 1670

At A publicke meeting of the Inhabitance of the towne to Chufe towne oficers

for Counftables ⎧ famuell Gofe
⎨ thomas prentis Junr
⎩ famuell Champnis

for felectmen { Captaine gookins
John ftedman
william Maning
Edward Oakes
thomas fox
John Cooper

furueyors of
high wayes
{ John Goue
Jofeph Rufell
Jeames Cutter fen^r
thomas Oliuer

granted to the owners of the kecthis that are to builded in the towne liberty to fell timber vpon the Common for the building of the fayd ketchis at that publicke meting that was for the Choyfe of towne oficers

[83] defember th 6 1670
at A metting of the felect men

liberty granted to Richard Jackfon to fell a tree for pofts —

liberty granted to m^r Jofeph Cooke to fell two trees to Repayer his fencis

agreed vpon by the felect men and thofe aded to them, as a Commity that the Rate made for the miniftry fhould Continue the fame ftill it was before. a part of It to gratifie m^r Chancy for his labours among vs and to be helpfull to Miftis Micthell and the Remainder to be Improued for the finifhing of the houfe for A minifter.

It was alfoe agreed vpon that theare fhould be a towne Rate made of a Rate and halfe of a fingell Country Rate for the defraying the towne Chargis   = 1½ of 1 —

defember th 23 1670.

Mr chauncy
£45
Mrs. Mitchel
£30

At A meeting of the Commity Chofen by the towne to order what fhould be allowed m^r Chancy for his labours amongft vs in preaching, and to miftris micthell It was agreed upon by the fayd Commity that theare fhould be allowed m^r Chancy for the yeere 1670 fourty-five pounds (the wood

that was Caried to him was to bee A part of It) and to be allowed to
miftris Micthell thirty pounds for the fame yeere, and what was Caried
her in wood to bee A part of It, and this to be payed out
for a houfe of the leauy made for the miniftry, and the Remainder to
built for a be Improued for the defraying of the Charges of the houfe
*minis
built for A minifter

January th 9 1670

at a metting of the felect men ———

liberty granted to feauerall to fell timber
to famuell Gofe a 100 pofts to Repayer his out fence
to thomas fox to Repayer his out fence ———
to william dixon timber for a payer of wheeles and to fence his garden ———
to thomas Androwes to Repayer his out fence
to John haftins to fence his garden ———
to John palfree two trees for his trade ———
to John Marrit to Repayer the out fence of his orchyard
to John Gibfon to Repayer his out fence ———

[84] January th 16 1670

At a metting of the felect men

Granted to John watfon to fell timber for a payer of wheeles and to Repayer leutenant winfhips fence neere John watfons houfe ———

granted to gilbert Crakbon three walnut trees to make fhores for his barne ———————

granted to Richard Jackfon to fell fome timber to Repayer his out fence and orchyard ———

granted to John ftedman timber to Repaer his garden fence ———

granted to daniell Cheauer timber to Repayer his out fence to the weft fielde

granted to John Cooper liberty to fell fume timber to Repayer his out fence and to ground fill his barne —

* Exact copy from manuscript.

liberty granted to Miſtris dunſter to fell ſume timber to Repayer her out fence ———

liberty granted to Elder froſt to fell ſume timber to Repayer his out fence ———

---

the order of the ſelect men for the Cattichiſing of the youth of the towne deuided as followeth

to Captaine gookins and Elder froſt the Eaſt ſide of the towne from the metting houſe to m^r Manings —

to m^r John ſtedman and Richard Jackſon the weſt ſide of the towne as far as Joſeph holmes — —

to m^r Danforth and thomas fox the Eaſt ſide of the Common from John taylors to nottime

to deacon ſtone and Edward Oakes the youth at the farmes —

to deacon Cheſholme and John Cooper the weſt ſide of the Common as far as notime

to m^r Maning and ſamuell Champnis thoſe beyound the Riuer as far as widdow woods

the Village on the ſouth ſide of the Riuer to Elder wiſwell and Edward Jackſon Cap prentis and John Jackſon ———

m^r Edward Collins leutenant winſhip and fracis Whitmore are to Catichiſe the youth beyound menotime ———

Catechiſing the youth

---

th 13 (12) 1670

At a metting of the ſelect men

liberty granted to ſeauerall to fall timber

to william barrit two trees for ground ſills

to Edward hall to Repayer his out fence in the ox paſtur

to thomas hall to Repayer his out fence

to Robert parker to Repayer his out fence

to leutenant winſhip to Repayer his out fence and about his Orchyard ———

[84] at a metting of the felect men
th 12 (i) 1670/1671

mr ftedman and thomas fox appointed to agree with the heardsmen to keepe the milch hearde

granted to Edward winfhip to fell fome timber to make A payer of wheeles and to ringe a payer

thofe appointed to looke after the yooking and ringing of the fwine ——

for the fwine at menotime and the fencis Nathanill pattin and william bull ——

for the towne Andrew fteuenfon and John goue

for the Common william towne ——

for the farmes dauid ftone ——

for the fouth fide of the Riuer Jeames prentis

driuers of the necke and vewers of the fence thomas longhorne and John ftedman Jun[r] ——

to driue the weft field Jeremiah holman —

and to vew the weft field fence John watfon and John gibfon Jun[r] —

march 12 1670/1671

at A metting of the Inhabitance of the towne the propofition was made that all the Common lands belonging to the towne without or beyound the Compas of the fiue mile line fhould be deuided into propriatyes this after Confiderable debate was put to the vote and voted on the Afirmatiue ——

and francis More and John watfon and John fheaperd and daniell Cheauer weare Chofen to be aded to the felect men to be A Commity to order and make deuifion of the faide lands granted to M^{tis} Micthell that her tennant at bilrica may dig as much Clay in Cambrigd bounds as will make a kill of brick for to make a ſtacke of Chimnies at her farme

---

March 20 1671
at a metting of the ſelect men

liberty granted to thomas ſwetman to fell ſume timber to make an adiſhon to his houſe ———
and to John ſheaperd two trees for his trade and timber to fence his garden
and to francis more to Repayer his out fence at Joniſis hill

---

21 (1) 1671

the Commity meeting togeather to Conſider about the deuiſion of the lands beyound the Cow Common and the farmes. m^r John ſtedman and m^r william Maning weare appointed to treate with the Comiſhon officers of the Artillery at boſton about theare farme granted them by the Court neere Concord to lay It out or Reſigne It vp becauſe our towne are about laying out theare lands adioining to It ———

[85] March 20 1671
at a metting of the ſelect men

John watſon dauid fiſke and daniell Cheauer weare appointed to take a vew of the lands voited to be layed out for to finde what damage is done by any perſons by felling of timber vpon the ſ^d lands and aqainte the ſelectmen with the ſame that they may be delt with all according to the towne order furthermore they weare appointed to Call vpon the owners of Any farmes adjoining to any of thoaſe lands to ſhow them theare lines that theare might be a true plot taken of the ſayde lands without damage to any propriator ———

Aprill 10 1671

at A metting of the select men

m^r Joseph Cooke and daniell Champnis weare appointed to Rune the line againeſt boſton bounds ———
 liberty granted to feauerall to fell timber to m^r danforth two trees for A payer of wheeles
 to John haſtins two trees for a payer of wheeles and a tree for pales
 to m^r Angier 3 trees to Repayer his fence and to build an out houſe
 and to Vmphry bradſhaw two trees for Clapbord to Couer his houſe
 to walter haſtins timber to Repayer his out fence ———
 Ordered by the townsmen that during the time that the highway ly through the farme that was m^r Androwes in the place wheare now It leade to John parkers houſe: It ſhall be lawfull for the occupiers of that farme to fence in and Improue the land that belonge to the towne for the olde high way that lead into boſton feilde — —

at A metting of the select men of Cambrigde the th 10 of Aprill 1671

At the reqeſt of m^r Edman Angier and others it Is ordered that m^r Oakes Richard Robbins and dauid fiſke bee A Commity to ſearch and Examine the grants and plats of the land on the ſouth ſide of the Riuer betwene m^r danforth farme and m^r Angiers farme and the lands belonging to ſamuell and daniell Champnis and ſee how far the high way betwene the ſaide lands is layed forth and to ſee wheather they Can finde any Common lands betwene the ſaide grant to perfit the ſaide high way vp into the lots or the highway leading from watter towne to Rokſbury and to Report to the towns men what they finde in the premiſis. ———

[85] May th 8 1671

At A metting of the select men
liberty granted to John Marrit to fell A tree to make Joyce ——
to samuell haftins two trees to make ground fills ——
and to Andrew belsher timber to build A barne ——

drain — granted to William barrit and Nathaniell Hancok to dige A fluce to dreane the ponde by theare houses in the townes land prouided they secure It from doeing damage as soone as may be and in Case the townes men see Reason for It, they are to stope It vp againe ——

an Order Concerning Cattill feeding vpon oure Common with out A keeper. ————

wheare as diuers Complaints are made to the selectmen that notwithstanding former orders: the breathren and Inhabitance of menotime now decline to hearde theare Cattill and not keepe them out of the bounds of the Cow walke Reserved for the towne within the fiue miles Contrary to towne orders and Couinants made with them and doe let theare dry Cattill and oxen goe with out a keeper and feede vpon the Cow Common and thearby preieduce the feede of the Cow hearde thearefore to preuent It It is ordered by the select men that noe dry Cattill nor oxen shall be Cept with out a keeper within the fiue miles vpon the Cow Common but If such Cattill be taken feeding theare of our owne Inhabitance It shall be in the liberty of our towne Cow keepers or any other Inhabitance to Impound the sayde Cattill eyther in the towne pound or in a yarde giuing leagall notice to the owners and the owners shall pay for pounding sixpence pr hed halfe to the pound keeper and the other halfe to the Impounder and all Cattill taken belonging to other townes wheather milch Cattill or dry Cattill taken feeding within the bounds of our towne in any place shall be alsoe Impounded as before and shall pay before they be Released one shilling pr head for poundage halfe to the pound keeper and halfe to the driuer — — —

m^r stedman and thomas fox are to vew the land that phillipe Joans desire to haue for to make and maintaine a stone wall against watertowne line and make Returne to the select men thearof ————

[86]   may th 29 1671

at A geanerall metting of the propriators of the towne lawfully warned to Confider about making A fence betwene watter towne bounds and ours It was Refeared to the felect men and m^r danforth deacon ftone and Richard Jackfon to make A Couinant with phillip Jones or any other able perfon to make a fufifhent fence of ftone of fower footes high with two gates vpon the high wayes one leading from Concord to water towne and the other leading from Cambrigd to watter towne by the farme fumtimes occupied by Richard hafell this fence to begin at the faid farme and goe on vpon the line to Rocky meddow and the faid phillip Jones or any other perfon that fhall make the faid fence and gates Is to maintaine the fame for euer in good Repayer and In Confideration whearof the towne grant lands vpon the Common wheare It is propounded fuch a qantity as they Can agree for to the faid perfon and his Eyers for euer prouided the land be bound to make good the fence and that It fhall not be fould to any perfon or perfons but an Inhabytant of Cambrigd and that the faid perfon to whom the land is granted fhall keepe noe heard vpon our Common nor more Cattill of his owne then his due proportion of what land of his ly in Common vnles hee haue liberty from the towne —— this was voited on the firmatiue

---

liberty granted to daniell Cheauer to fell A tree to make Joyce ——
and to henry boutill fix trees to Repayer his houfe and fume timber to Repayer his out fence. ——
the felect men doe not Except of henry boutill to be an Inhabitant in our towne

---

may th 29 1671

at A metting of the felect men

Mathew bregd appeering before the felect men being Conuicted of felling with in two yeers fifty trees vpon our Common land is fined three pound dauid fiſke appeering before the ſelect men being Conuicted of felling 40 trees at leaſt vpon our Common land without leaue is fined four ty ſhillings —— ——

and for taking of the Common land with out leaue into his farme is ordered to Remoue his fence and leaue It out againe with one yeere on penalty of paying 10ˢ amonth vntill It be done ———

[86] ſamuell ſtone being Conuicted of felling ten trees vpon our Common with out leaue is fined ten ſhillings

dauid ſtone appeering before the townſmen being Conuicted of felling at leaſt ten trees with out leaue vpon our Common is fined ten ſhillings. ———

Iſack ſtearns being Conuicted of felling timber vpon our Common with out leaue is fined ten ſhillings ———

Joſeph Meariam being Conuicted for felling timber Contrary to order is fined fiue ſhillings

Jeames Cutter for felling fower Clapbord trees Contrary to order is fined fiue ſhillings

Michaell bacon Junʳ for felling timber with out liberty on our Common is fined ten ſhillings ——— ———

william ſimons being Conuicted before the ſelect men for Cutting 800 of hop poles vpon our Common Contrary to order is fined twenty ſhillings

ordered by the ſelectmen that the fines aboue ſpeaſified be leauied by the Counſtable by the firſt of nouember next this Inſtant yeere 1671 and payed in Corne at the Country price deliuered at the towne vpon penalty of paying double for Neglect ——— ———

and It is further declared that if any perſon aboue named or aniother ſhall hearafter tranſgres in the like kinde the townsmen purpoſe to Require the like penalty according to the towne order ———

May 29 1671 : · ———

at A meeting of the propriators of the Common lawfully warned It was Refeared to the ſelect men with the breathren heerafter named to make A Couinant with phillip Jones or any other able perſon to make a ſufiſhent and firme ſtone wall of fower foote high with two gates vpon

the high wayes leading from Concord and Cambrigd land to watertowne (all allong the line from the farme late in occupation of Richard hafell vnto Rockey meadow and to maintaine the fame fence and gates in good Repayer for euer) in Confideration whear of the towne grant land vpon the Common whear it is propounded fuch a qantity as they can agree for turne ouer ———
[87] to the fayde perfon and his heyers for euer prouided the land be bound to make good the fence and that It fhall not be fould to any perfon or perfons but an Inhabitant of Cambrigd and that a perfon to whome the land is granted to fhall keepe noe heard vpon our Common nor more Cattill of his owne then his due proportion of what land of his ly in Common vnles he haue liberty from the towne: · ———

m^r thomas danforth ⎫
deacon ftone and ⎬ weare Chofen to Joine with the felect men in making this
Richard Jackfon ⎭ Contract ———

this was voited on the afirmatiue

at a meting of the Curch and towne
church

☞   July th 17 1671

1   to acknowlegd thankfullnes to m^r Oakes for his great loue, and felfe denial in parting with his frends and Concerns in England to Come ouer to vs ———

2   to manifeft unto him the Continuance of the earneft and affectionate defires of the Church and peaple that as foone as well may bee would pleafe to Joine in fellowfhip heere in order to his fettellment and becoming a paftour to this Church ———

m^r Oaks invited to move into the ministers houfe

3   to intreate him forthwith to Concent to Remoue himfelfe and family into the houfe prepared for the Ministry: · ———

the house prepaired for the ministry

4   that the deacons be furnifhed, and In abled to prouide for his accomadation at the Charge of the Church and towne and diftribute the fame feafonably for the Comfort of him and his family: ———

5. that halfe A yeers payment forthwith be made by euer one according to theare yeerly payment to the miniſtry; and the one halfe of It to be payed in money; and the other in ſuch pay as is ſutable to the end Intended ———
all theaſe perticulars weare Voted on the afirmatiue

August th 14 1671

at a meetting of the ſelect men

deacon John Jackſon ſamuell Champnis and thomas Oliuer weare appointed to Vew the high way from boſton bounds with boſton men to Captaine prentis and make thear of a Returne to the ſelect men — —

[87]   October th 9 1671

at A metting of the ſelect men ———

granted to m^r ſtedman liberty to fell a tree for pales to Repayer his fence ———

granted to m^r Cooke liberty to fell a tree to make fence about his kitchin ———

granted by the ſelect men that theare be ſume ded walnut trees felled for fireing for m^r Oakes vpon the day appointed to fell and Cary wood for him the day being the 16 of this Inſtant month of October 1671

at A publicke meeting of towne
Nouember th 13|1671

Choſen for Counſtables
- John kindrick ſen^r
- John Goue: · ———
- William barrit

Select men
- Captaine Gookin
- m^r danforth
- m^r John ſtedman
- m^r Edward Oakes
- thomas fox
- John Cooper

TOWN RECORDS

furuayors of
high wayes
{ william dixon
famuell haftins
Nathaniell fparhauke
Job hide
John Winter }

☛ granted to Avon bordman liberty to build a porch on the North fide of his houfe, three foote into the highway

th 27 (9) 1671

At a metting of the felect men ——

liberty granted to the deacons to fell three or fower ded trees vpon the plaine to fuply m^r Chancy with fume fire woode at the prefent the fnow being deepe that theare was noe tolerable pafing vnto the Rockes: · ——

defember th 10 1671

at a publicke meeting of the towne to Confider about the deuifon of the land beyound the eight miles and the deuifon of the woode vpon the Cow Common   It was voited on the afirmatiue that thofe that fhall with in one month after this metting that haue towne Right Come vnto the felect men, and voluntaryly fubfcribe this ingagment not to fell any fire wood out of the towne fhall haue his proportion in the Common wood fet out to him and for that Ende all the wood land with in the th 6 miles is to be meafured that the proportion of Each may be knowne —

[88]   defember th 10 1671

at the faide metting granted to Andrew belfher to Repayer the barne he bought of widdow beale fixteene trees —— ——

petter towne is Chofen to be the Repacker of meate and gager of Cafke, and fealer of weights and meafurs —— ——

£20 to Mrs Mitchel   Voited at the fame metting that theare be a Rate made of 20^l and payed in to M^{tis} Micthell for her fupply

granted to Nathaniell Green a tree to Repayer his out fence

feauerall perſons fined for felling of wood and timber on the Common with out liberty —— ——

Edward winſhip 20ˢ Richard Cutter 20ˢ Vmphry bradſheere 20ˢ· francis whitmore 20ˢ william dixon 20ˢ John watſon 20ˢ beniamin Crakbon 10ˢ.

At a meeting of the ſelect men
Jeanuary (15) 1671

granted to theaſe feauerall perſons liberty to fell timber ——
to mʳ danforth for his Orchyard and for mʳ pellams necke fence
to Cap gookins for neck fence and for A payer of wheeles
to william towne for his out fence
to thomas hall one tree
to thomas fox for his out fence
to mʳ Angier to Repayer his houſe
to Mathew bregd A Clap borde tree
to deacon ſtone a tree for poſts
to John Goue 2 trees to Repayer deacon Meariams houſe ——
to John Cooper for his out fencis and for ground fills for his barne and for a leanto
to danill Cheauer for a payer of wheeles

John Addams Nathaniell pattin Jonathan dunſter and Joſeph holmes appeering before the ſelect men weare Conuicted of fellin wood vpon our Common with out liberty weare fined ten ſhillings a peice for thear defalt

In the yeere 1671 december the 25 deliuered by the Counſtable william barrit the townes weights and meaſurs to petter Towne, he being Choſen ſealer namely one halfe buſhell one pecke one halfe pecke and one beere qart and one wine pinte and one halfe pinte — —— ——

one payer of braſe ſcales one leade weight of fower pounds and one leade weight of three pound (and ten braſe weights) one of two pound one of one pound one halfe pound one qarter one two ounce one one ounce one halfe ounce and one qarter of an ounce one halfe qaarter of an ounce and one fmaler all of brafe one open feale for the leade weights

one open brand to feale the wooden meafurs with the towne feale vpon them ———

and one yarde meafure

[88] the Returne of the Commity appointed to vew the highwayes from m^r hainefis farm to bofton bounds and to the Falls

---

Wee whofe names are heere Vnder written being Chofen and appointed by the felect men of this towne to vew the high wayes lyeing from M^r hainefis farme through Elder wifwals farme and other mens propriaties to boston bounds wee doe Judge It weare nedefull that theare fhould be an open and ftated Country high way layed out and bounded fower Rods broad from bofton bounds along through Elder wifwals farme and through M^r hainefis farme, now M^r wilifis farme and from thence to pas along through the fmall lots to the falls Commonly Called the lower falls and foe quite through vnto dedham bounds alfoe we Judg moft Coneunient that this way fhould bee ftated from M^r hainfis fearme, through Elder wifwals farme and other mens propriaties to bofton bounds it lyeth — —   famell Champnis
John Jackfon
thomas Oliuer

---

the agrement of Edward Gofe and thomas beale Concerning theare fence (and land) betwene theare lands in the necke being th 7 (2) 1651

Agreed as followeth that thomas beale accepteth of the land as It is now fet out in lew of his land that is left out of his fence to bro gofe alfoe bro gofe is to allow him 16 poles of fence when he have got vp his ftone wall of his owne ftufe according as it fhall then bee alfoe 20 Railes and at prefent to lend him 4^l for one yeere to be payed in like good pay at the yeers end and bro beale agreeth that the Common fence fhall be layed betwene bro gofe and him to the truth whearof they haue put to theare hands the day and yeere aboue written alſoe bro goſe agrees to ſecure all that part of fence betwene bro beale and him which is not of Right to be made by some other perſon without any Charge to bro beale

Memoran^d it is the true intent of this agrement that bro goſe ſhall be ingaged in noe fence betwene bro beale and him: ſaue only that fence which is vpon a new line by reaſon of his exchange of land — —

Edward goſe

thomas danforth   thomas beale
witnes — —

[89]   Feberwary th 11 1671
at a metting of the ſelect men

liberty granted to feauerall to fell timber vpon the Common ——

to Mathew bregd Clapbords to Repayer his houſe and poſts and Railes for his out fence heere at towne ———

to Nicolas wiith 2 trees for A payer of wheeles

to John watſon 2 trees for A payer of wheeles and for his out fence and A Cart ——

to umphry bradſhaw for A payer of wheeles and out fence ——

to Richard Ecels a tree to make ſtayers

to Jeremiah holman for a payer of wheeles and his out fence

to John bouttill for his out fence ——

to John ſtedman and benoni Eatton poſts and Railes for theare gardens ——

to petter towne one walnut tree and 2 trees for his trade — —

th 11 (j) 1671/1672
at A metting of the ſelect men

liberty granted to feauerall to fell timber

to william dixon A tree for pſts

to widdow Cooke 2 trees for poſts and 3 trees for Railes ——

to Roger buck A tree for Joyce ——

to ſamuell haſtins timber to Repayer his out fence ——

to John Marrit timber to Repayer his out fence ——

to thomas Longhorne timber to Repayer his out fence —
to Miſtis dunſter for a payer of wheeles —
to Joſeph ſill ſening ſtufe for his garden —
to Robert parker for his out fence ——
to Rober browne fenceing ſtufe for his weſt field fence
to Abraham Arington fence for his garden and bradiſhis lande and 2 ground ſills ——
to petter towne for his garden and for his houſe —
to John bouttill timber to Ring a payer of wheeles ——
to Joſeph Ruſell 50 Railes and ſume poſts
to Joſeph Cooke fence for his garden
to dauid fiſke 2 mapell trees for theare ſaw mill ——
to Elder froſt to Repayer his out fence

vewers of fencis driuers of the Corne fields and hoge Reues for the yeere 1672 to vew the fencis and driue the necke.
(thomas longhorne)
(John ſtedman —)
vewers of the weſt field fence
 francis More and John gibſon Junr
and to driue the weſt field
 Jemiah holman —— ——

[89] March th 11 1671 1672

vewers of the fencis in menotime field
 John Addams and william dixon ——
to driue notime feild Nathaniell pattin
to ſee the towne order excuted about ſwine for the towne
 Robert browne and petter towne ——
for the Common John palfre
for notime Joſeph Ruſell John ſquire
 to Rune lines betwene bilrica and our towne and the line betwene Concord and our towne m^r Joſeph Cooke and dauid fiſke and daniell Cheauers are appointed ——

and to Rune the line betwene Charls towne and Obourne and Cambrigd m^r Cooke and famuell Cooper are appointed

to agree with heards men m^r ftedman and thomas fox and william barrit are appointed —— ——

Aprill th 8 1672

at A metting of the felect men

liberty granted to feauerall to fell timber
to m^r ftedman for ground fills ——
to m^r Angier for his Orchyard in the towne
to m^r danforth A tree for his fluce ———

---

the felect men taking into Confideration the damag done by Cattill in Comon fields and the trouble of getting them to the pound Eyther by the Common driuer or by the owners of the land, the felect men doe order that for euery fuch beaft foe taken and Impounded the owner fhall pay eight teene pence pr hed to the driuers of the field, or the owners of the land

---

the tearmes of agreement of the felect men with thomas longhorne for the keeping of william healyes Childe as followeth that the fayde thomas longhorne is to bring vp hanna hely daughter of william hely borne in the yeere 1671 prouiding all Neffifaris for her of foode and Clothing in the time of her minority and futable Eaducation meete for one of her fects and degree and for his fatiffaction he is to be allowed out of the towne Rate fiue pounds A yeere for fiue yeeres and If fhe fhould dy before thofe fiue yeers be expired or It fhould be prouided for by any of Its freinds before that time then he is to haue not more then for the time he keepe It after fiue pounds perranum only forty fhillings of the fayde pay is to be in Cafh or If not then foe much in other pay at money price — —— ———

[90]   may th 4 1672
at A metting of the felect men

m^r ftedman and m^r Cooke weare appointed to meete watter towne and Concord men at watertowne may th 10 1672 for the fettelling of the Country Rode through watter towne towards Concord

---

July th 8 1672
at A metting of the felect men ———

granted to famuell green liberty to fell fume timber to make an addifhon to his houfe ——

---

29 (5) 1672
at A metting of the felect men

ordered about the fheepe

1   It is ordered by the felect men of Cambridge that all the fheepe owners in the towne that doe put theare fheepe with the flock doe before the tenth of the fixt month next bring in the number of theare fheepe and lames to Edward hall that they haue put to the flock when the flock firft went out togeather with the markes of them vpon penalty of ten fhilling fine for neglect thearof and It is ordered that for time to Come that they giue in the number of theare fheepe and lames before the laft of Aprill to Edward hall vpon the like penalty vpon any Complaints made againft them for neglect thearof

2   It is ordered that what euer perfon fhall fende for or fecth away any fheepe or lame frome the flock and doe not aqaint the fheapard or Edward hall thearwith and fhow him the marks thearof hee fhall forfit fiue fhillings for euery defect to the vfe of the towne ———

3   It is ordered that all the Rams and Rame lames be feaperated from the flock before the laft of July yearly excepting fuch as are Chofen for the vfe of the flock which Rams foe chofen fhall be put apart from the flock in fome fafe and Conuenient place at the appointment of the felect men or whome they fhall appoint (theare being

information giuen them by the fheaperd in feafon) and as for all other Rams and Rame lambs that weare not Chofen for the flock that fhall be founde with the flock after the tweluth of august next fhall be Impounded by the fheaperd and If after that they be fufered to goe with the flock the fayde owners fhall pay twelue pence aday for fuch Ram or Ram lambe that fhall goe with the flock notwith ftanding any Cuftome formerly ———

febtember th 9 1672

at A publicke meetinge of the towne to Confider about Repayering of the bregd It is ordered that the felect men doe caufe the bregd to be Exactly ferched and vewed and If upon ferching and vewing it be found that upon puting in of fume new ftrings and Caps and plankes and it will be Repayered foe as that It may be fafely Carted ouer for two or three yeers then they fhould Caufe the fame to be fpeedily Efected provided the Charge Extend not fourty pounds which the towne do voite to pay out of the next towne Rate ———

Repair of the great Bridge

[90] but If It be found vpon ferch that fuch a fume will not Repayer It to be fafe for Carting then the felect men are defired and ordered Eyther to prouide a feary boatt and A man to keepe It or other wife foe to Repayer the bregd that horfe and foote may pafe fecurly wheather of the two wayes they fhall finde to be beft for the publicke aduantage — prouided allwayes that this prefent order for Repayering notwithftanding it is Commited to the Care and prudence of the felect men and A Commity aded to them heerafter named or the maior parte of them to Confider and Contriue fume way to fill vp the brigd wharfe wife betwene the piles at each end leauing only three lengths for paffage in the midefts and to propofe fume way and mennes to fill the fame in a graduall way doeing A part euery yeere till the whole be done alfoe to Imploy fume perfons to get Contributions from other townes for, and toward the Efecting of the fame.

francis More vmphry bradftreet zacariah hickes and Jofeph fill weare Chofen to helpe ferch the bregd ———

Voted on the afirmatiue — ———

TOWN RECORDS

an order about the Cowes and fheepe ———

the felect men taking in to Confideration the Complaint of the heards men and fheaperd of the neglect of feauerall perfons in not keeping theare turns upon the faboth day or not fending a fufifhent keeper many Cowes are left in the woods and foe the owners are much damaged the felect men thearfor order that any that haue any Cowes goe with the heard or any that theare Cowes feede upon the Common and are ordered by the felect men to pay to the heards men fhall keepe theare turns upon the faboth day begining with thofe that haue moft Cowes goe with the heard and they fhall prouide afufifhent keeper and In Cafe any neglect to keepe theare turns hauing due warning by the heards men being two or three dayes before the faboth the fayde delinquincts fhall pay for euery fuch Neglect fiue fhillings to be leauied by the Counftable the one halfe to the heards men and the other halfe to the vfe of the towne ———

and the like order is for the fheepe : · ———

liberty granted to m^r danforth to fell fume timber for his kicthin and to thomas fox A fheepe houfe ———

At A publicke metting of the towne
Nouember th 11 1672

Chofen for Counftables { famuell haftins
daniell bacon
Marmaduke Johnfon

for felect men { Captaine Gookin
m^r John ftedman
m^r Edward Oakes
m^r william Maning
thomas fox
John Cooper

for furueyors { John winter
Juftinian houldin
daniell Champne
Noah wifall
John ftedman Junr

for fealing weights and meafurs petter towne
for fealing leather   Androw fteuenfon

[91]   11 (9) 1672
at A metting of the felect men

granted to John green fencing ftufe to Repayer his orchyard

and ·to Edward Mitchellfon fume pofts for his orchyard and 2 groundfills for his houfe ———

to Nathaniell handcoke fleepers for his barne

to Jonathan Cane timber for A Cart and wheeles —— ——

defember th (9) 1672
At A metting of the felect men

liberty granted to John ftedman Junr to fell fome timber to Repayer his gardin fence ——— ———

and to william dixon timber for A payer of wheeles and to Repay his out fence———

and to thomas Androwes a pale tree and fume Railes to fence in his garden ———

and to Jeremiah holman to build A dwelling houfe

agreed by the felect men that theare be a towne Rate made of A Country Rate and halfe for the defraying of towne Charges ———

and A Rate of twenty fiue pounds for m^{rs} Micthell to be leauied by the Counftables and 5^l of It If neede be with the wood that haue bine be payed her in be payed in woode ————

Jenuary th 13 1672
At A metting of the felect men

liberty granted to John watfon to fell fume timber to Repayer his out fence

liberty granted to petter towne to fell two trees for his trade ———

liberty granted to John Eames to make two kill of bricke on the Common beyonde me notyme prouided hee take nor by any woode that is taken of the Common —— ——

---

febrawary th[10] 1672
At A metting of the felect men ——

liberty granted to feauerall to fell timber

to leuetenant winfhip fower pine trees about beare fwamp or elfewheare upon the Common and timber for A Cart and wheeles ——

granted to John bouttill timber for A Carte

and to John palfre timber to build him an end of A houfe about 20 foote longe ——

granted to John fwane timber for A payer of wheeles

granted to famuell haftins timber for A 100 of Railes and eaqueuelente for them ——

granted to John Marrit two trees to make A fider pres ——

granted to M[tis] blowers timber to ground fill her houfe and to fence in A gardin ——

---

th 17 (12) 1672
At A metting of the felect men

liberty granted to Nathaniell hancoke timber to fence his gardin —

to william barrit ground fills for his houfe ——

to mr Angier fencing ftufe for his gardin and timber to Repayer his houfe ——

to doctor hore pofts and Railes to make A barricadoe againft his houfe ——

to Robert parker timber to ringe a payer of wheeles

to zacariah hickes fencing ftufe for his gardin and three groundfills for his houfe. ——

[91] to famuell gofe A tree for plancke for his floure

to Captaine gookin for his out fence

to John Jackfon for his out fence ——

to thomas longhorne 2 trees for pofts

to Joseph holmes for the west field fence
John green is to pay to m^r Angier what is in his hand due of his part of the towne Rate when hee was Counstable

---

In Answer to A motion made by Thomas Oliuer to the select men that hee might haue liberty to set vp his fence At the ende of his land, from the Corner stake Alonge by the trees that are marked, to the other Corner, stake, though not A straight line Joining to the highway that leade from Rocksbery to watertowne mill the premisis are granted, prouided hee leaue the high way fower Rods broad in the Narrowest place, and If It shall after warde appeere that the high way is damaged thearby hee shall take vp his fence againe, and set it in A straight line If the select men Require it — —
by the order of the select men ——

4 rods

March th^10 1673

At A metting of the select men ——

liberty granted to seuerall to fell timber ——
to Richard Cutter for A payer of wheeles ——
to Mathew bregd to Repayer his out fence to his land at towne and timber to build a house twelue foote sqaure ———
to Nicolas wiith for his out fence with 2 Railes and posts to them —
to vmphry bradshaw for his out fence —
to widdow Crakbon timber for A Carte —
to Edward hall for his yards and for the sheepe yards
to Nicolas fishington for the west field fence and for his yards ——
to Amoz woodward for his westfield fence ——
to John hastins for his out fence by his house and A tree for pales —
to Nathaniell pattin for his out fence and A tree for planke
to widdow Cooke for her out fence ——
to daniell Cheauer for his fence to the west field
to Abraham Arington for his west field fence and his gardin and groundsills for his house and for his land by samuell hastins ——

the names of the perſons that are to driue the Common fields and looke after the fencis and the ſwine ———

for the necke fence and to driue it
) John goue
} John ſtedman
) John bouttill ſen.ʳ

for the weſt field fence and to driue it
Jeremiah holman ——
(John watſon
{ francis More
(Amoz woodward

for menotime field fence and to driue it
(Nathaniell pattin
(John ſwane

for the farmes neere Concord to looke after the ſwine
Jſack ſtearns.

for hoge Reeues
(Edward winſhip
{ Androw ſteuenſon
(Jeremiah holman
(Jonathan ſanders

on the other ſide the water for the ſwine
(olde goodman kendrick
{ thomas prentis
(Jeames prentis

to agree with heardsmen
(mʳ ſtedman
{ thomas fox
(ſamuell haſtins

to agree with the ſheaperd
(John watſon
(thomas fox

[92] the Information giuen by thoſe heere vnder written of the pore and low Condition of Joſeph bartlit

theaſe are to Certifie our honered Captaine and the Reſt of the ſelecte men of Cambrigd that according to your order wee haue bine with Joſeph bartlit and wee doe finde him in a very poore Condition hauing noe houſe and very bad in Reſpect of foode and Rayment and thearfor if you would be pleaſed to Allow fiue pounds It may be A Comfortable ſupply to helpe to build him A houſe and A helpe to ſupply his preſent wants

March th 3 1673   thomas prentis
A Coppy of the Requeſt of the ⎫   John Jackſon
ſelect men ſent to the Reuerent ⎬   daniell bacon
Elder wiſwall and mr Nehamiah   Counſtable
hubbard preacher at the ſecond ⎮
Church at Cambrigd ——— ⎭

Vpon Information of the pore and low Condition of Joſeph bartlit and his family whoe is an Inhabitant of this towne and particularly hath his Reſidence among you wee thought It expeadiente: heereby to deſire and moue you to ſpeake to the Congregation upon the ſaboth
☞   day about his Condition and to moue them to make A Contribution towards his Releefe the ſaboth day folling wee ſhall allſoe moue our paſture to ſpeake to our Congregation to doe the like, and the Reaſon of our proceding in this way is becauſe theare is nothing to be ſpared out of the towne Rate for his Releeſe: and wee finde this way moſt feaſable to accompliſh the end hauing latly made A probation thearof for the Releefe of one John Coller A poore family on this ſide ſoe Commiting you to God, wee Remaine your louing friends and Neighbours
    dated at Cambrigd March th 12 167$\frac{2}{3}$

Aprill th 14: 1673   At a meeting of the ſelect men

granted to Richard Robbins liberty to fell ſume timber to Repayer his leantoes ———
    to Jonathan dunſter to Repayer his out fence
    to Jonathan Cane to Repayer his out fence
    to ſamuell gofe ſume for his orchyarde
    to mr Johnſon fence to Repayer his mothers garden
    to John Addams for his out fence by his houſe

---

* A Coppy of the Returne to the ſelect men
by mr thomas danforth and dauid fiſke Concering the land claimed by ſamuell and daniell Champne wee whoſe names are ſubſcribed being

---

* In the manuſcript the pen was drawn through this entry, as if with the intention of eraſure.

* defired to vew A parcell of land lying on the fouth fide of the Riuer
betwene part of the hed line of m^r Andrewes farme and m^r parhaukes
line and now Claimed by famuell and daniell Champne doe affert
that it is not part of that which the towne fould to Elder Champney
for 40 akers more or les when hee firft built in that place the head
line of that being terminated by the fame line that the fmall lots that
hee then bought of goodman fheaped thrumbl and others that had
lots theare ———

Vide fol. 117.

2 that it is noe part of the 100 akers which the towne granted him
and was layed out on the northerly fide of m^r Micthells lott ———

thomas danforth afertet to the firft articell of this teftimony
dauid fifke atefteth to the truth of the fecond article

13 (3) 1672.

[92]   2 (3) 1673

At A metting of the felect men ———

william Maning was appointed to pay for our deputies expencis for the yeere 1672 to John peafe of bofton ———

May th 12   1673

At A meeting of the felect men ———

thomas fox and walter haftins are appointed to lay out the high way into the neck of land againft m^r Jofeph Cookes line on the fouth fide of the way two Rods wide from the fence

our breatheren and Neighbors haue fubfcribed to giue to Jofeph bartlit for his Releefe fower pound one fhilling on the fouth fide of the Riuer ———

granted to Jonathan Remington to fell A tree for larth

July th 14   1673

At A metting of the felect men

m^r ftedman thomas fox walter haftins and John goue are appointed A Commity to treate with John Marrit for the exchange of the high way betwene water=towne and Cambrigd line; to lay the high way

* See footnote, page 210.

through John Marrits land, foe as may be moft Conueaniant for Carts, or any other ocation as the towne fhall haue neede to make vfe of It for

Alfoe m^r John ftedman and m^r Edward Oakes and m^r william Maning are appointed A Commity to Vew the highway on the other fide of the Riuer againft feauerall fmall lots and againft m^r Angiers farme and to fet out the highway that is neere his houfe that exchange was made with him to Remoue the way more Eafterly from his houfe and make Returne heer of to the feleƈt men ———

---

the Conditions of the grant of the feleƈt men to the perfons whofe names are heere Exprefed for to build A gallary on the north fide of the meetting houfe upon the beame ———

that they are build the gallary upon the beame from the gallary on the Eaft beame to the weft ende of the meeting houfe foe far as the Roofe doe not hinder and to make It like that on the Eaft end for workmanfhipe and to make the floure very Cloft and borde it vp upon the for part of It like the other gallary and to make a payer of ftayers to It wheare the feleƈt men fhall direƈt them

    turne ouer

[93] and If It appeere that theare be more Roome then for thofe 12 exprefed that then the feleƈt men will place in theare whome they pleafe ——— ——— ———

the names of the perfons	Eaphraim froft	thomas froft
	famuell prentis	phillipe Rufell
	william Cutter	Ephraim Cutter
	Jonathan dunfter	John Oldam
	Edward winfhip	John watfon
	John dickfon	John whitmore

---

13 (8) 1673

At A meeting of the feleƈt men

granted liberty to John watfon to fell A tree to make Joyce for A leanto ———

and one tree to Eaphraim froft to make a payer of wheeles ———

Nouember th 3 1673
At A meeting of the felect men
liberty granted to francis more to fell timber for A payer of wheeles

---

7 (9) 1673
At a meeting of the felect men

liberty granted to m^r danforth to fell fume timber for ground fills for m^r pelams barne

granted to dauid ftone liberty to fell fume hoope poles for his trade

It was ordered that thofe that weare delinqints in theare fwine fhould pay one halfe of theare fine to the hog Reeues ———

× × × × × × × × × × × × × × × × × × ×

Nouember th 11 1673
At A generall meeting of the Inhabitance
of the towne for the Choyfe of towne oficers

for Counftables
- Nathaniell hancoke
- famuell ftone
- daniell Champne
- Noah wifwall

felect men
- m^r John ftedman
- m^r Edward Oakes
- leutenant winfhip
- walter haftins
- francis More
- John Cooper

furueyors of high wayes
- Juftinian holdin
- Isack ftearns
- famuell Champne
- Jofeph fill
- Jeames prentis

[93] defember th 8 1673 : · —

At A metting of the felect men

liberty granted to feauerall to fell timber

to John taylor 2 trees for his trade

to Jeremiah holman timber for two mantel trees and fleppers for his houfe ——

to John Jackfon 2 trees for pofts and for A Cart and A payer of wheeles

to John Marrit 30 pofts and timber for one wheele

to Robert browne timber for a payer of wheeles and for 20 pofts and 50 Railes ——

to John watfon timber to make an Adifhon to his barne of twenty foote ——

to leutenant winfhip timber for his barne floure and for two payer of wheeles ——

Jenuary th 12 1673 At A metting of the felect men

granted to Andrew fteuenfon 3 ground fills one tree for pofts and 2 trees for Railes fence for his garden

to daniell Cheauer A tree for a ground fill for his houfe and for A payer of wheeles and fence for his garden

to John goue and famuell haftins for A payer of wheeles

to John palfre 2 trees for his trade ——

Jenuary th 26 1673

At a meeting of the felect men

granted to m^r ftedman liberty to fell fume timber upon the Common to build a leanto : · —— ——

2 (12) 1673
At A meeting of the felect men

an order made by the felect men for the Reftraining of perfons from felling wood with out liberty ———

the felect men taking into confideration the damage done in our Common woods by feauerall perfons Cutting downe gree wood with out liberty (they doe prohibit the Cutting downe any green oake or walnut or loping any tree upon the Common with out liberty from the felect men) and If any fhall prefume to fell any green oake or wall nut or lop any tree they fhall pay for euery fuch tree according to the former order fiue fhillings A tree —— ——

and in Cafe they Cut downe any fwamp wood they fhall forth with Cut It out and fet It vp or elfe It fhall be lawfull for any perfon that haue Intreft in our Commons to make vfe of the fame prouided they Cary It not out of the towne —— —— ——

Richard Cutter and Jeames hubbard are appointed to looke after the perfons that tranfgres in the premifis —— —— ——

m^r danforth leutenant winfhip m^r ftedman and m^r Edward Oakes and m^r Cooke are Chofen to Rune the line betwene the vilage on the fouth fide of the Riuer and Cambrigd — — —

william Maning and francis More and John Cooper are appointed to fet out the windmill hill neere Richard Ecels by the water fide, and the high way to It — — —

granted to walter haftins and John haftins timber to build A worke houfe — — — —

9 (12) 1673
At A meeting of the felect men

m^r John ftedman and walter haftins weare appointed to agree with A heards man to keepe the milch hearde of Cambrigd for the yeere 1674

P 94

Wood lott [94] At A generall meetting of the Inhabitance of Cambridg that are propriators in the Common lands and woods yet undeuided, the 9th day of february 1673: · ——

voted that A wood lot laid out for the ministers house

1 that theare be A wood lot layed out for the minifters houfe of the wood land with in the fiue miles, of fuch dimentions as the Committe heerafter named fhall thinke meete

2 that theare fhall be neyther any woodlot or wood or timber Alinated or fould of the woods within the fiue miles heerafter to be layed out, unto any perfon or perfons; of any other towne upon the penalty of the forfieture of fuch wood lot unto the publicke ufe of the towne of Cambridge : · —

3 that in the deuiding and proportioning of the wood lots now to be laid out within the fiue miles, Refpect be had principally unto the way and method ftated and Recorded in the Towne booke as men haue Right by Cow Commons prouided all wayes that the Commity haue liberty according to Rules of prudence to leffon fome propriators fhare that haue Confiderably more then others: and are well accomadated with farmes or other wood lots in the towne; and to make addition unto others that haue but A fmall proportion, by the former Rule, and haue neede of A fupply for theare vfe : · —

4 that If any mans wood lot fhall fall very bad with Refpect to the fmall quantity of wood thearupon, and fuch perfon haue noe other wood in the towne confiderable, in fuch A Cafe the Commity are Impowered to alot unto fuch a perfon or perfons fume meete proportion of wood out of the Common wood that ly intermixed among the fmall farmes beyonde the fiue miles

5 that all the Common woods within the fiue miles be layed out unto the propriators aforefaide: but the land to ly and Remaine in Common for euer: · —

6 that all the Common lands and woods beyound the Eight miles belonging to the towne of Cambrigd be proportioned and layed out unto the propriators Interefted thearin according to the Rule of deuifon, by Cow Commons, Recorded in the towne booke prouided alwayes that It Is left to the difcretion and prudence of the Commity to fet out and giue to fuch Inhabitance among us as haue noe Common Right and are fetteled houfholders and defray publick Charges: fuch

proportions of this land as they thinke meete: for which they are to drawe lots as others:: ——

7 that this affayer be tranfacted and Efected with all Conuenient fpeede: by Capt Gookin M^r thomas danforth m^r Jofeph Cooke thomas fox famuell gofe whoe together with the felect men of the towne are defired and Impowered A Commity or the Mayor part of them to Order and fettle this afayer according to the votes aboue Exprefed ————

all theafe votes aboue Exprefed weare voted in the affirmatiue in the fayde meeting, and ordered to bee Recorded by the towne Clarke, the 9th day of february in the meeting houfe at Cambrigd: · ——

february 16th 1673

the Commity meeting together did make Choife of of leutanant winfhip dauid fifke famuell gofe and daniell Cheauer to take a furvay of the Rockes ———

[94] March th 9 16$\frac{73}{74}$

At a metting of the felect men

to looke after fwine that they bee yooked and Ringed weare appointed for the towne   danill Cheauer and Common

for menotime Row Jeames hubbard   for the farmes towards Concord John Coller and thomas Cutter

for the vilage on the fouth fide of the Riuer Job hide and thomas hammond Ju^r and neere the towne Richard dana ———

for vewers of fences of Common fields

for the necke fence John goue and John ftedman Junr
for menotime field John fwane and Nathaniell pattin
for the weft field Richard Robbins Amos woodward and John watfon
for the vilage John fuller and John fpring
and for the fouth fide of the Riuer Nathaniell fparhauke and famuell Champne ———

for driuers of the Common fields

for the necke John ſtedman Juʳ and John goue
for menotime field John ſwane and Nathanill pattin
for the weſt field John Gibſon Juʳ and Jeremiah holman

for A ſheaperd   John Jackſon

and he is to haue two pence pr hed for euery ſheepe and lame the ſpeacia to be in Caſh or wooll one halfe after ſhearing time and the other halfe when hee leaue keeping them —— ——

thomas fox francis More and Vmphry bradſhaw and John watſon weare Choſen by the ſelect men to agree with the ſheaperd about the foulding the ſheepe and time of keeping of or what euer elſe is neſiſary for the flocke during the time hee keepe and to ſee hee performe the ſame and to looke after theare waſhing and Rames and what euer may bee needfull for the flock

Amos woodward being Conuicted before the ſelect men for felling 4 ſmall green walnut trees was fined 3ˢ which is to be leauied by the Counſtable and payed to Richard Cutter

---

4 (3) 1674
at the meting of the ſelect men

granted to fell timber on the Rockes
Vmphry bradſhaw timber to build an addiſhon to his houſe ——
and to Edward hall for A leanto ——
and to thomas Andrewes for his out fence

May 11th 1674
At A metting of the ſelect men

liberty granted to mʳ Corlit ſume poſts and Railes to Repayer his orchyard fence

and to walter haſtins ſume Railes and poſts for his out fence toward water towne ——

granted to Richard Cutter timber for his barne floure and groundfills for leanto ———

granted to Nicolas wiith timber for A hundred of Rails and three skore posts ———

granted to daniell Cheauer sume timber for his out fence and A groundsill for his house ———

[95] Amos woodward being Conuicted before the townsmen for felling sume green walnut trees upon the Rocks was fined fiue shillings and It was ordered by the select men that the Counstable should leauie It and pay It to Richard Cutter

solomon prentis being Conuicted before the select men for felling A green walnut is fined one shilling ———

Alsoe Richard hildreth is fined one shilling for felling a green walnut tree upon the Rockes (the rocks)

granted to Nicolas fishington twoo trees for to make A payer of wheeles ———

granted to benony Eatton one tree for A ground fill for his barne ———

granted to m^r stedman for his out fence against the Common and his oxe marsh sume timber of the Common ———

granted to John hastins sume Railes and posts for his out fence ———

granted to Joseph sill to fell sume timber upon the Rockes to make an adishon unto his dwelling house ———

May th 3 1674
At A meeting of the selectmen

M^r danforth hanging A gate upon the highway leading to the Ware house and desired the approbation of the select men. They doe
☞ allow of It, during the the time the Inhabitance of the towne, or the select men shall see meete

liberty granted to samuell gose to fell A 100 posts and 100 Railes upon the Rockes ———

granted to william barrit sume timber to ground fill his house ———

granted to John green sume timber to Repayer his fence about his yards

June 8th 1674
at A metting of the select men

John Eames appering before the select men to Anfwer for his diging Clay in our bounds neere milis ware with out leaue. The select men haue ordered him to pay for euery thoufand of brickes hee make of the fayd Clay, 7ᵈ pr thoufand in Cafh; and to fill up the pit againe, foe as A Cart may pas through it

Nouember th 2 1674
At A meeting of the select men

Granted to Captaine gookin to fell A lode of hoope poles upon the Common

granted to Mᵗʳˢ Michell liberty to fell fume timber to ground fell her barne or leanto

granted to leutenant winfhip liberty to fell fume timber to groundfill his leatos and to fence in his yarde

liberty granted to walter haftins to fell foe much timber as will make A 150 foote of planke

liberty granted to famuell gofe to fell fiue trees to Repayer his necke fence ———

[96] Nouember th 9 1674
At a generall meeting of the towne

Chofen for Counftables
for select men
- mʳ John ftedman
- mʳ Edward Oakes
- thomas fox
- walter haftins
- francis More
- John Cooper

- Job hide
- John palfre
- Jonathan Remington
- Isack fternes

for furveyors of high wayes, for the towne —
for menotime —
for the farmes —
for the vilage —
for the fouth fide of the Riuer —
for Cording of woode Robert browne

- John haftins
- Nathaniell pattin
- francis boman
- Jeames prentis
- fteuen francis

25 (9) 1674
At A metting of the felect men

liberty granted to Jonathan dunfter to fell two trees to make A payer wheeles and 2 fills A plate

further It was agreed upon that famuell and daniell Champne fhould take Care of the bregd to put in ftrings or what els nedfull for fafe pafage ouer till the felect men take further order

14 (10) 1674
At A meeting of the felect men

granted to Richard Cutter to fell fume timber for plank for his barne floure ———

granted to Jeremiah holman A tree to Ring A payer of wheeles and fleepers for his houfe ———

to famuell Cooke liberty to fell fume poft for his out fence

granted to william dixon liberty to fell fume timber to make planke for his barne floure ———

granted to petter towne 2 trees for his trade ———

28 (10) 1674

At A meeting of the felect men

Jonathan fanders appeering before the felect men and was Conuicted of felling 5 trees on the Common is fined 20^s

Jenuary th 11 1674
At A meeting of the felect men

liberty granted to m^r Angier and famuell gofe to fell 7 trees upon the Rockes to make A fider mill

granted to Edward hall 4 trees to fence his orchyard

granted to John fwane 4 trees to fence his Orchyard

February 8th 1674
A a metting of the select men

liberty granted t Andrew steuenson to fell 2 trees to ground fill his house — —

and to Gorge willowe to ground fill his house ———

8 (12) 1674

John watson Ju^r being ackused for loping of trees upon our Rockes our wood Reeves vewing the the woods neere aboute the place wheare hee did It doe finde Ninteene trees loped theare about that they Judged weare done with in les then A yeere of that time his father appeering to Answer for his sone owned hee loped soe many trees as made three lode of wood the select men fined him for those Ninteene trees according to the towne order fiue shilling A tree the whole being — 04 — 15 — 00

[97] 8 (12) 1674

Nathaniell pattin appeering before the select men was Conuicted of felling ten trees in the swampe on this side notime and one tree in the ware field was fined fifty shillings — 02 — 10 — 00

John swane appeering before the select men was Conuicted of felling A tree for A sleade and seauerall small trees was fined fifteene shillings — 00 — 15 — 00

10 (1) 167 4/75

At A meeting of the select men

persons appointed to looke after the swine that they be ringed and yooked for those on the south side of the Riuer neere the towne samuell Olddam ——————————

for the Vilage on the south side of the Riuer Noah wiswall and thomas prentis Ju^r. ——————

for the towne and Common daniell Cheauer ———————

for menotime samuell buck ————

for the farmes John winter ————

for to looke after the Common fencis ———
for the fencis in the weſt field (Richard Robbins and
                                 (John gibſon Ju^r
for the necke of land to looke after the fencis (John ſtedman Ju^r and
                                               (benony Eatton ———
for menotime field ——— (Vmpry bradſhaw and
                       (Nathaniell pattin
for the farmes neere Concord (Jeames Cutter ſen^r and
                             (ſamuell ſtone
for the Vilage on the ſouth ſide of the Riuer (John ſpringe and
                                              (Jeames prentis

---

for to driuers of the Common fields
for the weſt field ——— (Richard Robbins and
                      (John Gibſon Junr
for the necke of land ——— (John ſtedman Ju^r and
                          (benoni Eatton
for Menotime field ———⎛ Vmphry bradſhaw and
                      ⎝ Joſeph Ruſell
for the Vilage ———

---

granted to ſeauerall perſons to fell ſume timber
to m^r Angier three trees at the 100 Akers for poſts
to petter towne for ground ſills for his fathers houſe
to Robert parker for A leanto ———
to m^r danforth timber for his ſider mill to make A frame
to John Jackſon A tree to make felluoes
to John watſon for 24 poſts———
  to the taner goodman Reade A button wood tree to make two beames of at the 100 akers———
  to John Marrit A tree for poſts A tree for A wheele and A tree for A ground fill

the ware lot to Jeremiah holman for this prefent yeere 1675 upon theafe tearmes by the felect men —— ——

that hee is to vfe his moft prudent In deuor for the taking of the fifh in the feafon theareof and to fell them for twelue pence pr thousand to thofe in the towne that defire them and therfore to giue notice to thofe that defire them when the fifh are taken and If none of the towne will fecth them away hee may fell them to any other perfon and hee is to allow for the ware and the land belonging to It fower pound for this prefent [   ] and to pay It by thofe that haue fifh of him [   ] thofe perfons the felect men fhall make Choy_∧ [   ]

[97] Aprill th 12 1675
At A meeting of the felect men

william barrit and Nathaniell hancoks defired of the felect men that they might have liberty to Inclofe that part of the fwampe that ly againft william barits houfe and betwene theare owne land It being in bredth about twenty footes It is granted to the fayd william barrit and Nathaniell hancok to inclofe the fayde peice of fwampe upon this Condition that when the felect men fhall Require them they fhall lay It open againe unto the highway

timber granted to feauerall perfons ——

to m^r Angier 4 trees at the hundreth akers to Repayer his out fence at his farme ——

to Jonathan Cane timber for A payer of wheeles ——

to famuell haftins timber for A leanto : ——

to Nathaniell pattin timber for A payer of wheeles

to Richard Eccles two trees for to fence his garddin

10 (3) 1675

at A meetting of the felect men

vpon Complaint made to the felect men by famuell ftone and Jofeph Meriam of the low and pore Condifhon of John Johnfon the felect men doe Reqeft famuell ftone and Jofeph Meriam to take Care for his fuply

TOWN RECORDS 225

for his prefent nefefitye and to be fupplyed out of the towne Rate from the Counftable Ifack ftones not exceding fourty fhillings untill further order be taken

---

liberty granted to feauerall to fell timber upon the Rockes
to Nicolas wiith 3 trees to Repayer A leanto
to walter haftins A ground fill for A leanto
to Jonathan Cane timber for A frame ———
to John watfon for A leanto ———
to Richard Cutter 2 trees for ground fills
to m^r ftedman and Jeames hubbard for A ftable and fume grounfills ———

Nouember th 8 1675

At a publicke meeting of the Inhabitance towne for the Choife of towne officers

for Counftables { william Maning
mathew bregd
{ John Jackfon
John fuller

for felect men —— { m^r John ftedman
m^r Edward Oakes
thomas fox
walter haftins
francis More
John Cooper

furveyors of high wayes { for the towne   thomas longhorne
ouer the Riuer fteuen francis
for the vilage Jonathn hide
for the farmes
neere Concord famuell ftone

[98] 8 (9) 1675

At A meetting of the felect men

liberty granted to francis whitmore to fell fume timber upon the Rockes to ground fill his houfe ———

29 (9) 1675
at A meetting of the felect men

liberty granted to m^r danforth to fell fume timber upon the Rockes for A 100 pofts ———

liberty granted to thomas fox to fell foe much timber as will make A payer of wheeles ———

30 (11) 1675
At A meetting of the felect men

William healy and Danill Cheauer are appointed to looke after the fwine that they be Ringed in the towne and

Roger buck for the Common and menotime

14 (12) 1675
At a meeting of the felect men

william Maning and Nathanill hancoke and John Jackfon and John goue are appointed by the felect men to haue Infpection into familyes that theare be no by drinking nor any mifdemenor wheare by fine is Commited and perfons from theare houfis unfeafably

    granted to feauerall perfons to fell timber upon the Comon———

    to John fwane for groundfills for his houfe and timber for A floure —

    to John Marrit two trees for his fider mill

    to John palfree two trees for his trade

    to Richard Cutter fume poplers to make flankers about his houfe ———

John watfon and thomas fox and francis more are appointed to agree with A fheaperd to keepe the fheepe and what els is nefifary for the flock

    m^r ftedman and walter haftins are appointed to agree with A heards man to keepe the milch heard and provide bulls for the hearde

    liberty granted to Abraham Arington to fell fume timber to fence his orchyard

22 (12) 1675

At A meeting of the felect men

thofe appointed for to looke after the Common fencis and driue the fields ———

for to looke after the fence in the neke and driue It Is John ftedman Juʳ and Zacariah hickes and thomas longhorne

for the weft field: to looke after the Common fencis Richard Robbins and John watfon

and to driue the field Jeremiah holman

for menotime field to looke after the fence and driue the field Vmphry b₍ₐ₎ fhaue and Richard Cutter

thofe that are to looke after the fwine that they be yooked and Ringed on the fouth fide of the Riuer Richard dana and for the Vilage John fpring and febeas Jackfon ———

liberty granted to Jeremiah holman to fell fume timber upon the Rockes to groundfill a barne ———

francis More and John Cooper being appointed to agree with with famuell buck to keepe the ware in the yeere 1676 as followeth the fayed famuell buck is to allow for the ware and the paftur of the land thirty fiue fhillings for this yeere and to fell the fifh ant nine pence pr thoufand and to let noe man haue aboue A lode at A time while all that defire to haue any haue had A lode and noe man to fell his Intreft in the fifh unto Any other

[98]   27 (1) 1676

At A publick meetting of the Inhabitance of the towne to Confider about fortifieng of the towne againft the Indians It was agreed
☞ upon by a publicke vote of the towne as followeth ———

It is by the Inhabitance Joyntly agreed, that they Judge it necefary that fome thing bee done for the fencing in the towne with A ftockade, or fume thing Equiuolent; and In perfuance theare of, doe nominate and Impower the militia of the towne and felect men to fet out the place wheare, and to Each one theare proportion, and to doe what euer fhall bee neceffary for the Compleating theare of —

Fortification

24 (6) 1676
At A meeting of the select men

Granted to benoni Eaton to fell fume timber to Repayer the houfe that was m^r pealoms

---

At A meeting of the select men
9 (8) 1676

---

the select men doe Appointe walter haftins and francis More to Inquire about the accounts of the towne Rate of the parte of It that is in the hand of Ifack ftearns deceafed ⸺

liberty granted to m^r ftedman to fell fume timber upon the Rockes to Repayer his fence on Jonfis hill and fume pofts for his gardin ⸺

granted to brother hall liberty to fell two trees to make a payer of wheeles ⸺

granted to brother Robbins liberty to fell two trees to make a payer of wheeles and one tree for a ground fill

23 (8) 1676
At A metting of the select men

---

liberty granted to John Jackfon to fell fume timber upon the Rockes, to build him A houfe upon the place wheare his Oulde houfe ftande : · ⸺

liberty granted to Androw bordman to fell fume timber to build A leanto : · ⸺

Nouember th 13 1676

At a publicke meetting of the Inhabitance of the towne for the Choifeng of towne Officers — — — —

for Counftables
{
dauid fifke
Jonathan hide
petter towne
Androw bordman
}

TOWN RECORDS 229

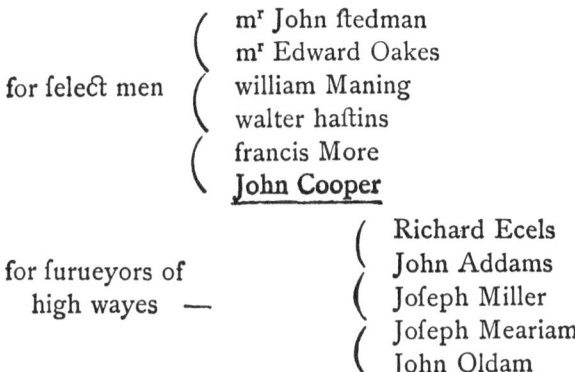

for fealer of leather   Andrew fteuenfon
for fealer of meafurs and weights   petter towne

[99]   defember th 29 1676
At A meeting of the felect men

liberty granted to Magor gookin to fell fume timber to Repayer his out fencis ——
liberty granted to John watfon fen^r to fell two trees for to make A payer of wheeles and timber for A Cart and to build A leanto ——

Nouember th 27 1676
At a metting of the felect men

the felect men taking into Confideration the vneaqality of abating the Counftables theare perticular towne Rate for theare feruice in that ofice It often fall out foe that they that doe the greateft part of the feruice haue the leaft Rats the felect men doe thearfor Agree to Alow our fower Counftables this yeere for theare feruice fifty fhilings out of the towne Rate and the two Counftables in the towne to haue two thirds of It and the other two Counftables to haue one thirds of It be tweene them ——————

12 (10) 1676

At A meetting of the felect men

liberty granted to feauerall to fell timber
to Mr danforth for A pres for his fider mill ———
to leutenant winfhipe for A leanto and A payer of wheeles
to william dixon two trees for pofts and foe many trees as will make A 100 of Railes and timber for A Cart

25 (10) 1676

At A meeting of the felect men

liberty granted to famuell bucke to fell A tree upon the Rockes to make fhouels ——
and to Richard Cutter two trees to Make A payer of wheeles
liberty granted to Mathew bregd to fell fume timber to make A frame upon our Common land beyonde the Eight Miles ———

8 (11) 1676

At A meetting of the felect men

John Jackfon is Appointed to take account of the Inhabitance of the towne wheare they had theare timber for to make theare part of theare fortification or of any other perfon and whoe they are that haue made non at all
liberty granted to feauerall to fell timber upon our Rockes
to Jonathan Remington A tree for pofts and two trees for Railes for his out fence
granted to Abraham holman to fell timber to build him A barne of 30 foote longe and 20 foote wiide
granted to francis More to fell foe much timber as will build him a fmall frame and for A barne floure
to walter haftins A tree for poft and Railes for his gardin and A tree for pales

22 (11) 1676
At A Meetting of the felect men

liberty granted to the worfhipfull m^r danforth to fell foe much timber upon the Rockes as will build A hay houfe of 20 foote wide and 30 foote longe ——

☞ liberty granted to the fellowes of the Colegd, to fell fume timber upon the Rockes for the fencing in of the Colegd orchyard ——

☞ danill Cheauer is appointed to fit Amongft the littill boyes at the North eaft Ende of the Meetting houfe to fee theare be noe diforder amongft them

29 (11) 1676
At A meetting of the felect men —— ——

liberty granted to Jeremiah holman to fell foe much timber as will groundfill and old barne and fume timber for fume fpares that are wanting

granted to Jofeph holmes two trees to make A payer of wheeles

and to John green fume pofts and Railes to fence his gardin

granted to John ftedman Ju^r to fell fume timber for ground fills for his barne and pofts and Railes for his gardin ——

granted to Androw bordman fume pofts and Railes for his gardin —

granted to benoni Eaton liberty to fell a Clapbord tree to [his houfe ——

[99] liberty granted to feauerall to fell timber

At A meetting of the felect men 12 (12) 1676

to Gorge willowes for to fence his garden and a tree for A ground fill ——

to Vmphry bradfhaw 2 trees for fleepers and one tree to make A Cart wheele

to Nicolas wiith for A leanto and to Repayer A leanto

to John Marrit A tree for pofts and 2 trees for a payer of wheeles

to John haftins fume timber to Repayer his out fence

232   TOWN RECORDS

 to famuell ftone for to Repayer his out fence upon Jonfis hill and upon the plaine neere Richard Robins

 to deacon John ftone timber for A payer of wheeles ———

 granted to thomas fox foe many trees as will make 30 pofts and 50 Railes

 to thomas Andrewes one tree for pofts and one tree for Railes

 to Nathanill green fume timber to Repayer his gardin fence

 to petter towne one tree for pofts

 to danill Cheauer for his out fence in the ox pafture

 granted to thomas longhorne to fell two trees for a payer of wheeles and timber for A 100 of Railes and one tree for pofts upon the hundreth akers

---

26 (12) 1676

 granted to thomas fofter to fell fume timber for his out fence by his houfe ——— ———

 granted to John watfon to fell fume timber to fence by his houfe upon the Common ——— ———

 m^r ftedman and deacon walter haftins are appointed to agree with A heardsman to keepe the milch heard

 william dixon and John watfon and Zacariah hickes are appointed to take Care about getting A fheaperd to keepe the fheepe and what euer is need full about the flocke for wafhing or Rames or what els is needfull

---

at A meeting of the felect men
th 12 (1) 1676/1677

 liberty granted to Richard Cutter to fell two trees for Railes and one tree for pofts for his out fence upon the Rockes

 liberty granted to m^r Edmond Angier to fell one tree upon the Rockes to Repayer his orchyard neere famuell gofes and two trees upon the hundreth akers ouer the water to Repayer his out fence

 to John palfree fence for his orchyard and timber for A leanto, granted to John fwane to fell foe much timber upon the Rockes as will Repayer his houfe and barne with ground fills and two Clapbord trees and Railes to fence his orchyarde

granted to famuell gofe to fell two trees for pofts and one tre for Railes upon the Rockes ———

granted to Nicolas wiith to fell tow trees for pofts and two trees for Railes upon the Rockes to make the out fence of land that was John frofts land ouer menotime ———

granted to Magor gookin to fell foe many trees as will make halfe A hundreth of Railes ———

granted to folomon prentis to fell fume timber upon the Rockes to fence his orchyard againft the Common ———

granted to thomas Androwes one tree for a groundfill

granted to John Cooper to fell one tree for pofts and 2 trees for Railes and one tree for timber for A leanto ———

15 (1) $\frac{1676}{1677}$

At A meeting of the felect men

to looke after the Necke fencis and driue the Necke
Zacariah hickes fen^r and John ftedman Junr
for the weft field to Vew the fencis John watfon fen^r and John Goue and John Gibfon Junr ———
to driue the weft field John gibfon and Jeremiah holman
for Menotime field to looke after the fencis and to driue It
John Addams fen^r william bull fen^r

[100]   to looke after the fwine

for the towne   william healy   Nathanill hancoke
for the Common   Roger bucke ———
for menotime   Richard Cutter   John Addams fen^r
for the fouth fide of the Riuer   Richard dana
for the farmes neere Concord   John Jonfon
the felect men doe order that the out fences

26 (1) 1677

at A meeting of the select men granted to thomas hall to fell soe many trees as will make A 100 of Railes and one tree for posts — — —

granted to william barrit to fence his gardin twoo trees for pales 2 trees for Railles and one tree for posts

granted to walter haftins to fell soe much timber as will build A small frame and one groundsill

granted to thomas longhorne A pale tree upon the hundreth akers

---

At A publick meetting of the Inhabitance of the towne
Aprill (30) 1677

to Consider about the settelling of the line betwene the Vilage, and the towne according to the Court order It being agreed upon by the Commity sent from the vilage namly Cap prentis leutenant strawbregd Noah wifwall Jonathan hide with the select men of Cambrigd to make Choise of A Commity of fiue men to settle the line. Two of them to be Chosen by the Inhabitance of the Vilage and two of them to be Chosen by the Inhabitance of Cambrigd and the fift man to be Chosen by the select men of Cambrigd and the Commity sent from the vilage and If they Cannot Agree then the fift man to be chosen by the Commity this was voted by the Inhabytance of Cambrigd the day aboue mentioned in the Afirmatiue and the two men Chosen by the Inhabitance of Cambrigd was Cap hammond and m^r William simes. but the pox being in Cap hamonds family, the select men of Cambrigd made Choise of sergant louden of Charls towne

[margin: Newtown]

Aprill (30) 1677
At A meeting of the selectmen

liberty granted to Jonathan dunster to fell 6 trees toward building him A house upon the land neere his mothers house ———

liberty granted to Israell Meade to fell two trees to make a payer of wheeles ———

granted to thomas post to fell fower trees to build A leanto

granted to umphry bradſhaw 4 trees for groundſills
granted to m^r Corlit to fell three trees to helpe fence his garden

[100]   13 (3) 1677
At A meeting of the ſelect men

liberty granted to ſiſter Arington A tree for poſts and A tree for Railes for to fence her yards

granted to leutenant winſhip to fell A tree for poſts and two trees for Railes for his out fence and two trees for Clapbords to Repayer his barne

granted to Jeremiah holman 4 trees for Clapbords to Couer his barne and two trees for A payer of wheeles

granted to Eaphraim froſt ſoe much timber as will builde A leanto and one tree for A ground fill for his houſe

granted to peeter towne A tree for poſts for his out fence

granted to Eaphraim froſt A tree to make a payer of wheeles

At A publicke meetting of the Inhabitance of the towne
21 (7) 1677

It was Agreed and ordered that the ſelect men doe forth with take Efectuall Care for the Repayering of the great brigd and for that Ende to Improue the timber that was brought for the fortifiecation and for the payment whearof they are to leuy A Rate upon the whole towne as the law direct, allowing to Each perſon for theare wood brought to the fortification as It ſhall be worth and Euery man is at his liberty to bring wood or doe other labour for his proportion ——

x · x · x · x · x · x · x · x · x · x · x

Nouember th 12 1677
At A publicke Meeting of the towne for the choyce of ſelect men and Counſtables and ſurueyers

236 TOWN RECORDS

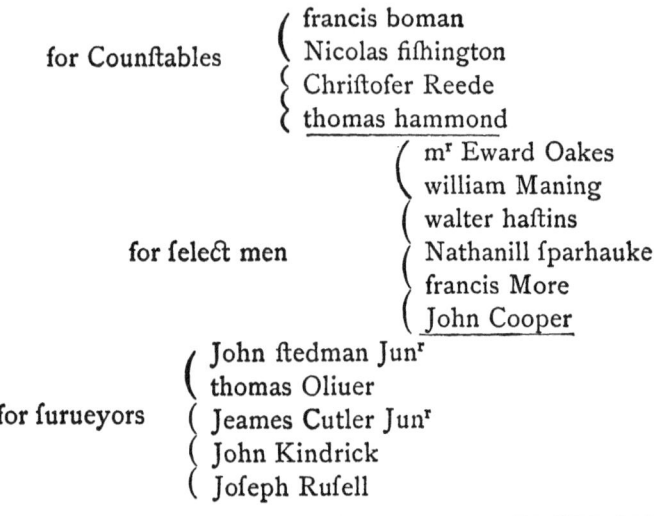

for Counstables { francis boman, Nicolas fishington, Christofer Reede, thomas hammond

for select men { m^r Eward Oakes, william Maning, walter hastins, Nathanill sparhauke, francis More, John Cooper

for surueyors { John stedman Junr, thomas Oliuer, Jeames Cutler Junr, John Kindrick, Joseph Rusell

liberty granted to seauerall to fell timber by the select men

30 (9) 1677

to John Jackson 2 trees to make A payer of wheeles

to francis More 2 trees to make A payer of wheeles

to John stedman 4 trees ground fills for his barne and sume for posts and Railes for his yards

to John Cooper timber to Ring 3 wheles and for to fence in his garden. ———

[101] 28 (10) 1677
At A meeting of the select men

granted to william Maning two trees for posts and one tree for Railes

granted to vmphry bradshaw 2 trees for A payer of wheeles and one tree for posts ———

granted to Maior Gookin 2 trees for fence for his gardin ———

granted to Robert parker sume timber to Repayer his hay house and his out fence and 2 trees for A payer of wheeles the felect men taking in to Confideration the prifing of the timber of the fortification It being by A publick Vote of the towne agreed that It fhould be Improued for the filling up of the brigd they doe order that hee that prouide his timber eyther by paying for It or of his owne fhould be allowed for It feauen fhillings fixpence a Rod and thofe that did take It of mens propriaty of land or wood lot fhould be allowed for theare felling Carting and fetting of It vp fouer fhillings fixpence A Rod and the towne to pay for the timber three fhillings A Rod

At A meeting of the felect men
11 (12) 1677

the felect men doe appoint Richard dana to giue Information to the felect men of Any that doe fell woode of the fmall lots out of towne that are on the other fide of the water or of the hundreth Akers

granted to leutenant winfhip liberty to fell two trees for A payer of wheeles and for A Cart

granted to thomas longhorne A tree for pofts and A tree for an axeltre

granted to John Marrit A tree for pofts and halfe A hundreth of Railes for the Cowes

m^r John ftedman and thomas fox are appointed to hire A heards man to keeke the milch heard and prouide bulls for the hearde

for the fheepe

the felect men doe appointe to take Care aboute the flock for to get A fheaperd and what euer is needfull for the flocke william dixon, John watfon and Vmphry bradfhaw

19 (12) 1677
At A meetting of the lect men

liberty granted granted to Nicolas wiith fen^r liberty to fell two trees for to make A payer of wheeles

liberty granted to John Jackfon foe much timber to Repayr his out fence to fell upon our Rockes

granted to John palfre timber to build A leanto and to fence his orchyard and 2 trees for his trade ———

22 (12) 1677
At A meetting of the felect men

liberty granted to Caleb Church to hange two gates upon his land on the placis hee defire during the pleasure of the felect men

liberty granted to petter towne to fell two trees for his trade and A tree for pofts and A walnut tre for hoopes

granted to John green to fell fume trees for the groundfills for his barne

25 (12) 1677
At A meetting of the felect men

liberty granted to Nathanill pattin to fell 2 trees for Railes and A tree for pofts and A tree for A ground fill

wheare as John Eames was fined 3ˡ for making brick upon our Common with out liberty the felect men doe agree that the one halfe of the fine bee Abated and hee pay thirty fhillings

11 (1) 1677/78
At A meeting of the felect men

liberty granted to william dixon to fell foe much timber as will make two ground fill for his houfe and one fill for A leanto and timber to build A leanto ———

[101] Men Chofen for hog Reeues for the yeere 1678
for the Vilage   John Mafon. Noah wifwall Ealiah kindrick ——
for to vew out fencis   John fpring and Job hide

---

for hog Reeues for the towne and Common

william healy and dauid ftone Junʳ
for the Common   John palfre and Ifraell Meade
beyond me Notime   Jeames hubbard and famuell bucke
for the farmes   John winter and John Rufell
ouer the water   thomas browne and John Mackoone
vewers of fencis   famuell Champne danill Champne

for the necke fence thomas longhorne and John ſtedman Junr
and to driue the Necke the ſame perſons ———

for the weſt field

to vew the fencis Richard Robins and John gibſon Junr
and to driue the field
Jeremiah holman and John Gibſon

for menotime field

to vew the fencis william dixon and Nathanill pattin
and to driue the field
Joſeph Ruſell and John Addams

for Runing of lines

for charles towne and Obourne and bilrica ———
m^r Joſeph Cooke danill Cheauer ſamuell Cooper ——
for Concord line ſamuell ſtone John winter
   liberty granted to thomas fox to fell ſoe many trees as will make 30 poſts and A 100 Railes
   liberty granted to piam blowers to fell ſoe many trees as will ground-fill his barne
   libertie granted to John haſtins to fell one tree for poſts for his out fence
   libertie granted to the worſhipfull m^r thomas danforth to fell ſoe much timber as will make A ſider pres
   granted to Jonathan Remington to fell A tree for poſts for his out fence
   liberty granted to william bull 4 trees for ground fills and two for plates

14 (1) $\frac{1677}{78}$

liberty granted to thomas Androwes to fell two trees upon our Rockes one for poſts and one for Railes ———
liberty granted to m^r Angier to fell two trees for two ground fills for his barne ———

8 (2) 1678
At A meeting of the felect men

granted to Jonathan Cane liberty to fell foe much timber as will make A payer of wheeles and to ground fill his houfe and to fence his yarde ———

granted to folomon prentis to fell foe much timber as will build A barne 18 foote longe ———

granted to Zacariah hickes 5 trees for groundfills for his houfe

granted to Androw bordman 3 trees to fence his garden

---

10 (4) 1678
At a meeting of the felect men

liberty granted to decon John ftone to fell fume timber to Repayer A leanto and ground fills for A leanto and bracis for his barne

granted to John Addams fen^r to fell 4 trees to groundfill his dwelling houfe in Refpect of nefefitie and not Right ———

granted to Edward hall foe much timber upon our Rockes as will make an Addition to his houfe about 16 foote longe

---

Cambrigd this 20 of febtember 1678

the felect men of Cambrigd hauing had many Complaints Come to them of the breaking the ground in the high wayes by perfons diging Clay or fand and being fenfable of the damage thearby doe order that whoe foe euer fhall digg any Clay or fande in any high way with in the bounds of the towne of Cambrigd fhall pay fiue fhillings for euery lode digged in the highway

At A Meeting of the felect men

liberty granted to thomas Androwes to fell A tree for pofts for his gardin ———

liberty granted to thomas fweetman to fell foe many trees as will groundfill his barne

[102] At A meeting of the select men
Nouember th 8 1678
granted to francis More the vse of the highway In the great swampe against his owne lot during the pleasure of the select men ——

Nouember th 11 1678
At A publicke Meeting of the Inhabitance of the towne
the Inhabitance of the towne Confidering It both duty and Reason that theare should be sume gratuity to our pastur m^r Vurian Oakes beside our anuall Allowance to him It was voted by the Inhabitance that for these two next yeares: god being pleased to Continue the Reauerant m^r Vrian Oakes with them they will Respectiuely double theare Anuall payments to him the one to be payed as hath beene Vseall by Contribution and the other to be payed in money for the Inableing him to purchase such lands as may bee for his nesary accomodation or otherwise as to him shall seeme meete the first payment to bee made the next september in the yeere 1679
Voted on the Affirmatiue
the persons Chosen to Joyne with the select men, Major gook $_\wedge$ m^r danforth m^r stedman and thomas fox to make these Rates
these seauerall officers weare Chosen upon the day aboue writen —

for Counstables
- John spring
- John Marrit
- John winter
- thomas foster

for select men
- m^r Edward Oakes
- m^r william Maning
- m^r Nathanill sparhauke
- francis More
- walter hastins
- John Cooper

for sureiyors of highwayes
- Ruben luxford
- william Ager
- Jeames hubbard
- Eaphraim winship

for the Vilage
- John Mason.

16

liberty granted to feauerall to fell timber

to thomas poſt for fencing for his gardin A tree for poſts A tree for pales 2 trees for Railes ———

to Nat hancoke A tree for poſts A tree for pales and two trees for Railes

to Edward hall

to Robert browne for his out fence one tree for poſts and two trees for Railes ———

to Androw bordman 2 trees for A payer of wheeles

to thomas longhorne 2 trees for A payer of wheeles at the hundreth Akers ———

to Chriſtofer Reede A tree for pales

to John haſtins 2 trees for A payer of wheeles

to william dixon A tree for Clapbords for his houſe

to m^r Angier to fence his orchyarde ———

to Richard Robins two trees for A payer of wheeles

to m^r danforth ſoe may Railes as will make 40 Rodes to fence his orchyard

to Vmphry bradſhaw A tree for poſts for his out fence

[102] Jenuary th 13 1678

at A meetting of the ſelect men

Complaint being made by ſume of our breathren to the ſelect men of theare neaſeacitie of fire wood the ſnow being deep upon the ground they Could not take up old woode that was upon the ground they doe allow that men for theare preſent Neceaſitie may Cut wood in the ſwampes upon the Rockes but not oake nor walnut and If any ſhall preſume to fell any green oake or walnut woode for fire woode they ſhall bee liable to pay for It according to the former order fiue ſhilling A tree and Vmphry bradſhaw is deſired to Informe of ſuch as ſhall tranſgres and this liberty to Continue during the preſent ſeaſon that the ſnow ſhall abide upon the ground

liberty granted to feauerall to fell timber

Roger bucke liberty granted to fell ſume timber to fence his orchyard and A Clapbord tree ———

granted to thomas Androwes A Clapbord tree

granted to william dixon to fell A 100 of Railes to fence his orchyard ———

granted to Jonathan dunfter timber to build a barne thirty foote longe ———

granted to dauid fifke liberty to make A Clampe of brickes neere Roger fhawes farme

granted to Danill Cheauer timber to make A Cart and two ground fills for his houfe

granted to Nathanill green Chandler liberty to fell foe many trees as will make A 100 of Railes and twenty pofts to fence his gardin ———

granted to petter towne liberty to fell foe many trees as will make A 100 of Railes to fence his fathers land againft the Common ———

granted to m^r Angier liberty to fell two trees for Railes and two for pofts at the hundreth akers for his out fence ———

granted to Magor gookin two trees for his out fence ———

liberty granted to John bradfhaw william Rufell and Jafon Rufell to lenthen the fouth galary at the weft end to accomodate them for a feate on the faboth day ———

Amoz Marrit appointed to fit in John watfons place on the galary—

the felect men haue appointed Noah wifwall to gather in the Reuertion of the Contributions at the Vilage on the fouth fide of the Riuer —

and Nicolas fifhington and Chriftofer Reede to gather in the Reuertion of the Contributions of the towne of Cambrigd according to law. —

10 (12) 1678

At A meeting of the felect men

the felect men haue appointed to get A fheaperd to keepe the flocke and to doe what Elfe is nefifary for the flock John watfon vmphry bradfhaw and thomas Androwes for the yeere 1679 ———

Alfoe the felect men doe order that the flocke bee not fed aboue two dayes in A weeke on this fide menotime

Alfoe walter haftins and francis More to agree with a man to keepe the milch hearde at prouide bulls

to folomon prentis timber granted to build A lento 17 foote long granted to John watſon to fell two trees for poſts and 30 Railes ——

granted to Eaphraim froſt one tree for poſts and ſoe many trees as will make fifty Railes

granted to ſamuell haſtins one tree for poſts and ſoe many trees as will make 30 Railes ——

granted to petter towne two trees for his trade and A walnut tree for hoopes ——

granted to John Jackſon two trees for poſts for his Orchyard

granted to Nicolas wiith one tree for poſts and 2 trees for Railes

granted to John haſtins to fell one tree for poſts and fower trees for Railes

[103] At A meetting of the ſelect men

for hog Reeues John haſtins for the towne and Common
for menotime ſamuell buck at the farmes John Coler
for the ſouth ſide of the Riuer Nathenill Robins

for the fencis of the Common fields

for the Necke thomas Longhorne and Aron bordman both to vew the fencis and driue the Necke ——

for the weſt field

John goue and ſolmon prentis to vew the fencis and Jeremiah holman to driue the weſt field ——

for menotime field

for to vew the fencis william dixon and John addams
to driue the field gerſhom Cutter —— ——
to Rune the line with Rokſbery and dedham ——
thomas foſter and Noah wiſwall are appointed for It and m^r ſparhauke alſoe to goe with them ——

10 (1) 1678 79

at A meetting of the ſelect of Cambrigd and ſeauerall of our breathren of the Vilage and wee deſire and appoint Job hide and thomas greenwoode to examine the account of thomas hammond about the towne and Country Rate that hee was to gather and to gather what is behinde and to giue account of It to the ſelect men of Cambrigd

granted to Richard Cutter two trees to make A payer of wheeles

granted to Robert wilſon one tree for poſts and ſoe many trees as will make A 40 Railes

the fiue trees felled by francis whitmore upon a grant to himſelfe and to Nathanill hancok in the yeere 1677 the ſelect men doe alow of It

granted to John Marrait A tree for to make A wheele

danill Champne and John Oldam are appointed to Joine with boſton men to Rune the line betwene boſton and Cambrigd upon the 15 day of Aprill in the yeere 1679

14 (2) 1679
At A meeting of the ſelect men

granted to leutenant winſhip to fell two trees for two groundſills for his houſe and ſoe much timber as will build A leanto to his houſe ——

granted to gerſhom ſwane to fell ſoe many trees as will make A hundreth of Railes and one tree for poſts for the Common fence betwene his houſe and william dixons barne ——

granted to Nathanill pattin two trees for Railes and one tree for poſts and A Clapbord tree

---

the Returne of francis More and walter haſtins of theare vewing of the line of John Rofe betwene his land and the Common ——

wee whoſe names are heere under written being appointed by the ſelect men to finde out and to ſettill the bounds of the land of John Rolfe firſt granted to Cap Gorge Cooke doe finde the Eaſt ſide to be bounded with Charles towne line at the north end of which ſtood A great black Oake marked and owned by ſeauerall perſons to be the bounds at that Corner the north ſide bounded by the fence now being and from the fence to A ſmall Oake upon the brow of the hill on the North ſide the brooke the ſouth ſide to bee A ſtreight line from the ſaide Oake to the ſouth ſide of his Mill houſe and the fence on the brow of the hill the bounds betwene menotime field and him 12 (3) 1679 walter haſtins francis More

thomas hall appeering before the ſelect men declared that he had ſould A Cow Right to francis More that ſumtimes belonged to the houſe that was m^r ſanders

[103] March 17th 1678/79 At A Generall Meeting of the towne and select men and propriaters of Cambrigd Common

1 It is ordered that all the Common land on the south side of the high way leading from Cap Cookes mill to water towne or further if the select men and Commity see Cause be fenced in for A Cow Common for such as haue Cow Rights Recorded in the towne booke and this is to bee done with all Conuenient speede and euery person that Cow rights and Commons shall doe theare proportion thearof as It shall bee set out by the select and Commity aded to them for the matter: and If any person that hath Right Refuse or Neglect to doe his or theare share in time Conuenient the select men and Commity are to let others that haue noe Right make up theare fence and shall and may haue the benifite thearof untill the propriators pay double the Value of the sayde fence which doing then they may Inioy the benifit thearof to theare Vse ─────────

2 It is ordered that the sayde fence be done with A stone wall eyther A whole wall or A halfe wall and sumething of brush upon It and not to be les than fower foote high ─── ───

3 It is Refered to the select men of Cambrigd together with the persons heere after named to Joine with them as A Commity to set out the lines and proportion euery mans share and make such orders for the Regulating the Commons and keeping of all Cattill and horses that haue noe liberty to goe theare as seeme good to them according to Reason

Maior gookin m^r thomas danforth william dixon John Goue or any three of them to Joine with the select men to Efect the mater

All theafe perticulers aboue writen weare Voted on the Afirmatiue

x · x · x · x · x · x · x · x · x · x

Nouember 17th 1679

At A publicke meetting of the Inhabitance of the towne for the Choice of Counstables and select men the Choice not standing upon Nouember th 10 by Reason of sume Earigularty in those that voted.

Counstables
{ m^r Jonas Clarke
  John Mason
{ Eaphraim winship
  John Oldam

select men
- william Maning
- m^r Nathanill fparhauke
- francis More
- william dixon
- walter haftins
- John Cooper

furuayers of high wayes
    for menotime   Jonathan fanders
    for the towne   Androw bordman
    for the fouth fide of the Riuer   Nathanill wilfon
    for the farmes   thomas Cutler

Nouember th 16 1679

the felect men haue Appointed for hog Reeues

for menotime   Nathanill pattin
for the farmes   John Rufell
for the towne   danill Cheauer
for the fouthfide of the Riuer   henry fmith

---

8 (10) 1679

At A meeting of the felect men

granted to Androw bordman foe many trees as will make an Addition to his barne of 14 foote longe ——

granted to m^r Angier two trees to make A floure for his barne

granted to Eaphraim froft to fell A tree to Ring A payer of wheeles

granted to Nat hancok A tree for pofts and A tree for Railes

granted to John Marrit foe much timber as will make A 100 of Railes and A poft tree

granted to John goue A Chefnut tree at the hundreth akers

granted to John haftins as many trees as will make 60 Railes and A tree for pofts for his out fence

granted to famuell gibfon 4 trees for Railes and 2 for pofts

[104]   granted to feauerall perfons to fell timber

to m^r Angier two trees upon the hundreth akers for his out fence to John watſon two trees for poſts and ſoe many trees as will make ſixty Railes ———

to John Cooper one tree for poſts and two trees for Railes for his out fence

granted to leutenant winſhipe for ſleppers for A floure for his houſe

granted to danill Cheauer two trees for groundſills one Raile tree and one Clapbord tree ——— ———

27 12 1679

At A meeting of the ſelect men

Liberty granted to Richard Cutter to fell two trees upon our Common to make borde for his floure ~ ~ ~

granted to M^{tis} Michell to fell ſume timber upon the Rockes to Repayer her orchyard and out fence ——— ———

John goue and John palfree are appointed by the ſelect men to get a heards man to keepe the Milch heard for the yeere 1680

15 (1) 1680

At A meeting of the ſelect men

Choſen for driuers of the Common fields and vewers of Common fencis

for the necke to Driue It and Vew the fenceis
  thomas longhorne and John Jackſon
for the weſt field to vew the fencis
  John watſon and thomas Androwes
and to driue the field   Jeremiah holman
for menotime field to vew the fencis and to driue the field
  John Addams ſen^r and Jeames hubbard

1680

Choſen to take Care about the flocke of ſheepe to hire A ſheaperd and take Care for the waſhing of the ſheepe and for Rams and what Elſe is Neciſary for the flock

Androw bordman Abraham holman and Joſeph Ruſell

Cambrigd this 22 of March $\frac{1679}{80}$

At A publicke meeting of the propriators of the Common
the Vote
thofe that are of the minde that the woods upon the Rockes Continue ftill as they haue been hitherto to be managed by the felect men are to manifeft it by holding up theare hand
this was Voted on the afirmatiue —— ——

12 (2) 1680

At a meetting of the felect men ——

liberty granted to Jonathan dunfter to fell foe much timber as will make two Rods and A halfe of fence againft william bulls next the Common——

June 26th 1680

the felect men going ouer the Riuer to the place Called the Indian lane and ordered John Mackoon to Remoue his fence, hee hauing taken in fume of the towne land and layed out the highway that gofhua fuller had taken in, and marked three trees below the ould track the Carts had made and the way to Extend fower Rods in bredth from the faide trees, and the felect men did order Jofhua fuller to make two payer of barrs for Carts to pas, till the laft of feptember next, and then to lay open the way for the futer

[104] The Returne of the Commity Chofen by Cambrigd
☞ felect men and the Inhabitance of the Vilage In fettelling the line betwixt them and the towne —— ——

wee whofe names are heere fubfcribed being Requefted and Impowered mutially by the felect men of the towne of Cambrigd and A Commity of the Inhabitance of Cambrigd Vilage In behalfe of both placis Refpectiuely Relating to a diference arifing betwene faide placis of the bounds betwene them after Reading and Confidering the Genarall Courts order Relating to the fame, alfoe hearing and waiing what both partyes had to say Relating to the Cafe doe determine as followeth.

hauing meafured fower miles from the Meeting houfe in Cambrigd, doe finde that line to terminate at A black Oake tree marked with fower Nochis upon the Roade which is fituate neere the North Eaft corner of widdow Jackfons Orchyard, and from the faide black Oake Northerly to A Chefnut tree In Mr Jackfons paftur, and to Continue the faide line till It Comes to Charles Riuer, and from the faide blacke Oake which is Marked with fower Nochis foutherly, to A heape of ftones which is the terminate of fower miles, from the faide meeting houfe in that place. and from the faide heape of ftones to Continue the faide line untill It Come unto bofton bounds as A teftimony that this is our yunanimus Conclution and full determination of the diferencis aboue faide wee haue heerunto fet our hands this 27th of the 7th 77

                         Richard Collicott
                         william fymes
                         william Johnfon
                         william bond
                         Richard lowden

At A meetting of the felect men   10 (3) 1680

liberty granted to Richard Cutter to fell foe many trees as will groundfill his and one Clapbord tree

liberty granted to vmphry bradfhaw to fell two trees for to groundfill his barne

liberty granted to M^{tis} Micthell to fell foe many trees as will make A hundreth and fifty Railes

liberty granted to the deputy gouernor to fell fume timber upon our Rockes as will ferue for to build A houfe at his farme neere water towne ———

liberty granted to thomas hall to fell foe much timber as will make A 100 of Railes for his orchyard

liberty granted to walter haftins one tree for a ground fill one tree for pofts and one tree for Railes

liberty granted to Jeremiah holman 2 trees for A payer of wheeles and 2 trees for Clapbord.

June 28th 1680

At A publicke meeting of the Inhabitance of the towne to Confider about the maintinance for the miniftry and the difpofing of It

1 Voted on the afirmatiue that the afefment upon the Inhabitance towards the miniftery in this towne be ftill Continued as formerly

2 that the maintinance that is anually allowed to the miniftry m^r Nathanill Gookin fhall haue one hundreth pound theareof for this prefent yeere, and the remainder to be payed to m^r Oakes this was voted on the afirmatiue

---

At A meeting of the felect men 11 (8) 1680

liberty granted to John gibfon fen^r to fell two trees for A payer of wheeles and timber for A Cart ———

[105] 8 (9) 1680

At A publicke meeting of the Inhabitance of Cambrigd for the Choice of towne oficers

for Counftables —
- John haftins
- Nathanill wilfon
- Joh Rufell
- for the Vilage
- Jeames prentis

for felect men —
- william Maning
- m^r fparhauke
- walter haftins
- francis More
- william dixon
- John Cooper

for furueyors of high wayes
- thomas longhorne for the towne
- famuell Oldam for the fouth fide of the Riuer
- famuell bucke for menotime
- dauid fifke Junr for the farmes

14 (10) 1680

At a meeting of the felect men

liberty granted to John wiith to fell foe much timber as will build A frame of 15 foote wide and 18 foote longe

liberty granted to Vmphry bradfhaw two trees to make A payer of wheeles ———

liberty granted to John Cooper to fell one tree to Ringe A wheele

liberty granted to Eaphraim Cutter to fell foe much timber upon our Rockes as will build him a frame of 26 foote long and two trees for Railes and one for pofts to fence in his yarde

liberty granted to m^r Angier to fell two trees at the 100 akers and one tree on the Rockes

liberty granted to Robert browne to fell A tree for Clapbord to Repayer his barne ———.

liberty granted to John watfon to fell fume timber for pofts for his orchyard and timber to build a houfe for his horfis

14 (12) 1680

At A meeting of the felect m

liberty granted to John fwane to fell fume pofts and Railes upon our rockes to fence his out fence and his orchyard and two Clapbord trees for his dwelling houfe ———

liberty granted to deacon haftins foe much timber as will make a payer of wheeles and A Cart ———

liberty granted to Nathanill pattin to fell one tree for Clapbords and three trees for groundfills upon our Rockes

liberty granted to thomas Androwes to fell trees for pofts and Railes upon our Rockes ———

10 (1) $\frac{1680}{81}$

At A meetting of the felect men

Phillip fhadduck Couinant with the felect men of Cambrigd to take Care about the gate upon the highway that goe to Concord to keepe

It ſhut for the ſekurity of our Common and for his paines we grant him the feede of fower hed of Cattill upon our Common for this preſent yeere 1681

for hogreeues

for the towne   Jonathan Cane
for the Common — Joſeph braddiſh
for thoſe beyonde menotime   Jeames hubbard
for thoſe on the ſouth ſide of the Riuer   ſamuell Oldum
for the farmes Neere Concord   John winter and beniamin Ruſell —
[105]   for ouerſeers of the fencis and driuers of the Common field
for the Necke for driuers and Vewers of the fencis   thomas longhorne and John Jackſon

for the weſt field

for Vewers of fencis   John Goue and ſolomon prentis
to driue the field   Jeremiah holman ———

for menotime field

for vewers of the fencis   thomas hall and Iſraell meede
to driue the feild   John Addams ſen[r]

24 (1) 1681

At A meetting of the ſeleċt men

m[r] Maning and francis More and John haſtins are appointed by the ſeleċt men to Anſwer the Complant of Jonathan ſanders before the worſhip[ll] danill gookin for ſume of his Cattill being put into to the Cow rate and hee refuſing to pay the ſeleċt men ordered the Counſtable to deſtrane upon his Eſtate

granted to widdow Cooke to fell A tree upon our Rockes for poſts for her out fence ———

granted to widdow Arington liberty to fell ſume poſts and Railes to fence her yarde at whome ———

widdow Cooke and her two ſons are fined for Cutting wood in the ſwampe on this ſide menotime the ſume of ten ſhilings and ſamuell Cooke for two lode of woode fiue ſhillings and Joſeph Crakbon fiue ſhillings

Nouember 14th 1681

At A publicke meetting of the Inhabitance of the towne for the Choice of towne Officers.

for Counſtables
(william barrit
(Abraham holman
(Jeames Cutler Junr
(febeus Jackſon

for ſelect men
/Deacon haſtins
| mr ſamuell Androwes
| william Maning
>francis More
| ſamuell Champne
| ſamuell ſtone
\John Cooper

ſuruayers of high wayes
(ſolomon prentis   for the towne
(John Addams   for menotime
(dauid fiſke fenr   for the farmes
(Noah wiſwall   for the Vilage

14 (9) 1681

liberty granted to John haſtins to fell A tree for poſts and ſoe many trees as will make 60 Railes for his out fence ——

liberty granted to mr Androwes to fell ſume timber to Repayer his out fence

At A metting of the ſelect men

Agreed with John willington to keepe the gate ſhut neere his houſe upon water towne line to Reſtraine Cattill for Coming on to our Common for which he is to haue the ſame liberty upon our Common that phillip ſhadduck had

12 (10) 1681

At A meeting of the ſelect men

granted to petter towne 4 trees for his trade
granted to ſamuell ſtone to fell two pine trees upon the Remote land

and to Nathanill green one tree for pofts and three trees for Railles for his out fence

[106] 12 (10) 1681

At A meeting of the felect men

the felect men taking into Confideration the Complaint of feauerall perfons of our Inhabitance that Cary wood of our Common Notwithftanding orders to the Contrary the felect men doe order that whoe foeuer fhall Cary any wood of our Common out of the towne fhall pay for euery lode Eighteene fhillings pr lode Notwithftanding any order to the Contrary ~ ~ ~ ~ ~

this order was publifhed

25 (11) 1681

At a meeting of the felect men

Jonathan dunfter hauing a grant of liberty to fell timber upon our Rockes to build him a barne but he made noe vfe of It the felect doe grant the fame liberty to him againe prouided he doe It this prefent yeere

granted to Robert parker to fell A tree for pfts and timber to Repayer his barne upon the Rockes ———

granted to famuell winfhip two trees for his trade upon the Rockes

granted to John Jackfon liberty to fell foe many trees as will make A hundreth of pofts

30 (11) 1681

At A meeting of the felect men

granted to John gibfon liberty to fell two trees to groundfill his houfe and two trees for Railes and one for pofts to repayer his out fence the timber to be felled upon our Rockes

9 (12) 1681

At A meetting of the felect men

granted to Jeremiah holman to fell two trees for A payer of wheeles upon our Rockes and foe many trees as will make A hundreth of Railes and 30 pofts for his out fence granted to thomas Androwes to fell foe much timber upon our Rockes as will Repayer his out fence ———

granted to John green to fell foe much timber upon our Rockes as will Repayer the out fence of his fathers orchyard or upon the hundreth akers

13 (12) 1681

At A meeting of the felect men

granted to John haftins to fell two trees upon our Rockes to make A payer of wheeles

granted to Zacariah hickes to fell fume pofts and Railes to repayer John ftedmans out fence and groundfills for the houfe ———

granted to Jofeph Rufell to fell foe much timber as will Repayer his out fence and timber to build A lento upon the rockes ———

granted to bro Maning 20 pofts to Repayer his gardin fence upon the Rockes

granted to mr Clarke 25 pofts to repayer his garden fence upon the rockes

granted to william hely A tree for pofts for his yards upon the Rockes

granted to william wiith to fell 50 Railes and 30 pofts to repayer the fence in the oxpaftur upon the rockes

granted to John Marrit to fell 4 trees upon the Rockes to repayer his fider pres ———

granted to Amos Marrit to fell foe much timber on our Rockes as build A fhop ———

granted to william dixon liberty to fell fume timber on our rockes to make an adition to his barne

granted to John watfon foe much timber as will build A leanto

granted to thomas Androwes to fell A ground fill for the houfe that was John frofts on the rockes

granted to John Cooper to fell 2 trees to repayer his houfe and 2 trees for railes and one tree for pofts

Vmphry bradfhaw and Martha bradfhaw his wife did fignifie by a note vnder theare hand that they ded give to theare fones william and Jafon Rufell the priuilgd that belong to theare houfe

TOWN RECORDS

[106]   27 (12) 1681

At A meeting of the felect men

granted to famuell gofe to fell two trees upon the Rockes to make a payer of wheeles

granted to william and Jafon Rufell to fell foe much timber upon our rockes as will build them a houfe of 26 foote long with a leanto at the Ende of It

francis More and Abraham holman and thomas Androwes are Appointed by the felect men to meafure the line betwene the wood lots and the fwampe lots in the old ox paftur from francis Mores Corner to the lot that was Edward fheaperds neere the highway that leade into the frefh pond meddow and to make returne thearof tò the felect men

the felect men doe Alfoe appointd Abraham holman to bee ouerfeer of the flocke to get a fheaperd and doe what euer Elfe is needfull for the flock for the yeere 1682 ———

for hogreeues for the yeere 1682

for the towne   Owin warlin
for the Common   folomon prentis
for menotime   famuell buck
for the fouth fide of the riuer   Jacob dana
for the farmes   thomas Cutler and John Jonfon

13 (1) $\frac{1681}{82}$

At A meetting of the felect m

granted to widdow Cooke one tree for pofts for her out fence and foe many trees as will make half A hundreth of Railes for her out fence which they are to fell upon the rockes

granted to Androw bordman to fell foe much timber upon our rockes as will make thirty pofts to fence in his yards

granted to walter haftins and thomas fox to fell foe much timber as will build Each of them A houfe upon our Common land

27 (1) 1682
At A metting of the select men

for the driuers of the Common fields and looke after the fencis to looke after the fencis John watson and Richard Robins for the west field

and to driue the west field samuell Cooper

for the necke of land to looke after the fencis thomas longhorne and danill Cheauer and they are alsoe to driue the neck for menotime field to vew the fencis and driue the field william dixon and Nathanill pattin

and for the farmes John winter and dauid fiske Junr to looke after the fencis

31 (1) 1682
At A meetting of the select

granted to Nathanill pattin 6 trees for ground fills for his house and barne and A tree for Clapbords for his barne and 2 trees for railes for his out fence

granted to william barrit a tree for posts and one tree for railes for his yarde fence

granted to Israell Meade to fell one tree for posts and soe many trees as will make halfe A hundreth of railes for his out fence

granted to thomas swetman A tree for a groundfill for his house and A Crocth and pole for his well

granted to richard Cutter one tree for posts and soe many trees as will make a hundreth of Railes

10 (2) 1682
At A meeting of the select men

granted liberty to John palfree to fell three trees upon the Rockes for his trade

[Page 107] 14 (2) 1682
At A publicke meeting of the propriators of towne Common ——

proposed at A towne meeting of the propriators and Voted that in order to the fencing in of the west field and the swamp lots that Eyther are, or may be made meddow of, the towne doe grant fume fmall qantity of the Common land adjoining to the hed of thofe fwamp lots, lying againſt the ox paſtur that may helpe in making up the fence about two or three Rods, or what the felect men fhall Judge Conuenient prouided that thofe whoe haue this addifhon of land doe make and mainetaine the fence for time to Come

granted on the afirmatiue

granted to John watfon twelue foote fquare on the north fide of his barne to build A porch upon

☞ granted to the felect men that theare may be A gate hanged at menotime bregd for keeping in or keeping of what Cattill may be ordered to be kept theare

A Coppy of the grant of the generall Court to the petition prefented by the felect men of Cambrigd for liberty to difpofe of the Eftate of Renold bufh for his necefary Releefe ~ ~ ~

At A generall Court held at boſton ixth of febuary <u>1682</u>

In Anfwear to the petition of John Cooper in behalfe of the felect men of Cambrigd in reference to Renold bufh the Court Judgeth It meete that the management of the whole affaire be refered to the management of the felect men of Cambrigd whoe are heereby Impowered to make fale of land or otherwife as they fhall Judge meete for payment of Juft debts fupply and Releefe of the faide bufh and family and that they fhall giue A true and Juft account of euery and difburfment when they fhall bee legally Called thearunto) this is A true Coppy taken out of the Court booke of Reccords

as Atteſt Edward Rawfon fecretary

<small>license to sell land</small>

At a Publik meetting of the Inhabitants of this Town of Cambridg this 8th of January 1682

<small>500 acres laid out to the use of the ministry in this town & place</small>

It was then voted and agreed that 500 acheres of the remote lands lyeing between Oburne Concord and our head line, fhall be layd out for the vfe & benefitt of the <u>miniſtry of this Town and place, and</u> to remaine for that vfe for euer; and as neer as may be that 500 ache^{rs} that hath bin alredy meafyered and the remaynder of thofe lands to be deuided amongſt the Inhabetants, by a Comittie hereafter named.

The Comittie Chofsen is the Honered Maio^r Gookins Elder Stone Deacon Cooper & Mr Nath: Sparahauke to Joyne with the Select men of Cambridg:

At a publike meeting of the Inhabitants of Cambridge the 8^t. 11mo. 1682

It was then agreed and voted that the widdow Rolffs land now in Contreverfy fhould be serveyed, and the lines in Contreverfie ftated, and setled by a Comittie hereafter named. the Comittie Chofsen is our honored Deputy Gouerner Tho: ffoxe & Samuell Andrew for the Setleing of the aboue written afayre according to beft direction, and Information;

[107]   Nouember the 13th. 1682

At a meeting of the Inhabitance of the Towne of Cambridge for the Choyce of Town officers

Town Counftables { Solomon Prentice
                  { Nathaniell Pattin

farme Counftable — ffrancis Whitmor
villedg Counftable — Edward Jackfon

ffor Select men {
  Leu^t Edward Winfhipp
  William Dickson
  John Wotson
  Samuell Chamne
  Samuell Andrewes
}

Chofe for Sveyors of ye fence in weft feild for the Insueing year 83
Abraham Holman & Sam^ll Cooper Junr

Chofsen for Servayer of ye high wayes in Town   Nicholas ffisenden

Hogreeues Chofsen for ye yeare 1683. {
  Ephraim winfhip & dauid fifk Junr for the farmes
  Tho: Hall for menotomie
  Tho: Andrew for the Commons
  Arron Bordman for the Town
  Henry Prentice South fide Riuer
}

Chofen for vewers of the fences on the neck   { Tho: Longhorne
and to driue it for the Infueing yeare 83   { Arron Bordman

Chofe for vewers of fences & dreeurs for menotomie feilds for ye Infueing yeare John Addames sen^r Jofeph Ruffells and John Addams senior Chofe for to servey the hyeway at menotomie

At ameeting of the Inhabitants of the Town Nouember 13th 1682 It was then voted that the Select men of this towne fhould Anually giue in an account to the Town of all Town charges and receipts on the day of Choyce of there Select men and voted on the affirmitiue;

At a meetting of the Select men (1st) 10mo 1682.

Granted to Amos Marritt. Two trees for timber for his Calling vpon the rocks

At a meetting of the felect men 18th: 10mo 1682

Granted to Thomas Longhorne one tree vpon the hundred ache^{rs} on South fid the riuer for posts

Chofe this day aboue written Sam^{ll} Chamne to be ouerfeer ouer the hundred ache^{rs} on the South fide the riuer that ther be noe Timber nor wood Cutt nor Caryed of it without liberty from the Townfmen

At a meeting of the selectmen the 22^d: 10mo 1682

Granted to petter Town liberty for 100 rayles & 25 pofts and two trees for his Calling of the rockes

At a meetting of the Select men of Cambrid: 5^t: 12mo 1682

Martin Townend of watertown was Choffen for the Infueing yeare to looke to the Gate by John willingtons feild and to looke after phillip Jones that he make vp the breaches in the stone wall

Granted liberty to Petter Town to Cutt hoops for his trade of ye rockes

At ameeting of the Selectmen the 12th 12mo 82

Granted liberty to the honered Maio^r Gookin to Cutt and Cary of the rockes fencing ftuff for his outfences

[108] The Town Rate for the yeare 1682 being a Rate 3 quarters _{Town} for the Town and one single Rat for ye vilidg and a quartor of _{tax} a rate is money

ffrancis Whitmors pt of the Town rat in Comon pay	*l*	*s*	*d*
	09	11	05
his money pay being a quarter of a rate is	01	11	06
Edward Jackſons pt of the Town rate in Comon pay is			
	10	11	10
his money pay is	03	10	06
Nathanill Pattin and Solomon Prentice there parts in Comon paye is			
	38	10	09
there money pt is	06	08	00
*	70	04	00

At ameetting of the Selectmen the 2^d march: 1682/3

Granted to our honered Deputy Gouerner liberty for to Cutt fencing ſtuff of the rockes for his out fences about ye Town

Granted liberty to william Dickſon to Cutt and gett off the rockes Two hundred and a half of rayles and poſts proportionable therevnto

Granted liberty to John wotſon to Cutt and gett off the rockes Two hundred & fifty rayles & poſts proportionable for his out fences

Granted liberty to Samuell Buck to Cutt ſoe much timber of the rockes to build a Leentoo to his barne of thirty foott long & tenn foott broad and foure foott ſtudd:

Granted liberty to Leut. Winſhip to Cutt and gett off the rockes one hundred & fifty rayles with poſts proportionable for his out fences

Granted liberty to Ephraim ffroſt liberty to Cutt & gett off the rocks 50 rayles & one tree for poſts for out fences & a tree for a groundſell

Granted liberty to Aron Boadman for 100 rayles & 50 poſts for his out fences to Cutt and Cary off the rockes

At a meetting of the Select men 19th March: 1682/3

granted to widdow Cooke 50 rayles & 17 poſts to be taken of the rocks for her out fences

Granted to Amos Marritt two trees for poſts & rayles of ye rocks

Granted to Jonathan Cane timber for a leentoo to the end of his

---

* In original record an entry appears here which was erased by drawing lines through the entry. It is not printed here because it appears in full on pages 263-264 marked *.

houfe and two trees for fence and timber for apayer of wheeles of the rockes

Granted to Danill Cheeuers fenfing ftuff for the prifson yard pofts for abought 10 rodd for a board fence off the rockes

Granted to Nathanill Pattin timber for a Leantoo to his barne and for hurdles for the ware off the rockes —— ——

Nathanill Pattin was Choffen for ouerfeer for the fheep to prouid a fheperd and take care about the foulding of them

Nathanill pattin hath taken the ware and for this Infueing yeare and is to pay to the Town for the same thirty ∧ llings in fuch pay as he generally fells his fifh for

*[108] December the 12th: 1682   Town orders

Whereas there is many Complaints made to the felect men of this town of the vnreafonable Stroy that is made by many prsons, of the wood and timber on the rocks & Commons in this Town notwithftanding all orders formerly made for the prevention thereof;

1- It is therefor ordered by the felect men of this Town, that if any prson or prsons whatfoeuer, fhall hereafter fall any tree or trees vpon any pt of the rockes or Comons of this Town, whether for wood or timber vnder one foott diameter two foott from the ground, or any other trees of greater diamiter that are fitt for timber, fhall pay for euery fuch tree, fiue fhillings for the vfs of the town, exept they haue a grant from the felect men foe to doe. and if any prson fhall fall or lopp any tree or trees vpon the Comon on this fide Menotomie Riuer without liberty from the felect men, fhall pay for each tree tenn fhillings to the Towns vfs.

2 It is further Ordered that whoefoeuer fhall cutt and cary away any wood out of any of the Comon fwamps on this fide menotomie Riuer, without liberty from the Select men, fhall pay for each loed fiue fhillings to the vfs of the Town.

3 It is further ordered that whoefoeuer fhall cutt and cary off any wood or Timber vpon any of our Comon lands to any other Town fhall pay Eighteen fhillings for each loed to the vfs of the Town

* See foot note, page 262.

4 It is further ordered that whofoeuer fhall fall any tree or trees for wood or timber vpon Mr Pelhams hundred ache^{rs} without liberty from the felect men, fhall pay for each tree fiue fhillings to the Towns vfs, and if any fhall cutt and Cary off thence to any other Town wood or timber, he fhall pay for each loed Eighteen fhillings to the vfs of this Town.

5 It is further ordered that whatfoeuer prson or prsons fhall Cutt any hoop poles either walnutt or oake off any of our Comon lands, without leaue from the felect men foe to doe, fhall pay for each hoop pole one peny to this towns vfs thefe orders was publifhed by pofting on the meeting houfe 13th: 12mo 1682

At a meetting of the felect men the 12th March: $\frac{1682}{3}$

Highway Marsh
Agreed with Mr Edmond Anger for the high way in the marfh one the South fide the riuer from the great brooke vp to the vpland he hath hired it for the Infueing yeare and is to giue for the same tenn fhillings in money: and hath liberty granted him to fhutt vp the high way that leadeth to the marfh below the Country high way; Recd of Mr Edmond Anger this 7th of december 1683: for the yeare paft tenn fhillings in Money.

At ameeting of the felect men the 9th Aprill: 1683

Granted to Tho: Danforth Efq^r three trees vpon the rockes for barrill heads & ftaues for his vfs

Granted to Richard Cutter a tree for pofts and one hundred rayles off the rockes

Granted to Tho: Andrewe fifty rayles of ye rockes

Granted to Amos Marritt three hundred poles for hoops for his trade off the rockes

Granted to william Barritt two trees for pofts off the rockes

Granted to Nath: Hancocke two trees for pofts off the rockes

At a meeting of the felect men the 14th of May 1683

Granted liberty to Ephraim Cutter liberty to Cut Sleepers for his kitchin and to Cutt a tree for Claboards for his vfs of the rockes

Granted liberty to John Marritt to Cutt Timber off the rockes for a leantoo on the backfide his barne fourty foott long and 10 ffoott broad:

At ameeting of the select men the 28th of May 1683

Granted liberty to Roger Bucke timber off the rocks for a fmale frame and Groundfells for his ould houfe

Granted to Mr Corlitt at a meating of the Select men 13th. Auguft 1683 Liberty for 60 rayles & 30 pofts and timber to mend his houell of the rockes

[109]   At a meetting of the Comitte and the select men of
Cambridg the 13th of Aprill 1683

It is ordered by the Comity and select men appointed to devid the lands Conteyned betwixt oburne Concord and our head line, Conteyned in a plat Drawn by Enfign Dauid ffifke, that each Squadrants be be drawn Each from the other, Eighty rode parrellell one from the other as neare as may be; and the firft Squadrant to begin at the place called m^r Cookes fouth Corner and there to be numbered one, and where the firft Squadrant doth end then the fecond to begin & foe to profeed fucceffiuely, vntil the whole be devided and the bredth of the squadrants, to be the length of the lotts, And enfign ffifk is Chofsen suruayer: & it is left to him, Samuell Chamne & Samuell Ston Senio^r and John watfon or any two of them whereof the serveiour to be one: firft to ftate and Setle all Country roeds that ly thorow this land of the width the law directs, and then to lay out high wayes from the farmes alredy setled, in the Common vnto this town, of two rode wide, and alfoe to leaue Convenient high wayes of two rod wide between the devifhons or Squadrents where need requires for a high way; and if ther be occation to lay a hy way thorow any mans land or lott he is to be allowed two ache^{rs} for one that is taken out of his lott for the high way;

At a publike meeting of the Inhabitants
of Cambridge the 15th of October 1683 =

It was then put to vote whether the former alottments of our remote lands Lyeing betwixt Oburne Concord & head line fhould ftand, whether euery mans number according there lotts then formerly drawn fhould ftand and it was voted on the affirmitiue and that they fhould beginn next Oburne Line, on the farther fid of the Eight mile line, makeing euery Squadrant eighty rod longe, & foe to profeed in the Number of lotts till they come to watertown Line, and where the laft lott in Number doth end in the firft Squadrant. there to begiñ the next number in the 2 d squadrant, & foe to profeed backe to Oburne Line agen, making euery Squadrant eighty rodd parrellell one to another foe farr as the land will beare it.

At ameeting of the Inhabitants of Cambridge
this 12th of Nouember 1683

It was then voted that Daniell Chamne Thomas Brown Zachariah Hickes Joseph Ruffell fhould take acco^{tt} of the Selectmen Now in being for the yeare paft of all the Towns Charges & Expense in the behalfe of the Town:

At ameeting of the select men the 17th of September 1683

There was then Choffen by the select men of Cambridge for the ordering and manidgment of the Contriverfie betwixt Mr Edward Pellam & this Town, about the meafureing of his fiue hundred acheres ouer agen that hath bin alredy Meafured by Enfign ffifke, and alfoe to meafure one hundred Acheres more if there be need of foe much or at leaft foe much as fhall make vp the former land meafured out by enfighn ffifke Sixe hundred ache^{rs} according to an anfhent grant of this Town to Mr Richard Harlackenden, there was then Choffen Samuell Andrews Leut: winfhip John watfon, Samuell Chamne Samuell fton & enfign ffifke,

we whofe names are aboue written haue Compleated the worke aboue mentioned for Mr Edward Pellum in the behalf of this Town in making the former land meafured by enfign ffifk in layeing foe much to it as fhall make it six hundred ache^{rs} wittneffe our hands this   of September 1683

[109] At a publick meeting of the Inhabitants
of Cambridge the 12th of Nouember 1683 =
for the Choyce of officers and made
Choyce as ffolloweth

TOWN RECORDS

for Counſtables
- Samuell Bucke for menotomie
- Abraham Jackſon for the villidg
- Sam^{ll}: Gookin for the Town
- John Tidd: for the farmes

for Select men
- Deacon Cooper
- Deacon Haſtin
- ffrancis More
- william Manning
- Nathaniell Sparahauk
- Samuell Chamne
- Samuell Andrews

& Survayors
- Ephraim Winſhip for Concord way
- Eſraell Mead for Menotamie
- Chriſtopher Reed for the Town
- John Smith South ſide the Riuer

Surveyors of fences
for ye south ſid ye riuer
- Mr Thomas Oleuer
- Thomas Brown

At ameeting of ye Inhabitants 12th: 9mo 83: of Cambridge there was then Choſen a Comitte to Joyne with the Towns men to make a Rate for the Miniſtry for ye Inſueing yeare and tell another reviſment

Choſſe Leut winſhip Samuell ſtone & Mr Tho: Oleuer

At ameeting of the Select men the 7th of Decembe^r: 1683

Made Choyce of Mr Samuell Chamne to Survay our great bridge and repayre the same, and alſoe the Cauſie on the South ſid the bridge that doth belong to the bridge ſoe farr as the villidge doe bare a ſhare of Charg with the Town;

At a meetin of the Select men y^e 17th: 1mo 168$\frac{3}{4}$

made Choyce of Tithingmen

for the Town Tithingmen
- Petter Town
- Andrew Bordman
- Chriſtopher Reed

for the Comōn Tithingmen	John watson Thomas Brown Abraham Holman
for menotomie Chofe Tithingmen ffor y^e farmes South fide the Riuer Tithingmen	Nathaniell Pattin Joseph Ruffell ——— Mr Daniell Chamne Mr Tho: Oleuer

At ameeting of the Select men Decemb^r. 10th. 1683

Granted liberty to Good: mead to take a Tree for Claboards vpon the right of the houfe he now liueth in;

At ameeting of the Selectmen the 10th 10mo. 1683

The high way marfh on the South fide the Riuer which Mr Edmond Anger hired of the towne the prefeding yeare was then lett to Andrew Boedman for twelue fhillings the yeare in money he runeing the rifque of all Inconveniences that may accrue it was let to him for the enfueing yeare 8th: 10mo 1684 Receiued of Andrew Boadman for the Towns high way marfh on the South fide the riuer for ye yeare paft 12^s money:

At ameeting of the Select men the 17th: 10mo. 1683

Granted liberty to Mr Anger timber vpon ye rockes for to make a paire of wheeles;

At ameeting of the select men 24: 10mo. 1683

Granted liberty to Leut winfhipe to Cutt timber of the rockes for the repaireation of his barne & leantoes.

Granted liberty to Mrs Michell to Cutt timber off our Comōns for to repaire here barne

At ameeting of the Select men the 26: 10mo 1683

made Choyce of Nathanill Pattin Israell Mead & Samuell Cooke, for wood reeues for the enfueing yeare

Granted to Nathaniell Pattin Liberty to Cutt timber for a paire of wheeles of the rockes

[110] At a meeting of the Select men 3ᵈ — 10ᵐᵒ 1683 made thefe ffollowing orders

Whereas there hath bine many Complaynts made to the select men of this Town, of the vnreafonable ftroy of wood vpon our Comons, and Efpefhally fmale trees vnder a ffoot diameter, notwithftanding any former order made by the Select men to the Contrary

It is therefor Ordered by the Select men of this Town as ane Addition to a former order made by them, beareing date the 12ᵗʰ day of December 1682 :

1 That whatfoeuer prfon or prfons fhall be found Carting downe any fuch fmale wood Contrary to order, if the prfon Carting of it downe, or fome other Conferned therein, will not teftefy, that that wood did not growe vpon any part of our Comon, he fhall pay for euery fuch loed of wood fiue fhillings, euery time he fhall be foe taken for yᵉ Towns vfs It is further ordered that if any prfon or prfons fhall fell any tree or trees, though decayed and foe vnfitt for timber and fitt for nothing but firewood & fhall onely lop of the boughs, and not Cutt and Cary away the bodyes thereof alfoe within tenn dayes after the felling of the same, fhall pay for euery such tree, fiue fhillings for the vfs of the Town:

pofted vpon our meetinghoufe dore the 3ᵈ : 10ᵐᵒ 1683

At ameeting of the select men 14ᵗʰ January 1683

Granted to Mʳ Edmund Anger liberty for one hundred and fifty rayles and pofts to them off the hundred acrers on the south fid the riuer for his outfide fences at his farme & fifty rayles and pofts to them off the rockes for his out fide fences in the Towne

Granted to Deacon walter Haftin liberty to Cutt timber off the rocks for a fmale frame

Granted to Mʳ Jofeph Cook liberty to Cutt timber of the roks for a Carte

Granted liberty to Nathaniell Hancock liberty to Cut timber for a fram of thirty fiue foott long & eighteen foott broad and thirteen foott ftude of the rockes

Granted liberty to John watſon liberty to Cutt Timber off the rockes for a frame of ſixteen foott ſquare & tenn foott ſtude

Granted liberty to Robert Parker for two trees for a payre of wheeles of the rockes

Granted liberty for two trees vpon the rocks to will wieth vpon the priuelidge of his mother for a payre of wheeles

Granted liberty to Richard Cutter to Cutt Timber for a paire of wheeles and Cart off the rockes

Granted to Nathaniell Pattin liberty to fell three pine trees in the great ſwamp;

At a meeting of the Select men the 4th ffebruary 1683

Granted liberty to Samuell Goff to Cutt Timber off the rockes for two paire of wheeles

At a meeting of the select men the 18th of ffebruary 1683

Granted liberty to m^r Thomas Oleuer to Croſs a high way of foure rode wide on the north Side of the sayd Oleuers feild betwine his feild fence and his new paſter, dureing the selectmens pleaſure;

At ameeting of the select men the 10th of March 168$\frac{3}{4}$

Choſe hogreeues for the Town and Comon for the Inſueing yeare

Choſe for y^e enſuing yeare   { Joſua woods
                                             { william wieth

and alſoe for Menotomie —   Jeremiah Holman
& Samuell Robbins for the South ſide y^e riuer

ffor the farmes towards Concord   { Thomas Cutler &
                                                      { Dauid ffiſk Juno^r

made Choyce of Nath Pattin to keepe the flock of sheepe for enſuing yeare

Choſe the vewers of fences for ye weſt fields is   { John Goue &
and driuers for the ſame is   { Thomas Andrewe

aded for driuer for the weſt feild   Jeremiah Holman

Chofe the vewers of ffences for the necke } Thomas Longhorne
and driuers for the same is } & Arron Boedman
Vewers and dreeuers for Menotomy feilds } Rich Cutter &
 Nathaniell Pattin

[110] At ameeting of the select men this 10th March 168¾

Granted liberty to the widdow Cooke liberty to Cutt fifty rayles & sixteen pofts of our Rockes

Granted Samuell Buck liberty to Cutt timber for a Leantoe eighteen foott Long & tenn foott wide of our Rockes

Granted Amos Marritt liberty to Cutt two trees off our Rockes for his trade and half a hundred of railes with pofts to them for outfid fences for his own fence and John Jackfons

Granted to Nathanill Pattin liberty to Cutt one hundred of rayles and twenty fiue pofts off the rocks for outfide fence

At a meeting of the select men this 12th: of May: 1684

Granted vnto John Haftin liberty for fixty rayles and one tree for pofts off the rocks for his outfide fences

Granted liberty vnto Robert Parker for one hundred of rayles and pofts to them off the rockes for his outfide fences;

Granted liberty vnto Richard Cutter for one hundred of rayles and poft sufifhent for them off the rockes for his outfide fences

Granted liberty to william Dickfon for one hundred of rayles with pofts for them of the rockes for his out fences

At ameeting of the Select men ye 9th: 4mo 1684

Granted liberty to Ephraim ffroft for timber for a barne off our Rockes on the Comon

At a meeting of the Inhabitants this 10th. of Nouemb^r 1684: ther was then Chofsen as Town offecers as followeth for ye year enfueing

Tithingmen chofs for y^e farmes
  David ffisk Senio^r
  John Tidd

Conftables

John Goue
Dauid ffifk Juno^r for farms
Jofeph Ruffell
John Prentice for y^e villidg

Tithingmen for Menotomie
  John Addames:
  Israell Mead:

Chofs for Cullers
of brick for the South
fid the riuer M^r
Daniel Chamne

    Selectmen $\begin{cases} \text{Leut Edward winfhip} \\ \text{Samuell Andrew} \\ \text{Samuell Chamne} \\ \text{william Dixfon} \\ \text{Daniell Chamne} \\ \text{Abraham Holman} \\ \text{John Watfon} \end{cases}$

Chofs for Culler of bricks
for the Town   Thomas Andrew
Tithingmen for y^e Town Chofs
Mr Joseph Cooke
william Barritt
Zechariah Hicks
Rubin Luxford

Tithingmen for $\Big\{$ the Comon
John Palfry
Solomon Prentice
Tho: Andrews

south fid the Riuer
Tithingmen
  Nath: Robbins   Survayors
  John: Oldum   of High wayes—

$\begin{cases} \text{Nicholas ffefenden for y}^e \text{ Town} \\ \text{Israell Mead for Menotomie} \\ \text{Jacob Dany for fouth fide Riuer} \\ \text{Phillip Ruffell for y}^e \text{ farmes} \end{cases}$

John willington of this town
Chofen to keep our gat at   Hogreeus Chofsen $\begin{cases} \text{Jacob Amfden} \\ \text{Amos Maritt} \end{cases}$
John willingtons feild   for the Town —

    Survayers fences and driuers $\begin{cases} \text{John Addams} \\ \text{will: Ruffell} \end{cases}$
    for y^e fences at Menotomie feild

        Hogreeues Chofsen — $\begin{cases} \text{Samuell Cooper} \\ \text{Samuell Cooke} \end{cases}$
        for the Comon to notomie

Surveyers fences & driuers of $\begin{cases} \text{Rich Robbins} \\ \text{ffrancis more} \\ \text{Jeremiah Holman} \end{cases}$
the feild weftfeild is ———

      Hogreeues Chofsen $\begin{cases} \text{Thomas Hall} \\ \text{Richard Cutter senio}^r \end{cases}$
      for Menotomie

Surveyers ffences & driuers $\begin{cases} \text{Daniell Cheuers} \\ \text{Zacheriah Hicks} \end{cases}$
for the necke is ———

      Hogreeues Chofsen for $\begin{cases} \text{Samuell Ouldum} \\ \text{Jacob Dany} \end{cases}$
      south fid Riuer

Surveyors fences on the   { John Ouldum
South fide the Riuer is   { Henry Smith

    Hogreeues Chofsen   { Ephraim winfhip
    for the farmes is   { will: Munroe

At a publik meating of the Inhabitants of this Town the 10th of Nouember 1684

It was then voted whether the Inhabitants of this Town that pay rats to the town Confiderable, fhould haue free liberty to Cutt wood off Mr Pellems hundred accers where the wood is referued for the townes vfs we mean that on the south fide the riuer, and it was voted on the affermitiue

at a meeting of the Selectmen the 24th: 9mo: 1684

Granted to Mr Cooke liberty to Cutt fix fcore pofts off the rocks for the outfide fence of his orchard

At ameeting of the Select men the 8^t of December 1684

Lett to Andrew Boedman the Towns high way marfh on the south fide the riuer that which was formerly lett to Mr Anger for 12^s the yeare in money for the enfueing yeare he ruñing the rifque of all Inconveniances that may accrue ye same

23 Nouember 1685 payd by Andrew Boedman 12^s money for the high way Marfh on the South fide ye Riuer

[111]   At ameeting of the select men 26^t: 10mo: 1684

Granted liberty to Peter Town for timber off the Rockes for a frame for a dwelling houfe.

At ameeting of the proprietors of the Comon
the 26ᵗ of January 1684

It was then voted whether the proprietoʳˢ of the rocks whether they would haue the rockes deuided into wood lots and it was voted on the negatiue

It was then alſoe voted whether they would haue the rocks Lye in Comon as they haue done and ſoe chuſe a Comite to take the beſt Courſe they cane to ſaue the wood from ～ — vnneſeſary Stroy and that none of it ſhould be Caryed out of Town and they bind themſelues to ſtand to the order that the Comitte Choſſen by them ſhould make and it was — voted on the affermitiue

There was alſoe then Choſsen for a Comitte to mak an order for the secureing the wood on the rocks as aboue written Elder Clarke Deacon Cooper Deacon Haſtin to Joyn with the Seleƈt men, then in being,

It was alſoe then voted by the proprietoʳˢ whether yᵉ afore mentioned Comitte ſhould take Care about the ſatiſſyeing Nicholas ffesenden for a prſell of land taken from him by the Town that lyeth in the great swamp in the weſt feild to be layd out in the great ſwamp in our ox-paſter or ſume other Convenient place in our Comon and it was voted on the affirmitiue.

It was alſoe then voted whether the high way running thorough
☞ Richard Eccles feild down to the wind mill hill ſhould be made an open high way, and it was voted on the affirmitiue;

It was then voted whether our Comon on this ſide menotomie riuer ſhould be preſerued for a paſter for the proprietoʳˢ of the Comon and a gate hanged at menotomie bridge and it was voted on the afirmitiue, and it was alſoe voted that our flocke of ſheep ſhould be kept off the aboue mentioned paſter and all other ſheep and that the ſheep ſhould be kept on the other ſide of menotomie bridge without yᵉ gate this was alſoe an affirmitiue vote: and the Seleƈt men ſhould order all that afaire with yᵉ Comity yⁿ Choſsen

At ameeting of the Seleƈt men the 2ᵈ of 12ᵐᵒ 1684

Granted liberty to Deacon Haſtin for a few poſts and rayles for ſum fence about his houſe; to be taken of yᵉ rockes.

At a meeting of the Select men the 2^d: 1mo $168\frac{4}{5}$

Granted Liberty to elder Clarke for Sum̄ pofts & rayles for his out fences of the rockes

Granted liberty to Joseph Ruffells for timber off the rockes for an end to add to his barne

Granted Nath: Hancock liberty for fom pofts for his outfide ffenfes of the rockes

Granted liberty to widdow Cooke to Cut fourty pofts and one hundred rayles for there outfide fences off the rockes

Granted liberty to Leut winfhip for timber of the rocks 2 repaire his barne & leantoe & 200 rayles & 50 pofts

Granted liberty to John watfon for 24 pofts and rayles to them to be taken of the roks

Granted Mr Anger liberty for to Cutt two hundred rayles and fifty pofts for his outfid fences in the Town to be taken off the rockes and alfoe fome Timber to repayre his ould houfe; & fome timber to repayre his fider mill

Granted liberty to our Honored Dep-ty Gouerner for to Cutt off the rocks four hundred of Rayles & pofts to them

At a meeting of the Select men of Cambridg 13th: Aprill 1685

Granted liberty to amofs Marritt for two trees vpon the rockes for his trade as Cooper

Lett the ware to nathaniell Pattin the ware & feild for 30^s the yeare and if the fifh doth not Come vp according to expectation the Select men promife to abate him what they fhall fe Caufe | the 22: 12mo $168\frac{5}{6}$

the Select men doe agree to abate Nathaniell Patin for y^e yeare paft tenn fhillings; & to pay twenty fhillings for y^e yeare paft & twenty fhillings for y^e yeare befor

22: 12: 85 payd for y^e yeare befor & that laft paft by Nath. Pattin to Danill Cheeuers Fortie fhillings in Corne

[111] At ameeting of the Select men the 20th of Aprill 1685:

Ther was then Chofsen Abraham Holman & Nathaniell Pattin for ouerſeers of the flocke of ſheep, for the prouiding of a sheperd and foulding of the ſheep and Carefully to Inſpect them in all Conſernes;

At ameeting of the Select men the 11th of May 1685

Lett to Richard Eccles for the enſueing yeare a high way lyeing in the weſt feild six rod broad lyeing betwixt his land & Deacon Haſtin the hole length of his land for Twelue pence the yeare in money.

11 May 1685 Granted to Ephraim Cutter liberty to take Timber off our rockes for a little barne

Granted liberty to Israell Mead for 100 rayles & 50 poſts off the rockes for outſide fences

Granted to widdow Cragbon liberty for 60 rayles & 17 poſts off the rockes for outſide fences

At ameeting of the select men the 25t day of May 1685

then made Choyce of Bro: John Watſon and Abraham Holman as a Comittee to looke to the Country High way that leads to Concord thorrow the ſmale farmes and to remoue all Incomberances therein and to make returne thereof vnder there hands.

wee the Comittee aboue Choſſen to vew the Country high way leading to Concord thorrow the ſmale farmes haue Carefully vewed the same and doe find it paſſable, returned vnder our hands this 8t of June 1685 ~ ~ John watſonn
Abraham holm

At ameeting of the select men 19th Auguſt 1685

Granted liberty to Thomas Hall to Cutt of our Rocks foure ſleepers of white Oake for his Barne flore about 7 foott Long

At a meeting of the select men the 22: ffebr: 1685

Granted liberty to John Jackſon timber off our Comon the roks for to biuld a barne on his ground by his houſe in Cambridge

At a meeting of the Select men the 26ᵗ of ffebruary 1685

There was then Chofsen Abraham Holman & Nathaniell Patin, for ouerfeers of the flocke of fheep, for the providing of a fheperd and foulding of the fheep, and Carefully to Infpect them in all Concernes;

The ware & ware feild was then Lett to Nathaniell Patin for Thirty fhillings for the enfueing yeare;

vpon a motion of Mʳ Samuell Gookins to the Select men his tendering to take the great gun from John Goue and repaire the Cariag and take care of it and keep it in repaire the Select men gaue there Confent that he fhould haue liberty foe to doe

The select men select men lett to Andrew Boedman ffebruary 1685: the high way Marfh on the fouth fide the riuer the he had the former year for the Infueing yeare for fourteen fhillings the yeare money

8ᵗ: 1ᵐᵒ 87: Andrew Boedman paid to the Town for the hyer of the ₐarfh for the yeare paft 14ˢ in money

[112] At ameeting of the Inhabitants the 9ᵗʰ day of Nouember 1685: there was then Choffen as town officers

Survayers for
yᵉ high ways
{ John Haftin yᵉ Town
Nath: Patin for menotomie
John Oleuer: South fide yᵉ riuer
Joseph Simons yᵉ farmes

Chofe Conftables
{ Town
menotomie
The vilidge
ffarmes.
{ Nath Hancocke
James Hubert
Tho: Parker senʳ
Tho: Cutler for the farmes

Hogreeues
{ Daniell Cheeuer Town
Solomon Prentic Comon
Israell Meed Girfham Cutter Menotomie
John Squire Joshua ffuller South fide Riuer
Edward winfhip John Winter yᵉ farmes

278   TOWN RECORDS

Select men
- Mr Sparrahauke
- Deacon Cooper
- Deacon Haftin
- Serieant More
- Samuell Chamne
- Abrahamn Holma
- Samuell Andrewe

Surveyers & driuer for fences for menotomie feild is as ffoll.
- Samuell Buck
- William Ruffell

Surveyers for the weft feild
- John watfon
- Nicholas ffefenden

Driuer for the weft feild
- Jer Holman

Surveyer & driuer for the Necke
- Arron Boedman
- William Barritt

Surveyer for the fences southfide Riuer
- Thomas Oliuer
- Thomas Browne

23^d : 2mo 1686 :

Nath: Patin is made Choyce of by select men to looke after the gate at Notomie bridge and the Crofs fence; for the enfueing yeare & he is to haue the rent of the ware allowed him: & he is ordered to hang that Gat the firft day of May next comeing.

Drummers

vpon the day of Election of Town officers It was voted whether the towne would pay our drumers demand of what they demand for drumeing for our foott Company, or ftand a futt at law with the drumers, and the Inhabitants vote was, that they would ftand a futt   Dated this 9th of Nouember: 1685.

It was alfoe voted by the Inhabitants of this Town that all our Conftables fhall pay ther prts of this Town rat at or befor the ffirft second day of october next after ther Choyce as Cunftables, and in deffect thereof fhall pay twenty fhillings a month tell they haue Compleated ther payment   Dated this 9th of Nouember 1685

At a meeting of the select men the 8^t: March 168$\frac{5}{6}$

Gaue libertie to Maio^r: Daniell Gookins to Cutt of our rockes 80: pofts & 100: rayles;

At ameeting of the select men the 23ᵈ Aprill 1686

There was then made Choyce of ffrancis More Abraham Holman Thomas Andrew for driuers of our neer Comon for the enfueing yeare

There was then Chofsen to looke after our Rocks that none did Cutt off any oake trees smale or great without liberty from the Townfsmen and a note vnder the Clarke of the Towns hand, to Carfully Infpect the fame was Choffen Samˡˡ Bucke & Nath: Pattin for yᵉ Infuing year

At ameeting of the Select men the 10ᵗʰ May : 1686 =

Granted to Ifraell Mead liberty for 50 rayles & two trees for pofts off our Rockes, for his outfide fence

Granted to Tho: Hall liberty for 50 rayles off our rockes for outfide fences

Granted to Deacon walter Haftin liberty for timber for an end to his barne off our Rockes

Granted liberty to Samˡˡ Andrew to tak timber off our rocks for a fmale frame

Granted to John Addams seniʳ liberty to Cutt 80 rayles off our Rocks for outfide ffences : & one Clabord Tree

Granted to liberty to Leut winfhip for timber for his Leentoo & a hundred of rayles & fifty pofts off our rockes

Granted liberty to John Haftin for 60 rayles and one tree for pofts off the rockes for outfide fences ;

Granted liberty to Mʳ Belcher to Cutt 30 pofts off our rocks Comon for outfid ffences ;

[112] At ameeting of the Select men the 10ᵗʰ May 1686

Granted liberty to James Hubert timber for a leentoo off our rocks ;

Granted to William Dikfon liberty to Cutt groundfells for his barne off our Rocks ;

Granted to Nath: Pattin liberty to Cut timber for a Leentoo off our rocks ;

Granted liberty to Mʳ Angeʳ to fell fome timber for groundfel˄ fhores for his houfe & pofts for fence off our Rocks ;

Granted liberty to Richard Cutter liberty to Cutt Timber off our rocks for an end to his houfe

Granted liberty to Ephraim Cutter for trees for a little barne off our rockes to fet vp neer his houfe in Town

At ameeting of the Select men the 17th May 1686

Granted to Abraham Holman liberty to Cutt off our rockes for fifty rayles and one tree for pofts for out fide fences in the weft feild;

At ameeting of the Select men the 26: of July 1686

Then the Select men ordered that John Watson for breach of Town order for cuting & Caryeing of wood off our Common out of Town & Cutting of Eleauen yong ftadles ofe our Comon Contrary to towne order fhould pay a fine to the Town of fourty fhillings this tranfgrefhon was in the yeare 1685:

At a meeting of the Selectmen the 9th Auguft: 1686

Then the Select men ordered that John Watson sen^r fhould pay Eighteen fhillings fine to the Towns vfs for breach of a publifhed Town order in Carying a loed of wood out of town in the yeare 1686: the fore prt of the sumer,

It was alfoe ordered at the same meetting by the Select men that the aforesayd John watfon vpon his Ingenious Confefhon and fubmition to y^e sentence of the Select men fhould haue half the fines abated him & that Twenty nine fhillings fhould satiffy for both his fines if payd to satiffacti$_\wedge$

At a meeting of the Select men the 9th : 6mo 1686

Then the Select men ordered that Girfham Cutter fhould pay to the vfs of the Town thirty six fhillings as a fine for Caryeing Two loed of wood out of Town, in the year 1686: in the fore prt of the Sumer which is according to a publifhed Town Order

at a meeting of the Select men the 13 Sep^t: 1686

Granted liberty to Daniell Cheeuers for fome fleepers for his houfe ouer his feller off our rockes

Granted Deacon Cooper liberty to take fome timber off our rockes for a new Carte

Granted liberty to Deacon Haftin liberty to take fome timber of our rockes for fleepers for a mill

At ameeting of the Select men this 13th of Octob^r 1686

The Select men then haue Excepted Twenty nine shillings that was due to John Watson for worke done at our bridge vpon the Towns account for fines layd vpon the aforesayd John Watson by the select men for breach of the Town order, the one fine being paffed the 9 of Auguft 1686: & the other the 26^t Jully 1686: as is aboue writtin;

[113] At a Meeting of the Inhabitants of Cambridge

regularly mett together to Chufe town officers and agree vpon a town rat for the infueing year the 8^t Nouember 1686 = which were Chofsen as ffolloweth

Conftables Chofsen for the Town { Arron Boedman
{ Thomas Andrewe

ebenezer wifwell for Cambridg villidge

for the farmes Chofs Phillip Ruffell

ffor Select men were Choffen {
Deacon John Cooper
Deacon Walter Haftin
ffrancis More
Sam^{ll} Chamne
Mr Sparrahauke
Daniell Chamne
Sam^{ll} Andrew
}

Surveyer for the Town   William Barritt
Surveyer for ye south fide the Riuer   Joshua ffuller
Surveyer for Menotomie — Nath: Pattin
Surveyer for the farmes — Joseph Simons

The Rate agreed vpon by the Inhabitants of the Town regularly mett together for the defraying the publike Charges of the Town was }   *l*   *s*   *d*
—100 — 00 — 00

A Committe Chofsen by the Inhabitants to make the rate for the minifter for the enfueing yeare and a rat for ye Town ffor the Town Chofs Mr Cook to Joyn with ye Select men to make a rate for the Town

ffor the Villidge Chofs Noah Wifwill to Joyn with Selectmen to make a Rate for the village;

ffor the farmes Chofs Sam^{ll} Ston sen^r to Joyn with Selectmen to make a rate for the farmes & to take an Invoice

At ameeting of the Inhabitants 28: 12mo 1686

It was then put to vote whether John Dikfon fhould haue about half an acce^r of land sould to them in the ware feild next Charlftown line to build a houfe and barne vpon and it was voted on the afirmitiue, and the Select men then in being were Choffen by the Inhabitants to agree with him for quantity and prifs

It was then alfoe putt to vote whether Abraham watson fhould haue about half an acce^r of our Comon land sould him by the Town, adjoyning to his father watsons feild next the widdow Cookes to Sett a houfe & barne vpon and foe Inhabitt amongft us and it was voted on the afirmitiue, and the selectmen then in being was made Choyce of by the Inhabitents to agree with him both about the quantity and prifs;

At a meeting of the selectmen the 13th of Decembe^r 1686

Granted liberty to will: wieth to Cut off our rockes 50 rayles and a tree for pofts for the outfide fence of his orchard;

At a Meeting of the Selectmen the 14th ffebruary 1686

Granted Good: watson liberty to Cutt off the rocks 120 rayles & 50 pofts for outfide fence in the weft feild;

Granted Thomas white liberty to Cutt off our rockes sufficient pofts & rayles for foure or fiue rode of out fide fence

Granted liberty to Joseph Ruffell to Cutt timber off our rockes for a frame of 20 ffoott longe to Joyne to his dwellinghoufe;

Granted to Petter Town of our rokes Two timber trees for his trade & hoope poles;

Granted to Arron Boedman of the rockes 10 quarter pofts and 40 rayles for out fide fence ;

Granted to John wieth of our Rockes 100 rayles & 30 pofts for outfide ffences;

Granted Thomas Andrew off our rockes 50 rayles & 25 pofts for out fide fence

[113]   At ameeting of the Selectmen ye 14th March: 1686/7

Chofs for the Infueing yeare
 Chofs Survayers for the weft   { Zecheriah Hicks Senr
  feild ffences — — — { Soloman Prentice
 Chofs Driuer for the weft feild { Jacob Hill
 Chofs Survayers of the necke fences { Sam^{ll} Goff
             { John Jackson
 Chofs driuer for the necke { Jacob Amfden
         { Israell Cheeuers
Chofs John wieth Hogreeu for ye Com͠on
Chofs Zecheriah Hicks Hogreeue for ye Towne
 Chofs Survayers for fences { John Addams Senr
  Menotomie feild { Israell Mead
Chofs driuer for Menotomie feild { Jafson Ruffell
Chofs Hogreeue for menotomie { william Ruffell
Chofs ouerfeers for ye flock of fheep { John Watson
             { Nathaniell Pattin

at a meeting of the select men the 28^t: March: 1687

The selectmen then Lett vnto Andrew Boedman the high way Marfh on the fouth fide the riuer which is the Towns land the same that he formerly hired: for fourten fhillings money a yeare for the Infueing yeare: 13: Aprill: 1689: Andrew Bordmans widdow paid fourteen fhillings money for the hire of the aboue said marfh for the yeare 1688

At ameeting of the Inhabitants the 4th of Aprill 1687

It was then propofsed to them whether they did agree that Mr John fteadman fhould haue layd out to him in our remott Coṁon neer the eight mile line fuch a tract of land as may anfwer 60 acce^{rs} that was apoynted for him in our laft diuifhon where the land fell fhort of acomadating him, and it was voted on the afirmitiue, And the Select men were made Choyce of as a Comitty to apoint the place & quantity

It was then alfoe put to vote whether the heires of Robert steadman defeafed fhould haue granted to him in thofe remott Coṁons of the Town a lott granted to them for a former lott that fhould haue bin layd out for him feuerall yeares fince, and that alfoe was votted on the affirmitiue & the select men were appoynted a Comitte to order that affaire

The select men now in being this 13th of Aprill 1689

Lett vnto Andrew Boedmans widdow the high way Marfh of the Townes on the south side of Charles Riuer for fourteen fhillings in money for this Enfueing Cropp

paid by the widdow Bordmans soñ this 23: 2mo: 1690: fourteen fhillings in money for the rent of the high way on the south fid the riuer aboue mentioned for the yeare 1689

The select men now in being this 13 Aprill 1690 lett vnto Andrew Bordmans widdow the Hye way marfh of the Townes on the fouth side of Charles Riuer for fourteen fhillings in Money the next enfueing Crop of Grafs

15: 7mo: 90: paid by Andrew Bordman for his Mother the widdow Bordman for the rent of the Marfh aboue written fourteen fhillings in money

[114] The 24th: July 1687

In anfwer to the vote of the Inhabitants of this Town the 28^t of ffebruary 1686: which is recorded on the other leef fide backward, the select men then Chofsen as a Coṁitte to laye out to John Dickson a Convenient accomidation in our ware feild next Charlftown line, hath on the day aboue written compleated that worke and have fet him out foure rode on the northeaft end: & Eleauen rode long on the North weſt ſid next yᵉ ware feild & fourteen rode ½ long on the Eaſt ſide againſt the ditch which is Charlſtown lines; and foure rode & a half or more on the south weſt end, Conteining about 38 rode or therabouts which the ſelect men then priſed at thirty foure ſhillings sixe pence in money: the aboue said land was sould to yᵉ sayd John Dickson to biuld a houſe & barne vpon to be an Inhabitant amongſt us, and the land being sould by yᵉ Town with out priuiledge belonging therevnto: & the said John Dickson is to mayntaine a ſufficient fence at his own coſt and charg againſt the Towns land ſoe long as it Continues to be Coõmòn land; and is hereby oblidged to the Town not to put a ſtranger into his houſe as an Inhabitant of this Town without the aprobation of the ſelectmen of this Town then in being; and the aforesaid John dickſon doeth agree to pay all aſſeſments in this Town both to Church Town and coõon wealth with the reſt of our inhabitants & to be as other Inhabitants without priuiledges 14 : 7 : 87 receiued the full of the thirty foure shillings & six pence for the vſs of the Town

Vpon the day aboue written was alſoe votted by the Inhabitants of this Town to sell to Abraham Watſon of this Town a Convenient peace of land to ſett a houſe & barne vpon on our Coõon land adjoyning to his father John watſons land in Charlſtown feild next the widdow Cooks, which the Select men of Cambridge being choſen a Comitte by the Inhabitents haue this 24 July : 1687 : ſett out to the sayd Abra: watſon as followeth three rode broad at each end and tenn rode long alongſt Charlſtown line Conteyning thirty rode for which he is to pay to the Town twenty nine ſhillings in money, and ſettle himſelf as an Inhabitent in this Town but hath not priuiledge layd by the town to the fore said prſell of ground he bought of the Town, and is to mayntaine a ſufficient fence againſt our Coõen while it doth Continue Comen land vpon his own coſt & Charge, and that he is not to put in any of another Town as tenant into the said houſe he ſhall biuld vpon the land he bought of the Town without the Conſent of the select men then in being, and to pay all aſſeſments to Town Church & County with our other Inhabitants of the Town as aboue Expreſt; and to be as other Inhabitants without priuiledges : 14 : 7ᵐᵒ: 87 Receiued twenty nine ſhillings in money in full for the aboue said thirty rod for the vſs of the Town

Mʳ Samuell Gookins payment to yᵉ Town for the Clay pits

To Clabords for the meetting houſe money is   00 — 01 — 00
To 32 ffoott of boards for the meeting houſe is   00 — 01 — 04

[114]   At a Publicke Meating of the Inhabitants the 14th Nouember 1687:

ther was then Choſsen officers for the Town-

Conſtables for the Town   { John wieth / Jacob Hill

Joseph Simons Conſtable for ye farmes
Joseph wilſon for the village

for Select men for the Enſueing year { Deacon Cooper / Deacon Haſtin / ffrancis More / Thomas Oliuer / Sam^{ll} Chamne / Daniell Chamne / Sam^{ll} Andrew

Choſe Survayer for the town   zecheriah Hicks
Choſe Survayer for ye south ſide ye Riuer   Sam^{ll} Oldum
Choſs Survayer for Menotomy   Sam^{ll} Bucke:
Choſs Survayer for ye farmes   John Ruſſell:

Survayers & drivers for the weſt field and vewers of ffences is   { Sollomon Prentice & Jeremiah Holman

Hogreeus for the Town is {   Survayers vewers of fences & driuers for the necke is —   { Sam^{ll} Goff / John Jackſon

Survayers vewers of fences & driuers for menotomy feild   { Nath: Pattin / Will Ruſſell

At ameeting of the Inhabitants the 28^t Nouember 1687 =

It was then voted on the afirmitiue by the Inhabitants that the Select men then in being ſhould Leuy arate of one hundred and Two pounds tenn ſhillings for defraying the Charges of the Town for the Enſueing yeare

Voted then on the Afirmitiue alſoe by the Inhabitants that Mrs Michell should be allowed out of the Town rate tenn pounds for the Enſueing yeare

Votted then on the affirmitiue by the Inhabitants

At a meeting of the Select men the 20th ffebruary 168⅞

Gaue liberty to Edward Winſhip to Cutt and Cary off our rockes one hundred of railes & poſts proportionable therevnto for outſide fences next the Com̃on:

Granted alſoe liberty to Leut winſhip to Cutt & Cary off our rockes two hundred of Rayles & poſts neſſeſary to them to repaire his out ſide ffences;

*Granted to Mr Danforth liberty for timber off the rocks for sider mil

At a meeting of the Inhabitants the 5^t March 168⅞

It was then votted whether they would giue liberty to the selectmen to make sale of the Claye pitt to Mr Sam^ll Gookin at a valuable priſe in money and it was votted on the aſermytiue;

At a publike meeting of the Inhabitants the 5^t of March 168⅞

It was then voted whether they would Sell Mr Samuell Gookins the Clay pitts neere the necke gat and it was votted on the afirmitiue,

And it was alſoe votted that the Select men then in being ſhould ſet the priſs of it which was an afirmytiue vote.

This 26 March 1688: mad this agreement. In pursuance of the aboue said vott of the Inhabitants the Select men haue agreed with Mr Sam^ll Gookins about the priſs of the aboue sayd Clay pitts as ffolloweth that in caſe the sayd Clay pitts doe Joyn home to Maio^r Gookins orchard then Mr Gookins ſhall pay for the ſame Eleauen pounds money, but in Caſe there be leagall proff that ther is a hygh way betwixt the Clay pitts and ſaid orchard then the said Mr Gookins ſhall pay but tenn pounds money for the aforesaid Clay pitts to the Town;

* Cancelled on original record, by a line drawn through.

[115] At a Publike meeting of the Inhabitants of Cambridge the 21 of May 1688, for the Choice Town officers according to the act of the Gouernour & Councill

Then Chofs for Conftables for the Town { John Wyeth & Jacob Hill

Then was Choffen Conftable for the farmes { Jofeph Simons

Then was Chofsen for Select men
{
  of ould ones
  Deacon John Cooper
  Deacon Walter Hastin
  Samuell Andrew
    chofs of New ones
  Samuell Ston Senr
  Jonathan Remington
  Dauid ffifk Senr

Mr Joseph Cooke Chofsen for Commifsione^r:

At ameeting of the Inhabitants of Cambridge the 21 May 1688

It was then put to Vott whether the Inhabitants would sell a peece of land on ye south fid ye Riuer of about fiue acce^r on the South fide ye Riuer neere Joseph Bartlitts & John Clarks, and it was votted on the affirmitiue, and the Inhabitants made Choyce of the select men, with Samuell Chamne and Daniell Chamne as a Committe to sell & set a price vpon ye said land to thofe that buy the same: This 21 May: 1688

It was alfoe then votted on the affirmitiue that the Inhabitants would giue to Thomas Stacy of this Town Smith a peece of ground behind his shop of twenty six ffoott long, and nineten foott broad, to sett a houfe vpon, to Continue a fettled Inhabitant amongft us;

Wee the Comitte aboue Mentioned in purfuance of the aboue Written Vott, haue bargained & sould, the aboue mentioned land vnto the aboue Adjacent Joseph Bartlet his heires and affignes, for foure pound tenn fhillings in money, a high way excepted of foure rode wide whofe wefterly fide bounds vpon Capt Noah wifwells land, which when the Country high way is taken out the prsell of land sould him will Conteine about foure acce^r. be it more or lefs, and being bounded on the Eaft with John Clark and Joseph Bartlets lands, about southeaft with

Cap Wifwell to a white Oake, and from that white oake it is bounded about South weft, and the reft of the Country high way about weft, and the reft of the peece of land is bounded with a high way & Cap. Thomas Prentice about northerly, we the aforesaid Comitte, haue alfo agreed with the said Joseph Bartlet, that in Cafe the Adjacent Clarke will fence the one fide of a rode wide high way thorow the tract of Land bought of the foresaid Comitte then the said Bartlet is hereby ingaged to fet him out one where may fut them both beft, right Crofs the land, from Clarks high way to the Country high way, and to the performance of the aforesaid premifses we the Comitte aforesaid in the behalf of the Town haue fet to our hands this Second day of March: 1690 the foure pound tenn fhillings being firft pd vnto Mr Samuell Chamne;

[115] September the 14th: 1688

Dauid ffifke sen^r & Samuell Stone sen^r, being appointed by the reft of the select men of Cambridge, to ftate the Lyne of Philip Chadwicks land (formerly Phillip Jonfes) next the High Way and to allow him Some recompence for Some land Claimed by Mr Cook of Boston. And wee haue drawn ye line as followeth Viz. from a white oake by the stone wall in watertowne Lyne, and from thence to a blacke Oake, and foe to a ftake on the west fide of the high way, and from thence to a black oake at the parting of the paths, from thence to a great rocke, thence to a blacke oake, then to a smale white oacke, thence to a gray oak, then to a red oak: and from thence to a white oake by the Rocky brooke

as attest } Dauid ffifke sen^r
          } Samuell Stone sen^r

At a meeting of the Select men the 18th March: 168$\frac{8}{9}$ made Choyce of seuerall officers as followeth

Driuers and vewers { Mr Joseph Cook
of ffences for the neck, { M^r Jo. Jackson

vewer of fences and driuers { John Watfon
for y^e weft feild { Jer: Holman
{ Will: Wyeth

Driuers & vewers of fences { Nath: Patin
for menotomy feild is ——— { Edw. winship

Hogreeu for menotomy: Girſham Cutter
Hogreeus for the Common { Tho: Andrew
{ Samˡˡ Cooke
Hogreeus for yᵉ Town { Zack: Hicks, Junʳ
{ Owin warland
Hogreeues for yᵉ farmes { Tho: Cutler
{ Will: Carly
Hogreeues for the south ſid yᵉ Riuer is { Isacc Wilſon
{ Jacob Dana

[116] at a meeting of the proprietors of the Town of Cambridg 29: 9ᵐᵒ: 89

It was then votted by them that none of them Will Cutt noe Green wood for fireing but what they ſhall find alredy fald vpon the penalty of fiue ſhillings for each loed nor noe yong wood

At a Generall meating of the Inhabitants of Cambridge for the Choice of Town officers the 11ᵗʰ: 9ᵐᵒ: 1689

Choſs Cunſtable { ffrancis Boeman:
for the farmes — {

Choſe Conſtables { Mʳ Joseph Cooke
for the Town — { John Cooper Junʳ

Their was then Choſsen for Select men
Deacon John Cooper
Deacon walter Hasting
Samuell Chamne
Leut. Remington
Samˡˡ Andrew

Survayers for the high wayes
Jakob Amſden for the Town
William Reed for the farmes
Joseph Ruſſell for Menotomy

22 March Hogreeues Choſsen for the yeare 1690
Hogreeue for the Town { Benonie Eaton
Hogreeue for the Coṁon { Henry Prentice
Hogreeue for Menotomy { william Ruſſell

at a meeting of the proprietors of the
Town of Cambridge 9: 5: 89
It was then voted by them that no one of them
will cutt nor fell wood for fiveing but what
they shall find already fell upon the penalty
of five shillings for each load nor no young wood

At a Generall meeting of the Inhabitants of Cambridge
for the Choise of Touñ officers the 11: 9mo 1689
Chose Cunstable { Francis Bowman   Cunstable { Mr Joseph Cooke
for the farms {   for the Town { John Cooper sen

There was then Chosen for Selectmen
Deacon John Cooper
Deacon Walter Hastings
Samuell Champney
Lout Remington
Sam. Andrew

Suveyors for the high wayes
Jakob Amsden for the Town
William Reed for the farms
Joseph Russell for Menotomy

Richard Hegiourous Chosen for the year 1690
Hegiouros for the Town { Benoni Eaton
Hegiouros for the farms { Henry Prentice
Hegiouros for Menotomy { William Russell
Hegiouros for ye isuings { William Roe / John Stone davids son
Hegiouros for the south side of Charles River { Beniamin Dany

Viewers of fences and divisors for the north { Sam. Gattson / [illegible]
Viewers of fences and divisors for west fields { Sam. Andrew / Solomon Prentice
Viewers of fences & divisors for Menotomy field { John Adams / Jason Russell

TOWN RECORDS 291

Hogreeus for for ye farmes	{ william Row.	
	{ John Ston Dauids son	
Hogreeues for the south fide of Charles Riuer	{ Beniamin Dany	
vewers of ffences and driuers for the neck	{ Sam^{ll}. Goff sen^r	
	{ Enfign Boardman	
vewers of fences and driuers for weft feild	{ Tho: Andrew	
	{ Solomon Prentice	
vewers of fences & driuers for Menotomy feild	{ John Addams	
	{ Jafson Ruffell	

[116]   At a meeting of the proprieto^{rs} of the rocks the 18th day of Nouember 1689: to Confider about the laying out the rocks and it was voted on the afirmitiue and the names of thofe that votted on the afirmitiue are Inferted as followeth and alfoe thofe few that voted on the Negetiue

Voted on the afirmitiue

Tho: ffox	Tho: Andrew	James Huberd
John ffroft	will: Bordman	Arron Bordman
Andrew Bordman	Deacon Hasting	John Jackfon
John Taylor	Jer: Holman	Abra: Holman
Nath: Hancock	John watfon	will: Manning
Herbert Peelham	Sam^{ll} Goff sen^r	Mr Day
Mr Belcher	Jacob Hill	Jofeph Sill
Benonie Eaton	Mrs Michell	John Cooper Junr
John Marritt	ffrancis More	Edward & Sam^{ll} winfhip
Robt Brown	Deacon Cooper	John wieth
John Holmes	Abra: Errington heirs	Georg Willice
will: wieth	John Hafting	Rich: Eccles
Edmond Angier	Joseph Cragbon	Zecheriah Hicks Senr
John Steadman Junr	John Palfry	Sollomon Prentice
Capt: Green	Elder Clark	Joseph Cook
Leu^t Remington	Sam^{ll} Gibson	Ephraim ffroft
Sam^{ll} Hafting	Owin warland	Sam^{ll} Andrew
John Swan	widdow Bowtell	Harvard Colledge
Nath: Patin	John Goue	widdow Michelson
John Green		

all aboue are votts on the affirmitiue
votts on the Negetiue are as followeth.

Tho: & Edward Hall   Tho Post   Jaſon & will Ruſſell
Jonath Dunſter   Richard Cutter   John Steadman sen^r

these were all that did then appear to giue in a negetiue vott
And their was then made Choyce of by written vots
Mr Joseph Cook John Jackſon John Goue and and Nathaniell Pattin to Joyne with the select men as a Comitte to order the maner and way and Method of laying out the rockes and how to Number the lotts. And Leut ffiſke was made Choyce of for the survayer thereof;

[**117**]   At a Generall Meeting of the Inhabitants of Cambridge for the Choice of Town officers the 10th of Nouember 1690 being the 2^d Munday in Nouember as followeth

Drivers and vewers   { Mr Joseph Cook
of ffences for the neck, { M^r Jo. Jackson

vewer of fences and   { John Watſon
driuers for y^e weſt feild { Jer: Holman
                       { Will: Wyeth

Survayer for Highwayes =
Sam^{ll} Haſtings is for the Town
James Clark for the South ſide the Riuer:
Jason Ruſsell for Menotomie.
Samuell Winſhip for the farmes.

Conſtables { Peter Towne hired by
           { Samuell Cooper for Town
           { Edward winship for menotomy.
           { Samuell Whitmor for y^e farmes

Selectmen { Elder Jonah Clarke
          { Deacon Cooper
          { Deacon Haſtings
          { Samuell Andrew
          { John Goue

Mr Thomas Oleuer Choſsen for Comitioner

TOWN RECORDS

for yᵉ neck vewers of fences & driuers — { Samᵘ Goff senʳ / John Jackson }

vewers of ffences for Menotomie feild
James Huberd &c
Joseph Winſhip

for the weſt feild vewers of fences — and driuer for the weſt feild — { Solomon Prentice / Samuell Kidder / Jer: Holman }

for driuers for menotomie
Joseph Adames &
Jaſson Ruſſell.

Hogreeus for menotomie { will: Ruſſell / Girſham Cutter }

Hogreeus for Town
Zech: Hicks Junʳ
Samᵘ Gibson

hogreeues for farmes { Will: Munroe / Tho: Cutler / John Comy }

Hogreeue for yᵉ Comͫon
Benj: Godward

hogreeues for the south ſide yᵉ Riuer — { Jacob Dany / James Clarke }

Tithingmen for the farmes { Samᵘ Ston / Leut ffiſke / Ephraim winſhip / John Tidd senʳ }

By yᵉ ſelectmen in behalf of yᵉ Town

5: 11ᵐᵒ 169¾ Called Sⁱʳ Hancock to keep ſcoole for the Town to teach both Gramer & Engliſh with writing & ſiphering

There being in yᵉ 91ˢᵗ folio of this Booke a Record Defaced not known by whom the said Record by order of the ſelectmen is in this place renewed

A Copy of yᵉ returne to yᵉ Select by Mʳ Thomas Danforth & David Fiske Concerning the land Claimed by Samᵘ & Danᵘ Champney: We whoſe names are Subſcribed being desired to View a parcel of land lying on the South Side of the River between part of the head line of Mʳ Andrews Farme & Mʳ Sparhawks line & now Claimed by Samuel & Daniel Champney: Do Aſsert that it is no part of that which the Town Sold to Elder Champney for 40 Acres more or leſs when he firſt built in that place the head line of that being terminated by the Same line that the Small lotts that he then Bought of Goodm̃? Shepard, Trumble, & others that had lotts there

2 That it is no part of y^e 100 Acres w$^{ch}_{.}$ the Town Granted him & was laid out on the westerly Side of Mr Mitchells Lott

13: (3) 1672: $\left\{\begin{array}{l}\text{Thomas Danforth afserteth to } y^e \text{ firft} \\ \text{Article of this testimony } \sim \\ \text{David Fiske attefteth to the truth} \\ \text{of the Second Article } \sim\end{array}\right.$

[**117**] At a meeting of the proprieto^{rs} of this Town Leagally warned and mett together this 13$^{th.}$ of Aprill 1691 =

A propofition was made to them whether they would devide all the Com̃on lands belonging to the Town without and within the Compafs of the fiue mile line, foe farr as was the ouerplufh of the laft Diuifhon vp^{on} the rocks, and it was then votted on the affirmitiue; and the proprieto^s did then make Choyce of Leut Remington Zecheriah Hickes sen^r. & Edward winfhip together with the selectmen, a Com̃itte for the ordering and fetling of this Matter and Concerne of the proprieto^{rs}

It was alfoe vpon the day aboue written propofsed to the proprieto^{rs} whether all the Common Lands on the south fide the High way leading from Capt. Cooks Mill to watertown or further if the Com̃itte fee Caufe be fenced in for a pafter, for such as haue Cow rights recorded in the Town Booke, and this is to be done with all Convenient speed, and euery prson that haue Cow rights and Com̃ons fhall beare their proportions thereof, as it fhall be fet out by the Com̃itte and the Com̃itte aboue mentioned are ordered and apoynted by the proprieto^{rs} to order and fetle this affaire, and all this was votted on the afirmitiue, and the pafter to be ftinted according to the proprieto^{rs} Cow rights according to beft accomadatioᴧ for the whole.

An order of the select men mad the 18th May 1691

Concerning the Numbere of working Catle and Cowes fhall be paftured on this fide Menotomie bridge

Firft That no proprieto^r fhall keep in the forementioned pafture aboue one Cow for Two Com̃ons, and one horfe for three Com̃ons, and that euery prson Concerned fhall pay towards the making of the gate and fence and driueing the pafter, three pence a head in money for euery Cow, and foure pence ahead for euery horfe;

2dly   It is further ordered, that whoefoeuer fhall put vpon the aboue mentioned pafter, more then his right aboue mentioned, fhall pay to the driuer twelue penc ahead for euery time they are taken therein, and that all horfes fhall be fettered as the law requires, and all other vnruely Catle restrayned if Complained off;

3dly   It is further Ordered, that the flocke of fheep fhall not come on this fide Menotomie bridge, (we mean the Towns fide) aboue once in fourteen dayes, and that no proprieto^r fhall put on more fheep vpon our our Coṁons, then they haue right to put on according to their priuiledges; this order mad$_\wedge$ by the select men was pofted vp at the meeting dore the 19th May 1691 =

[118]   At a meeting of the Inhabitants the 9th Nouember 1691 for the Choyce of Town officers

Chofe for Conftables for y^e Enfueing yeare   1st Peter Town
                                                2^d William Rufsell
                                                3^d Sam^{ll} Winfhip for the farmes

Chofe for Select men
  Mr Sam^{ll}: Andrewe
  Deacon Haftings
  Sam^{ll} Chamne
  Leut: Remington
  Edward winfhip
  Sam^{ll} Haftings
  william Munroe

Chofe survayers for the High wayes.
  Zacheriah Hicks Juner ye Town
  James Clark south fide
  Jason Ruffell for notomy
  Benia: Mury for farmes

Chofe Hogreeues for Menotome   Nathaniell Patin
                                  Joseph Addams
Chofe Hogreeues for the Town   John Haftings
                                  Owin Warland
Chofe Hogreeues for the south fide of Charles Riuer   John ffracis
                                                      Beniamin Dany
Chofe Hogreeues for the Coṁon   Thomas Andrew
                                  Beniamin Godward

Chofe vewers of fences | Sam[ll] Gibson — & Driuer
for weft feild | Amos Marritt
Added | John wyeth driuer
 | Sam[l] Kidder added servayer
Chofs vewers of fences | Sam[ll] Goff sen[r]
for y[e] necke and alfoe driuers | Zecheriah Hicks sen[r]
Chofe vewers of fences and | Jason Rufsell
driuers for menotomie feild | Joseph winfhip

Seuerall propofitons made to the Inhabitants vpon the day of Choyce of Town offecers: the 9th 9b[r] 1691 =

1. Choyce of a Comitte to make aminifters rat this was votted on the afirmitiue and their was Chofsen the select men and aded vnto them M[r] Thomas Oleuer Sam[ll] Stone sen[r] & John Goue

2dly It was put to vott whether their fhould be giuen by the Town in Comon pay Anually to a fcoolmafter twelue pound and it was votted on the afirmitiue to teach both latten & englifh and to write & fipher ;

3dly It was put to vote whether the Town would giue to the miniftry fourty acce[rs] of Common land for a fuply of wood Annually and it was voted on the afirmitiue;

Forty acres of wood land voted

4thly It was put vott whether we fhould make a Town rate for payment of Town debts and defray Town Charges and it was voted on the afirmitiue;

At a meeting of y[e] Select men novemb[r] 16th 1691

M[r] Samuel Andrewe was Chofen Clerke of y[e] Select men & to keep y[e] Towne Booke

It was the day aboue mentioned agreed by the Select to make a Town rate Conteining 2 fingle Country rates and the one quarter prt thereof to be leyed in money the other three quarters to be leuyed in Country pay

It was alfoe then agreed by the Select men that M[r] Samuell Chamne fhould be ouerfeer of our Great bridge

Chofs Hogreeues for ye farmes | John Johnson
for ye Noreft fide Concord roed | John Comy
Chofs Hogreeus for south weft fide | John Ston Dauids fon
Concord path for farmes | John Ston Sam[ls] fon

[118] At ameeting of the Select men the 13th of Juñ 1692

It was then agreed vpon by the Selectmen that John Green and Robert Webber fhould be Added to Samuell Goff sen[r] and Zecheriah Hickes sen[r] as driuers for our necke which aboue mentioned prsons were Chofsen for the better secureing of the Corne and paftures therein

At a meeting of the Inhabitants the twenty seauenth day of Juñ 1692 Leagally warned, and it was then votted by the Inhabitants that they would giue to a gramer fcoolmafter that fhould alfoe teach englifh that they would allow a Scoolmafter Twenty pound ayeare in Comon pay and this was votted on the afirmitiue by the majo[r] prt of the Inhabitants then present at leaft two to one;

Schoolmasters Salary

At a meeting of the Selectmen the 25[t] of July 1692

haueing teftimony of the defectiuenefs of Zecheriah Hickes sen[r] fence in the oxe pafter belonging to the weft feild they faw Caufe to fine him tenn fhillings — — — — } 00 — 10 — 00

And Solomon Prentice is likwife fined for the Same defect in his fence belonging to the weft feild — —} 00 — 18 — 00

Alfoe John wyeth for defect in his fence in the weft feild is fined — — — — — — —} 00 — 18 — 00

At a meeting of the Inhabitents the 14th of Nouembe[r] 1692 for the Choyce of Town officers

It was then Voted by the Inhabitants that the orders formerly made, according to the Inftructiones of the Inhabitants for the prefervation of the wood and timber in the Comon lands, be by the Selectmen be by the Selectmen vigouroufly prosecuted according to the true Intents of said orders

At a publicke meeting of the Inhabitants the 14th of Nouember 1692,

It was then voated that whereas Thomas Stacy is pofsefed of a houfe platt in the Town as now within fence which was formerly at a publik Towne meeting granted to him said Thomas Stacy his heires excecutor^{rs} for euer, and omitted entry in Town records, is at this prsent meetting renewed and Granted as aforesaid;

[119] At a publicke meeting of the Inhabitants of Cambridge the 2^d monday of Nouember 1692 : mett together to Chufe Towne officers according to an anfheant Town Order

Then Chofe for Conftables for the enfueing yeare
{ Nicholas ffesenden
  Jason Ruffell
  Will: Reed }

Then Chofe Seauen Selectmen as ffolloweth
{ Deacon Haftings
  Sam^{ll} Chamne
  Leut Remington
  Saml: Haftings
  Edward: Winfhip
  Saml: Ston Senr
  Saml: Andrew }

Chofe Survayer for the Town   Solomon Prentice
Chofe Survayer for the South fide ye Riuer   John Squire
Chofe for Menotomie Survayer their   John Dickson
Chofe Survayer for the farmes   John Rufsell

vpon this pulike meeting of the Inhabitants the day aboue mentioned, It was then put to vote whether the Selectmen fhould make a money rate to pay the Expence and defray the Charge of our <u>Paster Gookins</u> funerall Charges, which amounted to about <u>Eighteen pounds in money,</u> and it was voted on the afirmitiue;

At a meeting of the select men the 9th of January 1692

Then agreed with Zecheriah Hicks Juner that he fhould pay vnto the Town as an acknowledgement to the Town for the ftanding of his barne againft his houfe vpon the Towns land Twelue pence a yeare in money the firft payment being due next march at the choyce of Town officers and foe anually for the futer foe long as it fhall continue to ftand vpon the Towns land:

Then alfoe Agreed with Jonathan Nuting to pay to the Towns vfs twelue pence a yeare money as an acknowledgement vnto the Town for the standing of his fhop vpon the Towns land vpon our Common neer the pound the firſt payment to be next March at the Choyce of Town officers and foe Añually for the futur foe long as it ſhall Continue to ſtand their;

The Said Zecheriah Hicks hath pay^d this 2^d day of March in the year 169$\frac{8}{9}$: for four year laſt paſt: four ſhillings

Mr John Sparhauk began to keep ſcoole the 15th day of ffebruary 169$\frac{2}{3}$ being wedenſday

[119] At a meeting of the Inhabitants the 16th of January 1692

It was then votted by the Inhabitants whether the ſelectmen ſhould aply themſelues vnto the Gouernour & Counſell or the Generall Court, for ſome releeff or aſſiſtance for the maintenance of our great bridge, and it was votted on the afirmitiue that they should as foon as they had opportunity;

It was alſoe then votted whether we y^e ſelectmen ſhould make a rate for the Charge of repaireing our great bridge hitherto & it was voted on the afirmitiue;

It was alſoe then votted whether the Town would giue to menotomie people a quarter of an acce^r of land vpon our Comon neere ☞ Jaſson Ruſsells houſe neer the highway for the acomodation of a ſcoole houſe and it was votted on the afirmitiue foe long as it was Improued for that vſs and noe longer;

It was alſoe then put to vott whether the second monday in march next should be the day of our Choyce of Town offecers for the next yeare and it was votted on the afirmitiue

It was alſoe then votted whether the Inhabitants of this Town would
land sold for minister at lexington
sell to the farmes 5 or 6 acce^{rs} of land lyeing neer beniam̃ Muzes for the accomadation of their minister and it was votted on the afirmitiue provided they could agree vpon the prifs & pay & quantity

_ _ _ _ _ _ _

At a publick Meeting of y^e Inhabitants of Cambridge
March 13$^{th}_.$ 169$\frac{2}{3}$: for y^e Choice of officers for said towne ○

Then was Choſen for Conſtables $\left\{\begin{array}{l}\text{Abraham Hill}\\ \text{Amos Marrett}\\ \text{Matth: Bridge Jun}^r\end{array}\right.$

Chosen Five select men viz:
{ M{r} Sam{ll}. Andrewe
Deacon Walt{r} Hasting
John Jackson
Edward Winship
Jonath{n} Remington }

Samuel Stone sen{r}: Chosen Comissio{r}:
Chosen Leather Sealer   John Hasting sen{r}
Chosen Sealer of Weights & measures   Peter Towne
  Chosen Surveyo{rs} of high wayes
for y{e} towne & Comon   Solomon Prentice
for y{e} south Side y{e} River   John Squire sen{r}
for Menotomy   John Dickson
for y{e} Farmes   John Russell
Chosen for Towne Clerke   Jonath{n} Remington

  At a Meeting of y{e} Select men march 20{th} 169⅔
Chosen Viewers of fences for y{e} Neck   { Zech{h} Hicks Sen{r}
               Joseph Cooke }

Israel Chever { drivers of
Robert Webber   sd: neck: }

chosen viewers of fences for y{e} West field   { John Watson
                   Sam{ll}. Cooper }

Jeremy Holman { Drivers of
Jno: Wyeth ——   s{d} field: }

Chosen viewers of fences for menotomy   { Jason Russell
                  Joseph Winship }

Gershom Cutter
Jonath{n}. Butterfield { Drivers }

[120]   Chosen to Inspect the yokeing & Ringing of Swine
for y{e} Towne { Christoph{r} Mutchin
        Richard Ferguson }
for y{e} Comon { John Cooper
        Will Wyeth }
for Menotomy { Andrew Beard
        Sam{ll}. Bull: }

At a meeting of the Select men April 10th: 1693

John Watson Zechariah Hicks Senr & Sam^ll. Kidder are appointed a Comittee to agree wth a shepherd to keep the flock for this present yeare, also to take Care Concerning the Rams that they be kept from ye flock as is requifite & Customary also to take Care that ye flock be fed in such place as ye Select men shall appoint.

on ye motion of Jason Rufsell the Select men do desire m^r Andrew to state & settle the line between the Said Jason Rufsells land & the Comon according to ye Surveyo^rs. Plott y^t is wth ye records of the towne, he making a returne of what he shall do therein to the select men

Mr Andrew made report that he had stated the line as abovementioned according to the Surveyo^rs Plott on May the second Ann° Dom: 1693

At a publick Meeting of the Inhabitants of the Towne March 13th 169⅔: The Inhabitants of the Farmes requesting ye proprieto^rs to sell them a remnant of Comon land lying on this side the long Cawfey & likewife on the other side of said Caufey being neare to their Meeting houfe which said land they desire for the accomodacon of their Minister the Propriet^rs did Vote y^t it should be sold to the farmers for the end aforesaid, & for that purpofe made Choice of Joseph Rufsell & Nathan^ll. Pattin to Joine wth ye Select men in making said Sale

<small>Common lands voted to be sóld to lexington</small>

April 28th: 1693

The Select men & Comittee Impowered to make Sale of the Comon land to the farmers, have accordingly sold the Same, the termes being as followeth: that is to say, referring to the land on the further Side of ye long Caufey they are take it for more or less without Measuring for wch. they are to pay twelve pounds in money the land on this side the forementioned Cawsey to be meafured out to them & to pay for the same ten shillings p^r Acre in money, wch money for the land on this side the Cawsey to be paid forth with, or afsoon as it is meafured & the twelve pound for the land beyond the Causey to be paid w^thin a twelvemonth from ye Date abovesaid

<small>sold accordingly</small>

[120] At a meeting of the Propriet^{rs} of the town Comons May 12th 1693 It was then Voted that there shall be a herd of Cowes kept on the Said Comons this present yeare ⁓

1   It was also Voted that the present selectmen should Mannage that affaire referring to the Herd in providing an Herdsman & in taking effectuall order how he shall be paid for his paines ⁓

2   There being then a Motion made that there might be a sale of some remnants of Comon land for ye payment of some Debts due unto Mr John Hasting & Mr John Hancock for their keeping the schoole in the Towne the proprieto^{rs} did approve of said Motion & voted the sale should be made accordingly ⁓

It was then likewife Voted that John Gove Joseph Rufsell & Nathan^{ll} Pattin should be Joined wth the select men as a Comittee for to view the aforesaid Comon lands & to make sale of so much as may pay the Debts afore mentioned ⁓

3   At the meeting above said there being a Complaint made that severall persons had fallen short of their proportion in the former Divisions of land, the propriet^{rs} did then Vote that the above named Comittee should heare what each person hath to alledge & what shall be found due unto any person by falling short as aforesaid the said Comittee shall order them a recompence out of the Comon lands afore mentioned ⁓

4   The Select men have Nominated & appointed John Watson John Gove & Sam^{ll} Cooper for to provide & agree wth a Herdsman for the Cowes for this yeare ⁓

[121] May 22^d 1693 there being report made to the Select men of the number of acres of land sold to the farmers aforementioned for the accomodation of their Minister wch according to agreement they were to take by meafure being that on this Side of ye long Cawsey, they being according to said agreement to pay ten shillings p^r Acre for what it did amount to by meafure, & there being twelve acres so meafured wch Comes to Six pounds wch was paid to the Select men by Lt David Fifke & Sam^{ll} Stone sen^r: on said 22^d day of May on behalfe of said Farmers: the whole of the land on both ends of said long Cawsey both what was

meafured & not meafured is Bounded as followeth that is to say Bounded with the land of Mr Edward Pelham & John Mon Roe North East; wth ye land of Matthew Bridge Senr & Sam^{ll} Stone Senr Southweft & by that Called by the Eight Mile line North West excepting Meadow formerly laid out to Edw: Mitchelson John Cooper & Edward Goffe wch is Comprehended wthin the Bounds now mentioned

   Att a meeting of the Select men of Cambridge
   this 9th day of July 1694:

This wittnefeth that we the above faid have received of Leut: David ffifke, Sam^{ll} Stone Senr of Cambridge ffarmes, the Sume of Six pounds and eight Shillings, and nine pence this same day for and in consideration of part of payment of twelve pounds to be payd by them, for a parcel of Land Sold by us the Select men, by Order from the Inhabitants of the Town, as Attefts

              Samuel Green Clerke

  Att a Meeting of the Inhabitants orderly warned
   March 12th 169$\frac{3}{4}$

Then chosen for Conftables	⎧ David Demming — Amos Marrett ⎨ Samuel Kidder — peter Town ⎩ Benjamin Muzzy
ffor Selectmen	⎧ Deacon Walter Haftings ⎪ Jonathan Remington ⎨ John Jackson ⎪ Doct^r James Oliver ⎩ Samuel Champney
ffor Town Clarke	Samuel Green
ffor Surveyers of the High wayes	⎧ Abraham Hill ⎪ Amos Marrett ⎨ Matthew Bridge ⎩ John Oldham
Viewers of fences for west field,	⎧ Thomas Andrew ⎩ Solomon Prentice

Viewers of fences for the Neck: (Joseph Cook
                                  (John Stedman
    Viewers for Minotamy field   (Nathaniel Pattin
                                              (William Cutter

Sam^{ll} Cooper   )
Jeremiah Holman) drivers of the weft field
Israel Chevers   )
Samuel Goff   ) drivers of the neck fields

[121]   Cambridge ffarmers C^{rs}:

	£	fh	d
16 Decem^r 1701. By Cash paid by Mr Matt^h Bridge in part of what is due frō them for land Sold unto y^m for the accoṁodation of y^r Minist^r	01	06	3
13 Jan^{ry}: Paid by Deacon Hasting for Sam^{ll} Whittmore	00	10.	00
10 March 170$\frac{2}{7}$ By Cash pd: to y^e Town Treasu^r for m^r: ffrā: Bowman — —	£02	15-	00
9 ffeb^{ry} 170$\frac{7}{8}$ By Do: of ffrā Bowman in full for y^e Land Sold to y^e ffarmers	—01	—00	—00

Jaafon Russell   )
Joseph winfhip) Drivers of Minottomy fields
Liv^t: David ffifk Chosen Commissioner
Peter Town   Sealer of weights & measures
                Gager and Packer:
John Haftings Sealer of Leather
Abraham Watson) Chosen to execute the Act referring to
John Comy   ) horses going on the Town Coṁons
John Russell and)
Sam^{ll} winship   ) viewers of fences for the farmes
John Squire   )
Samuell Oldham) viewers of fence for the South Side of Charles River

Att a meeting of the Inhabitants orderly warned
March 30th, 1694

Then Chosen as the Law required
Mr Samuel Andrew Town Treasurer
and for Tything men

ffor the Town
  John Gove   )
  Nathaniel Hancock:)

for the Comon and Lane:
  Samuel Haftings   )
  Benjamin Goddard)

for Minotamy
  John Watson)
  John Addams)

ffor the ffarmes {Ens. Ephraim winfhip: John Tidd John Smith
[   ]

[**122**]   March the 30th. 1694

Agreeable to the 5th. Article referring to the Division of the Rocks vide: page 61: 62:

Gerfhom Cutter addressed himfelfe to the Select men

It was Ordered that Edward Winfhip and William Ruffel were Nominated and appointed on the behalfe of the Town to State Such high wayes and pafsage, as f^d Article directs unto, makeing return of their doings to the Select men of the Town within the Space of 28 dayes after:

The Lott propounded to be fenced and improved was Layd out to Isaac Day in the firft division

March the 30th: 1694:

Att a publick meeting of the Inhabitants of this Town, orderly warned, was then voted, that the Select men for the year Insuing, according to their best discretion fhould Order the prudentiall Affaires of the Town: viz: Ordering the enclosures of Comon fields, Ordering the Cow heards, flocks of sheep, and all appertaining thereunto; And for makeing all such by Lawes and Orders as the Law of this Province

allows, tending to the peace, Order and welfare of the Town, and for the preservation of all comon rights, Interests and propieties of this Town
Voted on the Affirmative

Att a meeting of the Select men the 4th. of Aprill

Ordered that Notice be giun to our Neighboures of Concord that Samuel Stone Senr is appointed to Settle the day running of the Line

Att a meeting of the Select men, Aprill the 4th.

It was then agreed vpon by desire of the proprieto^{rs} of the Cow Comons, that there should run a fence from Mr Danforths farme to Spie pond on the South end, and So from the north end of S^d pond to Ædward Winships the charge whereof was to be proportioned to the proprietors, for the feed of the Cowes of the proprietors and Such cattell as by agreement Should be put on it, and Deacon Walter Hastings and John Jackson, was to take a view of the Land what Cattell that percell of Land would be suitable to keep, and what proportion of fence would fall to every cow comon, and then give a Report therof Speedily, and so to forward that designe according to desire

At a meeting of the Select men Aprill the 9th. 94:

It was Ordered that Ædward winship and Samuel Kidder and John Jackson Shall be a Comittee to hire a Shepard for the year ensuing and to Order what may be requisite for the well ordering and governing the flock of Sheep:

Also Ordered att the Same time that Stephen Palm͜ Should be abated a Rate of twenty eight Shillings whereof he was assessed in the year 1690, and being comitted to Ædward winship then Constable to collect: he the Said Palmer produceing a certificatt from the Town Clarke of Woburn that Rates was payed for him by James ffowle for the Same Levie :

Also then Ordered, that the persons after named Should for the year ensueing carefully inspect the Law of the Province referring to yoaking and ringing of Swine   for the Town Israel Chevers

for Comon Jeremiah Holeman
[ ] Menotomie to the farmes   Joſeph winſhip
                                 Jaaſon Ruſsel

[122]   May the 7th: 1694:
At a publick Town meeting, Orderly warned

It was then voted for the defraying of charge due about the great Bridg, that the Select men Should make an aſſessment on the Inhabitants of the Town by a Rate of eighty pounds in Town pay.

Alſo a money Rate, of twenty pound for the Schoolemaſter and deputyes charges, and repairation of the meeting house, in this year 1694

July the 16th: 1694

Att a publick Town meeting, Orderly warned, purſuant to an order from the Treasurer of this Province Concerning Chooſing of Aſsessors for the Levying of a Rate or Tax for their Majeſtys Service, by Order of the Generall Court, and it was then voted to Choose three men for that affaire out of the Inhabitants of the Town as the Law directs; And there was then Chosen Deacon Walter Haſtings, Mr Samuel Stone, and Mr Thomas Oliver, to Attend that Service, they have accepted ot said place and have taken their Oath as the Law directs

January the 7th: 1694

It is ordered by the Select men for this year, that John Jackson, Nathaniel patten, Ædward winſhip, Jaaſon Ruſſell, are appointed to lay out high wayes and paſsage as may be accomadable for Joſeph winſhip William Ruſſel Jaaſon Ruſſel to their Lotts on the Rocks (explained)

January 7th 1694 Agreeable to the 5th Article for the devition of or Rocks, Joseph Winship: And Wll Russell adreſsed the Select men to Nominat prson according to ſd act for the Stating of Neſeſsary high ways over such Lotts as they propound to Incloſe ~ ~ The Select men doe order for Joseph Winship Jno Jackson and Nathaniell Pattin on behalfe of ye Towne As likewise for Wll Russell ~ ~

Jason Russell likewise Informed of his Intention to Incloſe as aboue Sd: The Sd prsons Jno Jackson and Nathaniell Patin are desired on ye

Towns behalfe, as aboue recited ~ ~ And to make theire returnes of theire doings herein wthin the Space of one Month after such high way or pafsag is apointed or stated ~ ~ ~ ~

March the 7th: 169$\frac{8}{8}$

Gerfhom Cutter haveing purchafed a Lott of Ifaak Day, of twenty accres, and being desirous to enclose the Same for improvement, according to the proposition in the 5th Article the Said Gerfhom Cutter addressing himfelfe to the Select men they appointing Nathaniel patten and Ædward Winfhip to view the Land and State an high way for carting, they make their return as followeth, that if the Said Cutter do att his own coft and charge make an high way for Carts to pafs on the north Side of his Lott next to John Coopers Lott, he then may enclofe his Lott, as by a return under their hands did appear,

Nathaniel patten
Ædward Winfhip

[**123**] February 4th 169$\frac{4}{5}$

At ameeting of the Inhabitants enjoined by law to maintaine the Miniftry in the towne legally warned It was propofed to them as followeth

1   That there shall be paid annually a hundred pounds in Money as a Maintenance for the next settled Minister during his Continuance in his Ministeriall worke ~ this vote was made void by the Inhabitants the 17th of May 1695, as will appear on the peage on the other Leafe

2   That for the better & more equall levying of ye said Sum on the Inhabitants; there be annually Chosen (on the day appointed for y^e Choice of town Officers) three persons, which wth the Select Men shall be a Comittee, to take a lift of persons & Estates & to afsefs the Inhabitants their p^{r}portions neare as pofsible to each persons ability~ Voted on the affirmative

Feb 4th 169$\frac{4}{5}$ the proprieto^{rs} of o^r Town^s Comon being mett together, It was proposed Whether all such p^{r}sons as claime Intreft in wood Lotts formerly granted to sundry p^{r}sons on the other side Minotomie, but the Land to lye in Comon to the Towns Vse, Should be Limitted wth in the Space of one yeare,

explanation

TOWN RECORDS   309

from y^e date hereof, to take of all such wood, and if any p^{r}son so claiming neglect so to doe wthin the forementioned and Limitted time, All such wood as shall be left standing, or lying; shall from thence forward be accounted Comon, and ordered and difposed of by the Major part of the proprieto^{rs} =
Voated on the afirmative

March 8th 169$\frac{4}{5}$ Then was the Towns Stock of powder and Amunition removed from Mr Sam^{ll} Andrews house, and comitted to the Cuftody of Sam^{ll} Maning, And the select men agreed wth said Sam^{ll} Maning, for his care to allow him Anualy Six shillings in comon pay:

[123]   March the 11th: 169$\frac{4}{5}$:

Att a publick meeting of the Inhabitants of Cambridge for the Choice of Town Officers, was then chosen for the year ensueing:

ffor Conftables
{ Mr John Bonner
  Abraham watson
  John Mirriam:
  Abraham Jackson

ffor Select men
{ Deacon walter Haftings
  Edward winfhip
  peter Town
  Abraham Hill
  John Oldham

ffor Town Treafurer   Mr Samuel Andrew
   Sallary 4^d pr pound receiving & delivering
ffor Town Clerke   Samuel Green
☞   Sallary twenty Shilling pr year money or as money:

for Surveyers of the high wayes
for the Town   Samuel Gibfon
for Minotimie   william Cutter
for the South fide river   Nathaniel Robbins
for the ffarmes   William Read

Veiwers of fences
for the weſt field   John Gove and John Cooper
for the Neck   Samuel Goffe Junr, Zechariah Hicks Junr
for Minottomie   Joseph Addams Jonathan Butterfield

Drivers of the fields,
ffor the weſt field   Samuel Kidder, Joseph Crackbone
ffor the Neck   Zechariah Hicks, Samuel Goffe Junr:

Howards for Horses,
Phillip Russel and Jacob Chamberline

Tithing men
for the Town   Nathaniel Hancock, Ruben Luxford
for the south side   James Clarke: Jacob Danie
for Minottamie   John Addams Nathaniel patten
for the farmes   Samuel Whitmore, Thomas Cutler

Nathaniel Patten, Amos Marrett, Joseph Winſhip then choſen to joyn with the Select men to vindicate the Towns intereſt, and particular proprieties, in laying out the high wayes, and other the Towns Intereſt; all these for the year enſueing:

March: 27: 1695

Perſons Choſen by the Select men then in being to Inſpect the Swine in and about this Town for the year enſuing: are
for the body of the Town   John Haſtings Senr:
for the Comon and plain to Menottamie   Jeremiah Holman Senr
for the South Side of the River   Benjamin Dana:
for Menottomie,   Samuel Bull and Jacob Chamberlin
for the ffarmes,   william Carter and John Stone the
           son of David   ſtone

Att a meeting of the Selectmen the 5th day of Aprill in the year 1695:

Granted unto Samuel Prentice the Sheep keeper for this year enfueing a Small piece of Land for the accomodatin of the Sheep in the night Season being next unto the Land of Abraham Watſon, and Samuel Cooke he the Said Samuel prentice allowing a Small acknowledgment of one Shilling in money for this present year, this grant is onely for this prefent year 1695: This acknowledgment of one shilling is pay^d this 20: day of Aprill 1696:

[124]   Cambridge Aprill, the 5th: 1695

Att A Generall Town meeting of the Inhabitants, Orderly warned, it was then voted theise particulars following:

1st: To Levy a Rate on the Inhabitants of ninety pounds in Co on pay, and of money twenty pounds, for the defraying of Town debts, and performing what was necessary to be done on behalfe of the Town,

voted on the Affirmative:

2^{ly}: It was voted that Leutenant Jonathan Remington and Mr Samuel Champney Senr: and John Gove was chofen for the year enfueing to overfee the Bridge over Charles River, and to look to the prefervation of it,

Voted on the Affirmative:

3^{ly}: That Corn Shall be payd in the Rate for the Town for this year enfueing att theis prizes following viz:

price of Grain

Wheat att five Shillings per bufhell:
Indian Corn att three Shillings pr bufhell:
Rye att four Shillings pr bufhell:
Barley att four Shillings pr bufhell:
Oates att two Shillings pr bufhell

Voted on the Affirmative

4^{ly}: Voted that the Select men in prefent being together with Leiutenant Jonathan Remington do farther prosecute an Orderly Ifsue of the Matter depending between the Town, and

Newtown the village or Newton So called, And that untill that Controverfie be determined, (and to gett Abraham Jackson Sworn as Conftable, and) that the Courts grant of one hundred and fifty pounds toward the Repairing of the great Bridge, be Respited and not Received by the Town and that before the Town be obliged by the Courts Act, they have Liberty to give their further vote herein, this alfo was Voted on the Affirmative;

5^{ly}: That the present Country Rate fhall be Levyed by the former Invoice, and that the Select men fhall make it, And that Leivtenant David ffifke then Chofen as a Comiffioner, to Joyn with the Select men to make both the Country, and Town Rate, this alfo Voted on the Affirmative:

Cambridge May the 13th: 1695:

proposed to the Inhabitants of s^d Town to give to the Next Minifter that the Church and Town Shall Settle among them, ninety pounds pr Annum in Money, so long as he fhall Carry on the worke of the Miniftry in Cambridge, and the vote entered in the Town Boak as the Agreement of the Town for maintenance of the Miniftry, ffebruary the 4th 169$\frac{4}{5}$ is hereby declared to be Null and void

Voted on the Affirmative

Alfo then Chofen as Assors, to joyn with the Select men to make the minifters Rate above mentioned:

Mr Samuel Champney
Mr Thomas Oliver
Leu^t: Jonathan Remington

[124] Cambridge, May the 13th: 1695

Alfo that wheras Nathaniel Patten, Amos Marritt and Joseph Winfhip, which were Chofen to Joyne with the Select men to enquire into, and afsert the Intereft of the Town, both referring to high wayes, and other Lands Incroached upon by particular p'fons: It was propofed, whether the Inhabitants will bear the Said perfons, with the Select men harmlefs as to what they Shall do Legally in that affaire

Voted on the Affirmative

March the 9th 169 6/5

At a publick Town meeting, orderly warned and assembled the day above expressed, for choosing of Town Officers, there was then chosen for Constables

    For the Town Thomas Andrews
                      John Withington
    for the farmes John Stone of the East
    ffor the village John Mixer:

For Selectmen:
- Deacon Walter Hastings:
- Edward Winship:
- Abraham Hill:
- John Oldham:
- Francis Bowman:

  For Town Treasurer Mr Samuel Andrew:
  for Town Clerk Samuel Green:

                for the Town Samuel Hastings Senr
                for Mixetimis
Surveyors for the highways William Russel
                for the South Sd of River Nathaniel _____
                for the farmes Jonathan Poulter

for Sealing of Leather, weights and measures John Hastings Sen

            for the Town, John Gove, Nicolas _____
            for the _____ _____ Amos Marrett
for tythingmen for the South Sd of River John Squiers Snr Joshua ____
            ffor Minotimis Nathaniel Patten, Aaron Russell

RECORD MADE BY SAMUEL GREEN, TOWN CLERK, 1694–1697

(See Folii 313–314)

July the 26th: 1695

By Order of the Great and Generall Court, holden att Boston, May the 29 last for the Inhabitants and free holders to Choose a Comissioner, to Joyn with the Select men then in being for the making of an Afsesment or tax for his Majestyes Service, att this day was then Chosen Mr Samuel Stone Senr: to be the comiffioner for that Service as Required by Order, and So entered in Book: the Inhabitants being Lawfully warned, and those then mett So agreed

The Same time and day It was voted by the Inhabitants then Affembled, to Return vnto Joseph Bartlett of Newtown the Sum of Money that the Town received of him about five yeares agone, for a fmall percell of Land that was Sold him att that time about five yeares Since, and he makeing complaint that he Could not injoy it quietly, the Inhabitants now met Voted on the Affirmative to return him his money again, and the Land to remain as before he bought it

August the 5th: 1695

Ordered by the Select men for the time being, that they have lett the high way on the South fide Charles River unto Samuel Green So farr as the Creek from the River Southward for five Shillings pr this present year enfueing

January 21: 95

Received by Deacon Walter Haftings of John Dixfon on the Towns accounts twenty Shillings for the use of the ware field, I say received &c: — 01 — 00 — 00:

[125] March the 9th: 169$\frac{5}{6}$

At a Publick Town Meeting, Orderly warned and Affembled the day above expreffed, for choofing of Town Officers, there was then Chosen for Conftables

    ffor the Town   Thomas Andrews
                            John Willington
    ffor the farmes John Stone of the Æaft:
    ffor the village John Mirack:

TOWN RECORDS

ffor Selectmen
{ Deacon Walter Haftings:
Ædward Winſhip:
Abraham Hill:
John Oldham:
ffrancis Bowman: }

ffor Town Treaſurer   Mr Samuel Andrew:
for Town Clerke — Samuel Green:

Surveyors for the high ways
for the Town   Samuel Haſtings Senr:
for Minottimie   william Ruſſel
for the South Side River   Nathaniel Sparhaw
for the farmes   Jonathan Prentice
ffor Sealing of Leather, weights and Meaſures,
John Haſtings sen^r

ffor tythingmen
{ for the Town,   John Gove, Nicolas ffeſsenden
for the Lane to watertown: Amos Marrett
for the South ſide ye River   John Squire sen^r:
Joſhua ffuller
for Minottomie   Nathaniel Patten, Jaaſon Ruſſel:
for the farmes,   John Ruſſel Iſaack ſterns
Joseph Symonds }

ffor Surveyors of fences,
for the neck of Land   Mr Sam^{ll} Goffe Senr:
Enſign Aaron Bordman
for the weſt field   Ruben Luxford, Benjamin Goddard
drivers of the weſt field   Jeremiah Holeman sen^r, Solomon prentice
drivers of the neck   { John Stedman
Iſrael Chevers }
ffor Minottomie.   { Joseph Addams
Eliſha Bull }
Haywards for the horſes   { John Dixſon
Gerſhom Cutter }

Hog Conſtables
ffor the Town   Joſeph Cook, Robert webber, Richard fferginſon
ffor Minottomie   Jacob Chamberlin, Jonathan Butterfield

ffor the Com̃on	William Withe, John Wales,
ffor the South fide	Daniel Champney, Iccabod Brown
ffor the farmes	John Coomie
	John Johnfon
	John Cutler Senr:

[125] March the 16th: 169$\frac{5}{6}$

At a meeting of the Inhabitants, Orderly convened att the meeting houfe in Cambridge Town, as followeth

1. whether the ninety pounds Granted by the Said Inhabitants May the 13 laft paft, for the maintenance of the next Settled Minifter, Should be Levyed on the Inhabitants for the year enfuing, to begin on the five and twentieth day of this Inftant March
2. The perfons Nominated to joyn with the Select men as a Comittee in this affaire of making the Rate for the maintenace of the next Settled Minifter among us, was then chofen.

Leu^t Jonathan Remington
Mr Thomas Oliver
William Rufsel:

3. That it Shall be left to the prudence of the then chofen Com̃ittee, to afsefs the Inhabitants their proportion of Said Minifters Rate for this prefent year:
4. Alfo that each perfon Afsefsed, Shall reackon and clear with the Deacon for their proportion in Said Rate on or before the laft day of the prefent year, which if neglected, it Shall be put into the Conftables hand to Collect the Same

All these Severall Articles were voted on the Affirmative

July the 27th 1696:

Att a publick meeting appointed by the Generall Court for the raifing of a tax or Afsefsment for his Majestys Service in this yere 1696: to choose Afsefsors to make the Rate or Afsefsment, there was then chofen for that Service att that time,   Deacon Walter Haftings
Mr Samuel Stone:
Mr Thomas oliver:

[126] March the 8th: 169⅞:

At a Publick Town meeting, orderly warned and Affembled the day and year above, for the Choofing of Town Officers, as Required by Law, then Chofen:

ffor Conftables
{ Owen warland:
  John Dickfon:
  Joseph Stone:

ffor Select men or Townfmen
{ Deacon Walter Haftings:
  Serg^t: Ædward winfhip:
  John Gove:
  John Oldham:
  william Ruffel:

Town clerke   Samuel Green

Assessors
{ Deacon walter Haftings:
  Mr Thomas Oliver:
  Mr Samuel Stone:

Surveyers of the high wayes
Ruben Luxford for the Town
Mr Jonathan Dunfter: Minotimy
Daniel Champney: South fide River
Jonathan Poulter the farmes

A Comittee Chofen to Lay out and to renew the marks of the Country high way from the five mile to Concord, and from Leut: ffisks to woburn line the perfons chofen was:

Leu^t: David ffifke
Mr Samuel Stone sen^r:
John watfon:
Matthew Bridge Junr.

A comittee chofen to make the minifters Rate for this year to joyn with the Select men then chofen

Mr Thomas Oliver
Nathaniel Patten
Jaafon Ruffel:

Tithingmen
{ Nathaniel Robbins sen^r: Daniel Danie: S. fide
  John Addams: Samuel Kidder: notomie
^

Surveyers for the fences
Leiut Remington, m^r Edmund Goffe for Neck
John Cooper, Jofeph Crackbone for weft field
Jeremiah Holeman Senr ₐior
ffence viewers for the neck: Leiv^t Remington: Mr Edmund Goffe
for the weft field   Amos Marret, John Cooper
for minotomie viewers and drivers   Jaafon Ruffel Nath: Patten
  ₐ for the Town   Zecheriah Hicks   Solomon Prentice
Tithing men for the farmes   Ifrael Mede   Ifaack Sterns
   for Minotomie   John Addams Samueₐ [   ]
   for South Sid River   Nath [   ] [   ]

[126]   Hog Conftables
for the Town: Daniel chevers:
for ye comon   Benj: Goddard
for the South fide: R: Benj: Dana   John Squire Junr
for the comon,   Benjamin Goddard, Joseph Crackbone
for Minotamie   Elifha Bull, Joseph Addams

A Return of the Comittee Chosen as on the other Lefte hand page chofen to Lay out an high way for the Country to Concord, from the five mile Swamp and onwards to Concord and from Leut: ffisks to Woburn, as was Ordered At the meeting on the 8th of March 169$\frac{8}{7}$ being the day of Choife of Town Officers

Upon the 17th day we mett, and began att the five mile Swamp and marked trees att a convenient diftance, till we came unto Samuel Wittamores fence; and then gave diftants Southweft of the fence, till we came againft his dore, then we marked a young Elme Northeaft of the high way; and So marked on both fides of the way, till we came to Samuel Winfhips; then the widdow Winfhip did Informe us, that her hufband had agreed with a former Comittee, that againft his fence Southweft, that the high way Should be Six Rodd wide and we accepted of it, and when we were paft the fence, we marked trees on both fides the high way again att a convenient diftance till we came to Mr Æftabrookes his fence, allowing that to be one fide of the high way, and Marked trees on the other fide, till we came into the Lane between M^r

Eaſtabrookes and John Poulter, and then aggreed that that ſhould be three Rodds wide, each of the propriators allowing their due diſtance the Land being good, we thought might be convenient: the like we did agree with Goodman Muzzey untill we was paſt his present fence, and aggreed with him for the ſeting up of his fence upon the one ſide of the Road, and mark the Other to the meeting houſe then we renewed the Marks to Concord. Then beginning att Leiut: Hicks, we renewed the Marks toward Woburn, that had been twice marked before, by ſome of the preſent Comittee, till coming to John Tidds field, we found the highway encumbered, with with fence and broken up Land, and when we were paſt that, we renewed the marks of the high way to Woburn Line.

David ffiſke sen^r: Samuel Stone Senr:
John Watſon Matthew Bridge Ju

[127] Cambridge March 14th: 169$\frac{7}{8}$

At a publick Meeting of y^e Inhabitants for Choice of Town officers, were Choſen as ffolloweth for the year Ensuing

Jonath^n Dunster ⎫
Nathan^{ll}: Hancock ⎬ Constables.
John Cuttler ⎭

Walter Hasting ⎫
Dr: James Oliver ⎮
John Oldham ⎮
Edward Winship ⎬ Select Men
Joseph Symons ⎮
William Read ⎮
Jonath^n Remington ⎭

Jonath^n Remington Town Clerke

Walter Hasting ⎫
Thomas Oliver ⎬ Aſseſso^{rs}:
Sam^{ll} stone sen^r ⎭

Tithing Men

Peter Town ⎫
Zech: Hicks Junr. ⎬ for ye Town

Reuben Luxford }
Benjam.^{n} Goddard } for ye Comon
John Adams }
Jason Rufsell } for Menotomy
Joseph Champney }
Daniel Dana } for South side ye River
John Rufsell }
John Tidd }
Thomas Cuttler } for ye ffarmes
ffrancis Bowman }

Surveyo^{rs}: of high ways

Joseph Hicks for ye Town
Nathan.^{ll} Sparhawk: for south side ye River
Joseph Winship for Menotomy
John Powlter for ye ffarmes

ffor to Infpect y^e yoking & ringing of swine

Daniel Chever }
Jno: Bunker } for y^e Town
Jno: Wyeth~ for y^e Comon
Elisha Bull }
Gershom Cutter } for Menotomy
Ebenez^r: Nutting }
George Adams } for y^e ffarmes

Viewers of fences

Ens: Aaron Bordman }
John Stedman } for y^e Neck

[127] 14 ffeb^{ery}: 170$\frac{3}{4}$

M^r: Jno: Oldham p^d: to the Town Treafu^{er}: One Shilling and 4^d: w^{ch}: he Received of Dan^{ll} Champney for the improoment of a parcel of Land belonging to the Town inclosed by the S^d: Champney S^d: Land being on y^e Northerly Side of m^{rs}: Phipps^s: farme

[128] Cambridge March the 14th 1698/7

At a publick Town meeting, Orderly warned and convened, for choice of Town Officers

Then Chofen for Conftables
for the Town — Nathaniel Hancok Junr
for Minotomy — Mr Jonathan Dunfter
for the farmes — John Cutter:

Select men
Deacon Walter Haftings
Leiv[t]: Jonathan Remington.
Doc[t]: James Oliver:
  John Oldham: defents
  Ædward Winfhip
  William Read ⎫
  Jofeph Symons ⎭ for the farmes

☞ Town Clerke Leiu[t]: Jonathan Remington

Surveiyers of the High wayes
for the Town Jofeph Hicks
for the South side Nathaniel Sparhawke
for Menotomie Jofeph Winfhip

Tything men:
In the Town Zechariah Hicks Junr Peter Town:
for the Lane watertown Ruben Luxford
for the Comon, Benjamin Goddard
for menottomie John Addams, Jaafon Ruffel:
for the South Side Jofeph Champney, Daniel Dana
for the farmes John Rufsel, John Tidd, Thomas Cutler ffrancis Bowman

Surveyers of fences
for the neck, Ens: Aaron Bordman, John Stedman
Drivers of the neck, Ifrael cheavers Robert Webber

for the weſt field Jeremiah Holeman sen^r Joſeph Crackbon
for Menottomie Joſeph Addams, Walter Ruſſel

Hog Conſtables
for the Town Daniel Chevers, John Buncker
for Minottomie Eliſha Bull Gerſham Cutter
for the Comon John Withe
for the farmes Ebenezer Mutting, George Addams

Aſſeſſors
Deacon walter Haſtings
Mr Samuel Stone Senr:
Mr Thomas oliver:
over leafe

[128] The names of thoſe y^t deſire that all the Lotts at Shaw ſhinn may bee ſudenly meaſured & euery one do engage themſelves to pay for ye meaſuring their owne portions

Daniel Gookin   Jonathan Mitchel
Richard Champney   Edward Jackſon
Edward Goffe   John Jackſon
Richard Jackſon   Tho: Danforth
William ffrench   Edward Winſhipp
Richard Parke   Andrew ſteuenſon
John Bridge   Richard Robins
William Manning   Eliah Corllett
William Pattin for himſelfe & mathew Bridge
ffrancis Whitmore   Richard Danee
ffrancis Moore ſenior Francis moore Junio^r
Abraham Arington   Daniel Kempſter
Jonathan Hide   Thomas ſwetman
Samuel Green   Robert ſtedman
Richard ffrancis   John Boutell
Stephen Daye: Dauid Stone;
Roger Bucke,   Gilbert Crackbone
M^r Joſeph Cooke   William Bucke

[129] The Same day on the other fide Lefe
Thofe that were then chofn to joyn with the Select men to make the Minifters Rate for the year enfuing were
>John Gove
>William Ruffel
>Samuel Sparhawke

There was then Granted a Rate for the defraying of Town Charges the Sume of fforty Pounds money:

Alfo a Rate of twenty pounds for thofe that belong to this meeting houfe

Alfo Voted that there Should be a peiw made and sett up between Mr Samuel Gookin's peiw and the Stairs on the South weft corner of the meeting houfe for the family of the Miniftry:

At a Meeting of the Select Men Aprill 14th 1698:

on the Motion of John Hasting in behalfe of his son Daniel Hasting the Select Men have Granted the said Daniel the Improvement of the houfe by ye Pound for a smiths shop he paying to the Town an acknowledgm^t of Twelve pence in Money for ye year ensuing

At a Meeting of ye Select Men July 11th 1698

on ye Motion of Mr Jno Leverett & Doct^r James oliver: the Select Men do grant that they shall have Convenient place in the Meeting houfe for the accomodation of their respective ffamilies, the place or places to be set out to them by ye Select Men ye Elders Consenting thereto: The places wch they desire are on each side of the Eaft Door of ye Meeting houfe

At a Meeting of the Inhabitants of Cambridge orderly Convened March 13th 1698/9 for ye Choice of Town Officers for the year ensuing, were Chofen as ffollows

Josiah Parker
Joshua ffuller } Constables
Joseph Teed

Jonath: Remington Town Clerk

John Shedman for the Town
Sam: Sparhawke for y: southside of y: River } Surveyors
Joseph Adams for Menotomy } of Highways
John Monroe for the Farmes

Nicolas Hosindon
Andrew Bordman } for y: Town
John Hasting for Watertown Eare
Henry Prentice for y: Common
John Watson for y: Plain
Nath: Pattinson } for
Jn°: Dickson } Menotomy } Tithing men
Nath: Robinsson } for South
Joseph Champney } side of y: River
Philip Russell
David Fisk jun } for y:
Sam: Whitmore } Farmes
Israel Mead

Sam: Goffe sen } for y:
David Deming } Neck
Solom: Prentice sen } for y:
Benjam: Goddard } Westfield } Fence Viewers
William Russell } for
Gershom Cutter } Menotomy

Mr Josiah Parker
Mr Thomas Oliver } Assessors
Mr Francis Bowman

Jonath: Nutting } for y:
Robert Wobson } Town

RECORD MADE BY JONATHAN REMINGTON, TOWN CLERK, 1693, 1698-1700
(See Folio 323)

Deacon Hasting
Mr Jno Leverett
Do&ct James Oliver   } Sele&ct Men
Jonath^n Remington
Edward Winshipp
Joseph Simons
William Read

[129]   Jonath^n Remington   Town Clerke

John Stedman for the Town
Sam^{ll} Sparhawke for ye southside ye River } Surveyo^{rs} of high ways
Joseph Adams for Menotomy
John Mon Roe for the ffarmes

Nicolas ffessinden }
Andrew Bordman   } for ye Town
John Hasting for watertown Lane
Henry Prentice for ye Com̃on
John Watson for ye Plain
Nath: Pattin sen^r }
Jno: Dickson   } for Menotomy   } Tithing men
Nath^{ll} Robins sen^r } for South
Joseph Champney   } fide ye River
Philip Rufsell
David Fisk Junr } for y^e
Sam^{ll} Whitmore } ffarmes.
Israel Mead

Sam^{ll} Goffe sen^r }
David Dem̃ing   } for ye Neck:
Solom^n Prentice sen^r } for y^e } Fence Viewers
Benjam^n Goddard   } weft field
William Rufsell }
Gershom Cutter } for Menotomy

Mr Josiah Parker
Mr Thomas Oliver   } Afsefso^{rs}
Mr Francis Bowman

Jonath^n Nutting }
Robert Webber   } for ye Town

[**130**] At a Meeting of the Select Men April 10th: 1699 ~

On the Motion of Severall persons on the South Side the River desiring that some high ways may be settled in order to the Improvement of their lands M.r Thomas oliver, John Oldham ~ and Nathan.ll Sparhawke are Nominated & appointed a Comittee to Settle Such high ways as they may Judge necefsary for the end aforefaid & to make report unto the felect Men of their doings therein at the next Meeting of the Select Men

At a Meeting of the Select Men May 8th. 1699 ~

Samuel Prentice y.e Shepherd moving that he might fence in & improve some land on the Comon on the North of Abr.ham Watfons Barn the Select Men have Granted the Same to him for this present year he paying for the Same to y.e Select Men for y.e ufe of the Town one shilling Money by way of acknowledgem.t:

At a Meeting of the Inhabitants of Cambridge May 15th. 1699 ~

there was then Granted a Rate for the Defraying of y.e necefsary Charges of the Town for this present year, the Sum: of Fifty pounds in Money ~

Alfo Voted that an Addrefs should in the Name of the Inhabitants be presented to the Gen.ll Court the next Sefsions, for some help & relief w.th reference to the great Bridge, & that affair to be Mannaged by the Select Men

Alfo by the Inhabitants of this part of the Town was then Granted a Rate of Ten pounds in Money for the Repairs of the Meeting houfe & paying for the Ringing y.e Bell & Sweeping the said Meeting houfe ~

Likewife then were Nominated & appointed Enfign Aaron Bordman, John Oldham & W.m Rufsell as a Comittee to Join with the Select Men to Make the Minifters Rate for y.e present year ~

At a meeting of the Select Men August 14th. 1699

By Information of severall that the Wife of Robert Webber has taken a Bastard Child of her Daughter living w.th Cap.t Gillam of Boston to nurfe S.d Child, the Select Men having Considered thereof Do order that Josiah Parker Constable do forthwith give notice to Robert Webber & his Wife that within two days they procure security to be given that s^d Bastard child [130] shall be no Charge to the Town: wch if they neglect to do, then the S^d Constable the next day to Convey said Child to Boston to its Mother

August 16th 1699 ~ Mr Thomas Oliver Mr Josiah Parker & m^r ffrancis Bowman Chosen to be Afsefso^rs for this p^rsent year were sworn to the due discharge of their office for the p^rsent Tax ~ Coram Jonath^n Remington Town Cler?

At a Meeting of the Select Men Decemb^r 11th 1699

On a Motion made to the Select Men by John Lawrence, James Wilson, Thomas Mead, Nathan^ll Duntlin & Joseph ffassett Inhabitants of Cambridge ffarmes, that a high way might be settled leading to their respective houfes & for pafsage to the Meeting & to Market. The Select Men do Nominate & appoint Deacon Samuel Stone Matthew Bridge Junr: & ffrancis Bowman as a Committee to take a view & to Consider what may be necefsary & Convenient for the settlement of said high way & to make report thereof to ye Select Men at their next Meeting on the Second Monday of January next

The return of ye s^d Comittee.

We whofe names are under written being appointed a Comittee by ye Select Men of Cambridge as appears by an order bearing date ye 11th of December 1699: to Consider of a Convenient high way for sundry of o^r Neighbo^rs living Northward of o^r Parrish to come to ye publick Meeting and to Market: Accordingly we did attend it ye 18th day of this Instant, and do Judge it most Convenient to be where it now is allowed and fenced from John Lawrence his houfe to ye Brook Southerly & so continuing along by Goodman Nuttings ffence that now is till it come to Mr Goffes Lott, & then upon ye Edge of Mr Goffes Lott till we come to Goodman Kerlys land, & so through his land where it has formerly been laid out, Continuing till it come at a Swamp upon Mr Aaron Bordmans land (as we were Inform'd, wch we think will be inconvenient by reason of ye chargeablenefs it will attend to make it pafsable, and the small inconveniency that will be to the Proprieto^r:

to compaſs yᵉ weſt end of the Swamp till we come to Joseph Teeds land, & so continuing where yᵉ way is now trodden till we come unto yᵉ Countrey Road yᵗ leads from Concord to Oburn between Joseph Teeds and John Johnsons : and further we think it may be convenient that yᵉ way go up by the Widow Teeds & so continuing till it come at yᵉ Meeting houſe where it is now trodden

{ Samuel Stone
ffrancis Bowman
Matthew Bridge Junʳ

By reaſon of ſome objection made againſt what is above returned yᵉ select Men did deſire the abovesᵈ Comittee once more to take a view of said high way & did Join wᵗʰ them Capt Read, Enſign Symonds

&

[131] & Mʳ Edward winshipp for effecting that affaire ~ And they made their report of what they had done as followeth : We whoſe names are Subſcribed were ordered a ſecond time to take a further care about a high way for oʳ neighboʳˢ as is within expreſt & to Join wᵗʰ three of yᵉ Select Men to do it, & we have Jointly ~ agreed a Confirmation of what was formerly agreed upon

Samuel ſtone   William Read
ffrancis Bowman   Edward Winſhipp
Matth Bridge   Josep Symonds

Alſo Mʳ Aaron Bordman is allowed the two Rod in breadth of land that lyes between Shaws ffarm & the Small lotts the whole length of his lott towards his recompence for yᵉ high way going through his land

At a Meeting of yᵉ Select Men Decembʳ 18ᵗʰ 1699

Mʳ Thomas Oliver Nathanˡˡ Sparhawke & Joseph Champney are Nominated and appointed a Comittee to take a view of Some land in Elder Champneys hundred Acres now in yᵉ Poſseſsion of Henry Smith in order to yᵉ ſetling & laying out of a high way ~ through Sᵈ land : and some persons Informing that a high way of twenty foot wide may be ſufficient : If therefore that be so Judged by Sᵈ Comittee it will be by the select Men approved of, Also yᵉ sᵈ Comittee are desired to take a view of yᵉ land allowed for a highway between sᵈ hundred acres & the head of some small lotts purchaſed by s^d Henry Smith being two Rod in breadth, wch is to be allowed to s^d Henry Smith in recompence for that laid out in his land as aforeſ^d, & if they Judge that be not sufficient to make recompence, that they would signify what it falls short in value And s^d Comittee are defired as speedily as pofsible to perform ye aboves^d service & to make report in writing under their hands of ye Same to ye Select Men ~

The Nineteenth of December 1699 ~ ~

We whofe names are underwritten have in obedience to the within written order have taken a view of S^d land & do give in o^r Judgment as followeth (1) that it is convenient that ye s^d way be laid through that land wch Henry Smith lately bought of Joseph Champney on ye Eaft side of it (2) the s^d way hath need to ly Thirty foot wide at ye South end of s^d land unto the foot of ye Hill wch is about Twenty Pole & that from thence Twenty foot wide to ye North end of s^d land (3) That ye s^d Henry Smith over & above the two Rod way which belongeth to ye Town there be allowed him fforty five shillings in Money in satisfaction for ye s^d way

       Thomas Oliver
       Nathan^{ll} Sparhawk
       Joseph Champney

 Memrd the day above mentioned

Henry Smith Recd: forty five Shillings in Money in Satisfaction for ye way a bove mentioned. viz:

   of Jno: Oldham.   .01 .02 .6
   & of Dan^{ll} Dana.   .01 .02 .6

Capt Remington & m^r Jno Bunker prefent when the money was paid.

[131] At a Meeting of the Inhabitants of Cambridge orderly Convened March 11th 1700 for the Coice of Town Officers for ye year ensuing there were then Chofen a ffolloweth ~

  Mr Edmond Goffe ⎫
  Jofeph Winshipp ⎬ Constables
  Joseph Mirriam ⎭

Deacon Hasting
Jonathⁿ: Remington
Edward Winshipp
John Oldham } Select Men
William Rufsell
Francis Bowman
Philip Rufsell

Jonathⁿ Remington Town Clerke

Jonathⁿ Remington Town Treafurʳ.

Andrew Bordman
Jonathⁿ Butterfield } Surveyoʳ of yᵉ high ways
John Squire senʳ
Benjamⁿ Muzzey

Nathanˡˡ Hancock Junʳ
Samˡˡ Manning
David Deming
Solomⁿ Prentice senʳ
John Cooper } Tithing Men
Samˡˡ Kidder
Jafon Rufsell
John Adams
Nathˡˡ Sparhawk
Benjamⁿ Dana
Matth: Bridge Junʳ
John Rufsell
John Lawrence

Zech: Hicks senʳ } viewers of fence for yᵉ neck
Ephraim ffroft

John Watson } viewers for yᵉ Weft field
solomⁿ Prentice Junʳ

Gerfhom Cutter } Viewers for Menotomy field
Elisha Bull

Sam^{ll}: Gibson }
Israel Chever } Hawards for ye Neck
  Jeremy Holman }
  John Wyeth } Hawards for ye weft fjeld
    Abrah^m: Hill }
    Walter Russell } Hawards for Menotomy field

John Hafting   Sealer of Leather

Peter Town   sealer of Weights & Meafures

Owen Warland
Joseph Cooledge
Thomas Prentice
John Collis   Perfons to Infpect
Philip Cooke   } ye yoking & Ringing
Matth: Abdy   Swine
Ebenez^r swan
John Squire Junr
Nath^{ll} Robins

[132] George Mon Roe }
Sam^{ll} ftone Davids son } perfons to Infpect ye yoking
Jofeph Bowman } & Ringing swine for ye ffarms

On S^d: day of Choice was voted to give the the little Meeting houfe Bell to the ffarmers

Voted then that the Select Men in the name of the Inhabitants do give their thanks to Capt Andrew Belcher for the Bell for their Meeting houfe he has given them

Voted then that the land that was formerly belonging to Reynold Bush wch ye Town had by Execution for his Maintenance, shall be sold & the Money to be Improved for repairing the fchool houfe, & the Select Men are appointed to make ye Sale

Mr Edmond Goffe John Jackson & Jason Rufsell are by ye Proprieto^{rs}: of the Town Commons Nominated & appointed to make Enquiry into

ye state of the five hundred Acres of land Granted for ye ufe of
☞ the Ministry in this Town & place & to make report thereof to
the Proprieto^{rs} at their next Meeting: Alfo to make enquiry
concerning sundry parcels of land undivided & to take an acc^t of y^e
quantity & quality of said lands & make report as aboves^d for wch pains
and labo^r they are to be satisfyed

William Pattin requefting of the Proprieto^{rs} y^t he might have halfe an Acre of land where his houfe standeth wch he is willing to purchafe it was voted by ye Proprietors that he fhall have that liberty & give what the s^d committee above mentioned shall determine

John Bunker having set his shop upon the Comon land by y^e
Meettng houfe did requeft the Propriet^{rs} that his shop might
☞ stand where it is: wch was granted him he payin fuch rent yearly
as shall be agreed on

On the requeft of David Deming to have liberty to hang a Gate Crofs the way y^t leads to ye Wind mill hill at the north part of his land it was granted he fhould have the liberty for ye p^{r}fent year

At a Generall Town Meeting of the Inhabitants of Cambridge y^e: 18th May 1700 there was then Chofen Jno Leverett Esqr Select Man, and And^r Bordman, Town Clerk

there was Then alfo Voted y^t ye Sum thirty pounds Should be levied upon them, for the defraying nefcefeary Charges among them. it was also voted by the Inhabitants belonging to y^e: Old Meeting houfe in this town, y^t ye Sum of ten Pounds Should be Levied upon them for the defraying of Charges arifeing among them Selves

[132] At a Generall meeting of the Inhabitants of Cambridge y^e: 24th of June 1700. It was then Voted that ye Schoolhoufe Should be forthwith fitted up By Rebuilding ye Same. And that ye Charge y^t Should arife thereby Should be added (by ye Select Men) to ye town Rate granted by ye Inhabitants ye 18th of May 1700 ~ ~ ~

Cam.^{r} 30: July 1700

At a meeting of Jno Leverett Esqr Justice of the Peace and the Select men of ye town, Agreed and Ordered that a Suitable watch be kept In the town nightly from time to time After nine of ye clock In the Evening untill sun rife in the Morning, from and After ye first Evening in Augst next Insueing ye Date hereoff untill the last Day of Sep.^{t} following. And ye Town Clerk is hereby Ordered to give Notice to ye Constable for ye Town, y.^{t} he do from time to time as afore said Warn or Cause to be warned two Meet persons qualified as ye Law Directs, And order y.^{m} to attend him In ye Evening to Receive their Charge as is set forth in ye Law.

Sep.^{t} 9th 1700 ~

At a Meeting of the Selectmen

John Leverett Esqr: & Deacon Hasting were appointed to Treat wth Zach^{ry}: Hicks Ju.^{r} and Jos: Hicks, or some other Sutable person or persons Concerning the Rebuilding the Schoolhouse wch s.^{d} house is to be 20 foot wide & 26 foot In length, the above mentioned persons are also appointed to take care that ye above mentioned House be speedyly done, In good Workman like order — — — —

At a Meeting of ye Select men 2 Octr 1700. ~ ~

Nat.^{ll} Hancock sen^r: is appointed to take Care for ye Supply and Reliefe of ye Widdow Sawtle and to Render an account (of his Disburstments In y.^{t} affair) to ye Select men when Called thereunto — —

At a Meeting of the Select men 11. Novr 1700.

Whereas there hath been of late a publick Contribution In this Town for ye Reliefe of Joseph Bemus and Wm Chamberlin their Substance having been of late Consumed by fire the Select men have Ordered 03 : 00 . 0 of S.^{d} Money to be disposed of for Wm Chamberlins vfe & ye Remainder for Jos: Bemus: ~ Deacon Hasting & m.^{r} Fra^s: Bowman are appointed to Lay out S.^{d} money for ye vfe above mentioned.

[**133**] 11 . Nov.r 1700 ~.

At a Meeting of the Select men.

Whereas Sundry persons have manifested their dissatisfaction concerning a High way lay.d out Some time the last year by Deacon Sam.ll Stone, m.r: Fra.s Bowman & m.r: Math: Bridge as ap.rs by their Return Entred in the Town Book. ~ the Select men have Nominated & appointed m.r Jn.o Oldham m.r: Phillip Russel, m.r: W.m Russel & m.r: Benj.a Muzzey, to Join w.th the above mentioned Comitte to make a final Issue of y.e matter, either by confirming y.e above mentioned Return, or by laying out the Way in some other place as they Shall Judge most Convenient; And make Return of their doings therein under their hands on y.e Second Monday in Decemb.r next.

[**133**]   25 June 1700 ~.

At a Meeting of the Select Men ~.

Complaint being made by Liev.t Thomas Cuttler & others for want of a High way for their passage to Meeting & Market. ~ the Select men do Nominate & appoint Jn.o Russel, David Fiske Ju.r: & Math: Bridge a Comitte to lay out & Settle Such High way for y.e above S.d persons as they (y.e Comitte) Shall think most Convenient; and make Report of their doings therein to y.e Select men on y.e Second Monday in July next.

We whose hands are under written were ordered by the Select men to Consider of & lay out a High way for Liev.t Cuttler and the rest of y.e Neighbours in y.t: part of the Neighbourhood to y.e Meeting house &c. as appears by an Order bearing Date. 25. June. 1700 Accordingly we have attended it. ~ And began at y.e Northerly part of Liev.t Cuttlers land, and came into a lane y.t: is fenced on both Sides between Tho.s Cuttler Jun.r & Jn.o Cooper . for Sundrey Rods; & then y.e a bove s.d Tho.s Cuttlers lane wholy a little further; then into wast land Some Rods further; then through a corner of Ro.t Mirriams land leading into more wast land of Sam.ll Stones Son of David Stone; then we came into a lane through David Stones land; and it is to be under stood y.t: so far as we have pafsed is where it is now trodden and also two Rods wide: then through Ro.[t] Mirriams land again leading to Deacon Sam[ll] Stones, fenced on one Side; then we came to Deacon Stones turning Easterly a bout 20 Rods; then we went through an inclosure of Deacon Sam[ll] Stones fenced on y[e] East side and an Inclosure of Deacon Jn[o] Mirriams where we marked the High way on the West Side; then we came into Widdow Mirriams land fenced upon y[e] South Side by Jn[o] Mirriams then we went between Deacon Sam[ll] Stones & Deacon Jn[o] Mirriams marked on both sides, then we came onto Deacon Samuel Stones land for Somthing a bout halfe a Mile & marked on both Sides; then we came on to y[e] Parrish land marked it on both sides till we came into the Countrey Road where it is now trodden.

5 July. 1700 David Fiske
Jn[o] Russel
Mathew Bridge

[134]   At a Meeting of the Proprietors of the Comon lands in Cambridge orderly Convened y[e] 2nd of December. 1700. ~

There was then Voted that Jn[o] Leverett Esq[r] Deacon Walter Hasting, Edward Winshipp & W[m] Rufsel, Should be a Comitte to receive y[e] acct[s] of m[r] Edm: Goffe, Jn[o] Jackson & Jason Rufsel (who were appointed in March last by S[d] Propriet[rs] to take a Survey of Sundry parcels of Comon & undivided land) and also to agree wth S[d] persons refering to y[t] affair The Comitte afore S[d] are impowered to proportion y[e] Proprieto[rs]: of y[e] Comon & undivided lands according to their Respective Intrests or proprieties, & give a list of the Same to y[e] Constables together wth a Warrant to Collect y[e] Same as in other Town Rates. ~ ~ ~ ~ ~

m[r] Edm: Goffe & Jason Rufsel being present at y[e] Voting of what is a bove written did promife to Suspend y[e] prosecution of s[d] Propriet[rs] in a Course of law ~ ~ ~

Also the a bove mentioned Comitte are Impowered to Order the Collecting of y[e] proportions Set upon y[e] Proprieto[rs] who have hither unto Neglect[d] to pay their proportions for y[e] Satisfieing a Comitte by S[d] proprieto[rs] appointed on the 24th of Sep[t]: 1695. —   —   —

At a Meeting of the Select Men.
y[e] 9th of Decem[r] 1700.

The Town Clerke is Ordered to pay unto m[r] Tho[s] Willis three pounds In Money for a parcel of timber at the South end of the great Bridge, & Deacon Hasting is appointed to Receive Said timber of m[r] Willis.

At a Meeting of the Proprietors of the Common lands in Cambridge, Orderly Convened the 16th of Decem[r] 1700.

There was then Voted that the Comon & undivided lands belonging to s[d] Proprieto[rs] Should be layed out to Each Proprietor his proportion of s[d] lands. ~ Excepting a High way on the South fide of Charls River from s[d]: River to the Rhoad now leading to Roxbury w[ch] S[d] way is on the East of m[r] Edw: Pelhams Farme, & on the East or South of m[r] Sam[ll] Angers farme.

A way voted for the use of the ministry.

The above mentioned way was on s[d] day Voted by s[d] Proprieto[rs] for the Vfe of the Ministrey in this Town & place; Reserving a Convenient pafsage to the Severall lotts of Marsh butting on S[d] High way.

There was at S[d] Meeting also Voted that John Leverett Esq[r] Deacon Hasting, Liev[t] Aaron Bordman Jason Rufsel & John Jackson should be a Comitte [**134**] to lay out f[d] Comon lands Reserving Convenient High ways a Training field Clay pitts and Watering places for Cattle.

13 Jan[ry]: 1700. I

Paid by y[e] Select Men to m[r]: Jn[o] Oldham

£ s
02 . 05 . 0 wch money was due from the Town for damage done to Henry Smith by a high way being lay[d] thrû: his land 19. Dec[r] 1699

10: ffeb[r] 1700. I

Whereas at a Meeting of y[e] Select men 9 Sep[t] 1700. Jn[o] Leverett Esq[r] & Deacon Hasting were appointed to treat wth Zech[r] Hicks Jun[r]: & Jos: Hicks Concerning y[e] taking down and building a Schoolhoufe: Accordingly y[e] above mention[d] persons did Cov[t] and agree wth Zech[r] Hicks Jun[r]: and Jos: Hicks for y[e] Sum of   to take down, build

& finish in good workmanlike Order S^d houſe on or before ye 16: Nov^r: 1700 for payment for Sd: houſe Vid: ye book of accompts page. 71.

At a Meeting of the Inhabitants of Cambridge Orderly Convened (March . 10th 1700 . 1) for the Choice of Town officers for ye Year Ensuing there were then Chosen — — — — — — —

Joseph Coolidge
Gershom Cutter ſen^r: } Constables
John Munroe

Deacon Hasting
John Oldham
Edwd Winshipp
William Ruſsel } Select Men and Aſsessors ~ ~
Sam^{ll} Sparhawke
Fra^s: Bowman
Phillip Ruſsel

And^r Bordman . Town Clerke

And^r Bordman Town Treasur^r ~.

Surveyo^{rs} of
High Ways
{ Zch^{ry}: Hicks Junr: for ye Town.
  Elisha Bull for Menotomy
  Nat^{ll} Longley for ye South ſide ye River.
  Wm Munroe Ju^r: for ye Farmes.

Peter Town ~
Nat^{ll} Hancock ſen^r } for ye Town
John Gove ~

Sam^{ll} Hasting for ye Lane
Benj^a Goddard } Tithing men
Solomon Prentice Ju^r. } for the Coṁon
Abraham Watson for ye Plain
Nat^{ll} Pattin ſen^r }
Joseph Winshipp } for Menotomy

Turn over.

[135] Sam:ll Champney ⎱ South fide
   Dan:ll Dana . . ⎰ y:e River.
    Ensigne Jos: Symonds ⎫
    David Fiske Jun:r ⎬ for the Farmes   Tithing Men
    Tho:s Smith fen:r ⎭

Joseph Cooke ⎱
Sam:ll Gibson ⎰ for the Neck
Ens: Sam:ll Cooper ⎫
Tho:s Prentice ⎬ West field   Fence Viewers
Sam:ll Kidder ⎭
Ab:r Hill ⎱
Sam:ll Bull ⎰ Menotomy field. ~

Nat:ll Hancock Ju:r ⎱
Jonathan Nutting ⎰ for the Neck
Jer. Holman ⎱
John Cooper ⎰ West field   Hawards. ~
Walter Rufsel ⎱
W:m Pattin ⎰ Menotomy field ~

John Hasting fen:r Sealer of Leather

Peter Town Sealer of Weights & Meafures. ~

John Mañing ⎱
W:m Barret ⎰ for the Town
Amos Marret for y:e lane
Jn:o Collis ⎱
Jn:o Wyeth ⎰ Comõn
fam:ll Cooke y:e Plain   Persons to
Jn:o Phillebrown ⎱   Inspect the
And:r Wilson ⎰ Menotomy   Yoaking
Sam:ll Robbins ⎱   and Ringing
Henry Smith ⎰ South fide y:e River.   of Hoggs.
Jn:o Comey ⎫
George Munroe ⎮
Nat:ll Whittemore. ⎬ for the Farmes
Jos: Stone ⎮
Tho:s Mirriam ⎭

Liev^t: Aa^r Bordman } to Joine wth ye Select Men
Jason Rufsel } in making ye Ministers Rate

Voted on s^d 10: March. 1700 . 1. that Liev^t David Fiske, Jno Cutter fen^r Nich^o Fissenden & Israel Cheever fhould be a Comitte, to Joine wth a Comitte y^t may be appointed by ye Inhabitants of Watertown to make Search for ye old bounds between Watertown and Cambridge, (betwixt black Pine and Mount Tabor,) and make Report of their doings therein to ye Select Men on the Second Monday in May next.

Voted that m^{rs} Hanah Gookin Should be payed three pounds to pay the Rent of her houfe this prefent year. ~ ~ ~ ~ ~ ~

[135] At a Meeting of the Select Men. 10 March 1701. 1 . ~ ~

Liev^t: Aaron Boedman Requesting that he might have the improvement of the Burying yard (to keep fheep in) the felect Men did consent y^t he fhould have the improvement of S^d yard (for ye vfe a bove mentioned) for One year next Ensuing provided he would cutt ye gate of f^d yard in funder & hang the fame wth futable hooks & hinges, also fix a ftub post in the ground & a Rayle from poft to poft Crofs the gates for them to fhutt against, all to be done in good workman like Order wch the S^d Boedman promifed to do . ~ ~

At a Meeting of the Select Men.
14 Ap^r 1701.

Jason Rufsell, Sam^{ll} Kidder & Nicholas: Fifsenden were appointed a Comitte to take care of the Sheep (y^t go on the Comons) this present year, by Causing them to be kept in one or two flocks as they Shall Judge most proper. ~ ~ ~ ~

14 Ap^l 1701. Recd of Sam^{ll} Prentice one fhiling money In part for Rent for a piece of land near Ab^r Watson's Barn. ~ ~ ~

At a Meeting of ye Inhabitants Orderly Convened 19 May . 1701.

there was then Voted y^t: ye Sum of forty five pounds Should be levied on ye Inhabitants of s^d town for ye defraying of Charges arifing

In yᵉ whole Town. Also the Sum of Ten pounds Should be levied on yᵉ Inhabitants belonging to yᵉ Old Meeting house In yˢ: Town for Defraying of Charges amongst them. ~ ~ ~

There was also voted yᵗ the Select Men Should Informe oᵣ Representative that yᵉ building a Mill on Medford River will be prejuditial to medows In oᵣ Town, & that he make his objections at yᵉ Genᵣˡˡ Court against building a mill on sᵈ River. ~ ~ ~

[136] We the Subscribers being appointed to make Search for yᵉ old bounds betwixt Black pine & Mount Tabor (as appears by a Vote of yᵉ Inhabitants 10 March 1701.) Accordingly we did attend sᵈ Service on yᵉ 14 Apʳ: 1701 & found yᵉ most ancient bounds between Watertown & Camʳ In yᵉ place above mentioned, althô: not to yᵉ Satisfaction of yᵉ Comitte appointed by yᵉ Inhabitants of Watertown by Reason of its being a Bow line. ~ Lievᵗ Fiske further Sais yᵗ he being one of yᵉ first yᵗ was appointed to Run sᵈ line wᵗʰ persons appointed from Watertown sᵈ persons from Watertown did Shew yᵐ most of yᵉ bounds yᵗ we have now found. ~ ~ ~

David Fiſke Senʳ:
Nichˢ Fiſsenden

At a Meeting of yᵉ Select Men. 9ᵗʰ June . 1701 . ~ ~
the Cler: is to Send a Notification to yᵉ fence Viewers at Menotomy, to Signifie to them yᵗ they are appointed to take a view of the Stone Wall Called by yᵉ Name of Phillip Joneses Wall between Watertown and Camʳ: & to make Report to yᵉ Select Men in what Condiçon it is at preſent in on the Second Monday in July next . ~ ~ ~

We the Subscribers being appointed by the Select Men to take a view of yᵉ Stone Wall Called by yᵉ name of Phillp Jonesˢ: Wall, as appears by an Order bearing date yᵉ 9ᵗʰ of June, 1701. ~ Accordingly we did (Sometime in Sᵈ month of June) take a view of Sᵈ wall and then found it down in twenty & two places, Some of which a loaden Cart might be driven through: also without gates in yᵉ places where they were appointed to be Set up. ~

14. July. 1701   Abraham Hill
                 Samᵤˡ l. Bull.

TOWN RECORDS 339

At a Meeting of y:̊ Select Men the 13?ͭʰ Octo?ͬ 1701. ~

The Treasurer is Ordered to pay to y:̊ Widow Teed thirty Shillings on Condition She give bond to y:̊ value of three pounds to Secure y:̊ town from any further Charge concerning a high way layd thrû her land by Deacon Sam¹¹ Stone Fraˢ: Bowman & Math: Bridge a Comitte appointed for y:ͭ affair.

[136] At a Meeting of y:̊ Select Men 12?ͭʰ Jan?ͬʸ: 170½. ~ ~

☞ It was then Ordered that John Bunker Should pay to o?ͬ Town Treaſurer Six Shillings money for y:̊ Rent of land where his Shop Stands for y:̊ two years last past. ~ ~

Also that Zech?ͬʸ: Hickes Jun?ͬ pay to o?ͬ S:ͩ Treaſur?ͬ: twelve pence p?ͬ year for for what remains due for y:̊ rent of land on w?ͨʰ his barn Stands.

Also that Fra:ˢ Bowman & Phillip Ruſsel take care for the reliefe of Lidia Knite. ~ ~ ~ ~ ~ ~

At a Meeting of y:̊ Select Men. y:̊ 9?ͭʰ ffeb?ͬʸ: 170½. ~ ~

It was then Ordered that Deacon Hasting and And?ͬ: Bordman Should take care to procure Staves for the Tything Men of our Town. as the Law Directs. ~ ~ ~ ~

At a Meeting of the Inhabitants of Cambridge Orderly Convened (9?ͭʰ March 1701 . 2) for y:̊ Choice of Town Officers for y:̊ year Ensuing, there were then Chosen ~ ~ ~ ~ ~

John Stedman ⎫
Samuel Sparhawke ⎬ Constables
Thomas Blogget ⎭

Deacon Hasting ⎫
John Oldham ⎪
William Ruſsel ⎬ Select Men
Sam¹¹ Cooper ⎪
Fraˢ: Bowman ⎭

And?ͬ Bordman Town Cler;
And?ͬ Bordman Town Treaſu?ͬʳ ~

Deacon Hasting ⎫
Fraⁿ: Bowman ⎬ Aſseſsors
Andʳ: Bordman ⎭

~ ~ Joseph Cooke. ⎫
    Danˡˡ: Dana.   ⎪ Surveyoʳˢ of
    William Pattin ⎬ high ways. ~.
    Joseph Teed.   ⎭

(turn Over.)

[137] mʳ: William Andrewe ⎫
      Owen Warland   ⎪
      John Hasting Senʳ: ⎪
      John Collis   ⎪
      Benjᵃ: Goddard   ⎪
      John Watson   ⎪
      Jason Ruſsel   ⎬ Tithingmen
      Gershom Cutter senʳ: ⎪
      Samˡˡ Oldham   ⎪
      Benjᵃ: Dana   ⎪
      Nichˢ: Fiſsenden senʳ:⎪
      Lievᵗ: Cuttler   ⎪
      William Munroe Senʳ: ⎪
      John Ruſsel.   ⎭

~ ~ Amos Marrett   ⎫   ⎫
    Solomon Prentice ⎬ West field   ⎪
    Elisha Bull ~ ~ ⎫ Menotomy   ⎪
    Jonathⁿ Butterfield ⎬ field   ⎬ fence
    Joshua Fuller   ⎫ South Side   ⎪ Viewers
    Samˡˡ Oldham   ⎬ yᵉ River   ⎪
    Benjᵃ Muzzey   ⎫   ⎪
    Jamˢ Wilson   ⎬ yᵉ: farmes.   ⎭

Jeremiah Holman ⎫   ⎫
Thoˢ Prentice   ⎬ yᵉ: Weſt field ⎪
Abrā: Hill   ⎫ Menotomy   ⎬ Hawards.
John Williams   ⎬ field. ~   ⎭

    John Hasting Senʳ: Sealer of Leather
    Samˡˡ Mañing Sealer of Weights & Meaſurᵉˢ:

Sam:ll Gibson
John Pattin
Jn:o Hasting Ju:r
Sam:ll Bowman
Jn:o Dickson
Walter Rufsel   to Inspect y:e yoaking
Sam:ll Bull   & Ringing of Swine
Jam:s Clerk
Jn:o Squire Jun:r
Jonathan Poulter
David Rufsel
Jn:o Cuttler Jun:r
George Addams

[137] John Gove   } to Joine w:th the Select Men
       Tho:s Whittemore } in making the
       Nath:ll Sparhawke } Ministers Rate.

it was also Voted on S:d day that the Select Men Should make up accounts with y:e Town Treafu:r ~ ~ ~

At a Meeting of y:e Select Men 31 March 1702. ~ ~ ~

It was then concluded that Liev:t Aaron Bordman Should have y:e Improvment of y:e Burying yard for this present year he paying for y:e Same Six Shillings ~ ~

It was then also concluded that Solomon Prentice sen:r Sam:ll Cooper & Jason Rufsel Should Joine with Charlstown Perambulators In Renuing y:e Bounds betwixt their town & ours   Also y:t Nat:ll Sparhawke and Daniel Dana. Should Joine with Boston Perambulators. ~

Also y:t Deacon Hasting, Jn:o Oldham Nat:ll Hancock & Joseph Champney Should Joine w:th Newton Perambulators

Also y:t Liev:t Fiske, Sam:ll Kidder & Tho:s Prentice Should Joine with Watertown Perambulators;

Also: y:t David Fiske Jun:r & Jos: Stone Should Joine w:th Concord Perambulators

Also y:t Jn:o Lawrance; & Jam:s Wilson Should Joine w:th Billericah Perambulat∧

Also y:t Phillip Rufsel & W:m Munroe Ju:r Should Joine w:th Woborn Perambulators

At a Meeting of y^e: Select Men 13. Ap^{ll}: 1702.

John Watson, Jason Rufsel & Zech^{ry}: Hickes Junr were appointed a Comitte to take care of ye Sheep (y^t go on ye Comons) this p^resent year, by caufing y^m to be kept in one or two flocks as they Shall Judge most proper. ~ ~ ~

[138] At a Meeting of ye Inhabitants Orderly Convened 15 May 1702. ~

There was then Voted y^t ye Sum of fifty-eight pounds be Levied on ye S^d Inhabitants for ye defraying of Charges arising in o^r Town, the One halfe of S^d Rate to be payed in mony, & the other halfe to be payed in grain. Merchantable grain y^t: is to Say Indian Corn at three Shillings pr Bus^{ll} Rey at four Shillings pr Bus^{ll} Barley at 3^s – 6^d: Peafe at 4^s: & Oats at 18^d pr —

Also that ye Sum of twelve pounds be Levied on ye Inhabitants belonging to this Meeting house for ye defraying of Charges arising among themselves — ~ ~ ~

Whereas Capt William Read, Lieu^t Thos Cuttler & Ensigne Joseph Symonds have (on behalfe of ye farmers) Requested the Inhabitants that their proportion of Ammunition may be kept in their precinct. ~ It was on S^d 15 May Voted y^t: the Select Men Should proportion & Deliver unto the above mentioned Capt Read, Lieu^t: Cuttler & Ensigne Symonds, the ffarmers proportion of our Town Stock of Ammunition, Provided they give Bond (to ye Satisfaction of ye Select Men) to Secure ye Town from any trouble or Charge y^t: may happen to arise by reason of their Receiving of their proportion of Amunition as above S^d ~.

There was Also on s^d day Voted that the Select Men take care y^t Mrs Hañah Gookin be Decently buryed at ye Charge of the Inhabitants belonging to this Meeting house, & y^t: the Charge of S^d funeral be added to ye Town Rate granted this year.

— — — — — — — —

At a Meeting of ye Comifsion officers & Select Men ye 10th: May 1703.

There was then Ordered y^t part of the Town Stock be removed to ye ffarmes ~

At a Meeting of the Inhabitants of Camb&. Orderly Convened. 3rd March 1702. There were Chosen for y° year Ensuing —

John Bunker
Sam&. Oldham } Constables —
Joseph Lock

Deacon Hasting
Fra: Bowman
John Oldham } Select Men
Sam&. Sparhawke
Lt. Sam&. Cooper

Deacon Hasting
Fra: Bowman } Assessors
Sam&. Sparhawke

And&. Bordman Town Cler & Town

✗ Cam&. Manind

RECORD MADE BY ANDREW BORDMAN, TOWN CLERK, 1700–1730
(See Folio 343)

[138] At a Meeting of y:e Select Men of Cambridge & y:e Select Men of Newton, 9:th Nov:r 1702. Present from Newton Lieu:t: Jn:o Spring and m:r Jn:o: Ward it was then mutually agreed by y:e s:d Select men, that m:r John: Oldham take care of y:e Great Bridge over charls River in Cambridge to put & keep the Same in good Repair untill y:e Second Monday in March next, And to give an acct: of his disbursturnents on s:d Bridge unto y:e s:d Select Men, in order to his having Satisfaction for his expences in that affair. ~ ~ ~ ~ ~

At a Meeting of the Inhabitants of Camb:r Orderly Convened, 3:rd March 1702. There were Chosen for y:e year Ensuing ~ ~

John Bunker
Sam:ll Oldham } Constables ~
Joseph Lock

Deacon Hasting
ffra:s: Bowman
John Oldham } Select Men
Sam:ll Sparhawke
L:t Sam:ll Cooper.

Deacon Hasting
ffra:s: Bowman } Afsefso:rs;
Sam:ll Sparhawke

And:r Bordman Town Cler & Town Trea:r

Sam:ll Maning
Benjamin Dana } Surveyo:rs of high Ways.
Sam:ll Cook
John Coomey

Zech:ry: Hickes sen:r:
Jn:o Gove
Nath:ll Hancock sen:r:
Reuben Luxford } Tything Men
Ephraim ffrost.
Solomon Prentice sen:r:
Sam:ll : Kidder ~ ~

(turn over)

[139] John Watson
  Nath.ll Pattin sen.r
  Nath.ll Robbins
  Nath.ll Sparhawke   } Tything Men
  Phillip Rufsel
  Ensigne Symonds
  Matthew Bridge ~ ~

  Nich.s ffifsenden } fence Viewers for
  Benj.a Goddard   Weft field

   Jos: Winship   }
   Ab.r Hill   for Menetomy field

  Dan.ll Champney }
  Benj.a Cheney   South Side y.e River

   John Lawrence }
   John Poulter   for y.e ffarmes

   Jer: Holman ~ ~
   Solomon Prentice Jun.r }
   Walter Rufsel   Hawards
   Nat.ll Pattin Jun.r

Nat.ll Hancock sen.r : Seal.r of Leather
Sam.ll Mañing   Sealer of Weights & Meas.rs

    Israel Cheever
    Robert Webber
    Stephen Hasting
    John Green
    Phillip Cook
    Elisha Bull   } To Inspect y.e yoaking
    Ebenez.r Swan   & Ringing Swine
    Gershom Davies
    Icabod Brown
    Tho.s Smith
    Jn.o Stone West
    Nath.ll Dunklin
    George Munroe

Nich.ˢ ffiſsenden ⎫
Abra: Watson ⎬ to aſsiſt In making
Wᵐ: Ruſsel ⎭ yᵉ Minᵗʳˢ Rate ~ ~

Capt Tho.ˢ Oliver & ⎫ to take care yᵗ the great Bridge
mʳ Sam.ˡˡ Oldham ⎭ Over Charls River be kept in good Repair
(go forward)

The five hundred acres before voted to be lett for the use of the ministry in this part of the Town

[139] Also Whereas there is a tract of land Containing about five hundred Acres Layd out for the Uſe of the Ministrey in this Town & place it was on s.ᵈ Day
Voted that the Select Men, or Major part of them (with the consent of our Rev.ʳᵈ Pastour) Should & hereby are impowered to Rent out S.ᵈ Land So that it become Proffittable to the Ministrey in this part of the Town which was the end for which it was designed.

At a Meeting of the Select Men 3.ʳᵈ March. 1702 ~~

mʳ: Edm.ᵈ Goffe mʳ: W.ᵐ Ruſsel & mʳ: Abraham Watson Were then appointed to provide a Shepard for the flock of Sheep for the Ensuing year, & to give s.ᵈ: Shepard Directions concerning y.ᵉ Managment of s.ᵈ flock so as may be most for the advantage of the Same, & to take care that the Sheep Owners have the benefitt of folding s.ᵈ flock as Near as May be according to the Number of Sheep they turn thither, also to take care y.ᵗ s.ᵈ Shepard have satisfacōn for his Service in that affair. ~

Ord.ʳᵈ to Pay Tho.ˢ : Belknap $\overset{£}{01}$. 00. $\overset{d}{08}$, the full of what is Due to him for keeping Jos: Bradish. ~ ~ ~

At a Meeting of y.ᵉ Proprieto.ʳˢ of the Comōn Lands Orderly Convened 10 March 1702

There was then Voted that each proprietor Shud draw One Lott for y.ᵉ whole Intrest which he hath (at this time) in the Lands Now to be drawn for. Also that y.ᵉ first Lott in in this division of Lands Shall be layd on the South Side of y.ᵗ tract of Land known by y.ᵉ Platt No: 1 & to proceed succeſsively & y.ᵗ every parcel of Land in this Division be begun, on y.ᵉ South Side thereof

Also that nefscefsary High ways be allowed before y.̊ division of s.ᵈ land. It is here to be understood that thefe Votes Refer Only to y.ᵉ Remote parcels of Land. ~ ~ ~

There was also Voted at s.ᵈ Meeting that Nat.ˡˡ Hancock sen.ʳ Ensigne Marrett, & m.ʳ Jos: Cooke Shud be a Comitte to take a view of a tract of Land near y.ᵉ lower falls on y.ᵉ South Side of Charls Riv.ʳ w.ᶜʰ is apprehended to be belonging to said proprieto.ʳˢ & to Make Return to s.ᵈ prpriet.ʳˢ at their Meeting on Monday Next Concerning that affair. —⁓⁓⁓⁓

[140] At a Meeting of the Proprietors of the Comon Lands Orderly Convened 15 March 1702/3

there was then Voted y.ᵗ: S.ᵈ Proprieto.ʳˢ meet on the third Tuesday of Aprill next at Nine of y.ᵉ clock in y.ᵉ Morning to draw their Lotts of y.ᵉ Land then Represented to y.ᵐ by y.ᵉ Comitte. It is here to be understood y.ᵗ this Vote Refers to the Comonlands viz.ᵗ Mill.ˢ: Ware, y.ᵉ Ox Pasture, Ware feild &c. —⁓⁓⁓⁓

first clerk of the Proprietors.   Also Voted And.ʳ Bordman Cler of S.ᵈ Proprieto.ʳˢ ———

Also voted y.ᵗ y.ᵉ Comitte appointed (10.ᵗʰ: March 1702.) to take a View of Land Near the lower falls Make return of their doings in that affair on y.ᵉ above s.ᵈ third Tuesday in April next ———

At a Meeting of y.ᵉ Select Men 12. Ap.ʳ 1703. ~ ~ ~

the Treafu.ᵉʳ is Ordered to pay Henry Prentice what is Due to him for bell Ringing in y.ᵉ year 1702 & to m.ʳ : ffifsenden what mony can be procured for him. Also Ord.ʳᵈ to Sink Jn.ᵒ Blower, Tuckerman, George Lawrence & Jn.ᵒ Mattucks, in y.ᵉ Town Rate made in y.ᵉ year.: 1702. & Doct.ʳ Willington, in all his Rates made in o.ᶠ Town in s.ᵈ year. 1702

At a Meeting of y.ᵉ Inhabitants Orderly Convened y.ᵉ 19 Ap.ʳⁱˡ: 1703.

There was then Chosen Cap.ᵗ: Josiah Parker Comifsioner to Join w.ᵗʰ y.ᵉ late Afsefsors in taking a List of y.ᵉ Polls & Ratable Estate of this Town, as y.ᵉ Law Directs.

At a Meeting of y:̊ Select Men 19th: Apll: 1703. ~

Whereas y:̊ late Select Men of this Town at their meeting on y:̊ 11th: Decemr: 1699, Did appoint mr: Samll: Stone Senr: mr: ffra:̊ Bowman & mr: Matth: Bridge to consider of what may be Nefscefsary & convenient for y:̊ Settlement of a Highway for Sundrey of their Neighbours Northward of their Parrish, as appears by their Return bearing Date y:̊ 18th: day of sd: Decembr: And Whereas it is thought by some persons that sd: Return pursuant to sd: appointment is Not a Suffitiant stating out of sd: Highway ~ ~

The Select Men therefore Do hereby appoint
[140] the aforesd: Comitte, vizt: mr: Stone, mr: Bowman & mr: Bridge to State out & Determine sd: High Way the Same being No where lefs then two Rods Wide, & to make Return of their doings therein unto y:̊ Select Men.

Ordered on sd: Day yt: y:̊ Arms Delivered by Lievt: Cooper to ye Select Men, y:̊ year last past, be Delivd: to Capt: Josiah Parker Pursuant to his Excellency's Order — — — — — —

— — — — — — —

At a Meeting of y:̊ Select Men, 10 May 1703 ~ ~

There was then Ordered yt: the above sd: Comittee vizt:
mr: Stone, mr: Bowman & mr: Bridge be a Comitte to State out the land Reserved in y:̊ ffarmes for Clay pitts Near mr: ffiskes Meadow, & y:̊ land Near Ebenr: Nuttings Reserved for y:̊ end aforesd: Also to State out y:̊ way to y:̊ land aforesd: Near Ebenr: Nuttings Sd: Comitte are appointed to state a High Way from y:̊ Easterly part of Matth: Brige's land or Brige's Gate to Concord Road sd: way being two Rods wide ~

Also Ordrd: y:̊ Treaserr: to Pay
  Capt: Oliver   01 . 06 — 0
  Capt: Reade   01 . 12 — 6
y:̊ Afsefsrr: for y:̊ Service }
 in y:̊ year 1702.

At a Meeting of y:e Select Men   24 May 1703

The above mentioned Comitte Viz:t : m:r : Stone, m:r Bowman & m:r Bridge are appointed to take an account of y:e Quantity of Land taken frō: each proprieto:r in y:e High Way firſt above mentioned & to Value y:e Same & to make Return of y:r Doings therein to y:e Select Men

Also Ord:rd : to Sink   Winter & Tho:s Paul in their Rates Comitted to Cons:t Blogget to Collect, that is to Say   Winter in y:e Province, County & Town. & Tho:s : Paul in y:e Town Rate

Also Tho:s Grant & Tho:s Baverick in y:r Rates

28 ffeb:ry· 170¾ Recd: of And:r Bordman Town Treaſu:r Eighteen Shillings mony in full satisfaction for a parcel of Land taken frō me for y:e accommodation of a high way as appears on Record bearing Date y:e 19:th Aprill 1703

         his
  I say Recd pr me Joseph ⟋ Symonds
         mark.

[141]   At a Meeting of y:e Inhabitants Orderly Convened 12 July 1703. there then was Voted that the Sum of fifty Eight Pounds Ten Shillings be Levied on s:d Inhabitants for y:e Defraying of Charges arising in s:d Town & that the Sum of five pounds be Levied on y:e Inhabitants belonging to this meeting house for y:e Defraying of Charges arising amongst them selves. ~ ~ ~ ~

At a Meeting of y:e Inhabitants belonging to y:e Old meeting house in Cam:de Orderly Convened 12 July 1703. There was then Chosen Jn:o· Leverett Esq:r Moderat:r Also Voted By S:d Inhabitants that they apprehend it Neſceſsary at this time to proceed to y:e Building a New Meeting houſe: & in Order there unto there was then Chosen.

  Cap:t And:r Belsher Esq:r
   Tho:s : Brattle Esq:r
  Jn:o : Leverett Esq:r
  Col: Fra:s ffoxcroft Esq:r :
  Deacon Walter Hasting
  Cap:t Tho:s Oliver &
  m:r : W:m Ruſsel

A Comitte to advise & Consider of the Moddel & Charge of Building s^d: Meeting houfe. ⌣⌢⌢⌢ and to make report of ye Same to s^d Inhabitants ⌢

Also Voted y^t ye Rev^{rd} m^r Brattle Signifie to Capt Belsher y^t: he is Desired to Deliver ye Mony w^{ch}: is in his hands (wch was Collected in o^r: Congregation for ye Redemption of Captives) unto Deacon Walter Hasting ⌣⌢⌢⌢

⌢ ⌢ ⌢ ⌢ ⌢ ⌢ ⌢ ⌢ ⌢

At a Meeting of ye Select Men 14 ffeb^{ry}: 170¾

Ordered that m^r Jason Rufsel take care of Wm Chamberlin's youngest Child & provide Nefscefeary clothing for her & that he bring an acc^t: of his Difburstments on s^d Child to the Select Men on ye Second Monday in March next, in order to his being Satisfied for the Same.

Also Ordered y^t m^r: Sam^{ll} Oldham procure for the Town a good Suffitiant pound and that he keep an acc^t of his time and disburstments in that matter in order to his being pay^d: for the Same. ⌢⌣

[141] Att a Meeting of y^e: Select Men
13th: March 170¾

Ord^{rd} to pay m^r: Jason Rufsel twelve shillings for ye keeping Wm Chamberlins Child to this day & Agreed s^d Rufsel to keep s^d Child untill y^e: Second Monday in May Next, for which he is to Receive of y^e: Town 18^d pr week

TOWN RECORDS

		s	
* Robert Parker	49 — 08 —	2
Thomas Bredghm	44 — 07 —	8
Rich Wyeth	26 — 04 —	4
Will man	16 — 02 —	8
Holman	10 — 01 —	8
Elder ffroſt	15 — 02 —	6
Grene	18 — 03 —	0
Danffurth	6 — 01 —	0
Crackbone	13 — 02 —	2
ffrench	05 — 00 —	10
Holms	28 — 04 —	8
Shaw	12 — 02 —	0
Gibſonn	11 — 01 —	10
hildreth	8 — 01 —	4
Coopr	6 — 01 —	0
Oak₍	2 — 00 —	4
Braudiſh	10 — 01 —	8
Eld^r Chpns	4 — 00 —	8
		47

perſons defectiue in y^r ſwine 4 (1) 1657
   Phillip Cooke
        of thoaſe ſwine Lot [   ]
Thomas Gleaſon 11 ſwine with out Rings 3 with out yookes and 8 on Ringed and 2 on yooked
   John Greene 2 with out yookes and Ringes
   bro belſher — —

* The entries following this star, or pages 350, 351, 352, 353, and 354, are recorded in the last pages of the record book, upside down, and are printed in the corresponding place in this volume.

May: 6: 1646: Concerning Cunftables

A Copy of ye order of Court at [ ]

It is ordered that every Cunftable hath b_ vertue of his office full power to make figne & fet forth purfuites or hues & Cries after murtherers Man flayers peace Break_ Theeves Robbers Burglaries, when no mageftrate is at hand, allfoe to apprehend with out warrant Such as are overtaken with Drinke. fwearing, Breakin_ the faboth lying, vagrant prfons night walkers, or any that shall breake or har_ in any of theefe. provided they be taken in the manner eyther by ye fight of the Cunftables them felves, or by prefent information by others. As allfoe to make fearch for all fuch prfons, eyther on ye faboth Days, or at Any other time when there fhalbe any occaffions in all houfes licenfed to fell Bee_ or wine, or in any other fufpected houfes or difordered places. & thofe to aprehend keepe in fafe Cuftody vntill oportunity for to Bring them before the next magestra_ for further examination, provided when any Cunftable is imployed by any of ye magestra_ for ye aprehending of any, he fhall not doe It with out a warrant in writting : & if an_ prfon shall refufe to affift any of ye Cunftables in ye execution of his office in any of the thinges aboue mentioned, Being by [ ] required there vnto, fhall pay for y^r negl_ of It. ten shillings, to ye vfe of the Cou_ to be leavied by Any magestrate before whome Any Such offender shalbe Broug_ & if It shall appeare By good teftimony that any shall willfully & obftinately & Contemptuoufly refufe to giue affiftance to any Such Cunftables, as is before expreffed he shall pay forty Shillings [ ] ye vfe of ye Country: uppon the Juft Comp_ of ye Cunftable as aboue faide; & that no man may pleade ignorance, when a Cunfta_ shall require affistance, It is ordered that euery Cunftable shall haue a ftaffe w_ fome remarkable diftinction provided [ ] ye towne wch shalbe as a figne or badg_ of his offices, & this ftaffe to take alo_ with him, when he shall goe forth to difcharge any part of his office, wch ftaffe shalbe blacke & about fome five foote, or five & a halfe long, bein_ tipped at ye upper end fiue or fix inches with Braffe ———

ffor yᵉ Better Keeping of watches & wards. (An order made by yᵒ Gener͜ Court, May. 6. 1646.) By yᵉ Cunſtables in times of peace,

It is ordered that every Cunſtable ſhall preſent to one of yᵉ next mageſtrates yᵉ name of every prſon who ſhall uppon lawfull warning refuſe or neglect to watch or ward, eyther in prſon or ſome oth͜ ſufficient for yᵉ ſervice, & if being ſoe Convented he Cannot giue a Juſt excuſe ſuch mageſtrate ſhall grant warran͜ to yᵉ Cunſtables to Levy 5ˢ on ſuch offender for every default the ſame to be imployed for ye vſe of yᵉ watch for ye ſame towne, & It is yᵉ intent of yᵉ law yᵗ every prſon of able Body (not exempted by law) or of eſtate, to hire an other ſhalbe liable to watch or to ſuply by another when they ſhalbe th͜ to required, & if there be in yᵉ ſame houſe divers ſuch perſons (whether) ſon͜ ſervants or ſurjourners, they ſhalbe allſoe Compelled to watch as afore ͜

The Number of prſons & of the eſtate of the [   ] as It was taken by the townſmen By the order of the Court, in yᵉ yeare, 1647. (1) mo.

	s
135 prſons, at 20ᵈ pr heade, one peny in the pound comes to 11ˡ. 5ˢ	11 — 05 — 00
90 houſes at 2537ˡ 10ˢ.	10 — 11 — 05
Broaken land 776. ac at 1ˡ pr acʳ — 3ˡ 4ˢ. 8ᵈ .	03 — 04 — 08
vnbroaken land. 1084. acʳ. at 10ˢ pr acʳ.	02 — 05 — 04.
Marſh land. 500 acʳ at 10ˢ pr acʳ	01 — 01 — 08
ffarr medows 258 acʳ at 6 pr acʳ	00 — 06 — 05
208. Cowes. at 5ˡ pr. Cow 1040.ˡ·	04 — 06 — 08
42. thre yearelings, at 4ˡ pr heade.	00 — 14 — 00
74. two yearelings at 2ˡ 10. pr heade.	00 — 15 — 05
79. one yearling at 1ˡ 10ˢ pr. heade.	00 — 09 — 10½
14. steers at. 5ˡ pr heade.	00 — 05 — 10
131 oxen. at 6ˡ pr heade.	03 — 05 — 06
20. horſe. at 7ˡ pr heade.	00 — 11 — 00
6. thre yearlings at 5ˡ pr heade,	00 — 02 — 06
9. two yearlings at. 3ˡ pr heade,	00 — 02 — 03

5. one yearlings. at 2ˡ pr heade,	00 — 00 — 10
37. sheepe at 1ˡ 10ˢ pr heade,	00 — 04 — 07½
62. Swine at 1ˡ pr heade.	00 — 05 — 02
58. Goates. at 8ˢ pr heade.	00 — 01 — 11
totall. 40ˡ — 01 — 4ᵈ	40 — 01 — 04
It. more in a Barke of mʳ ſparahauks ⎫ 50ˡ at peny pr l. ⎭	00 — 04 — 02
more in goods of mʳ Tanners. 70ˡ 19ˢ at peny pr l. ⎭	00 — 05 — 10∧
a Hoy of John Thrumbles at . 50. l.	00 — 04 — 0∧
Halfe a ſhallup of Bro: Hutchins 5ˡ	00 — 00 — 0∧
It. 10. men to be added to there rate ⎫ 3ˢ 4ᵈ. pr heade, 1ˡ 13. 4. ⎭	01 — 13 — 04
	02 — 07 — [ ]
more halfe a Barke of mʳ Andrews ⎫ doth Come to a 140. l. ⎭	00 — 11 — 0∧
Halfe a Boate 2ˡ	00 — 00 — 0∧
	02 — 19 [ ]
	40 — 01 [ ]
	43 — 00 — [ ]
in ſtocks 55ˡ 4ˢ 7ᵈ	00 — 04 — 0∧
in sheepe 3ᵈ.	00 — 00 — 0∧
	43 — 05 — 0∧

The Country rate 1651. for perſons 132 rates at 3ˢ. 9ᵈ pr head, and eſtates at 1½ prˡˡ the rate amounting to 56ˡˡ — 06ˢ — 02ᵈ the cunſtables, and Colledg prſons being free

19. (11) 1662.

The Comittee for ordering the Seating of people in the meeting houfe, Being mett at the Ordnary.

Appoynted. Br. Ri: Jacksons wife to fitt there where sister Kempfter was woont to fitt.

m^{rs} Vpham, with her moother.

Efter Sparhauke, in the place w^r m^{rs} Vpham is removed from

Daniel Champny. ⎫
Ephraim Winship ⎬ on the South Gallery.

Jno Stedman, on the fore gallery on ye South Side.

Joanna winship, in ye place w^r Efter Sparhauke was woont to fitt.

Mary Lemon, where old fifter Jackson was woont to fitt.

Mr Day to sitt in the 2: Seats from ye table.

Ens. Samuel Greene, to sitt at the Table.

Ri: Robbins to sitt in the place w^r Ens: greene was woont to sitt:

Jno Gibson where m^r Day was woont to sitt.

Richard Eccles where Jno Gibson was woont to sitt

Benj: Crackbone w^r Ri: was woont to sitt.

Juftinian Holden to sitt in y^e foremoft Seats.

Robert Stedman to sitt in y^e second seats.

Good.e Gates at y^e end of y^e Deacons seats.

11. 1. 6$\frac{2}{3}$ Jno Taylor & Ri: Eccles are appoynted to sitt in the seate w^r Br. Stedman & Mr Robins satt.

Ri: Dana where Br. Gibson satt.

James Hubbard where Jno. Taylor satt.

Index of Names

Index of Names

ABDY, Matthew, 329.
Abbott, Daniel, 19.
Abot, Daniel, 13.
Abott, Daniel, 11.
Adames, Joseph, 293.
Adams, George, 319.
    Jer., 13.
    John, 116, 119, 140, 148, 150, 154, 319, 328.
    Joseph, 323.
Addames, John, 271.
    John, Senr., 261.
Addams, ——, 26.
    George, 321, 341.
    Jer., 5.
    John, 117, 118, 148, 153, 162, 173, 176, 181, 184, 198, 201, 210, 229, 244, 254, 272, 291, 305, 310, 316, 317, 320.
    John, Senr., 233, 239, 240, 248, 253, 261, 279, 283.
    Joseph, 295, 310, 314, 317, 321.
    Will., 19.
Ager, William, 241.
Aires, Mr., 57.
Aldis, Nathan, 66, 68.
Allen, Mathew, 5, 6, 7, 13, 15, 18.
    Mr. Mathew, 16.
Amsden, Jacob, 272, 283, 290.
Andrew, Mr., 165, 293.
    Samuel, 259, 272, 279, 281, 286, 288, 290, 291, 292, 298.
    Mr. Samuel, 163, 305, 309, 314.
    Thomas, 260, 272, 279, 283, 290, 291, 295.
Andrewe, Mr., 43, 211.
    Samuel, 278.
    Mr. Samuel, 295, 296, 300.
    Thomas, 264, 270, 281.
    Mr. William, 340.
Andrewes, Samuel, 260.

Andrewes, Thomas, 218.
Andrews, Daniel, 165.
    Mr., 16, 71, 98, 107, 117, 136, 143, 154, 164, 173, 353.
    Old Mr., 173.
    Samuel, 167, 266, 267.
    Thomas, 166, 176, 270.
    William, 10, 13, 14, 15, 18.
Andrewse, Mr., 23.
Androwes, Mr., 191, 254.
    Mr. Samuel, 254.
    Thomas, 187, 206, 232, 233, 239, 240, 243, 248, 252, 256, 257.
Angeir, Edmund, 43, 46, 48, 57, 80.
Anger, Mr. Edmund, 264, 268, 269.
    Mr., 268, 273, 275, 279.
    Mr. Samuel, 334.
Angier, Bro., 55, 92, 98.
    Edmund, 19, 104, 131, 232, 291.
    Mr., 117, 120, 121, 127, 140, 141, 146, 147, 152, 154, 165, 174, 179, 184, 191, 198, 202, 207, 208, 212, 221, 223, 224, 239, 242, 243, 247, 252.
    Mr. Edmund, 85, 110, 181, 191.
Arington, Abraham, 208, 226, 321.
    Sister, 235.
    Widow, 253.
Arnold, John, 9, 13, 18.
Austin, 13.
Austine, Jonnas, 18.

BACON, Daniel, 181, 205, 210.
    Michael, 51.
    Michael, Junr., 194.
Bambrig, Guy, 13.
Bambrige, Guy, 9, 11, 18.
Bambrigg, Mr., 15.

INDEX OF NAMES

Banbricke, Widow, 97.
Bancroft, Bro., 55.
   Roger, 46, 52, 57, 83, 84, 87, 93, 98.
Barit, William, 224.
Barnard, John, 9, 13.
Barnet, William, 336.
Barratt, William, 164, 175.
Barrett, William, 117, 137.
Barrit, William, 188, 192, 196, 198, 202, 207, 219, 224, 234, 254, 258.
Barritt, William, 264, 272, 278, 281.
Bartlet, Joseph, 288, 289.
Bartlit, Joseph, 209, 210, 211.
Bartlitt, Joseph, 288, 313.
Baverick, Thomas, 348.
Beal, Thomas, 91, 92, 98.
Beale, Bro., 61, 199, 200.
   Thomas, 9, 13, 16, 18, 51, 56, 70, 73, 75, 77, 101, 116, 117, 123, 131, 199, 200.
   Widow, 137, 177, 197.
Beall, Thomas, 90, 93.
Beard, Andrew, 300.
Beats, Richard, 18.
Beckeells, Richard, 36, 43.
Belcher, Andrew, 117, 120, 122, 139, 144, 153, 154, 158, 169.
   Capt. Andrew, 329.
   Mr., 279, 291.
Belknap, Thomas, 345.
Belshar, Andrew, 65, 95, 100.
Belsher, Andrew, 192, 197.
   Bro., 350.
   Capt., 349.
   Capt. Andrew, Esq., 348.
Bemus, Joseph, 331.
Beniamen, 13.
   John, 4, 5, 7, 8, 9, 11, 12, 16, 18.
Beniamin, Mr., 16.
Benjamin, Mr., 19.
Benyt, James, 23.
Besbeche, Mr., 27.
Besbeg, Mr., 43.
Besbege, Mr., 27.
Besbeth, ——, 19.
Betts, Goodman, 77.
   John, 33, 48, 49, 59, 66, 67, 68, 69, 75, 76, 87, 89, 97.
Bicklestone, William, 40.
Bittlestonn, Sister, 55.
Blogget, Daniell, 97.
   Thomas, 26, 339.

Blower, John, 346.
Blowers, Mrs., 207.
   Piam, 239.
Blunfeld, William, 17.
Boadman, Aaron, 262.
   Andrew, 268.
Boardman, Ensign, 291.
Boedman, Aaron, 271, 278, 281, 283.
   Lt. Aaron, 337.
   Andrew, 268, 273, 277, 284.
Boeman, Francis, 290.
Boman, Francis, 220, 236.
   Mr., 92, 97.
   Nathaniel, 162.
Bond, William, 250.
Bonner, Mr. John, 309.
Bordman, Aaron, 197, 244, 260, 283, 291, 320.
   Ensign Aaron, 314, 319, 324.
   Lieut. Aaron, 334, 337, 341.
   Mr. Aaron, 325, 326.
   Andrew, 228, 231, 240, 242, 247, 248, 257, 267, 286, 291, 323, 328, 330, 335, 339, 340, 343, 346, 348.
   Widow, 284.
Bosworth, Jonathan, 9.
Boswith, Jonath., 5.
Bosworth, Jonah, 5.
Boswth, Jona, 13.
Bourne, Jane, 145.
Boutell, John, 98, 137, 321.
Boutill, Henry, 193.
Bouttaile, John, 56.
Bouttill, John, 200, 201, 207.
   John, Senr., 209.
Bower, Ben, 98.
   George, 109.
Bowers, Jerah, 159.
   Widow, 116.
Bowman, Francis, 304, 314, 319, 320, 325, 326, 328, 335, 339, 340, 343.
   Mr. Francis, 304, 323, 325, 331, 332, 347.
   Nathaniel, 164, 166.
   Samuel, 341.
Bowtell, John, 131, 156, 157, 164.
   Widow, 291.
Braddish, Joseph, 253.
Bradish, Joseph, 345.
   Robert, 18.
Bradshaue, Humphry, 227.
Bradshaw, John, 243.
   Martha, 256.

INDEX OF NAMES 359

Bradshaw, Vmphry, 191, 200, 208, 218, 223, 231, 235, 236, 237, 242, 243, 250, 252, 256.
Bradsheere, Vmphry, 177, 184, 198.
Bradstreet, Mr., 22.
  Mr. Symon, 2, 4, 6, 11, 16, 18.
  Vmphry, 204.
Brattle, Rev. Mr., 349.
  Thomas, Esq., 348.
Braudish, ——, 350.
Bredge, John, 50.
Bredsha, Vmphry, 133, 154, 165, 167, 169, 174, 175.
Bregd, Mathew, 181, 193, 198, 200, 208, 225, 230.
Bregdhm, Thomas, 350.
Bridg, Bro., 47.
  John, 4, 14, 17, 25.
Bridge, Deacon, 111, 112, 128, 134, 155.
  Deacon John, 121, 122, 131, 132.
  John, 8, 15, 16, 18, 22, 25, 27, 29, 32, 34, 36, 41, 45, 46, 47, 49, 51, 57, 64, 66, 70, 73, 81, 84, 86, 87, 98, 99, 100, 106, 321.
  John, Senr., 52.
  Matthew, 64, 91, 98, 118, 137, 139, 149, 160, 165, 171, 176, 303, 321, 332, 333, 339, 344.
  Matthew, Junr., 299, 316, 318, 325, 326, 328.
  Matthew, Senr., 303.
  Mr., 347, 348.
  Mr. Matthew, 304, 332, 347.
  Thomas, 98.
Brige, 347.
  Matthew, 347.
Briggam, Thomas, 39, 41, 43, 46, 47, 98.
Briggame, Thomas, 36.
Brigham, Bro., 54.
  Thomas, 53, 54, 63, 65, 67, 69, 70, 73, 79, 101, 156, 157.
Broadish, Goodman, 63.
  Robert, 55, 64, 66, 67, 104.
Brodish, Robert, 98.
Brown, Ichabod, 315, 344.
  Robert, 291.
  Thomas, 266, 267, 268.
Browne, John, 140, 142, 148, 150.
  Robert, 87, 98, 104, 108, 121, 138, 142, 158, 163, 169, 176, 201, 214, 220, 242, 254.
  Thomas, 118, 131, 132, 147, 176, 238, 278.
Buck, Roger, 115, 177, 200, 226.

Buck, Samuell, 222, 227, 244, 257, 262, 271, 278.
Bucke, Roger, 86, 97, 117, 128, 153, 165, 167, 233, 242, 265, 321.
  Samuell, 230, 238, 251, 267, 279, 286.
  William, 87, 98, 321.
Bucklie, Mr., 67.
Buckly, Mr. Peter, 18.
Bukly, Mr., 33.
Bull, Elisha, 314, 317, 319, 321, 328, 335, 340, 344.
  Samuell, 300, 310, 336, 338, 341.
  William, 97, 118, 119, 138, 140, 150, 151, 154, 157, 162, 173, 176, 184, 189, 239.
  William, Senr., 233.
Buncker, John, 321.
Bunker, John, 319, 330, 339, 343.
  Mr. John, 327.
Bur, Benjamyne, 23.
Bush, John, 108.
  Renold, 60, 69, 98, 108, 137, 259.
  Reynold, 329.
Butler, ——, 13.
  Richard, 5, 8, 46.
  William, 8, 13.
Butterfield, Jonathan, 300, 310, 314, 328, 340.

Cabot, Mr., 26.
Cane, Bro., 54, 62.
  Christopher, 73, 83, 87, 90, 93.
  Jonathan, 142, 154, 161, 162, 185, 206, 224, 225, 240, 253, 262.
  Sister, 166.
Carly, Will., 290.
Carter, William, 310.
Chadwick, Philip, 289.
Chamberlin, Jacob, 310, 314.
  William, 331, 349.
Chamberline, Jacob, 310.
Chamne, Daniel, 266, 272, 281, 286, 288.
  Mr. Daniel, 268, 272.
  Samuell, 261, 265, 266, 267, 272, 278, 281, 286, 288, 290, 295.
  Mr. Samuell, 287, 289, 296.
Champne, Daniell, 205, 210, 211, 213, 221.
  Danill, 238, 245.
  Samuell, 210, 211, 213, 217, 221, 238, 254.
Champnes, Elder, 26, 33.
  John, 19, 33.
  Richard, 18, 21.

Champney, Daniell, 293.
  Daniel, 315, 316.
  Dan^{ll}., 319, 344.
  Elder, 175, 211, 293, 326.
  Joseph, 309, 320, 323, 326, 327, 341.
  Richard, 99, 321.
  Samuel, 293, 303, 336.
  Mr. Samuel, 312.
  Mr. Samuel, Senr., 311.
Champnies, Elder, 53, 95.
Champnis, Daniell, 191.
  Elder, 57, 62, 63, 66, 98.
  Richard, 61.
  Samuell, 185, 188, 191, 196.
  Samell, 199.
Champny, Daniel, 354.
  Elder, 101, 106, 122, 164.
  Richard, 45, 65, 93, 138.
  Mr. Richard, 79, 92, 171.
Champnye, Elder, 104.
Chancy, Mr., 182, 186, 197.
Chaplin, C., 15.
Chapline, ——, 21.
  Clement, 14, 18.
  Mr., 14, 16, 17.
Chauncey, Mr. Charles, 166.
Chauncy, Mr., 182.
Cheauer, Daniell, 97, 102, 122, 177, 184, 185, 187, 189, 190, 193, 198, 208, 214, 217, 219, 222, 231, 232, 236, 239, 243, 247, 248, 258.
Cheauers, Daniell, 201.
Cheaver, Daniel, 91, 103, 108, 116, 130, 142, 163, 174, 176.
Cheavers, Daniel, 109, 123, 148, 151, 164, 165, 167.
  Israel, 320.
Cheeuers, Daniel, 263, 275, 277, 280.
  Israel, 283.
Cheever, Israel, 337, 344.
Cheney, Benjamin, 344.
Cheny, Thomas, 130.
Cherry, Thomas, 131, 139.
Chesholme, Deacon, 175, 188.
  Thomas, 37, 65, 66, 67, 93, 98, 117, 120, 132, 133, 135, 137, 152, 153, 180.
Chester, Mrs., 10.
Chever, Daniel, 319.
  Israel, 329.
Chevers, Daniel, 317, 321.
  Israel, 300, 304, 306, 314.

Ch.p.n.'s, Elder, 350.
Church, Caleb, 238.
Clark, ——, 289.
  Elder, 291.
  James, 292, 295.
  John, 5, 288.
  Jonas, 96.
Clarke, ——, 289.
  Elder, 274, 275.
  Elder Jonah, 292.
  James, 293, 310.
  John, 9, 18, 20, 24.
  Jonas, 98, 125, 131, 145, 169.
  Mr., 256.
  Mr. Jonas, 246.
  Nicholas, 9, 11, 15.
  William, 22.
Clearke, William, 82.
Clemance, William, 88, 97, 128 143.
  William, Junr., 161.
  William, Senr., 88, 92, 97.
Clemans, Ould, 68.
Clerk, James, 361.
Coale, Jacob, 160, 161.
Cobbett, Josiah, 19
Coke, George, 47.
Colby, Anthony, 5.
Coll, 148, 160.
Colledge, 64, 66, 139, 144, 169.
Colledges, 67.
Coller, Goodman, 180.
  John, 210, 217.
Collicott, Richard, 250.
Collines, Mr., 64.
Collings, Edward, 43.
Collins, Edward, 45, 66, 67, 188.
  Mr. Edward, 75, 82.
Collis, John, 329, 336, 340.
Comey, John, 336, 343.
Comie, John, 315.
Comy, John, 296, 304.
Conry, John, 293.
Convars, James, 163.
Cook, Capt., 50, 294.
  Joseph, 23, 24, 45, 291.
  Mr., 282, 289.
  Mr. Joseph, 269, 272, 289, 292, 304, 314.
  Philip, 344.
  Samuel, 343.
  Widow, 285.
Cooke, Bro., 118.

INDEX OF NAMES

Cooke, Capt., 49, 51, 71, 116, 246.
   Capt. George, 245.
   George, 33, 36, 47, 48, 49, 67.
   Gregory, 167.
   Joseph, 14, 15, 22, 25, 27, 29, 32, 33, 34, 36, 38, 40, 41, 42, 43, 45, 46, 47, 157, 167, 201, 217, 300, 336, 340.
   Mr., 14, 16, 23, 64, 77, 90, 96, 116, 151, 159, 170, 176, 196, 202, 203, 215, 265, 273.
   Mr. George, 34.
   Mr. Joseph, 15, 34, 36, 45, 49, 52, 59, 65, 67, 76, 77, 81, 83, 84, 87, 90, 91, 93, 95, 100, 106, 108, 121, 128, 153, 156, 162, 163, 167, 184, 186, 191, 201, 211, 239, 288, 289, 290, 321, 346.
   Philip, 3, 56, 63, 86, 88, 98, 99, 101, 108, 111, 115, 117, 137, 138, 147, 151, 152, 155, 163.
   Samuel, 221, 253, 268, 272, 290, 311, 336.
   Widow, 200, 208, 253, 257, 261, 271, 275, 282.
Cooledge, Joseph, 329.
Coolidge, Joseph, 335.
Coomey, John, 343.
Coomie, John, 315.
Cooper, ——, 350.
   Bro., 54, 63, 128, 140.
   Deacon, 170, 175, 260, 267, 274, 278, 281, 286, 291, 292.
   Deacon John, 170, 177, 281, 288, 290.
   John, 52, 57, 58, 64, 65, 67, 70, 77, 78, 86, 87, 89, 90, 91, 94, 98, 99, 104, 105, 107, 108, 109, 111, 115, 121, 123, 124, 129, 130, 131, 132, 133, 135, 138, 139, 142, 147, 149, 150, 152, 156, 158, 159, 161, 162, 163, 164, 167, 175, 181, 183, 184, 186, 187, 188, 196, 198, 205, 215, 225, 227, 229, 233, 236, 241, 247, 248, 251, 252, 254, 256, 259, 300, 303, 308, 310, 317, 328, 332, 336.
   John, Junr., 290, 291.
   Samuel, 202, 239, 258, 272, 292, 300, 302, 304.
   Ensign Samuel, 236.
   Lieut., 347.
   Lieut. Samuel, 343.
   Samuel, Junr., 260.
Coopper, John, 106.
Corlet, Eliath, 66.
   Mr., 77, 83, 106, 154, 173, 182, 235.

Corlet, Mr. Elijah, 97, 153, 162.
Corlett, Mr., 138.
Corlit, Mr., 218.
Corlitt, Mr., 265.
Corllett, Eliah, 321.
Couldbey, Anthony, 11, 19.
Couldby, Anthony, 13.
Couldbye, Anthony, 7.
Cracbone, Gilbert, 64, 86, 97, 99, 109.
Crackbon, Benjamin, 198.
   Gilbert, 149, 187.
   Joseph, 321.
Crackbone, ——, 3, 350.
   Benjamin, 150, 151, 354.
   Bro., 54, 60, 63.
   Gilbert, 19, 57, 65, 70, 90, 92, 106, 118, 120, 130, 139, 147, 157, 161, 163, 165, 166, 169, 171, 176, 184, 321.
   Joseph, 310, 317.
Cragbon, Joseph, 291.
   Widow, 276.
Cragbone, Gilbert, 105.
Crakbon, Joseph, 253.
   Widow, 208.
Crosbe, Symon, 29.
Crosbee, Symon, 23.
Crosbey, Symon, 18, 25, 29.
Crosby, Goodie, 44.
   Ould, 67.
   Simon, 27, 34.
   Thomas, 66.
Crosbye, Sister, 40.
   Widow, 68.
Cutler, James, 60.
   James, Junr., 236, 254.
   John, Senr., 315.
   Thomas, 247, 257, 270, 277, 290, 293, 310, 320, 332.
Cutter, Ephraim, 212, 252, 264, 276, 280.
   Gershom, 244, 277, 280, 293, 300, 305, 308, 314, 319, 321, 323, 328.
   James, 194.
   James, Senr., 186, 223.
   John, 320.
   John, Senr., 337.
   Richard, 54, 76, 80, 97, 117, 119, 120, 140, 145, 151, 162, 166, 172, 173, 174, 178, 183, 198, 208, 215, 218, 219, 221, 225, 226, 227, 230, 232, 233, 245, 248, 250, 258, 264, 270, 271, 280, 292.
   Richard, Senr., 272.

362   INDEX OF NAMES

Cutter, Thomas, 217.
  Widow, 98.
  William, 38, 50, 52, 56, 66, 68, 212, 304, 309.
Cuttler, John, 318.
  John, Junr., 341.
  Lieut., 332, 340, 342.
  Lieut. Thomas, 332, 342.
  Thomas, 319.
  Thomas, Junr., 332.

DAMFORTH, Thomas, 50.
Dampford, Mr., 24, 29.
  Thomas, 33.
Dampforde, Mr., 23.
  Nicholas, 25, 29.
Dana, Benjamin, 310, 317, 328, 340, 343.
  Daniel, 319, 320, 327, 336, 340, 341.
  Jacob, 257, 290.
  Richard, 82, 89, 98, 110, 111, 135, 141, 151, 158, 164, 217, 227, 233, 237, 254.
Danee, Richard, 321.
Danffurth, ——, 350.
Danforth, Mr., 14, 16, 188, 191, 193, 196, 198, 200, 202, 205, 213, 215, 219, 223, 226, 230, 231, 241, 242, 287, 306.
  Nicholas, 15, 18, 27.
  Thomas, 44, 45, 52, 56, 57, 58, 59, 62, 63, 64, 66, 68, 69, 70, 73, 75, 76, 77, 79, 80, 81, 83, 85, 86, 88, 89, 90, 91, 92, 93, 94, 95, 97, 99, 101, 102, 105, 106, 107, 108, 109, 111, 113, 115, 121, 122, 123, 125, 126, 127, 128, 129, 130, 131, 132, 133, 135, 136, 137, 139, 141, 142, 143, 145, 147, 149, 150, 152, 153, 155, 156, 157, 158, 159, 160, 162, 163, 164, 165, 166, 167, 170, 173, 174, 175, 177, 182, 183, 210, 211, 294.
  Mr. Thomas, 142, 173, 180, 181, 195, 217, 239, 246, 293.
  Thomas, Esq., 264, 321.
Danie, Daniel, 316.
  Jacob, 310.
Daniel, Robert, 70.
Daniell, Robert, 43.
  Widow, 126.
Danniell, Robert, 45.
Dany, Benjamin, 291, 295.
  Jacob, 272, 293.
Dauenport, Thomas, 47.

Dauis, Dollard, 8.
Davies, Gresholm, 344.
Day, Isaac, 305, 308.
  Mr., 64, 117, 291, 354.
  Robert, 9, 13, 18.
  Stephen, 98, 171.
Daye, Stephen, 321.
Deming, David, 323, 328, 330.
Demming, David, 303.
Denison, Daniel, 5, 12.
  Mr. Daniel, 17.
Dennison, Daniel, 10.
Deputy Governor, 250, 260, 262, 275.
Dickson, John, 212, 282, 284, 285, 298, 300, 316, 323, 341.
  William, 260, 262, 271, 279.
Dixon, William, 98, 110, 115, 137, 140, 143, 151, 158, 159, 163, 164, 167, 168, 173, 174, 175, 176, 184, 185, 187, 197, 198, 200, 201, 206, 221, 230, 232, 237, 238, 239, 242, 243, 244, 245, 246, 247, 251, 256, 258, 272.
Dixson, John, 313, 314.
Dosse, Thomas, 111.
Druse, Vincet, 98.
Dudlie, Mr., 95.
Dudly, Samuel, 5, 13.
  Mr. Samuel, 16.
  Thomas, 4.
  Thomas, Esq., 2, 4, 6, 12, 16, 18.
Dunklin, Nathaniel, 344.
Dunster, Bro., 47.
  Jonathan, 185, 198, 210, 211, 221, 234, 243, 249, 255, 292, 318.
  Mr., 46, 66, 70, 71, 78, 95, 109, 112, 132, 138.
  Mr. Henry, 53, 75, 79, 82, 91, 106.
  Mr. Jonathan, 316, 320.
  Mrs., 140, 159, 164, 171, 188, 201.
Duntlin, Nathaniel, 325.

EAKE, Mr., 127.
Eames, John, 207, 220, 238.
  Thomas, 103.
Eason, Joseph, 9, 13.
Eaten, Mr., 33.
  Mr. Nathaniel, 33.
Eaton, Benoni, 153, 228, 231, 290, 291.
Eatton, Benoni, 200, 219, 223.
Eccles, Richard, 120, 132, 133, 135, 141, 151, 154, 159, 167, 172, 224, 274, 276, 291, 354.

INDEX OF NAMES

Ecels, Richard, 181, 200, 215, 229.
Ecles, Richard, 64, 71, 80, 86, 98.
Eldred, Samuel, 76.
Elly, Nathaniel, 9, 13.
Elmer, Edward, 5, 9, 13.
Ensigne, James, 9, 13, 18, 21.
Erington, Abraham, 57, 98, 111.
Errington, Abram, 65, 116, 135, 137, 153, 164, 291.
Esigne, James, 11.

FASSETT, Joseph, 325.
Ferginson, Richard, 314.
Ferguson, Richard, 300.
Fesenden, Nicholas, 272, 274, 278, 298.
Fesington, John, 75.
Fessenden, Nicholas, 314.
Fessinden, Nicholas, 323.
Fessington, John, 65, 66, 87, 101, 102, 106, 111, 114, 121, 123, 125, 131, 135, 137.
Fisenden, John, 147, 148, 152, 153, 158, 159, 161, 163.
 Nicholas, 260.
 Widow, 168.
Fishenden, Bro., 152.
 John, 67, 129, 132, 133, 134, 135, 139, 141, 142, 143, 162.
Fisher, Thomas, 9, 18.
Fishingdin, John, 149.
Fishington, Nicolas, 208, 219, 236, 243.
Fisk, David, 51, 190.
 David, Junr., 270, 271, 323.
 David, Senr., 271, 288.
 Lieut., 315, 317.
 Lt. David, 304.
Fiske, David, 55, 57, 97, 107, 117, 125, 128, 130, 133, 144, 149, 152, 155, 163, 181, 191, 194, 201, 210, 211, 217, 228, 243, 293, 294, 333.
 David, Junr., 251, 258, 260, 332, 336, 341.
 David, Senr., 254, 289, 318, 338.
 Ensign, 265, 266.
 Ensign David, 265.
 Lieut., 292, 293, 338, 341.
 Lt. David, 302, 303, 312, 316, 337.
 Mr., 347.
Fissenden, John, 163, 164.
 Mr., 346.
 Nicholas, 337, 338, 344, 346.
 Nicholas, Senr., 340.
Fissher, Thomas, 13.

Flint, John, 174.
 Mr., 141.
Foster, Thomas, 232, 241, 244.
Fowle, James, 306.
 John, 163.
Fownell, John, 97.
Fox, Thomas, 83, 87, 93, 94, 97, 99, 102, 106, 107, 111, 123, 125, 132, 134, 135, 137, 139, 140, 142, 146, 147, 150, 151, 152, 153, 158, 161, 162, 163, 164, 165, 166, 167, 172, 173, 175, 181, 183, 186, 187, 188, 189, 192, 196, 198, 202, 205, 209, 211, 217, 218, 220, 225, 226, 232, 237, 239, 241, 257, 291.
Foxcroft, Col. Francis, Esq., 348.
Foxe, Thomas, 260.
Fracis, John, 295.
Frances, Richard, 35, 97, 150.
Francis, Richard, 133, 143, 145, 153.
 Stephen, 220, 225.
French, ——, 350.
 Bro., 56.
 Richard, 63, 97.
 Lieut. William, 97.
 William, 18, 321.
Frenche, John, 29, 73, 97.
 William, 26.
Frost, Edmond, 59, 66, 138.
 Elder, 26, 55, 63, 64, 102, 137, 160, 172, 175, 182, 186, 201, 350.
 Ephraim, 212, 235, 244, 247, 262, 271, 291, 328, 343.
 John, 154, 166, 233, 291.
 Mr. Edmund, 98.
 Thomas, 212.
Fuller, John, 158, 163, 181, 217, 225.
 Joshua, 249, 277, 281, 314, 322, 340.

GARDEN, Richard, 143.
Gates, Goodie, 354.
Gearner, Edmond, 9.
Gerner, Ed., 13.
Gibbines, Capt., 48.
Gibson, Bro., 54, 350.
 John, 9, 13, 19, 28, 77, 78, 98, 117, 118, 143, 161, 187, 233, 239, 255, 354.
 John, Junr., 189, 201, 218, 223, 233, 239.
 John, Senr., 251.
 Samuel, 247, 291, 293, 296, 309, 329, 336, 341.

Gibsonn, ——, 350.
Gillam, Capt., 324.
Gipson, Bro., 63.
    John, 66, 67.
Girling, Mr., 173.
Girlinge, Richard, 19.
Gleason, Thomas, 350.
Gleison, Goodman, 122.
    Thomas, 117, 119, 123, 155.
Glouer, John, 76.
    Mrs., 368.
Glour, John, 64, 65.
Goave, John, 130, 133, 143, 149, 157, 161, 167, 172, 176.
Goddard, Benjamin, 305, 314, 317, 319, 320, 323, 335, 340, 344.
Godward, Benjamin, 293, 295.
Gof, Edward, 23.
Gofe, Bro., 199, 200.
    Edward, 36, 58, 199, 200.
    Samuel, 181, 185, 187, 207, 210, 217, 219, 220, 221, 232, 233, 257, 304.
Goff, Capt., 41.
    Edward, 27, 38, 40, 41, 42, 45.
    Samuel, 270, 283, 286, 304.
    Samuel, Senr., 291, 293, 296, 297.
Goffe, Bro., 60, 62, 78, 120, 124.
    Bro. Edward, 119, 123.
    Edmund, 327.
    Edward, 29, 33, 45, 46, 49, 50, 51, 53, 56, 58, 63, 64, 65, 66, 68, 69, 70, 71, 72, 73, 75, 76, 77, 79, 80, 83, 84, 85, 86, 89, 90, 91, 93, 94, 95, 98, 99, 100, 101, 105, 106, 108, 109, 113, 115, 117, 119, 121, 141, 156, 157, 303, 321.
    Mr., 325.
    Mr. Edmund, 317, 329, 333.
    Mr. Edward, 84, 87, 93, 121.
    Samuel, 118, 131, 137, 139, 154, 160, 165, 176.
    Samuel, Junr., 310.
    Samuel, Senr., 323.
    Mr. Samuel, Senr., 314.
Goodman, Richard, 4, 13.
Goodn, Richard, 5.
Goodwine, Mr., 12.
    Mr. William, 17.
    William, 5, 13.
Goofe, Edward, 46, 47.
Googine, Capt., 75.
    Daniel, 82.

Gookin, Capt., 90, 113, 133, 135, 137, 148, 149, 150, 153, 154, 159, 163, 173, 175, 181, 196, 205, 207, 217, 220.
    Capt. Daniel, 132, 135, 136, 139, 147, 152, 158, 161, 162, 167, 175.
    Daniel, 142, 253, 321.
    Major, 229, 233, 236, 241, 243, 246, 261.
    Mr. Nathaniel, 251.
    Mr. Samuel, 287, 322.
    Mrs. Hanah, 337, 342.
    Samuel, 267.
Gookins, Capt., 177, 186, 188, 198.
    Major, 260, 287.
    Major Daniel, 278.
    Mr., 287.
    Mr. Samuel, 277, 285, 287.
    Pastor, 298.
Goue, John, 182, 186, 187, 196, 198, 209, 211, 214, 218, 226, 233, 244, 246, 247, 248, 253, 270, 271, 277, 291, 292, 296, 335.
Gove, John, 302, 341, 343.
Grant, Seth, 9.
    Thomas, 348.
Green, Bartholomew, 10.
    Capt., 291.
    Ensign, 137.
    John, 206, 208, 219, 238, 256, 291, 297, 344.
    Mr., 16.
    Nathaniel, 197, 232, 243, 255.
    Samuel, 13, 203, 303, 309, 313, 314, 316, 321.
Greene, Bro. John, 120.
    Ensign, 354.
    Ensign Samuel, 354.
    John, 116, 117, 122, 139, 152, 153, 166, 350.
    Mr., 27, 31.
    Nathaniel, 97.
    Samuel, 10, 31, 55, 58, 63, 64, 66, 98.
    Widow, 19.
Greenhill, Samuel, 9, 13.
Greenwood, Thomas, 244.
Grene, ——, 250.
    Bro., 41.
    Mr., 26.
Greshold, Frances, 24.
Greshould, Frances, 33.

HADDON, Garrad, 5, 19.
Hadon, Garrad, 5, 13.

INDEX OF NAMES

Haines, Mr., 33, 68, 199.
Hall, Bro., 228.
  Bro. Edward, 124.
  Edward, 84, 90, 97, 104, 118, 126, 143, 147, 149, 159, 164, 179, 184, 185, 188, 205, 208, 218, 221, 240, 242, 292.
  John, 98.
  Thomas, 55, 61, 86, 97, 104, 115, 140, 142, 143, 149, 160, 169, 174, 183, 188, 198, 234, 245, 250, 253, 272, 276, 279, 292.
Hamlet, William, 87, 92, 98.
Hamlett, William, 115, 131.
Hammond, Capt., 234.
  Thomas, Junr., 217, 236, 244.
Hamond, Goodman, 98.
  Thomas, 121, 128.
  Thomas, Junr., 176.
Hancock, Mr. John, 302.
  Nathaniel, 269, 275, 291, 305, 310, 318, 341.
  Nathaniel, Junr., 320, 328, 336.
  Nathaniel, Senr., 331, 335, 343, 344, 346.
  Sir, 293.
Hancocke, Goodman, 59.
  Nathaniel, 11, 19, 59, 77, 165, 260, 264, 277.
  Widow, 97.
Hancok, Nathaniel, 13, 185, 192, 245, 247.
Hancoke, Nathaniel, 207, 213, 226, 233, 242.
Hancoks, Nathaniel, 224.
Handcoke, Nathaniel, 206.
Harlackenden, Mr., 16, 34.
  Mr. Richard, 266.
  Mr. Roger, 13, 18, 41.
Harlackinden, Mr., 23.
Harlackingden, Mr., 25, 29, 30, 33.
  Mr. Richard, 26, 31.
  Mr. Richard, Esq., 31.
  Mr. Roger, 27, 31, 32, 33.
Harlakenden, Roger, 27.
Hart, Stephen, 4, 5, 7, 13, 17.
Harvard College, 291.
Hasell, Richard, 183, 193, 195.
Hassell, Richard, 177.
Hassull, Goodman, 167.
Hassull, Richard, 80, 92, 98, 127, 131, 149, 150, 168, 171, 172.
Hasteings, John, 83, 101, 107, 111, 116.
Hastin, Deacon, 267, 274, 276, 278, 281, 286.
  Deacon Walter, 269, 279, 281, 288.
  John, 271, 277, 279.

Hasting, Daniel, 322.
  Deacon, 291, 304, 323, 325, 331, 334, 335, 339, 340, 343.
  Deacon Walter, 290, 300, 348, 349.
  John, 291, 322, 323, 329.
  John, Junr., 341.
  John, Senr., 300, 336, 340.
  Mr. John, 302.
  Samuel, 291, 335.
  Stephen, 344.
  Walter, 318.
Hastings, Deacon, 292, 295, 298.
  John, 86, 98, 103, 116, 168, 171, 174, 295, 304.
  John, Senr., 300, 314.
  Samuel, 122, 174, 175, 292, 295, 298, 305.
  Samuel, Senr., 314.
  Walter, 132, 135, 137, 151, 153, 159, 160, 163, 164, 166, 176.
Hastins, Deacon, 252, 254.
  Deacon Walter, 232.
  John, 185, 187, 191, 208, 215, 219, 220, 231, 239, 242, 244, 247, 251, 253, 254, 256.
  Samuel, 192, 197, 200, 205, 207, 209, 214, 224, 244.
  Walter, 177, 181, 182, 191, 211, 213, 215, 218, 220, 225, 226, 227, 229, 230, 234, 236, 241, 243, 245, 247, 250, 251, 257.
Haugh, Mr., 105.
Haukins, Timothy, 73.
Haynes, John, 4.
  John, Esq., 4, 6, 7, 10, 11, 16.
  John, Esq., Governor, 18.
  Mr., 44, 127.
Hayward, Thomas, 15.
Healy, William, 202, 226, 233, 238.
Heate, Thomas, 5, 13.
Hely, William, 202, 256.
Henbury, Arthur, 160.
Heywarde, Thomas, 18.
Hibbins, Mr., 84, 89.
Hichecocke, Mathew, 35.
Hickes, Zachariah, 154, 204, 207, 227, 232, 240, 256, 266.
  Zachariah, Junr., 339, 342.
  Zachariah, Senr., 233, 283, 297, 343.
Hicks, Joseph, 319, 320, 331, 334.
  Lieut., 318.
  Zachariah, 137, 139, 163, 272, 283, 286, 299, 310, 317.

Hicks, Zachariah, Junr., 290, 293, 295, 298,
    310, 318, 320, 331, 334, 335.
  Zachariah, Senr., 291, 296, 297, 300, 301,
    328.
Hide, Job, 197, 217, 238, 244.
  Jonathan, 97, 106, 132, 139, 155, 157, 169,
    225, 228, 234.
  Samuel, 88, 101, 108, 115, 122, 137, 148,
    151, 174.
Hides, Samuel, 89, 97.
Hildreth, ——, 350.
  Bro., 61, 63.
  Richard, 51, 56, 75, 80, 87, 90, 91, 92, 99,
    102, 104, 109, 219.
  Sergent, 108.
Hill, Abraham, 299, 303, 309, 314, 329, 336,
    338, 340, 344.
  Jacob, 283, 286, 288, 291.
Holden, Justinian, 149, 155, 354.
Holeman, Jeremiah, 307.
  Jeremiah, Senr., 314, 317, 321.
  Mr., 47.
Hollman, William, 63.
Holman, ——, 350.
  Abraham, 230, 248, 254, 257, 260, 268,
    272, 276, 277, 278, 279, 280, 291.
  Abram, 117, 171.
  Jeremiah, 148, 164, 169, 176, 184, 189,
    200, 201, 206, 209, 214, 218, 221, 224,
    227, 231, 233, 235, 239, 244, 248, 250,
    253, 255, 270, 272, 278, 286, 289, 291,
    292, 293, 300, 304, 329, 336, 340, 344.
  Jeremiah, Senr., 310.
Holmes, Bro., 63.
  John, 150, 154, 180, 184, 291.
  Joseph, 171, 188, 198, 208, 231.
  Robert, 46, 76, 84, 85, 87, 97, 109, 121,
    132, 139, 140.
Holms, ——, 350.
Homan, William, 97.
Homes, Robert, 64, 65, 68, 73, 121.
Hompste, Edm., 40.
Homsteade, Nicolas, 29.
Homsted, James, 17.
Hooker, Mr., 7, 12.
  Mr. Thomas, 6, 17, 18.
  Thomas, 7.
Hopkins, John, 9, 11, 13, 15, 19.
  Mr., 6.
Hore, Doctor, 207.
Hosmer, James, 15.

Hosmer, Thomas, 5, 7, 13, 14, 15, 16, 18.
Hossmer, Thomas, 14, 23.
Hotchins, George, 45.
Hough, Mr., 42.
Houghe, Mr. Atterton, 8.
Houldin, Justinian, 205, 213.
Hubbard, James, 116, 137, 140, 154, 215, 217,
    225, 238, 241, 248, 253, 354.
  Mr. Nehemiah, 210.
Huberd, James, 291, 293.
Hubert, James, 277, 279.
Hudson, Raph, 18.
Hunt, Edmond, 9, 13, 18.
Hutchin, George, 43.
Hutchine, Bro., 56.
  George, 69.
Hutchins, Bro., 353.

Isaacke, Joseph, 37.
Isack, Joseph, 38, 42, 45.
Isacke, Joseph, 34.

Jaakson, Richard, 46, 47.
Jackson, Abraham, 267, 309, 312.
  Bro. Richard, 114, 126, 354.
  Deacon John, 196.
  Edward, 188, 260, 262, 321.
  John, 115, 122, 128, 152, 157, 160, 172,
    174, 175, 183, 188, 199, 207, 210, 214,
    218, 223, 225, 226, 228, 230, 236, 237,
    244, 248, 253, 255, 271, 276, 283, 286,
    291, 292, 293, 300, 303, 306, 307, 321,
    328, 333, 334.
  Mr., 111, 121, 163, 174, 175, 250.
  Mr. Edward, 122, 148, 158, 161.
  Mr. John, 259.
  Old Sister, 354.
  Richard, 23, 25, 27, 29, 33, 34, 37, 38, 45,
    46, 105, 115, 118, 125, 128, 131, 136, 149,
    150, 157, 160, 164, 166, 168, 170, 173,
    175, 179, 181, 182, 186, 187, 188, 193,
    195, 321.
  Sebeas, 227, 254.
  Widow, 250.
Jacksonne, Bro. 57.
  Richard, 50.
Jacson, Bro. John, 78.
  Bro. Richard, 80, 81, 93, 102.
  John, 58, 69, 84, 87, 89, 91, 97.
  Mr., 71, 78, 88, 98.

INDEX OF NAMES

Jacson, Mr. Edward, 58, 77, 78, 83, 84, 87, 89,
    93, 102, 108, 110, 155.
  Richard, 53, 64, 66, 68, 69, 71, 82, 98, 99,
    100, 106, 108, 111, 156.
  Sebeas, 227, 254.
  Widow, 250.
Joanes, William, 19.
Joans, Philip, 192.
Johnson, John, 224, 296, 315, 326.
  Marmaduke, 205.
  Mathew, 163.
  Mr., 210.
  William, 250.
Jones, Philip, 193, 194, 261.
  William, 13.
Jonse, Philip, 289, 338.
Jonson, John, 233, 257.
Jud, Thomas, 13.
Judd, Thomas, 9, 18.
Juitt, Joseph, 127.

KANE, Jonathan, 137.
Kelse, Will., 5.
Kelsy, William, 9, 13.
Kemball, ——, 26.
Kempster, Bro., 96.
  Daniel, 86, 92, 97, 123, 131, 145, 321.
  Goodman, 57.
  Sister, 354.
Kemstere, Bro., 116, 126.
Kendall, John, 54, 69, 77.
Kendrick, Old Goodman, 209.
Kene, Christopher, 9, 13.
Kerly, Goodman, 325.
Kidder, Samuel, 293, 296, 301, 303, 306, 310,
    316, 328, 336, 337, 341, 343.
Kindrick, Ealiah, 238.
  John, 236.
  John, Senr., 196.
Kinsbury, Goodman, 3.
Kirnan, John, 2.
Knite, Lydia, 339.
Knowls, Goodman, 56.
Knox, ——, 3.
Knyght, John, 29.

LAMBSON, Barnabas, 14, 18, 23, 24.
Lamson, Barnabe, 25.
  Goodman, 23.

Lamsonn, Barnabe, 27.
Lathan, Carath, 68.
Lathum, Carie, 47.
Lawrance, John, 341.
Lawrence, George, 346.
  John, 325, 328, 344.
Lemon, Mary, 354.
Leverett, John, Esq., 330, 331, 333, 334, 348.
  Mr. John, 322, 323.
Lewis, ——, 19.
  William, 5, 7, 13, 17.
Lock, Joseph, 343.
Lockwood, Mr. Edmond, 2.
Longhorn, Thomas, 88.
Longhorne, Thomas, 56, 91, 97, 104, 117, 120,
    126, 128, 129, 130, 132, 135, 142, 144,
    155, 157, 161, 166, 167, 169, 176, 183,
    189, 201, 202, 207, 225, 227, 232, 234,
    237, 239, 242, 244, 248, 251, 253, 258,
    260, 261, 271.
Longley, Nathaniel, 335.
Lord, Richard, 5, 6, 13, 18.
Louden, Sergeant, 234.
Lowden, Richard, 250.
Luxford, Reuben, 241, 272, 310, 314, 316, 319,
    320, 343.

MACKOON, John, 238, 249.
Man, Will, 9.
  William, 13, 54, 63, 75, 89, 98, 104, 107,
    109, 117, 118, 120, 127, 130, 350.
  Wm., 3.
Maning, Bro., 256.
  John, 336.
  Mr., 188, 254.
  Mr. William, 180, 190, 205, 212, 241.
  Samuel, 309, 340, 343, 344.
  William, 183, 186, 211, 215, 225, 226, 229,
    236, 247.
Mann, William, 19.
Manning, Bro., 48.
  Mr., 164.
  Mr. William, 163, 167.
  Samuel, 328.
  William, 64, 69, 93, 94, 98, 99, 105, 117
    133, 142, 170, 175, 267, 291, 321.
Mariot, Thomas, 34.
Maritt, Amos, 272.
Marrait, John, 245.
Marratt, ——, 19.

Marret, Amos, 317, 336, 340.
  Bro., 96.
  Deacon, 96.
  Thomas, 29, 38, 41, 42, 43, 45, 57, 66, 68, 70, 83, 85, 97, 99.
Marrett, Amos, 299, 303, 310, 314.
  Deacon, 133.
  Ensign, 346.
  John, 174.
  Thomas, 36, 46, 59, 66, 67, 70.
Marriot, Thomas, 28, 73.
Marrit, Amos, 243, 256.
  John, 116, 182, 187, 192, 200, 207, 211, 212, 214, 223, 226, 231, 237, 241, 247, 256.
Marritt, Amos, 261, 262, 264, 271, 275, 296, 312.
  Deacon, 127.
  John, 149, 150, 161, 165, 166, 167, 168, 265, 291.
  Thomas, 50, 73, 138, 140.
Mason, Capt., 165.
  Capt. Hugh, 151.
  John, 238, 241, 246.
Masters, John, 5, 7, 9, 13, 18.
Mattucks, John, 346.
Maynard, John, 9, 13, 18.
Mead, Goodman, 268.
  Israel, 267, 268, 271, 272, 276, 279, 283, 323.
  Thomas, 325.
Meade, Israel, 234, 238, 253, 258.
Meariam, Deacon, 198.
  Joseph, 194, 229.
Mede, Israel, 317.
Meed, Israel, 277.
Meriam, Joseph, 224.
Michell, Mr., 65, 93, 96, 121.
  Mrs., 220, 248, 268, 287, 291.
Michelson, Edward, 64, 75, 76, 98, 144, 154, 156.
  Widow, 291.
  William, 120, 156.
Micherson, Bro., 55.
  Edward, 65, 67, 90.
Miller, ——, 3.
  Joseph, 3, 97, 229.
Mirack, John, 313.
Mirriam, Deacon John, 333.
  John, 309, 333.
  Joseph, 132, 135, 141, 327.

Mirriam, Robert, 332, 333.
  Thomas, 336.
  Widow, 333.
Mitchel, Jonathan, 321.
  Mr., 143.
  Mrs., 136.
Mitchell, Mr., 138, 154, 211, 294.
  Mrs., 179, 182, 186, 187, 190, 197, 206, 250.
Mitchellson, Edward, 206.
Mitchelson, Edward, 303.
Mon Roe, George, 329.
  John, 303, 323.
Monsell, Deacon, 157.
Moore, Bro. Goulden, 53.
  Francis, 107, 111, 118, 119, 123, 130, 137, 147, 159, 171.
  Francis, Junr., 98, 101, 125, 133, 134, 154, 156, 169, 174, 176, 321.
  Francis, Senr., 57, 77, 98, 160, 167, 321.
  Goulden, 66, 68, 86, 98.
  John, 28, 29, 59.
More, Enoch, 29.
  Francis, 189, 190, 201, 204, 209, 213, 215, 218, 220, 225, 226, 227, 228, 229, 230, 236, 241, 243, 247, 251, 253, 254, 257, 267, 272, 281, 286, 291.
  Francis, Junr., 150, 177.
  Francis, Senr., 321.
  Gouldin, 47.
  John, 29, 34, 36, 41.
  Sergeant, 278.
Morrill, Abraham, 5, 13, 18, 86.
Munroe, George, 336, 344.
  John, 335.
  William, 273, 293, 295.
  William, Junr., 335, 341.
  William, Senr., 340.
Munrow, William, 119.
Mury, Benjamin, 295.
Muse, Hester, 5, 7, 13.
Musse, Hester, 5, 19.
Mutchin, Christopher, 300.
Mutting, Ebenezer, 321.
Muze, Benjamin, 299.
Muzzey, Benjamin, 328, 340.
  Goodman, 318.
  Mr. Benjamin, 332.
Muzzy, Benjamin, 303.
Myat, Joseph, 10.
Mygat, Joseph, 16, 17.
Mygate, Joseph, 9, 13, 19.

INDEX OF NAMES 369

NICHOLES, Walter, 19.
Nichols, Walter, 22.
Norcras, Mr., 83.
Nuting, Jonathan, 298.
Nutting, Ebenezer, 319, 321, 347.
    Goodman, 325.
    Jonathan, 323, 336.

OAK, ——, 350.
Oakes, Bro., 47, 63, 152.
    Bro. Edward, 62, 75.
    Edward, 46, 47, 49, 50, 51, 56, 57, 58, 108, 121, 122, 125, 129, 132, 133, 134, 135, 136, 139, 142, 144, 146, 147, 148, 152, 163, 165, 167, 174, 175, 186, 188.
    Mr., 154, 179, 191, 192, 196, 251.
    Mr. Edward, 196, 205, 212, 213, 215, 220, 225, 229, 236, 241.
    Mr. Vurian, 241.
    Thomas, 65, 71, 75, 101, 143.
Oaks, Edward, 83.
    Goodman, 44.
Okes, ——, 3.
    Edward, 58, 77, 80, 84, 93, 96, 99, 101, 102.
    Thomas, 75, 86, 96.
Oldam, John, 212, 229, 245, 246.
    Richard, 3, 91, 97, 101, 110.
    Samuel, 222, 251.
Oldham, John, 303, 309, 314, 316, 318, 319, 320, 324, 327, 328, 335, 339, 341, 343.
    Mr. John, 332, 334, 343.
    Mr. Samuel, 349.
    Samuel, 303, 340, 343, 345.
Oldum, John, 272.
    Samuel, 253, 273, 286.
Oleuer, John, 277.
    Mr. Thomas, 267, 268, 270, 292, 296.
Oliuer, Thomas, 186, 196, 199, 208, 236, 278, 286.
Oliver, Capt., 347.
    Capt. Thomas, 345, 348.
    Doct. James, 303, 318, 320, 322, 323.
    Mr. Thomas, 307, 311, 315, 316, 321, 323, 324, 325, 326.
    Thomas, 318, 327.
Olmsted, James, 10, 11, 12, 13, 18.
Omsted, ——, 5.
    James, 5, 8.
Ouldum, Samuel, 272.

PADLEFFOOTE, Jonathan, 97.
Padlefoote, Jonathan, 116, 128.
Page, John, 27, 43.
Paine, Mr., 35, 40.
Palfraye, John, 116.
Palfre, John, 201, 207, 214, 220, 237, 238.
Palfree, John, 187, 226, 232, 248, 258.
Palfrey, John, 130, 165.
Palfry, John, 291.
Palmer, Stephen, 306.
Parishe, Thomas, 36.
Parke, Richard, 19, 45, 66, 69, 98, 321.
Parker, Capt. Josiah, 346, 347.
    John, 87, 97, 174, 191.
    Josiah, 322, 325.
    Mr. Josiah, 323, 325.
    Robert, 26, 53, 54, 63, 73, 74, 78, 79, 94, 98, 101, 108, 109, 111, 114, 123, 126, 128, 137, 142, 150, 151, 159, 164, 169, 175, 188, 201, 207, 223, 236, 255, 270, 271, 349.
    Thomas, Senr., 277.
Parkes, Mr., 64.
    Richard, 111, 122, 166.
    Thomas, 158.
Parks, Mr., 65.
Parrish, Thomas, 43, 44, 66.
Parrishe, Thomas, 39, 71.
Patin, Nathaniel, 177, 277, 278, 289, 291, 295, 307.
Patrik, Capt., 5, 13.
Patrike, Capt., 5.
    Daniel, 18.
    Mr. Daniel, 2.
Patten, Bro., 54.
    Nathaniel, 307, 308, 310, 311, 314, 316, 317.
    William, 20, 30, 79, 80, 83, 98, 117, 118, 171.
Pattin, John, 341.
    Nathaniel, 178, 184, 189, 198, 201, 208, 209, 217, 218, 220, 223, 224, 238, 239, 245, 247, 252, 258, 260, 262, 263, 268, 270, 271, 275, 276, 279, 281, 283, 286, 292, 301, 302, 304, 307.
    Nathaniel, Junr., 344.
    Nathaniel, Senr., 323, 335, 344.
    William, 133, 142, 145, 149, 150, 157, 159, 164, 166, 167, 321, 330, 336, 340.
Pattine, William, 21, 143.
Paul, Thomas, 348.

INDEX OF NAMES

Paulfere, John, 170, 173, 175.
Paulfree, John, 159.
Pealoms, Mr., 227.
Pease, John, 211.
Peelham, Herbert, 291
Peintre, William, 5.
Peintree, William, 9.
Peintry, William, 16.
Peirce, Thomas, Senr., 163.
Pelam, Mr., 213.
Pelham, Herbert, 56.
    Herbert, Esq., 51, 67, 68.
    Mr., 55, 64, 68, 94, 96, 104, 105, 126, 139, 141, 142, 144, 154, 264.
    Mr. Edward, 303, 334.
    Mr. Herbert, 75, 76.
Pellam, Herbert, Esq., 49, 50.
    Mr., 198.
    Mr. Edward, 266.
Pellem, Mr., 273.
Pellm, Mr., 57.
Pellum, Harbert, 33.
    Mr. Edward, 266.
Pentry, William, 13.
Perce, Thomas, 157.
Philips, Mr., 66, 67, 84, 105, 109.
Phillebrown, John, 336.
Phillips, Mr. George, 50.
Phipps, Mr., 319.
Poast, Stephen, 10.
Polly, George, 118, 122.
Poole, John, 2.
Post, Thomas, 234, 242, 292.
Poulter, John, 318, 344.
    Jonathan, 316, 341.
Powlter, John, 319.
Prat, John, 5, 13.
    Mr., 15.
Pratt, John, 7, 11, 18.
    Mr., 11.
Prentic, Solomon, 277.
Prentice, Capt. Thomas, 155, 289.
    Henry, 53, 84, 85, 260, 290, 323, 346.
    James, 161, 169.
    John, 271.
    Jonathan, 314.
    Lieut., 135.
    Samuel, 324, 337, 340.
    Solomon, 260, 262, 283, 286, 291, 293, 297, 298, 300, 303, 311, 314, 317, 323.
    Solomon, Junr., 328, 335, 341, 344.

Prentice, Solomon, Senr., 328, 343.
    Thomas, 106, 336, 340, 341.
    Thomas, Junr., 139, 161.
Prentis, Capt., 188, 196, 234.
    James, 189, 209, 213, 220, 223, 251.
    Samuel, 212.
    Solomon, 219, 233, 240, 243, 244, 253, 254, 257.
    Thomas, 209, 210.
    Thomas, Junr., 184, 185, 222.
Prentise, Henry, 98.
    Thomas, 98.
Prfessor (The), 33.
Prince, John, 9, 11, 13.

Raines, Henry, 131.
    Samuel, 131.
Rawson, Edward, 259.
Read, Capt., 326, 342.
    Capt. William, 342.
    William, 318, 320, 323, 326.
Reade, Capt., 347.
    Christopher, 242, 243.
    Goodman, 223.
Readinge, ——, 19.
    Joseph, 5.
Redfin, 69, 78.
Reding, Joseph, 13.
Reed, Christopher, 267.
    William, 290, 291, 309.
Reede, Christopher, 236.
Remington, Capt., 327.
    Jonathan, 161, 165, 174, 182, 184, 185, 211, 220, 230, 239, 288, 300, 303, 318, 323, 325, 328.
    Lieut., 290, 291, 294, 295, 298, 317.
    Lieut. Jonathan, 311, 312, 315, 320.
Reskie, William, 22.
Reyner, Samuel, 162.
Rice, Richard, 19, 21.
Richads, Nathaniel, 5.
Richards, Nathaniel, 5, 13, 18.
Rindge, John, 18.
Robbines, Richard, 104, 107, 108, 128.
Robbins, Brother, 228.
    Goodman, 146.
    Nathaniel, 272, 309, 344.
    Nathaniel, Senr., 316.
    Richard, 87, 98, 99, 125, 143, 144, 147, 148, 152, 155, 157, 191, 210, 217, 223, 227, 272, 354.

INDEX OF NAMES

Robbins, Samuel, 270, 336.
 William, 135.
Roberts, Nicholas, 18.
 Richard, 93.
Robins, Mr., 354.
 Nathaniel, 244, 329.
 Nathaniel, Senr., 323.
 Richard, 88, 152, 239, 242, 258, 321.
Rofe, John, 245.
Rolfe, John, 246.
Rolff, Widow, 260.
Rosse, Thomas, 140.
Row, William, 140, 176, 291.
Rusell, Benjamin, 253.
 Jason, 243, 255, 257, 283, 291, 292, 293, 295, 296, 298, 299.
 John, 238, 247, 251, 319.
 Joseph, 186, 201, 223, 236, 239, 248, 256.
 Philip, 212.
 William, 243, 256, 257.
Rusells, John, 35.
Russel, David, 341.
 Jason, 307, 314, 316, 317, 320, 333, 334, 337, 339, 340, 341, 342.
 John, 314, 320, 332, 333, 340.
 Mr. Jason, 349.
 Mr. Philip, 332.
 Mr. William, 332, 345, 348.
 Philip, 341, 344.
 Walter, 321, 341, 344.
 William, 307, 322, 333.
Russell, Jason, 300, 301, 304, 307, 319, 325, 329, 337.
 John, 37, 46, 47, 49, 50, 57, 65, 67, 77, 79, 80, 83, 90, 98, 286, 298, 300, 304, 328, 329.
 Joseph, 150, 154, 157, 160, 168, 169, 176.
 Mr., 29, 61.
 Philip, 272, 281, 323, 328.
 Walter, 329, 336.
 Widow, 137, 140, 150.
 William, 73, 79, 85, 89, 98, 110, 111, 115, 116, 117, 118, 119, 121, 123, 272, 278, 284, 286, 290, 292, 293, 295, 305, 323, 324, 328.
Russells, Bro., 35.
 John, 31, 38, 45, 52, 68.
 Joseph, 261, 266, 275.
Russill, Joseph, 268, 271, 282, 290, 301, 302.

Sackett, Symon, 2.
 Widow, 18.
Saket, Symon, 5, 13.
Sakt, Symon, 5.
Saltingstal, Sir Richard, 31.
Saltingstall, Sir Richard, 41.
Sanders, ——, 67.
 Jonathan, 209, 221, 247, 253.
 Mr., 245.
 Robert, 37.
Santly, John, 18.
Saunders, Robert, 43.
Sawtle, Widow, 331.
Scill, Joseph, 148.
Scott, Thomas, 9, 10, 13, 17.
Sell, B., 57.
 John, 40, 42.
Shadduck, Philip, 252.
Shaw, Bro., 63.
 Richard, 44.
 Roger, 36, 45, 46, 47, 48, 50, 51, 66.
Shaw, ——, 326, 350.
Shawe, Abraham, 43.
 Bro., 47.
Sheapard, Edward, 257.
Sheaperd, Goodman, 211.
 John, 184, 189, 190.
 Samuel, 41.
Sheaprd, Mr., 33.
 Mr. Thomas, 33.
 Samuel, 34.
Shearman, Ensign, 165.
 Mr., 93.
Shepard, Edward, 98, 111, 137, 140, 142, 143, 152, 155.
 Goodman, 35, 294.
 John, 64, 97, 99, 101, 102, 103, 104, 115, 124, 134, 137, 140, 142, 150, 152, 154, 155, 169.
 Mr. Samuel, 92.
 Mr. Thomas, 19, 88.
 Samuel, 34.
Shephard, Mr. Samuel, 65.
Shepherd, Ed., 69.
 Mr. Thomas, 66, 69.
Sill, Joseph, 201, 204, 213, 219, 291.
 Widow, 98.
Simes, Mr. William, 234.
Simons, Joseph, 277, 281, 286, 288, 323.
 William, 194.
Sims, Mrs. Sarah, 98.

INDEX OF NAMES

Sims, William, 94.
Skidder, James, 64.
Skidmore, Thomas, 67.
Smith, Abram, 55.
   Henry, 247, 273, 326, 327, 334, 336.
   John, 267, 305.
   Thomas, 344.
   Thomas, Senr. 336.
Sparahauk, ——, 83.
   Mr., 59, 61, 62, 66, 353.
   Nathaniel, 267.
Sparahauke, Mr., 57, 68.
   Mr. Nathaniel, 260.
   Nathaniel, 72, 92.
Sparauhau, ——, 85.
Sparauhauk, Mr., 87.
   Nathaniel, 92.
Sparauhauke, Mr. Nathaniel, 87.
Sparhauk, Mr., 94.
Sparhauke, Ester, 354.
   Mr., 121, 211, 244, 251.
   Mr. John, 299.
   Mr. Nathaniel, 241, 247.
   Nathaniel, 98, 110, 124, 197, 217, 236.
Sparhaw, Nathaniel, 314.
Sparhawk, Mr., 293.
   Nathaniel, 319, 327, 328.
Sparhawke, Nathaniel, 320, 324, 326, 344.
   Samuel, 322, 323, 335, 339, 343.
Sparohawke, Nathaniel, 46, 341.
Sparrahauke, Mr., 278, 281.
Spencer, ——, 13.
   Garrad, 10.
   Michael, 10.
   Mr., 23.
   Thomas, 5, 13, 18.
   William, 2, 5, 7, 8, 9, 10, 12, 13, 14, 15, 16, 17, 18.
Spring, John, 175, 217, 227, 238, 241.
   Lieut. John, 342.
Springe, John, 223.
Squa Sachem, 48.
Squire, John, 201, 277, 298, 304.
   John, Junr., 317, 329, 341.
   John, Senr., 300, 314, 328.
Stacy, Thomas, 288, 297.
Standly, Tymothy, 9, 13, 15, 21.
Stanly, Tymothy, 11, 18.
Starr, Mr. Comfort, 18.
Steadman, John, 68, 86, 101, 130.
   John, Junr., 291.

Steadman, John, Senr., 292.
   Mr. John, 284.
Stearns, Isaac, 209, 213, 228.
Stebing, ——, 13.
   Edward, 18.
Stebinge, Edward, 5.
Stedman, Bro., 124, 354.
   Bro. John, 111, 123.
   John, Ensigne, 49.
   John, 43, 46, 50, 52, 53, 56, 57, 63, 64, 66, 68, 73, 75, 76, 77, 78, 80, 83, 84, 85, 87, 93, 94, 95, 98, 103, 104, 105, 106, 107, 108, 110, 111, 113, 115, 121, 125, 128, 132, 136, 176, 186, 187, 200, 201, 209, 236, 256, 304, 323, 339, 354.
   John, Junr., 153, 176, 184, 189, 205, 206, 217, 218, 223, 227, 231, 233, 236, 239, 314, 319.
   Mr., 117, 120, 121, 129, 133, 143, 148, 165, 167, 175, 179, 181, 185, 189, 192, 196, 202, 203, 209, 211, 214, 215, 219, 225, 226, 228, 232, 241.
   Mr. John, 142, 155, 161, 177, 181, 188, 190, 196, 205, 212, 213, 215, 220, 225, 229, 237.
   Robert, 55, 71, 73, 97, 110, 115, 133, 144, 150, 151, 164, 354.
Steele, ——, 13.
   George, 4, 5, 7, 12, 15, 18.
   John, 5, 10, 13.
Steeuenson, Andrew, 80.
Steevenson, Andrew, 109, 113, 161.
Sternes, Charles, 118, 123, 124.
   Goodman, 120.
   Isaac, 158, 175, 220.
Sterns, Charles, 117.
   Isaac, 163, 317.
Steuenson, Andrew, 79, 177, 182, 189, 206, 209, 214, 222, 229, 321.
Stevenson, Andrew, 3, 86, 97, 143.
Stockin, George, 13.
Stockine, George, 9, 11.
Ston, John, 291.
   John (David's son), 296.
   John (Samuel's son), 296.
   Mr. Samuel, 6, 7.
   Samuel, 266, 282, 293.
   Samuel, Senr., 288.
Stone, ——, 3.
   Daniel, 55, 64, 97.
   David, 97, 131, 189, 194, 213, 310, 321, 332.

INDEX OF NAMES 373

Stone, David, Junr., 238.
  Deacon, 64, 121, 125, 130, 132, 133, 138, 141, 150, 154, 155, 159, 167, 168, 172, 173, 175, 177, 182, 183, 188, 193, 195, 198, 333.
  Deacon Gregory, 131, 140.
  Deacon John, 231, 240.
  Deacon Samuel, 325, 332, 333, 339.
  Elder, 260.
  Gregory, 26, 63, 66, 91, 98, 99, 100, 136.
  John, 310, 313.
  Joseph, 316, 336, 341.
  Mr., 347, 348.
  Mr. Samuel, 307, 315, 316.
  Mr. Samuel, Senr., 313, 316, 347, 321.
  Samuel, 131, 147, 152, 167, 176, 196, 213, 223, 224, 225, 232, 239, 254, 267, 332.
  Samuel, Senr., 265, 267, 286, 296, 298, 300, 302, 303, 306, 318, 326, 329, Sam^{ll}, David's son, 329.
Stones, Isaac, 225.
Stonn, Mr., 8, 12.
  Mr. Samuel, 7.
  Samuel, 13.
Straiton, Samuel, 81, 82.
Stratton, Goodman, 153.
Strawbregd, Lieut., 234.
Swætman, Thomas, 97, 115, 116, 123, 135, 240.
Swan, Ebenezer, 329, 341.
  John, 98, 104, 115, 116, 117, 118, 119, 120, 124, 167, 174, 175, 291.
Swane, Gershom, 245.
  John, 207, 209, 217, 218, 221, 222, 226, 233, 252.
Swann, John, 140, 166, 173.
Swetman, Bro., 73.
  Thomas, 58, 89, 190, 258, 321.
Symes, William, 250.
Symonds, Ebenezer, 329.
  Ensign, 326, 342, 344.
  Ensign Joseph, 336, 342.
  Joseph, 314, 326, 348.
Symons, Joseph, 318, 320.
  Mr. Sara, 40.

TAILCOTT, John, 13.
Talcott, John, 4, 18, 21.
Tanner, Mr., 353.
  Mr. William, 127.
Taylcot, John, 15, 354.

Taylcott, John, 7, 9, 11.
Taylor, John, 97, 135, 169, 188, 214, 291.
Teacher, ——, 25.
Teed, Joseph, 322, 326, 340.
  Widow, 326, 339.
Thesington, Goodman, 44.
Thoms, Bro., 40.
Thrumble, ——, 211, 294.
  John, 56, 69, 77, 95, 96, 313.
Tidd, John, 267, 271, 305, 318, 319, 320.
  John, Senior, 293.
Tomlins, Tymothy, 8.
Tompson, Mr., 127.
  Mrs., 91.
Tomson, An——, 65.
Town, Peter, 303, 304, 309, 318, 320, 329, 335, 336.
  William, 3.
Towne, Peter, 124, 132, 137, 143, 157, 159, 161, 165, 167, 169, 175, 176, 180, 183, 184, 197, 198, 200, 201, 206, 221, 223, 228, 229, 232, 235, 238, 243, 244, 254, 261, 267, 273, 282, 292, 295, 300.
  William, 15, 19, 40, 48, 86, 98, 107, 130, 189, 198.
Townend, Martin, 261.
Trowbridge, James, 163, 165.
Tuckerman, 346.

USHER, ——, 67.
  Hezechiah, 45.

VINCENT, Humphrey, 11, 13, 18, 21.
Vpham, Mrs., 354.

W——, John, 7.
Waban, 60.
Wachman, Samuel, 10.
Wadsworth, ——, 13, 19.
  William, 16.
Wadswth, William, 4, 5.
Wales, John, 315.
Ward, John, 124, 132, 167, 169, 170, 174.
  Mr. John, 343.
Warland, Owen, 290, 291, 295, 316, 329, 340.
Warlin, Owen, 257.
Warner, Andrew, 5, 6, 7, 12, 13, 14, 15, 16, 17, 22.

INDEX OF NAMES.

Watson, Abraham, 282, 285, 304, 309, 311, 324, 335, 337, 345.
  Bro., 119.
  Bro. John, 276.
  Goodman, 282.
  John, 64, 97, 101, 104, 108, 111, 115, 120, 121, 122, 133, 134, 137, 143, 154, 157, 158, 162, 163, 164, 166, 173, 174, 176, 184, 187, 190, 198, 200, 206, 209, 212, 214, 217, 218, 223, 225, 226, 227, 229, 232, 237, 243, 248, 252, 256, 258, 259, 260, 262, 265, 266, 268, 270, 272, 275, 278, 280, 281, 283, 285, 289, 291, 292, 300, 301, 302, 305, 316, 318, 323, 328, 340, 342, 344.
  John, Junr., 222.
  John, Senr., 233, 280.
  Mr. Abraham, 345.
Wattsonn, John, 276.
Web, Richard, 5.
Webb, Richard, 9, 13.
Webber, Robert, 297, 300, 314, 320, 323, 324, 325, 344.
Wellington, Doct., 346.
  Roger, 150.
Wells, Thomas, 18.
Welsh, Thomas, 55.
Wenshepe, Edward, 50.
Wenship, Edward, 98, 107.
West, John Stone, 344.
Westwood, William, 5, 11, 16, 17.
Wetherall, William, 19.
  Mr. William, 18.
White, ——, 13.
  John, 5, 10, 11, 16.
  Thomas, 143, 163, 177, 282.
Whithead, Samuel, 11.
Whitheade, Samuel, 15.
Whitmor, Francis, 262.
  Samuel, 292.
Whitmore, Francis, 65, 98, 119, 133, 138, 140, 143, 147, 150, 151, 154, 161, 169, 172, 175, 188, 198, 225, 245, 260, 321.
  John, 212.
  Samuel, 310, 323.
Whitney, Richard, 172.
Whittamore, Benjamin, 160.
Whittemore, Nathaniel, 336.
  Thomas, 341.
Whittmor, Samuel, 304.
Whyte, Goodman, 40.

Whyte, John, 42.
Wieth, John, 283, 286, 291.
  William, 27, 282, 291.
Wiith, John, 252.
  Nicholas, 200, 208, 219, 225, 231, 233, 237, 244.
  William, 256.
Wilcocke, Mr., 127.
  William, 64, 68, 98.
Wilcok, William, 26, 30, 31.
Wilis, Mr., 199.
Wilkerson, Widow, 66, 68, 97.
Wilkinson, Widow, 64.
Willard, Symon, 18.
Willcocke, William, 36.
Willcoke, William, 47.
Williams, Isaac, 147, 152.
  John, 340.
Williard, Symon, 8.
Willice, George, 291.
Willington, John, 254, 261, 272, 313.
Willis, Mr. Thomas, 334.
Willow, George, 222, 231.
Willowes, Bro., 55.
  George, 40, 80, 81, 90, 98, 130, 138, 141, 165.
Willows, George, 118.
Wilson, Andrew, 336.
  Isaac, 290.
  James, 325, 340, 341.
  Joseph, 286.
  Nathaniel, 247, 251.
  Robert, 140, 154, 162, 245.
Wincett, Humphry, 9.
Wines, Daniel, 98.
Winshapp, Edward, 15.
Winshep, Edward, 13.
Winshepe, Bro., 47.
  Sergeant, 46, 47, 49.
Winship, ——, 29.
  Edward, 29, 34, 45, 62, 63, 65, 66, 68, 70, 77, 79, 80, 83, 85, 87, 88, 89, 90, 93, 94, 100, 106, 118, 120, 147, 149, 184, 189, 198, 209, 212, 274, 277, 287, 289, 291, 292, 294, 295, 298, 300, 306, 307, 308, 309, 314, 318, 320.
  Ensign, 108, 109, 111, 115, 123, 126, 128.
  Ensign Edward, 115, 119, 120.
  Ensign Ephraim, 305.
  Ephraim, 172, 173, 241, 246, 260, 267, 273, 293, 354.

INDEX OF NAMES

Winship, Joanna, 354.
  Joseph, 293, 296, 300, 304, 307, 310, 312, 319, 320, 344.
  Lieut., 135, 137, 139, 140, 142, 150, 155, 166, 168, 171, 172, 174, 175, 177, 187, 188, 207, 213, 214, 215, 217, 220, 235, 237, 245, 262, 266, 267, 275, 279, 287.
  Lieut. Edward, 131, 136, 149, 150, 160, 161, 162, 171, 260, 272.
  Samuel, 255, 291, 292, 295, 304, 317
  Sergeant, 68.
  Sergeant Edward, 316.
  Widow, 317.
Winshipe, Lieut., 230, 248, 268.
Winshipp, Edward, 23, 25, 47, 51, 56, 59, 321, 323, 326, 328, 333, 335.
  Ensign, 115.
  Joseph, 327, 335.
  Mr. Edward, 326.
Winshop, Bro., 47.
  Edward, 58.
Winter, ——, 348.
  John, 197, 205, 222, 238, 239, 241, 253, 258, 277.
Wisall, Noah, 205.
Wiswal, Elder, 199.
Wiswall, Elder, 165.
  Mr., 175.
  Noah, 213, 222, 234, 238, 243, 244, 254.

Wiswall, Rev. Elder, 210.
  Thomas, 111.
Wiswell, Capt., 289.
  Ebenezer, 281.
  Elder, 188.
  Noah, 288.
Wiswill, Noah, 282.
Withe, Bro., 55, 71.
  John, 320.
  Nicholas, 59, 62, 64, 66, 67, 98, 104, 107, 117, 118, 123, 128, 130, 137, 143, 151, 153, 166.
  Richard, 83.
  William, 315.
Wittamore, Samuel, 317.
Wodsworth, William, 171.
Woodes, Richard, 97, 151, 157.
Woods, Joshua, 270.
  Richard, 163, 169, 176.
  Widow, 188.
Woodward, Amos, 208, 209, 218, 219.
  Goodman, 146.
  Widow, 164.
Woolcott, John, 13.
Wyeth, B., 57.
  John, 288, 296, 297, 300, 319, 329, 336.
  Richard, 350.
  William, 289, 292, 300.

Index of Subjects

Index of Subjects

ABATEMENT of fines, 4, 8, 39, 48, 120, 130, 154, 173, 238, 280.
About the meeting-house, 3.
Account, town and country rates, 244.
    of town charges and receipts, 261, 266.
Accounts, inquiry into, 228.
Acres granted, 7, 8, 9, 10, 11, 12, 13, 16, 17, 26, 32, 33, 40, 51, 52, 59, 66, 67, 68, 69, 72, 77, 78, 83, 91, 92, 127, 131, 132, 133, 136, 139, 165, 173, 211.
    on West side the River, 8.
    of meadow ground, 12, 13.
    of salt marsh, 12.
    of pine swamp, 15.
    within west end field gate, 15.
    on South side the River, 17, 44, 136, 173.
    for common ox pasture, 32.
    400 of upland to Joseph Cooke, 41.
    400 of upland to Samuel Shepard, 41.
    600 upland and meadow to Cooke, Goffe, and Bridge, 41.
    100 to Thomas Parrish, 44.
    at Alewife Meadow, 45.
    200 of upland to Roger Shaw, 50.
    100 to Richard Champnis, 61, 62.
    200 at head of eight-mile line to Gregory Stone, 63.
    1000 at Shawshine for use of the church, 74, 96.
    500 to President Dunster, 82.
    500 to Mr. Daniel Googins, 82.
    500 to Edward Collins, 83.
    300 to Mr. Thomas Shepard, 88.
    Division of Shawshine, 96, 97, 98.
    200 to Richard Hildreth, 91.
    on Strawberry Hill, 122.
    laid out, 139.
    of swamp north side Menotomy River, 154.

Acres, 50 to farm south side the river, 174.
    500 for use and benefit of ministry, 259, 330, 345.
Action on Mr. Dunster's proposal, 109.
Address to General Court, 324.
Agreed,
    impale ground shall be divided, 3.
    sale of, offered to town, 3.
    town shall not be enlarged, 4.
    houses not to be thatched, but slated, 4.
    division of planting ground in neck, 7.
    seven men to do whole business of town, 11.
    man to keep the goats, 17.
    to keep 100 cows, 19, 28.
    to make a weir, 20.
    to keep 100 cattle on the other side the river, 20, 28.
    house for hog-keeper, 21.
    to fetch alewives from the weir, 22.
    with Mr. Bradstreet, 22.
    for boy, 23.
    for man to keep the calves, 23, 36.
    to take up all the stubs, etc., 23, 29.
    to keep three score cows, 30.
    for lad to help keep dry herd, 35.
    to keep milch cows, 36, 43.
    possession of meadow, 43.
    to keep dry herd on other side the water, 44.
    concerning hogs without a keeper, 44.
    right for a house lot, 46.
    care of the town spring, 46.
    payment of debt due the town, 46.
    use of meadow, 47.
    out-fences to be made sufficient, 47.
    to pay Squa Sachem, 48.
    fence to secure Indians' corn, 48.

INDEX OF SUBJECTS

Agreed, on exchange of land, 51.
   price for rent of marsh, 53.
   satisfaction for money expended, 60.
   to divide wood lots, 64.
   common meadow land laid out, 68.
   land for small farms, 71.
   dry herd keeper, 72.
   farm at Shawshine for use of church, 74.
   to do part of fence, 76.
   land sold for gratuity to Mr. Corlet, 77.
   constable to make and levy rate, 77.
   cow common to be stinted, 78.
   five men to examine old records, 79.
   not to exceed nnmber recorded, 79.
   hogs at liberty, 79.
   to make up and maintain fences, 81.
   pay for trespass of beasts, 81.
   swine to be ringed or yoked, 81.
   highway granted, 82.
   rate made and gathered, 84.
   land to be viewed, 84.
   on repairing meeting-house, 85.
   to build a new meeting-house, 85.
   to keep milch herd, 86, 91, 103.
   grant to be entered in town book, 88.
   highway laid out, 89.
   on land added to lot, 89.
   land recovered from Dedham, 89, 90.
   land laid out, 92.
   meeting to consider of Shawshine, 92.
   town rate made, 93.
   concerning land at Shawshine, 98.
   at general meeting in 1652, 99, 100.
   instructions to townsmen, 99, 100.
   use of weir, 103.
   grant of 100 acres, 104.
   concerning swine, 113.
   rate for pay for school-house, 113.
   to set out of the Rocks, 115.
   grant to Mr. Pelham, 126.
   in consideration of a highway, 131.
   levy for payment to executors of Mr. Dunster, 132.
   division of common lands, 136, 147.
   division of swamps, 136.
   meadow made from swamp, 136.
   to refer difference about fences, 157.
   stone wall for security of cow common, 167.
   meeting to consider division of land in the Rocks, 168.

Agreed, touching dividing common woods and timber, 168.
   committee to order survey, 169.
   care for building house for ministry, 180.
   rate made for ministry, 182, 186.
   town rate made, 186, 206.
   care of the bridge, 221, 235.
   stockade against Indians, 227.
   gate upon Watertown line, 254.
   hire of highway in marsh, 264.
   acknowledgment for standing barn on town land, 298.
   fence to Spy Pond, 306.
   tax for his Majesty's service, 313.
Agreement about paling on the Neck, 3.
   for monthly meeting, 4.
   common pales, 15.
   fences at Pine Swamp, 15.
   for purchase of land, 90.
   with carpenters, 93.
   care of milk herd, 103, 123, 124.
   with Mr. Jackson, 110.
   with Richard Dana, 110.
   of thirteen men, recorded in the Towne booke, 155.
   concerning fence and land, 199.
   for keeping child, 202.
Alcock's Meadow, 88.
Alewife Meadow land, 41, 45, 47, 138.
Alewives, division of, 20, 22.
   from the weir, 22.
Alienation of land, 50.
   without consent of townsmen, 168.
Allowance for attendance at General Court, 93.
   for land, 104.
   for wharf, 105.
   from fines concerning swine, 20.
   for grain to cow-keepers, 124.
   for maintaining gate, 135.
   for grammar-school master, 138.
   for passage of highway, 148.
   for wolf killed, 155.
   to Mr. Corlet, 182.
   to constables, 229.
Ammunition, 309, 342.
Annual account, 261.
   meeting, 112, 113.
Answer for being from under family government, 160.
   for falling trees, 174.

INDEX OF SUBJECTS 381

Answer for digging clay without leave, 220.
Apple trees, etc., 39.
Appointed
  to view the pales about west end field, 21.
  to see a cartway made to the weir, 22.
  to make a pound, 22, 91.
  to mend pen for dry cattle, 22.
  to make a house for the cow-keeper, 22.
  to look to fence in west field, 31, 80, 86, 90, 104, 107, 109, 111, 123, 128.
  for fencing new field on south side, 38.
  to fetch away wood or timber cut contrary to order, 58.
  to divide land on South side the Water, 58.
  to stake out land, 59.
  to see execution of order concerning hogs, 61, 80.
  to look unto Pine Swamp fields, 61, 80, 90, 104, 107.
  to look unto Neck of land, 61.
  to see to the cow common, 61.
  to gather certain fines, 62.
  to execute orders concerning fences about the Neck, 80, 90, 104, 108, 109, 123, 128, 150, 157.
  to execute orders concerning fences Menottime fields, 80, 90, 104, 108, 109, 123, 128, 162, 176.
  to levy penalty for breaking order concerning hogs, 80.
  to run line between towns, 81, 91.
  to measure land sold for Mr. Corlet, 83.
  to lay out highway on Wigwam Neck, 83.
  to present names of trespassers, 83, 143.
  to oversee meeting-house repairs, 85.
  to agree with cow-keepers, 86.
  to agree with workmen, 86.
  to agree about the weir, 86.
  to make up common fence, 86.
  townsmen to keep milk herd, 86.
  to view complaints, 88.
  to lay out highway to the meadows, 88.
  to take notice of want of ladders, 90.
  to see order executed concerning swine, 92, 104, 108, 109, 115, 128, 143, 151, 157, 163, 166.
  to lay out land, 101, 104, 107, 149, 165.
  to lay out land on Strawberry Hill, 101.
  to lay out highways on south side the water, 102.

Appointed to determine differences about highways, 105.
  to bargain with a herdsman, 108.
  to levy fine for inhabitant without leave, 108.
  to view fences about ox pasture field, 109.
  to stake out highway, 111.
  to execute orders concerning trees for firewood, 115.
  on order concerning improvement in spinning and clothing, 115.
  to present defects to townsmen, 115.
  to make levy for maintenance of pastor, 121.
  concerning ringing and yoking of swine, 128, 143.
  to consider complaints concerning land, 123, 128.
  to present names of delinquents, 128, 143.
  to lay out land at head of eight-mile line, 133.
  to mark bounds in Great Swamp, 134.
  to lay out highway, 142, 148.
  to drive the neck, 143.
  to see to painting the bridge, 143.
  to clear field of cattle, 157, 169.
  to settle bounds of small farms, 163.
  to lay out ten acres of meadow, 165.
  surveyors of fences, 166, 169, 176.
  to erect a pound, 170.
  to settle neck fence, 170.
  for catechising, 175.
  to run bounds, 176.
  to drive cow common, 177.
  sealer of leather, 177.
  to agree with workmen on school-house, 180.
  on damage done to our lands, 182.
  to agree with herdsmen, 189, 202, 209, 215, 226, 232.
  to treat with artillery officers, 190.
  to view lands voted to be laid out, 190.
  to obtain lines of farm lands, 190.
  to run lines against Boston bounds, 191.
  to run highway from Boston bounds, 196.
  to run lines Billerica and Concord, 201.
  to run lines Charlestown and Woburn, 202.
  for settling of country road towards Concord, 203.

INDEX OF SUBJECTS

Appointed to agree with shepherd, 209, 232, 243.
  to pay deputy's expenses, 211.
  to lay out highway into neck of land, 211.
  concerning highways, 211, 212.
  to look after transgressors, 215.
  to set out Windmill Hill, 215.
  to look after swine, 217, 226.
  to have inspection into families, 226.
  to inquire about accounts of town rate, 228.
  to take account of the inhabitants, 230.
  to sit amongst little boys in the meetinghouse, 231.
  to gather in contributions, 243.
  to examine account, 244.
  for hog reeves, 247.
  to answer complaint, 253.
Arbitrators, 157.
Arms delivered, 347.
Ash, 147, 151.
  timber from 100 acres, 183.
Assessment, 251, 307, 313, 315.
Assessors, 307, 312, 315, 325.

BARGAIN with Waban, 60.
  for house sold, 109.
Bark not to be conveyed out of town, 158.
Barn, place for, 25.
  porch on, 29.
  encroachment of allowed, 83, 88.
Bastard Child, 324, 325.
Bear Swamp, 207.
Beast found in planting fields, 61, 129.
  to be paid for to cow keeper, 103.
  impounded, pay for, 202.
Beer and Bread, 100.
Bell, 78, 329.
Bell-ringing, payment for, 346.
Billerica (Shawshine), 106.
  church farm at, 180.
  tenant at may dig clay in Cambridge, 190.
  lines run at, 201.
Book, orders entered in, 40, 88.
  keeping of, 40.
Boston, 37, 38, 295, 313.
  bounds, 191, 196.
  line, 72, 80, 104, 136, 166.

Bounds of grant, 8.
  erected, 12.
  of land of John Rolfe, 63.
  Watertown and Cambridge, 337, 338.
Boy employed, 23.
Boys in meetinghouse, 231.
Breach of town orders about wood and timber, 54, 101.
  of town orders about oxen, 54, 55.
  of hog order, 53, 54, 77.
  of orders felling trees, 78.
  concerning cattle & fences, 153.
  of orders concerning oxen and hogs, 54, 55.
  concerning cattle and fences, 153.
  of orders by swine, 117.
  of orders by swine, timber, and wood, 120.
Brick, liberty to make kilns of, 207.
  to pay per thousand, 220.
Bridge to low-water mark, 14.
  at the mill, 71.
  over Charles River, 113, 134.
  wood for, 134.
  to be painted, 143.
  maintenance of, 164.
  repairing of, 173, 204, 299.
  searchers, 204.
  care of, 221.
  timber for, 237.
Burying place paling, 15.
  pound at, 91.
Burying yard, 337, 341.
Bush, Renold, entertaining inhabitant without consent, 108.
  estate of, 259.

CALVES, 23, 36, 44, 76.
  wrongfully retained, 76.
Cambridge, 30, 70.
  village, 249.
  farms, 343.
Cartway, 6, 7, 22.
Catechising, 175, 188.
Cattle, 9, 80.
  on south side the river, 16, 17, 20, 28, 35.
  Mr. Green's, 16.
  driving from planting fields, 21, 161, 162, 169.
  from cow commons, 21, 80.

INDEX OF SUBJECTS 383

Cattle and keeper, 22, 28, 72.
  pasture for, 25.
  in the Neck, 25.
  fences against, 47.
  lost, 60.
  over the water, 72.
  to be impounded, 80, 92.
  trespass of, 80, 92, 95, 129.
  damages from, 95, 129, 146.
  without a keeper, 192.
  from other towns prohibited, 149.
  feeding on cow common, 129.
  in neck of land, trespass of, 129, 153.
  trespassing, 145.
  in herd without consent, 145.
  driven from west field, 157.
  in pasture, 162.
Causey to Roxbury, 30.
  the long, 302.
  repairs of, 267.
Cedars for posts, 78.
Charles River, 12, 30, 31, 33, 38, 39, 41, 42, 44, 48, 52, 60, 77, 87, 110, 113, 133, 134, 250, 313.
Charlestown, 6, 9, 24, 25, 33, 41, 42, 62, 70, 76, 157, 176, 202, 234, 245.
  field, 75, 76.
  path, 16.
Chauncy, Rev. Mr., Allowance to, 186.
Cheaver's Meadow, 173.
Cheescake Brook, 41.
Chestnut Hill, 44.
Children, educating of, 47.
Chimneys to be clean swept, 88.
Chosen to draw up instructions, 99.
Church farm at Shawshine, 74, 94, 180.
Churches, division of, 107.
Clapboards, 53, 57, 58, 63, 73, 83, 87, 91, 105, 140, 142, 144, 145, 153, 163, 165, 172, 178, 180, 191, 194, 198, 200, 286.
Claypits, 14, 15, 133, 287, 334, 347.
Clerk of the market, 77.
  for selectmen, 177.
Collectors of fines, 62, 120.
College, 33, 66, 95, 231.
Commissioner, 218, 292, 304, 312.
  to make assessment, 313.
Commissioners to fix bounds, 8.
  to end small causes, 77, 84, 87, 93, 106, 108, 121, 125.
  to make assessments, 313.

Committee
  on Cow Common, 100, 168, 246.
  concerning Shawshine, 106, 143, 181.
  on bridge over Charles River, 113, 133, 204.
  to divide wood, 121.
  concerning highways, 122, 155, 211, 212, 276, 316, 317, 324, 325, 326, 327, 332, 339, 347.
  to consider complaints, 128.
  on fence upon Watertown line, 131.
  to view land and set a price, 132.
  on division of swamps, 125, 136.
  to draw up list of inhabitants, 155.
  to divide common lands, 156, 189, 294, 246.
  on common woods and timber, 168, 169.
  on old line of farm, 174.
  on satisfaction to Mr. Danforth, 177.
  on a ministry house, 170, 179, 182, 186.
  help to Mrs. Mitchell, 186, 187.
  to make rates, 186, 282, 315, 316, 324.
  allowance to Mr. Chauncy, 186.
  on division of lands, 189, 190, 294.
  to treat with Artillery Company, 190.
  to examine grants on south side the river, 191.
  return on highways, 199.
  on repairing bridge, 204.
  on lands and woods, 216, 217.
  on town lines, 234, 249.
  for regulating the Commons, 246.
  land of Widow Rolfe, 260.
  lands for the ministry, 260.
  to divide lands, 265.
  for securing wood on the Rocks, 274, 292.
  to lay out land, 284.
  on sale of land, 288, 301.
  to agree with shepherd, 301, 306.
  to assess provision for ministry, 308, 315.
  common lands belonging to proprietors, 333, 334.
  old bounds between Watertown and Cambridge, 337, 338.
  care of sheep, 337, 342.
  on lands, 346, 347.
  on meeting-house, 349.
  for seating people in meeting-house, 354.
Common divided, 4, 5, 8.

INDEX OF SUBJECTS

Common ground, use of, 7.
  pales, 8, 16, 21.
  fields, 21.
  meadow, 68, 76.
  meadow at Shawshine, 89, 101.
  land set out, 95.
  lands, division of, 147, 189.
  south side the river, 155, 156.
  land taken without leave, 194.
  orders concerning, 203, 204.
  woods and timber, 215, 297, 308, 309.
  within five miles, 216, 294.
  beyond eight miles, 216.
  to be fenced, 246, 259.
  on this side Menotomy River, 274.
  sale of land to farmers, 302.
  belonging to proprietors, 333, 334.
Compensation to Richard Jackson, 81.
  to William Russell, 116.
Complaints, 52, 62, 76, 87, 88, 94, 95.
  on other side the water, 85.
  stroy of timber, 94.
  cattle in corn fields, 95.
  neglect in payments, 103.
  need of highway, 110.
  want of land, 128.
  stroy of corn in the neck, 129.
  of fence at West field, 130.
  expenses about school-house, 132.
  of town's poor, 145, 146.
  obstruction of highway, 146.
  about wood lots, 149.
  for felling trees, 150.
  breach of town orders, 153, 164.
  not full due of land, 166.
  incorrect invoice, 174.
  disorderly conduct, 178.
  inhabitants of Menotomy, 192.
  of herdsmen and shepherds, 205.
  condition of Johnson, 224.
  want of firewood, 242.
  digging in highway, 240.
  taking wood from common, 255.
  stroy of wood, 269.
  want of highway, 332.
Concord, 20, 41, 45, 51, 63, 96, 176, 193, 195, 201, 203, 205, 209, 259, 276, 306.
Conditional grants, 7, 8, 15, 26, 27, 31, 32, 41, 42, 43, 47, 75, 84, 120, 125, 126, 147.
Conditions of grants, 26, 32, 41, 69, 78, 111, 132, 134.

Conditions of farms, 75.
  of land sale, 135.
Confession of carrying away bark and wood, 162, 280.
Consideration for expenditure of time, 81.
Constable to pay for making highway, 8.
  reckoning with, 16.
  to make and gather the town rate, 63.
  to levy, 100, 119, 120.
  to pay deputy at General Court, 102.
  delivers weights and measures, 198.
  ordered to distrain, 253.
Constables to be chosen yearly, 1.
  chosen, 10, 11, 12, 14, 45, 46, 49, 50, 69, 77, 87, 99, 101, 106, 108, 111, 121, 124, 130, 132, 135, 139, 147, 152, 158, 163, 167, 175, 181, 185, 196, 205, 213, 220, 225, 228, 236, 241, 246, 251, 254, 260, 267, 271, 277, 281, 286, 288, 290, 292, 295, 298, 299, 303, 309, 313, 316, 318, 320, 322, 327, 335, 339, 343.
  as surveyors of new lands, 29.
  joined with townsmen, 34, 36, 93, 111.
  to give in a yearly account, 100.
  care for repairs on meeting-house and school-house, 112.
  to repair the Great Bridge, 173.
  allowance to, 229.
  duties and powers of, 351, 352.
Contracts, performance of, 109.
  about land and fence, 195.
Contributions to the Ministry, 157.
  from other towns for the Bridge, 204.
Controversy, 260, 266.
Cording wood, 220.
Corlet, Mr., 77, 106, 182.
Corn to Indians, 48.
  for cattle in dry herd, 72.
  payment in, 103.
  price of, 168, 311.
  preservation of, on the Neck, 61, 62, 129.
  fields, 162.
Covenant to make and maintain fence, 130.
Cow common, 21, 47, 49, 61, 78, 79, 80, 92, 100, 163, 167, 197, 216, 306.
Cow-keeper, 19, 22, 28, 86, 103, 124.
Cow-right, sale of, 243, 245, 246.
Cow yard row, 18.
Cow yards, 5, 6, 7.
Cows, 17, 19, 21, 22, 30, 36, 70, 108.
  duty of owners of, 28.

INDEX OF SUBJECTS 385

Cows, damage done by, 48, 49.
   detained, 87.
   and sheep, 205.
Coxall, 127.
Creek, the, 107.
Cullers of brick, 272.

DAMAGE by highway, 104, 120, 334.
   to the Commons, 158.
Damages done by swine, 34, 35, 42, 52, 53, 62, 74, 102.
   by cattle trespassing, 48, 81, 95, 129, 154, 163, 202.
   for detention of calves, 76.
   done by dogs, 83.
   granted, 141.
   for neglect of fences, 143, 153, 154.
   by felling timber, 190.
   by cutting down green wood, 215.
Danforth, Thomas, house and land sold to, 105, 109.
Day of monthly meeting, 37.
   of election of town officers, 43, 45, 49, 113.
Debt, 46, 77, 85, 87.
Dedham line, 81, 89, 90.
   highway, 86, 88, 89.
   land recovered from, 89, 90.
   path, 185, 186.
Deed of sale demanded, 109.
   school-house and land, 138.
Defect in yoking and ringing swine, 140.
   in highway work, 164.
   in fence, 297.
Defective fences, 86.
Delinquent in breach of hog order, 53, 54, 117, 128.
   in felling trees, 53.
   leaving tops of trees, 117.
Delinquents to pay, 72, 177.
   in bringing corn, 72.
   about swine, 128, 213.
Deputy paid, 102.
   to General Court, 113.
   expenses of, 211.
   Governor, 262.
Detention of calves, 76.
   of oxen and cows, 87.
Difference referred, 83, 124.
   about highways, 105, 124.

Directions for cutting wood and brush, 126.
Ditch, 30, 47.
Division of Common pales, 4.
   of lands, 7, 13, 16, 57, 58, 71.
   of planting ground, 7.
   of Fresh Pond Meadow, 12.
   of meadow ground, 13.
   proportions of, 13.
   of ground between Charlestown and Common pales, 16, 17.
   of alewives, 20, 22.
   of old ox pasture, 32, 33.
   of fences, 60, 62, 70, 76.
   of wood lots, 63.
   of Shawshine, 96, 97, 98.
   of town not encouraged, 107.
   of Great Swamp, 125, 127.
   common lands south side the river, 156.
   wood on the Rocks, 168.
   land beyond cow common, 190.
   land beyond eight-mile line, 197.
   woods on cow common, 197.
   lands between Woburn, Concord, and our head line, 265.
   of the Rocks, 291.
   of common lands, 294.
Dogs, 22, 83.
Domestic fowls, 21.
Draft cattle, 16.
Drain, 192.
Drivers of field at the Neck, 167, 176, 184, 201, 218, 223, 233, 239, 253, 258, 271, 283, 291, 297, 304, 310, 314, 320.
   of West field, 145, 169, 176, 184, 201, 218, 223, 227, 233, 239, 253, 258, 270, 283, 291, 293, 304, 310.
   of Menotomy, 162, 169, 176, 184, 218, 223, 227, 233, 239, 253, 258, 261, 271, 291, 314, 321.
   of Common fields, 218, 223, 227, 253, 258.
   for the Village, 223.
Drummers, grant to, 24, 56.
Dry cattle, 17, 21, 22, 35, 44, 49, 60, 61, 70, 72, 80, 192.
   and oxen without a keeper, 192.
   South side Charles River, 60.
   corn for, 72.
Dry herd keeper, 72.
   herd on Common, 149.
Dunster, Mr. Henry, 53, 82, 109.

Duty of owners of cows, 28.
Dwelling-houses, 22.

EDUCATING children, 47.
Eight-mile line, 63, 133.
Enclosure, 16, 17, 32.
Engagement, 82.
English commodity, 60.
Entertainment of strangers, 24, 100.
Estate of Mr. Dunster's wards, 53.
Exchange of lands, 51, 62, 107.
   of highways, 211, 212.

FALLS, the, 147.
Families, inspection of, 226.
   improvement in spinning and clothing, 112.
Family government, submission to, 160.
Farm at Shawshine, 74, 75, 82, 91.
   Thomas Shepard, 88.
   on Boston line, 136.
   on south side the river, 104, 173, 189.
   house on south side the river, 131.
Farms granted, 31, 41, 50, 51, 59, 67, 68, 75, 127.
   on south side the river, 31, 127.
   exchange of, 51.
   laid out by majority, 59.
   division of, 71, 76.
   conditional, 75.
   at Shawshine, 75, 91.
   rate for, 282.
Fence, ground between pine swamps, 15.
   or ground forfeited, 17.
   between planting field and ox pasture, 31.
   in West field, 31, 39, 61, 73, 80, 86, 90, 104, 107, 109, 111, 123, 127, 128, 130.
   on south side Charles River, 33, 34, 38, 39, 40.
   for securing the corn, 34, 48.
   removal of, 39, 249.
   on Watertown line, 39, 131.
   in neck of land, 42, 49, 73, 80, 86, 90, 104, 108, 109, 111, 123, 128.
   liberty to erect, 50, 84, 110, 208.
   Menotomy field, 60, 62, 70, 80, 90, 93, 104, 105, 109, 111, 123, 125.
   pine swamp field, 73, 80, 86, 90, 92, 104.

Fence divided, 73, 76.
   insufficiency of, 74, 86, 95, 130.
   in old ox pasture, 75, 76, 109.
   against Charlestown field, 76.
   of common fields, 81, 86, 95.
   of meadow, 84.
   across highways, 84.
   at house of correction, 113.
   covenant concerning, 130.
   surveyor to be paid, 130.
   at Rocky Meadow, 131.
   between Watertown bounds and ours, 193.
Fences, 15, 17, 23, 34, 47, 48, 50, 73, 74, 75, 76, 83, 84, 90, 108, 109.
   marked stakes at, 23.
   at the Neck of land, 31, 42, 44, 49, 73, 80, 86, 90, 104, 108, 109, 111, 123, 128, 142.
   between corn and pasture ground, 47.
   in West field, 31, 39, 73, 80, 86, 90, 104, 107, 109, 111, 123, 127, 128, 130, 143.
   Menotomy field, 104, 108, 109, 111, 123, 128.
   in pine swamp field, 61, 73, 80, 86, 90, 102, 104, 107.
   appertaining to common fields, 81.
   return of defects in, 86.
   order of General Court, 90.
   against cattle, 102.
   neglect of, 102.
   insufficiency of, 152.
   and swine orders, 161.
   defective about corn fields, 162.
Fence Viewers, 15, 31, 38, 39, 42, 47, 49, 62, 70, 73, 74, 80, 90, 104, 107, 108, 109, 111, 123, 128, 130, 131, 142, 143, 151, 157, 161, 189, 201, 209, 217, 220, 223, 227, 233, 239, 244, 248, 253, 258, 260, 261, 267, 271, 273, 278, 283, 286, 289, 291, 292, 293, 296, 300, 303, 304, 310, 314, 317, 319, 320, 321, 323, 328, 336, 340, 344.
   of Common fields, 217, 223, 227, 244, 248, 253.
   of the West field, 90, 104, 184, 189, 201, 209, 217, 223, 227, 233, 239, 244, 248, 253, 258, 260, 270, 278, 283, 286, 289, 291, 292, 293, 296, 300, 303, 310, 314, 317, 321, 323, 328, 336, 340, 344.
   of the Neck, 90, 104, 157, 161, 189, 209, 217, 220, 227, 233, 239, 244, 248, 253,

INDEX OF SUBJECTS 387

258, 260, 271, 278, 283, 286, 289, 291, 292, 293, 296, 300, 304, 310, 314, 317, 319, 320, 323, 328, 336.
Fence Viewers of Menotomy field, 90, 104, 151, 162, 209, 217, 223, 227, 233, 239, 244, 248, 253, 261, 271, 278, 283, 285, 289, 291, 293, 296, 300, 304, 310, 317, 321, 323, 328, 336, 340, 344.
of the Farms, 223, 258, 304, 340, 344.
of the Village, 217, 223.
south side the river, 157, 217, 268, 273, 278, 304, 340, 344.
Fencing, 88, 140, 149, 154, 166.
highway, 147.
Fencing Stuff, 47, 58, 60, 70, 71, 83, 86, 88, 104, 107, 111, 114, 130, 134, 137, 138, 150, 155, 161, 162, 165, 170, 173, 201, 206, 207.
Ferry, 15.
Ferry-boat, 96, 204.
Field on south side Charles River, 39, 40.
beyond Menotomy River, 123, 137.
Field Drivers, 80, 104, 145, 162, 169, 176, 184, 201, 218, 223, 227, 233, 239, 253, 258, 261, 270, 271, 283, 291, 293, 297, 304, 310, 314, 320, 321.
Fine for felling trees, 6, 215, 222.
for inhabitant without leave, 108, 109.
remitted, 148.
for horse, 178.
digging in highway, 240.
Fined, 48, 54, 55, 56, 63, 77, 78, 87, 116, 117, 118, 119, 120, 131, 137, 138, 140, 148, 150, 151, 154, 160, 166, 172, 173, 174, 175, 177, 193, 194, 198, 218, 219, 221, 222, 253, 280, 297.
Fines, 3, 49, 61, 62, 90, 114, 144, 145, 152, 160, 213.
abated, 120, 150, 154, 173, 238, 280.
to be levied, 194.
to be paid in corn, 194.
Fire, no child to carry, 23.
danger of, 83, 156.
Firewood, common to every inhabitant, 6.
on South side the River, 83.
price of per load, 114.
Mr. Chauncy, 197.
granted, 137, 196.
during deep snow, 197, 242.
Fish, 22, 78, 103, 224.
Five surveyors of town lands, 12.
mile end, 59, 67.

Five surveyors, with seven selectmen, 67.
men to examine old records, 79.
men to apportion Cow Common, 79.
Footbridge, 15.
Forfeit, 58, 81, 85, 115, 126.
Forfeited land, 17, 27, 31, 69, 87, 136.
Fort Hill, land on, 25.
Fortification, 230, 235.
against Indians, 227, 237.
timber for bridge, 237.
Fresh Pond Meadow, 12, 13, 125.
land at, 19, 127.
Funeral charges, 298.

GALLERY in meeting-house, conditions for leave to build, 134.
permission to build, 212.
Garden plot granted, 8, 15.
trespass of poultry on, 21.
Gate, 4, 135, 141, 253, 254, 261, 278.
Gate keeper, 252, 254, 278.
Gates, 80, 110, 193, 195, 238.
removal of, 135.
on highway, 193, 219.
Gauger, 93, 99, 101, 197.
General Court, 37, 38, 49.
Glass about meeting-house, 164.
Goat, 17, 20, 26, 39, 59.
damages by, 59.
without a keeper, 139.
Goatherd, 17.
Gookin, Mrs., house rent of, 337.
Grain, price of, 311.
for cow-keeper, 124.
Grant of acres, 7, 9, 26.
of money, 8.
of marsh, 11, 42, 44.
of land, 7, 8, 9, 10, 12, 15, 26, 27, 31, 32, 41, 42, 43, 44, 45, 59, 61, 63, 66, 67, 68, 69, 71, 72, 74, 75, 77, 82, 88, 89, 93, 94, 95, 96, 97, 98, 104, 107.
of plough land this side Vine Brook, 52.
of Fort Hill, 25.
and alienation of land, 37.
liberty to build a house, 40.
to cut timber, 53, 57, 59, 79, 80.
of timber and firewood, 83.
of trees and timber, 151.
for the ministry, 259.

INDEX OF SUBJECTS

Grants, conditional, 7, 8, 15, 26, 27, 31, 32, 41, 42, 43, 47, 69, 75, 84, 120, 125.
   order respecting, 11, 32.
   recorded as town grant, 123.
   land South side the River, 136.
   of highway, 120, 139.
Grass, liberty to mow, 111.
Great Bridge, 173, 235, 237.
Great Swamp, town lines in, 50, 58, 82, 87, 125, 126, 127, 134, 159.
   wood from, 72, 81, 82, 126, 127.
   division of, 125.
Ground granted, 10.
   forfeited to town, 17.
   division of, 9, 16, 17.
   use of, 7, 49.
Gun, 277.
Gunpowder, 3.

HARVARD COLLEGE, 82.
Hay, 9, 84.
Haywards, 310, 314.
Heifer, 55, 56.
Herbage in Great Swamp, 159
Herdsman, 108, 226, 232, 237.
Highway, 8, 139.
   to be mended, 14, 38.
   in the Neck, 38, 211.
   between towns, 38, 99, 111.
   South side the River, 82, 89, 102, 110, 111, 122, 124, 144, 212, 324.
   from Roxbury, 88.
   to Dedham, 89, 165, 197.
   Menotomy field, 93.
   payment for, 110, 116.
   into Pine Swamp field, 118.
   damage done by, 120, 142, 159.
   towards Watertown Mill, 131, 208.
   to Roxbury, 141, 142, 144, 191.
   laid out, 148.
   to maintain forever, 147.
   into Boston field, 191.
   from Concord to Watertown, 193.
   from Cambridge to Watertown, 193.
   from Boston bounds, 196, 197.
   from Roxbury to Watertown, 208.
   between Watertown and Cambridge line, 211.
   exchange of, 211.
   removal of, 212.

Highway to Windmill Hill, 215.
   digging in forbidden, 240.
   from five-mile swamp, 317.
   recompense for, 326.
Highways, 3, 18, 40, 59, 82, 83, 89, 94, 105, 111, 116, 120, 121, 122, 133, 167, 199, 274, 276, 307, 325, 326, 332.
   gates on, 193, 195, 219, 238.
   committee to consider and lay out, 105, 111, 122, 155, 212, 312, 316, 320, 325, 332.
   return of committee, 199, 317, 326, 327, 332, 333.
   complaint for closing of, 146, 152.
   surveyors of, 14, 18, 99, 100, 101, 106, 108, 111, 121, 132, 135, 139, 152, 158, 163, 167, 175, 176, 181, 186, 197, 213, 220, 225, 229, 236, 241, 247, 251, 254, 260, 267, 277, 290, 292, 303, 309, 316, 319, 320, 328, 335, 340, 343, 347.
Hog constable's order, breach of, 53, 54, 55, 56, 97.
Hog-keeper, 21.
Hogreeves, 24, 61, 113, 115, 144, 169, 176, 184, 201, 209, 213.
   beyond Menotomy, 169.
Hogs, 23, 30, 42, 60, 61, 79, 80.
   without a keeper, 44, 53, 54, 55, 56.
   yoked and ringed, 60.
Hoop poles, 93, 195, 213, 220.
Horse on cow common, 21.
   in planting fields, 21.
   in corn fields, 178.
Horse-block at meeting-house, 159.
House, leave to build, 40, 42.
   lots granted, 29.
   lots in Neck of land, 46.
   and land sold, 105.
   of Correction, 113.
   right, resignation of, 171.
   for the Ministry, 179, 180, 183, 187, 195.
Houses, order concerning, 4, 17, 22, 24.
   owners of, 17, 18, 19.
   not to be let or sold without consent, 19, 22, 24, 50.
   by the Fresh Pond, 19.
   towards Watertown, 26.

IDLERS in time of public worship, 178.
Impaled ground, 3.

INDEX OF SUBJECTS 389

Impounded, 192, 202.
Impounding cattle, 146.
Impowered in marriages and oaths, 125.
Improvement of families in spinning and clothing, 112, 115.
Indian corn, 60, 82.
Indian Lane, 240.
Indians, 20, 84, 85, 87.
Information of low condition of inhabitant, 209.
Inhabitant refused, 155, 193.
Inhabitants, 3, 50, 288.
    South side the River, 107, 130.
    without leave, 108, 147.
    to pay for cattle on cow common, 129.
    beyond four miles from old meeting, house, 136.
    · having interest in common lands, 155.
Inspection of families, 226.
Instructions to townsmen, 99, 100.
Invoice, errors in, 674.
Islands among swamps, 66.

JACKSON, Richard, recompense to, 81.
Judges of fence, 47.

KEEPER of cattle, 28.
    of dry cattle, 35.
    of milch herd, 86, 87, 91, 103, 105, 123, 124.
    of cows on Sabbath, 205.
Keeping cattle on South side the River, 20.
    the calves, 23, 36, 44, 76.
    milch cows, 28.

LAD, 23, 25.
Ladders, 14, 88, 90, 175.
Land,
    by the farms, 2.
    sale of, 3, 24, 61, 78, 89, 90, 92, 95, 132.
    division of, 7, 13, 16, 17, 40, 58.
    grants of, 7, 8, 9, 10, 12, 15, 26, 32, 41, 42, 57, 59, 61, 63, 66, 67, 68, 69, 71, 72, 74, 75, 77, 82, 83, 84, 87, 88, 89, 92, 93, 94, 95, 96, 97, 98, 104, 107, 149, 282, 284.
    to be measured, 9, 12, 62.
    behind Pine Swamp, 11.

Land, to non-residents, 17.
    on South side Charles River, 17, 19, 31, 33, 35, 44, 77, 87, 95, 156, 177, 211, 288.
    forfeited, 17, 27, 31, 69, 87, 125.
    not to be sold without consent of townsmen, 24.
    at the Brook, 26, 31, 52.
    behind the new lots, 32.
    for ox pasture, 32, 156.
    adjoining Great Swamp, 32.
    for School or College, 33.
    on South side the water, 35, 57, 58, 68, 69.
    record of, 37.
    at Alewife Meadow, 45, 138.
    use of, 50.
    alienation, 50.
    exchange of, 51, 52, 62, 82, 92, 102, 107, 174, 200.
    grant of, confirmed, 59, 61, 72.
    for small farms, 67, 68, 71, 75, 91.
    head of eight-mile line, 63, 133.
    at Menotomy, 66, 67, 69.
    beyond five miles, 67.
    at Watertown Mill, 68, 69.
    at Shawshine, 74, 75, 82, 91, 96, 97, 98.
    for schoolmaster, 77, 83.
    for President of Harvard College, 82.
    yielded to town, 85, 87, 96.
    planted by Indians, 87.
    on which meeting-house stands, 89, 95.
    recovered from Dedham, 89.
    satisfaction for, 89, 104.
    purchase of, 90.
    proposal for, 95.
    on Strawberry Hill, 101, 122.
    allowance for, 104.
    on the Neck, 132, 133.
    to those belonging to new meeting-house, 135.
    to be set out by selectmen, 139.
    in lieu of damages, 141.
    in recompense for loss of wood-lot, 149.
    for preservation against fire, 156.
    shares of, in swamps, 149.
    beyond the eight miles, 197.
    on the Common, 195.
    Return concerning, 210, 245.
    of John Rolfe, 245.
    of Widow Rolfe, 260.

INDEX OF SUBJECTS

Land of Reynold Bush, 259.
  for the Ministry, 259.
  remeasuring of, 266.
  in Great Swamp, 274.
  in remote Common, 284.
  set out in Weir field, 284, 285.
  sold, 288, 299.
  sale of, to farmers, 302.
  at Alewife Meadow, 138.
  on South side, division of, 152.
  of Common to be divided, 147.
  Common, names of those having interest in, 155.
  damage to, 182.
  for the Ministry, 250.
  between Woburn, Concord, and our head line, 265.
  Committee for dividing, 294.
  sale of Common, 301, 302.
Laying out the Rocks, 291.
Leather sealing, 77.
Lecture days, 15.
Levy for schoolmaster, 106.
  maintenance of Pastor, 121.
  on proprietors of Commons, 131.
  for payment to executors of Mr. Dunster, 132.
  bridge over Charles River, 134.
Liberty to fell timber, 57, 59, 63, 71, 73, 74, 78, 79, 80, 81, 84, 85, 86, 88, 89, 90, 91, 92, 93, 94, 95, 96, 101, 102, 103, 104, 109, 110, 111, 113, 114, 115, 116, 118, 119, 121, 122, 123, 124, 126, 130, 131, 132, 133, 134, 137, 138, 140, 141, 145, 147, 154, 161, 163, 170, 178, 180, 181, 183, 185, 188, 202, 203, 204, 205, 206, 207, 208, 210, 213, 214, 218, 220, 221, 223, 229, 230, 231, 240, 242, 252, 256, 265, 268, 269, 271.
  to fell trees, 53, 57, 58, 60, 63, 70, 71, 73, 74, 78, 80, 83, 86, 87, 105, 107, 116, 130, 131, 221, 230, 233, 234, 235, 239, 240, 244, 248, 250, 254, 258, 264, 270.
  to take trees on the Rocks, 51, 126, 137, 219, 225, 226, 227, 228, 231, 232, 233, 248, 255, 256, 257, 262, 271, 273, 275, 276, 278, 279, 280, 287.
  to encroach, 83, 88.
  to mow, 76, 83, 111, 116, 149, 151.
  to use and fence highway, 110.
  to take pines in the Swamp, 133.

Liberty to young men to build a gallery, 134.
  to take trees marked out, 137.
  for wood on South side the River, 137.
  for timber for workhouse, 148, 150.
  to the College for posts and rails, 144.
  to fell timber, pages following 150.
Line between towns, 91.
  in Great Swamp, 50, 58, 82, 87, 125, 126, 127, 134, 159.
  between the Village and Cambridge, 215, 234, 249.
  between Boston and Cambridge, 245.
  between wood lots and swamp lots, 257.
Little Spy Pond, 66, 177.
Little Rock Meadow, 149.
Location on Watchhouse Hill, 86.
Lots not built on, 4.
  granted for cow yards, 5, 6, 7.
  not improved to revert to town, 10.
  granted in West end field, 9, 10.
  division of, 7, 8, 13, 16, 17, 40, 58.
  for sale to be first offered to town, 10.
  out of Cow Common, 11.
  on West side the River, 10.
  behind the Pine Swamp, 11.
  laid out by committee, 96.
  forfeited to use of town, 161.
  on South side the River, 161.
Lost Goods, 37, 38.
Lower Falls highway, 197.

MAGISTRATES, 112, 125.
Maple trees, 201.
Marriages and oaths, 125.
Marsh, grant of, 9, 11, 42, 44, 105, 107, 142.
Meadow, 13, 31, 34, 45, 47, 68, 69, 84, 88, 96, 107, 125.
  south side Charles River, 27, 41, 43, 45, 47, 50, 51.
  Alcock's, 68.
  at Shawshine, 83, 89.
  liberty to mow, 76, 83.
Measure of meadow ground, 12, 13.
Measurers of land, 12, 62, 83.
Measuring to be paid for, 69.
Meeting to consider of Shawshine, 92.
  of inhabitants and proprietors of commons, 155.
  day, 12, 37.

INDEX OF SUBJECTS 391

Meeting-house, 3, 85, 86, 87, 93, 112, 127, 159, 164.
Mending highway on the Neck, 38.
Menotomy, 34, 67, 68, 71, 176, 184, 188, 189, 192, 201, 207, 209.
  River, 20, 21, 32, 58, 66, 155.
  field, 60, 70, 80, 90, 93, 143.
  land at, 69.
Michaelmas, 60.
Milch Cows, 16, 28, 36, 43.
  herd, 86, 103, 215, 226.
Mill, 58, 82, 338.
Minister, house for, 179, 182, 186.
  land sold for, 299.
Minister's rate, 296, 315, 316, 341.
Ministerial grant, 96.
Ministry allowance, 130, 251.
  supply for, 178.
  house, 179, 182, 186.
  land for, 259, 296.
  pew, 322.
Mitchell, Mr., grant of land, 136.
  of tree, 138.
Mitchell, Mrs., 186, 187, 197, 287.
Moderator, 348.
Money, 8.
  for redemption of captives, 349.
Monthly meeting, 4, 14, 37.
Mortgage, 104.
Mowing ground, 16.

Names of proprietors, 13.
  of owners of houses, 18, 19.
  of delinquents, 128.
Neck of land, 25, 38, 42, 61, 108, 109, 128, 129, 161, 169.
  fence, 73, 76, 90, 128, 169, 184, 201, 208.
Neglect of records, 37.
  of fences, 102.
  to pay cow keeper, 103.
  of trees felled, 117, 162.
  to pay fines or rates, 119.
  in yoking and ringing swine, 119, 120.
  to keep turns on the Sabbath day, 205.
New meeting-house, 85, 86, 135.
  ox pasture, 128.
Newtown, 2, 12, 26.
Nominated to treat with Southside, 136.
  to view land and report, 152.
  to view necessity of highway, 165.

Non-attendance, 87.
Non-residents, 17.
Notice, 113.

Oaken timber, penalty for felling, 279.
Oakes family, 179.
Oakes, Mr., invited to move into minister's house, 195.
  payment to, 196, 241.
Occupiers of farms, 191.
Offer from Fuller, of Woburn, 95.
Officers to order prudential affairs, 69.
  chosen, 69, 77, 84, 87, 93, 101, 106, 121, 147.
Old meeting-house, 95, 135.
  ox pasture, 33, 65, 75.
Order concerning houses, 4.
  concerning wood and timber, 6, 7.
  concerning common pales, 7.
  concerning out fences, 47, 72, 73.
  respecting further grants, 10.
  respecting Mr. Green's cattle, 16.
  of General Court, 49.
  made null and void, 112.
  to remove fence, 194.
  about cows and sheep, 205.
  restraining felling of wood, 215.
Orders, breaches of, 53, 54, 55, 77.
  concerning timber and firewood, 114, 269, 297.
  concerning wood and timber on the Rocks and Commons, 263, 264.
Ordinary, 78.
Other side, 35, 47, 57, 66, 67, 68, 69, 70, 71, 209, 212.
Over the water, 35, 72.
Overseers, 167, 184.
Owners of houses in the town, 18, 19.
  of cattle and of fences, 129.
  of fence in the Neck, 184.
Ox pasture, 22, 25, 32, 33, 65, 75, 76, 109, 121, 188.
  fence in, 49, 76, 109.
  wood in, 131.
Oxen trespassing, 49, 55.
  fines concerning, 62.
  detained, 87, 90.

Pale and gate over highway, 23.
Pales, 4, 25.

INDEX OF SUBJECTS

Pales, about the Neck, 21.
    with posts and rails, 25.
    about West End field, 21.
Paling in the Neck, 3, 7, 8.
Parish tax, 179, 338, 348.
Pastor, maintenance of, 121, 150.
Pasture, 25, 162.
Path from Cambridge to Roxbury, 30.
    from the Mill to Watertown, 58.
Pauper, 224.
Pay of Representative, 93, 102.
    of schoolmaster, 153.
    for bricks made, 220.
Payment for making highway, 8.
    for cattle lost, 60.
    in corn for wood taken, 82, 103.
    to Mr. Corlet, 83.
    of debt to town, 87.
    for detaining oxen, 90.
    of dues, 157.
    for cattle, 171.
    of town rate, 168, 208.
    to Mr. Oakes, 241.
    to Deputy at General Court, 102.
    in corn, 103.
    to Mr. Gookin, 251.
Pelham, Mr., satisfaction to, for damages, 104.
Pen for calves, 23.
Penalties for breach of law about swine, 113.
    for letting felled trees lie on Common, 114.
    for letting felled trees lie on highway, 128.
    for felling trees under 12-inch diameter, 114.
Penalty for deficient fence, 73, 102.
    for non-attendance, 78.
    for exceeding number of cows allowed, 79.
    for want of yoke on swine, 81.
    for damage by dogs, 83.
    for damage by swine, 102.
    neglect of ladders and chimneys, 88.
    felling trees without consent of townsmen, 94, 102.
    non-payment to keeper of milch herd, 103.
    not removing trees felled, 114.
    felling trees under 12 inches in diameter, 114, 115, 127.
Penalty for swine without rings, 116.
    disposing of wood out of town, 125, 216.
    cutting down second growth, 127.
    felling tree upon highway, 128, 138.
    trespass of cattle, 141.
    forfeiture of land, 136.
    for cattle kept without consent, 145.
    for removing sheep or lamb from flock, 143.
    digging sawpit in highway, 161.
    felling trees contrary to orders, 170.
    neglect of payment of fines, 194.
    neglect concerning sheep, 203.
Perambulation, 91.
    Charlestown and Woburn, 163, 202.
    Billerica and Concord, 201.
Pew for minister's family, 322.
Pine Swamp, 9, 15, 16, 17, 73, 80, 86, 90, 92, 104, 118.
    trees granted, 207.
Pines, the, 110, 133.
Plank, 115, 130.
Planting ground in Neck, 7.
    field, 9, 21, 31, 33, 61.
    fields on South side the River, 33.
Porch, liberty to build, 197.
Possession of meadow, 43.
Posts and rails, 25, 128, 144, 177, 200, 201, 206, 207, 214, 218, 219.
Pound, 22, 39, 91, 170.
    keeper, 91.
    regulations of, 91.
Powers of officers, 43.
Precaution against fire, 23.
Preservation of wood and timber, 101, 112, 170.
Price for rent of marsh, 53.
    of grain, 168.
    of wood, 114.
Privileges, 17.
Prohibition of felling wood on South side, 137.
Proportion of division, 13.
    of land divided, 75.
Proposition for discharge of 40 pounds, 109.
Proprietors of Common to be levied on, 131.
    general meeting of, 215.
    names of, 13.
    of wood lots, 64.
    new ox pasture, 128.
Provision for Cattle, 17.

INDEX OF SUBJECTS 393

Provisional grant, 27, 120.
Public School or College, 33.
Public Worship, 178.
Publishing of orders, 112.
   by posting on meeting-house, 128.

RAILS, 25, 107, 128, 140.
Ram lambs and rams, 203, 204.
Rams impounded and fined, 204.
Rate, 77, 84, 85, 183.
   for bridge, 113.
Rates abated, 48, 85, 130.
   levied, 138, 141, 206.
Receipt for land purchased, 92.
Reckoning, 16.
Recompense to Joseph Cooke, 32.
Record defaced, 211, 293.
Recorders of town lands, 43, 50.
Records, 37, 43, 79, 100.
Reference of difference, 83.
Register of births, etc., 40, 45.
Relief of poor family, 210.
   of sufferers by fire, 331.
Rents to be paid, 339.
Repacker of meat, 197.
Repairing meeting-house, 85, 159.
   bridge, 204.
Repairs, 112.
Representative, pay of, 93, 102.
Request to Second Church, 209, 210.
Resignation of house-right, 171.
Restraining from felling wood, 215.
Restrictions upon inhabitants, 50.
   upon voters, 128.
Return concerning land, 210, 245, 293.
   of committee to view highways, 199, 249, 250.
Ringing of swine, 23, 30, 52.
Road to Roxbury, 30.
Rocks, the, 57, 126, 197.
   division of wood in, 168.
Rocky Meadow, 21, 22, 41, 131, 193, 195.
   land in, forfeited, 27.
Rowley, 127.
Roxbury, 30, 88, 91, 92, 99, 104, 141, 142, 191, 208.
   path to the Pines, 110.
Running of lines, 81, 91.

SALARY of minister, 312.
Sale of land to be first offered to town, 3.

Sale of swamp land, 7.
   of land of the Common, 77.
   and delivery of bark, 162.
Sales of land restricted, 24, 52.
Salt marsh South side Charles River, 12.
Satisfaction for damage done by swine, 53.
   for land to be determined, 89.
   by grant of land, 166.
   for making and maintaining fence, 166.
   for land taken from Danforth's farm, 177.
   for land of Richard Dana, 110.
Sawpit in highway, 161.
School, 77.
School-house, outlay for, 109, 112, 113.
   repair of, 112.
   expense about, 132.
   building, 335.
Schoolmaster, 106, 293, 296, 297, 299.
Sealer of leather, 1, 77, 101, 206, 329.
   of weights and measures, 84, 197, 206.
Seating in meeting-house, 127, 160, 354.
Security for pay to town, 135.
Selectmen, 104, 105, 111, 121, 125, 132, 135, 139, 147, 149, 152, 153, 163, 167, 175, 181, 186, 196, 205, 213, 220, 225, 229, 236, 241, 247, 251, 254, 260, 267, 272, 278, 281, 286, 288, 290, 292, 295, 298, 300, 303, 309, 314, 316, 318, 320, 323, 328, 335, 339, 343.
   consent of, necessary to voting, 112.
   powers of, 305.
Selling wood out of town, 161, 263, 280.
Seven men to be chosen townsmen, 11.
Seventh mile South side the River, 136.
Shawshine, 92, 93, 98, 99, 106.
   river, 51, 96, 97.
   church farm, at, 74, 94, 181.
   farms at, 75, 82, 91, 143.
   meadow at, 83, 89, 93, 101.
   division of, 97, 98.
Sheep of non-residents to pay for feed, 130.
   to be ear-marked, 144.
   and lambs put to flock, 203.
   kept on other side Menotomy Bridge, 274.
   care of, 276, 277.
Shepherd, 218, 226, 232, 237, 243, 248, 276, 277.
Shrubs and small trees in ox pasture, 121.
Sizer of cask, 93.
Small causes, 77, 84, 87, 93, 106, 108, 121, 125.
   farms, 67, 71, 75, 127, 216.

INDEX OF SUBJECTS

Snow deep, 197, 242.
South side Charles River, 12, 30, 31, 33, 38, 39, 42, 44, 48, 58, 60, 77, 87, 95, 127.
   the River, 17, 80, 82, 83, 107, 130, 136, 137, 144, 147, 155, 156, 157, 166, 170, 176, 177, 184, 191, 211, 215.
   inhabitants, 107.
   the Water, 58, 61, 62, 72, 102.
Spinning and clothing, 115.
Springs at the Pines, 110.
Spy Pond, 57, 64, 65, 111, 116, 120.
Squa Sachem, 48.
Stakes to be set up, 8.
Staves for tythingmen, 339.
Steers, 22.
Stone wall against Watertown line, 192, 194.
Strawberry Hill, 77, 101, 122.
Street free from obstructions, 10, 18, 29.
Stroy of wood, 101, 114, 126, 162.
   of corn, 129.
Stubs to be taken up, 23, 29.
Subscription for relief of poor inhabitant, 211.
Suit in law, 81.
Surveying woods and commons, 120.
Surveyors of fences, 157, 166, 167, 169, 174, 176, 260, 267, 272, 273, 278, 283, 314, 320.
   of land, 12, 24, 29, 34, 37, 45, 52, 57, 125, 174, 205, 217, 236, 267, 281, 286, 298.
   of highways, 10, 14, 18, 23, 29, 34, 36, 43, 45, 49, 50, 52, 57, 70, 85, 93, 99, 100, 101, 106, 108, 111, 121, 125, 132, 135, 139, 147, 152, 158, 163, 167, 175, 181, 186, 197, 213, 220, 225, 229, 241, 247, 251, 254, 260, 272, 277, 290, 292, 295, 300, 303, 309, 310, 314, 316, 319, 320, 323, 328, 335, 340, 343.
   of woods and commons, 162.
Swamp ground, sale of, 7.
   oak, 138.
   shares, 149.
   land, 165, 166.
   near Little Spy Pond, 177.
   at Menotomy, 189.
   farms near Concord, 209.
Swamp lots, price of, 62.
Swamps, 1, 7, 50, 51, 66, 111, 116, 120, 133, 224.
   division of, 136.
Swine, 1, 7, 11, 34, 52, 53, 56, 62, 73, 81, 102, 104, 109, 112, 113, 128, 157, 162, 167, 176, 201, 222, 226.

Swine, yoking and ringing of, 31, 35, 52, 62, 73, 74, 81, 108, 113, 115, 140, 161, 300.
   without rings, 115, 116.
   breach of order respecting, 119.
   on South side the River, 128, 151, 157, 167.
   to be yoked, 143.
   on west side Menotomy River, 151.
   on common, 151, 226.
   to be ringed, 102, 226.

Tax for 1651, 353.
   for his Majesty's service, 307, 313, 315.
Taxes abated, 48, 85.
Tavern, first, 100.
Thirteen men recorded in Town Book, 155.
Three men to end small causes, 77.
Timber to be moved or forfeited, 6, 10.
   on the Rocks, 57.
   forfeit for taking, 58.
   not to be felled without leave, 25, 34.
   not to be sold out of town, 52, 87.
   and wood, 52, 83, 114.
   liberty to fell on the Common, 63, 71, 73, 78, 79, 80, 81, 84, 85, 86, 88, 89, 90, 91, 92, 93, 94, 95, 96, 102, 103, 104, 105, 109, 110, 111, 113, 114, 115, 116, 118, 119, 121, 122, 123, 124, 136, 137, 148, 149, 162.
   for school-house, 71.
   for bridge, 71.
   common, other side the water, 71.
   payment for, 82.
   great stroy of, 94, 101, 114, 162.
   felling and stroy of, fined, 131.
   for fencing, 149, 154, 158, 164.
   for fencing at House of Correction, 113.
   oaken, on one hundred acres, 164.
   granted, 95, 96, 116, 169, 171, 179.
   maintenance of bridge, 164.
   liberty to fell, see pages following 164.
Tithingmen, 267, 268, 271, 272, 293, 305, 310, 314, 316, 318, 319, 320, 323, 328, 335, 336, 343, 344.
Town, the, 2.
   book, 12, 14, 40, 88, 155.
   clerk, 93, 101.
   cows, 108.
   debt, 46, 77, 116.
   division of, 107.
   gate, removal of, 135.

INDEX OF SUBJECTS 395

Town lines, 91.
  lot granted, 16.
  meeting, 45, 46, 49, 50, 51, 56, 84, 99, 106, 112.
  officers, 1, 43, 45, 46, 49.
  duties of, 99, 100.
  orders concerning timber and wood, and swine, 120.
  privileges, 17, 112, 123.
  rate, 63, 77, 84, 85, 93, 113.
  right for building a house, 123.
  spring, 46.
  tax, 325, 338, 342.
  treasurer, 309, 314.
Townsmen, 1, 11, 13, 14, 20, 23, 29, 34, 36, 43, 45, 46, 49, 50, 51, 57, 70, 77, 84, 87, 93, 99, 101, 106, 108, 111, 129, 159.
  duty and power of, 11, 12, 14, 99, 100
  to see to educating children, 47.
  of Charlestown, 70.
  to lay out small farms, 75.
  on expenditure of time, 81.
  instructed, 99, 100.
Training field, 334.
Transcript to be delivered to General Court, 24, 29, 35, 45.
Transfer of grants, 15, 31.
Tree on path from Watertown to Charlestown, 6.
  forfeit for selling out of town, 8.
Tree, 57, 71, 114, 138.
Trees not to lie on ground, 6, 8, 114.
  not to lie on highways, 6, 128.
  felling of, without leave, 25, 34, 53, 54, 58, 78, 94.
  not to be sold out of town, 87.
  felled for firewood, 94, 102.
  granted, 57, 71, 73, 78, 79, 86, 110, 138, 169, 184, 197.
  on Common, 71, 162.
  on the Rocks, 126.
  from College lot of wood, 171.
  not to be felled without special license, 172.
  lopped, 222.
  liberty to fell, 57, 58, 60, 70, 71, 73, 78, 80, 83, 87, 105, 116, 123, 124, 126, 137, and pages following.
Trespass, felling great white oak, 162.
  of cattle, 80, 92, 95, 120, 129.
  of swine, 74.

Trespassers in Great Swamp, 81, 82.
Trespasses on highways, 128.

UNDERWOOD and brush on common Great Swamp, 72.
Upland granted, 41, 45, 50, 51.
  and meadow, 26, 41, 96.
  pay for, 62.
  and pay for swamp, 62.

VALUATION in 1647, 352.
Viewers of land, 84.
Village South side the River, 188.
Voted, on proportion of Cow Common, 79.
  meeting-house to be repaired, 85.
  meeting-house, new, to build, 85.
  meeting-house to stand on Watchhouse Hill, 86.
  Church farm at Shawshine leased, 94.
  lean-to may project into street, 94.
  highway may be taken in, 94.
  Common land granted, 95.
  Sale of old meeting-house land, 95.
  instructions to townsmen, 99.
  instructions to constables, 100.
  instructions to surveyors of highways, 100.
  business of stinting cow common, referred, 100.
  house and land sold to Thomas Danforth, 105.
  levy for grammar school master, 106.
  time of annual meeting, 112.
  concerning swampy piece of land, 120.
  Committee to divide wood east side Winottime River, 121.
  Committee to divide Great Swamp, 127.
  concerning seating persons in meeting-house, 127.
  to abate rate to inhabitants South side the River, 130.
  fence to be erected on Watertown line, 131.
  Committee to determine about fence on Watertown line, 131.
  for building bridge over Charles River, 134.
  Levy for bridge over Charles River, 134.
  Division of swamps and other lands, 136.

INDEX OF SUBJECTS

Voted grant of marsh, 142.
  bridge to be painted, 143.
  property of wharf and ground, 167.
  property in wood lot, 168.
  Committee on house for the minister, 179.
  compensation allowed Mrs. Mitchell, 179, 197, 287.
  to sell Church farm at Billerica, 180.
  Committee to sign deed of sale, 180.
  Common lands to be divided, 189.
  Covenant concerning fence and gates, 193.
  Contract concerning fence and gates, 195.
  relating to settlement of Mr. Oakes, 195.
  relating to selling firewood out of town, 197.
  repairing of bridge, 204.
  wood lot for minister's house, 216.
  Common wood within five miles, 216.
  Common woods and lands beyond eight miles, 216.
  a gratuity to Mr. Oakes, 241.
  on orders regulating the commons, 246.
  concerning the woods upon the Rocks, 249.
  concerning West field and swamp lots, 258.
  land for the Ministry, 259.
  of Widow Rolfe, 260.
  annual account to be given, 261.
  concerning allotments of remote lands, 265.
  Accounts of Town Charges and expenses, 266, 337, 338, 341, 342, 348.
  liberty to cut wood, 273.
  division of the Rocks, 274.
  Suit at law with the drummers, 278.
  Constables to pay town rate, 278.
  land, sale of, 282, 284, 285, 288.
  town rate, 286, 296, 330, 338.
  not to cut green wood for firing, 290.
  Cow-rights and Commons, 294.
  wood land for ministry, 296.
  schoolmaster, 296, 302.
  preservation of wood and timber, 297.
  maintenance of Great Bridge, 299, 324.
  grant to Menotomy of land for school-house, 299.
  day for choice of officers, 299.

Voted land, sale of to the Farms (Lexington) for minister, 299.
  cows on common, 302.
  payment of debts due, 302.
  selectmen for year 1694, duties of, 307.
  levy for maintenance of ministry, 308, 315.
  wood lots on other side Menotomy, 308.
  pew for minister's family, 322.
  bell, gift of, 329.
  school-house, 330.
  Committee concerning common and undivided lands, 334.
  house rent of Mrs. Gookin, 337.
  concerning old bounds, Watertown and Cambridge, 337.
  burial of Mrs. Gookin, 342.
  Common lands, 345, 346.
  new meeting-house, 348.
  money for redemption of captives, 349.
Voters, orders concerning, 112.
  about laying out the Rocks, 291, 292.
Votes on division of wood and timber, 216.
  on remote parcels of land, 346.
Vyne Brook, 26, 31, 32, 50, 76.

Waban hired to keep cattle, 60.
Walnut trees felled, 219.
Warned to answer for felling trees, 173.
Warning by surveyors of highways, 85, 148, 160.
Watch from 9 P. M. to sunrise, 331.
Watches and Wards, 352.
Watchhouse Hill, 86.
Watering place for cattle, 46, 334.
Watertown, 3, 6, 16, 17, 20, 26, 27, 39, 41, 50, 58, 71, 73, 76, 81, 82, 91, 110, 115, 134, 191, 192, 193, 203, 208, 211, 218.
  lane, 175.
  line, 111, 131, 141.
  mill, 69, 82, 88, 110, 131, 135, 208.
  pond herd, 151.
  stone wall, 192, 194.
  bounds, 193.
  weir, 12, 16.
Weights and measures delivered, 198, 199.
Weir, 20, 22, 77, 86, 103.
  house Wharf, 167.
Well, construction, 46.
  at Swamp, 120.

INDEX OF SUBJECTS 397

West field, 9, 10, 15, 21, 31, 73, 80, 90, 109, 111, 127, 128, 130, 145, 157, 161, 166, 171, 184, 207, 208, 209.
   cattle at liberty in, 61.
Wharf, 94, 105.
Wharfing, 94.
Wigwam Neck, highway to, 83.
Windmill Hill, 7, 215.
Winottime Brook, 125.
   field, 104, 108, 109, 111, 125, 128, 162, 164, 166, 169, 176.
   River, 121, 123, 137, 138.
Woburn, 95, 96, 104, 176, 202.
Wolf, bounty for killing, 155.
Wood and timber not to be sold out of town, 52, 58, 59, 101, 112, 114, 136, 168.
   on island in swamp, 66.
   grant of, 71.
   overplus of, 71, 72.
   to be cut and fetched, 77.
   out of the Weir, 77.
   in Great Swamp, 72, 81, 82, 125, 126.
   in 100 acres, reserved, 104.
   preservation of, 101, 112, 114, 170.
   to lie in common, 126.
   great stroy of, 126.
   disorderly taking, 131.
Wood E. side Winottime River, 121.
   S. side Charles River, 137.
   for the bridge, 134.
   in ox pasture, 131.
   not to be sold or alienated out of town, 125.
Wood, division of, on the Rocks, 168.
   for Mr. Oakes, 196.
   division of, on Cow Common, 197.
   of Common prohibited, 207.
   for Mrs. Mitchell, 206.
   felling without liberty, 215, 216.
   to the ministry, 296.
Wood land to be measured, 197.
Wood lot for minister's house, 216.
Wood lot not to be sold or alienated, 216.
Wood lots at neck of land, 64.
   next Spy Pond, 65.
   in old ox pasture, 65.
   on other side Menotomy Bridge, 66.
   in Common Great Swamp, 72.
   sale of, 105.
   laid out, 139, 144, 149, 216.
   complaint concerning, 149.
   orders concerning, 215.
   method of division, 216.
Wood reeves, allowance from fines, 170, 268.
Workhouse, timber granted for, 148, 215.
Working cattle, 11.
Workmen about meeting-house, 87.
Wrentham, 109.

YARD, to build on, 35.
Yokes and rings, 113, 217.
Yoking and ringing of swine, 35, 42, 52, 60, 61, 62, 63, 73, 74, 115, 119, 123, 128, 140, 181, 189, 217, 319, 329, 336, 341, 344.
Youth in time of public worship, 164.

www.ingramcontent.com/pod-product-compliance
Lightning Source LLC
Chambersburg PA
CBHW070058020526
44112CB00034B/1433